THE FRENCH

Portrait of a People

Sanche de Gramont

THE FRENCH

Portrait of a People

G. P. Putnam's Sons

New York

58933

FOR GABRIEL, WHO CAN READ

Contents

Introduction

➤➤➤-➤➤➤-➤➤➤-➤➤➤-➤➤➤-➤➤➤-➤➤➤-➤➤➤-➤➤➤-➤➤➤-➤➤➤-➤➤➤-➤➤◄◄◄-◄◄◄-◄◄◄-◄◄◄-◄◄◄-◄◄◄-◄◄◄-◄◄◄-◄◄◄-◄◄◄-◄◄◄-◄◄◄-◄◄◄

I AM the product of French parents, French secondary schools, and French military service; I am also the product of Yale and Columbia universities, a ten-year career on New York City newspapers and national magazines (I had two horses shot from under me, the New York *Herald Tribune* and *The Saturday Evening Post*), and finally, I am in the custody of an American wife. As someone who has lived twenty years in the United States and fifteen years in France, and who writes and thinks in English but still counts and occasionally dreams in French, the study of natural character has become my particular form of introspection. In adjusting to my dual origin I have become a bivalve like the oyster, in order to separate the contradictory traits I have acquired. I feel by turn nomadic and sedentary, hearty and formal, confident and suspicious, an adept of time-motion studies and a fanciful idler, and I suffer from both a French liver and American blood pressure.

I have seen France as someone who, accustomed to a garden, does not think to identify its flowers, but who, returning after a prolonged absence, acquires the curiosity of a horticulturist. I have had a sense of the country in the dual meaning of that word:

through the disorderly perceptions of the senses, and through intelligible impressions, or what makes sense. To sort these out, I began by asking myself the most obvious question, Why is a Frenchman not a German or an Irishman? But to approach national character head on seems as risky an enterprise as hunting for the unicorn. As Antisthenes said, I have known such and such a horse, but I have never known horseness. I wanted to avoid the stereotypes that have been thrust upon us since the Bible lumped together as incorrigible revelers all the inhabitants of Sodom and Gomorrah. Are there no virtuous Gomorrheans, no lazy Germans, no placid Spaniards, no hot-blooded Swedes, no teetotaling, dull-witted, unpatriotic and puritanical Frenchmen?

If there is a French *volksgeist,* or collective soul, it is not in Caesar's description of the Gauls as irascible and brave, quick-tempered and undisciplined, nor in the observations of the debarking Englishman at Calais about the smell of the Continent, nor in the familiar cutouts like short plump Dupont, sitting in the Café du Commerce in front of a glass of wine, smoking a rice-paper Gauloise and making over the world. The statistical approach seems equally unrewarding. Does it help to know that France has more washing machines with centrifugal dryers than any other Common Market country, that 53 percent of French housewives like to cook, or that 13 percent of the male population uses deodorants?

But a number of factors can be studied to help isolate the compound called Frenchness. "The millions of men who compose a nation," said Jean de La Bruyère, "find themselves assembled on a common soil to speak the same language, live under the same laws, and agree on common customs, usages, and beliefs." The French occupy an area colored green in my atlas, with borders and terrain features. They speak a language distinguishable from other languages, which French writers have used to compose a literature. They obey (or disobey) the same laws, and are ruled by and overthrow the same governments. They recognize certain events as forming their history, and some of these events are reinterpreted to contribute to a sense of national kinship. The past is a lesson to be learned and a legacy to draw from. France is atavistic in the sense that the same diseases tend to recur after a lapse of several generations.

The French can also be examined through the different forms of exchange that allow any society to survive—the exchange of words, on which education, culture, and the mass media are founded; the exchange of money and goods, which keeps the economy going; and the exchange of women, which keeps the species going.

Finally, there is a common frame of reference by which the nation's inhabitants know one another to be French. It is not revealed by the study of physical appearance or personality traits, for there again one falls into the stereotypes such as the *bon vivant* anarchist or the rationalist-libertine. It is a fund of data acquired by being raised in a country, knowledge less learned than absorbed through the pores as well as the mind: a mixture of proverbs like "Long as a day without bread" and trademarks like the Michelin-tire man, sermons and travelogues, prohibitions and platitudes, menus and metro tickets, the inbred notion of a certain way things are done and said. The Frenchman is not someone who possesses a navy blue passport and speaks the language of Descartes, but someone who knows who broke the Soissons vase, what happened to Buridan's donkey, why Parmentier gave his name to a hash, and why Charles Martel saved Christendom.

Part I

Data

Part 1

Data

I

The Epic Land

HUMAN attributes have been conferred upon the land since the first century B.C., when the Greek geographer Strabo praised its virtues "as though coming from an intelligent prevision." Later on, some geometrically minded geographer decided that France was a nearly perfect hexagon, with three sides on the sea and three on the land. What other people have made the shape of their country an esthetic value and a source of moral satisfaction? The hexagon became a treasure and an emblem. It developed a life of its own, and the dogma that France is a person became useful to rouse patriotic feelings. The ideology of the land was connected with divine interference: France, like Adam, had been modeled by the finger of God, and was thus perfectly proportioned and balanced (at equal distance between the equator and the Pole), fertile of soil, and temperate of climate. Its people were, by virtue of living there, a chosen people. There was no reason to stray outside the sacred hexagon, which provided an endless variety of good things. This was the European Eden, as the Germans knew when they coined the expression, "As happy as God in France."

Other countries are neuter in gender, but France is feminine. French leaders see her as an object of masculine passion. To Gambetta she was a mother, to General de Gaulle she is a fairy-tale princess. Thanks to historians like Michelet, who developed a doctrine of personalism in the nineteenth century, and to geography textbooks, which sing of territorial perfection in naïve terms, the French have come to think of their country as a noble lady blessed with natural wealth, envied by jealous neighbors, but always victorious in adversity—sometimes after being saved in extremis by a miracle worker.

She has a rare and complex beauty: French soldiers die for her *beaux yeux*. It has become an automatic reflex for French writers to give their country human traits. She has an eternal soul. She is, says the textbook used in elementary schools, "the friendliest and most generous nation in the world." Nourished by fable and myth, the reassuring catechism of a "clear and legible country" took root and became fixed in the self-indulgent notion of a providential shaping. Lyrical stanzas on the harmony of her contours are a set piece of French literature: She is "the only country in the world which has three distinct coastlines," wrote Paul Valéry, as if this were a magnificent achievement. Perfection in balanced variety is the Frenchman's gift by birthright. It has existed ever since elephants drank in the Seine. Other countries have made their geography epic: great land masses like the United States, with Frederick Jackson Turner's hymn to the frontier, and Russia, with the mystique that its territory can never be conquered, but only France boasts a God-given anatomy.

The French further believe there is a symmetry between the land and the people: The qualities of the land are to be found in the national character, and vice versa. A sky in the Île-de-France will be called "essentially French" because in its color and cloud formations it seems to embody qualities of lightness and subtlety. The French temperament is manifest in its landscapes. Every major French writer has explored this idea. André Gide wrote that just as the land is varied, "neither is French genius all heath, all pasture, all shadow or all light, but organized in a harmonious balance of these diverse elements." In difficult periods of history, however, the distinction arises between the ideal, harmonious France and the undeserving inhabitants of this Camelot, a nation of rude complainers, improvisers, fosterers of nepotism, and lovers of dishonest schemes. Jean Giraudoux in 1940 wrote a tirade on the glory of the land and the unworthiness of its people, and General de Gaulle often fell into somber moods brooding over the same theme.

In point of fact, France is no more a hexagon than England without Ireland is a triangle, and in any case, what does it explain about a country to try to fit it into an abstract, perfectly regular geometric shape like a cookie mold, dispensing with all the troublesome asperities? This idealized, romantic vision is necessary precisely because France, far from being predestined to be a nation, is not a geographical unit but a quilt of regions stitched over many centuries and after many wars, history's choice of one of several possible arrangements of Western Europe. The hexagon represents the longing for an orderly universe in compensation for a turbulent national history.

The hexagon obsession and the view of the land as an extension of national character is one origin of the belief in the superiority of French civilization and of Gallocentric *nombrilisme*—the conviction that France is the navel of the world. But the French, far from being at the center of the world, cannot agree on where the center of their own country is located. The controversy pits the inhabitants of Bruère-Allichamps, a few scattered houses on either side of a national road, against those of a rural hamlet called Vesdun. Each community has its experts and historians who have devoted their lives to this dilemma. Allichamps' claim rests on the discovery in 1757 of a Roman milestone which made vague references to marking the center of Gaul. It was placed on a pedestal at the crossroads and topped with a French flag and the caption: "Tradition designates this monument as the center of France." But Vesdun, according to its inhabitants, is the precise point at which a straight pin can balance a cardboard cutout of France. A sign there says: "According to the mathematical calculations of the mining engineer Monsieur Dumont . . . we find that Vesdun is the halfway point of 22 diagonals of France. This is the maximum number of diagonals intersecting the same point. Vesdun owes this privilege to its position as center of gravity of our national territory." Vesdun has science on its side, and Bruère-Allichamps has tradition, thereby summing up one of the basic conflicts of modern France. To paraphrase General de Gaulle's story of the three hundred cheeses, How can you govern a country which cannot even agree as to the location of its own center?

Instead of defending the sacred hexagon and searching for its exact center, instead of propounding the myth of a predestined nation, the French should see themselves as the triumph of human will over accidents of geography, as a nation not granted by God but forged by man, not given by birthright, but continuously fought for and refined. The illusion of a France complacently sheltered behind perfect natural borders betrays the reality of a permanent struggle.

A Geography Lesson

France is a country in Western Europe which occupies 212,659 square miles, not counting the offshore island of Corsica. It is about the same size as Texas without the panhandle. It is the thirty-fourth largest nation in the world, slightly smaller than Kenya, slightly larger than Thailand. France is sparsely populated. With 49,795,010 inhabitants (according to the 1968 census), it has the lowest population density of any Common Market country: 86 per square kilometer, compared to Italy's 167 and West Germany's 220. The two principal reasons for this spaciousness are that so many French soldiers have died young, and that the less children there are in a family, the more property there is to divide.

World atlases were once colored with the green of French possessions from Pondicherry to Gabon, but France today, for the first time since Richelieu, is virtually locked within its continental borders, which are roughly those defined by the Treaty of Utrecht in 1713. France was not geographically predestined to be a nation, as were such spatially defined units as the British Isles, Italy, and the Iberian peninsula. It is the creation of history more than geography. French greatness is a projection of French history rather than an expression of present power based on size, population, economic and military strength, or any of the other factors geographers use to measure nations of the first rank. The historic quest for natural borders and the myth of the hexagon have made up for the absence of natural ramparts. Geology's trick on France was to offer a natural border where it was least needed, while leaving exposed the main invasion routes from the north and east. What would the nation have become if the Pyrenees had been more strategically located on its German and Belgian fronts?

The odd idea arose that the Rhine was a natural border, whereas the vocation of any river is to be navigated and bridged. World War I battles bear the names of French rivers such as the Marne and the Somme. These and the hundreds of other names of places where armies have fought testify that France is easily penetrated from almost every direction. Hannibal crossed the Pyrenees, the Franks used the same broad boulevard later chosen by the Germans, the armies of the European coalition against Louis XIV crossed the Alps in 1707 and reached Toulon, and the Allies landed in Normandy in 1944. The northeast border is a pencil line on a map, indifferent to the terrain. Another imprecise but equally important French border is the inner division where two worlds meet, where *langue d'oc* (the dialects of southern France) meets *langue d'oïl* (the dialects of the north), where round Roman tiles change abruptly at Tournus to flat tiles, blue and gray skies touch, written Roman law gives way to Frankish common law, and the Latin faces the Celt.

There is no more ethnic than geographic unity in France. Defenders of the concept of a French race are divided into two camps. One holds that northern invaders such as the Franks furnished the country's elite, while the defeated Gallo-Romans became serfs; the other defends the country's Latin heritage. This division of opinion shows France turning one profile toward the northern land mass of Europe and the other toward Mediterranean civilization. If France has a geographic mission, it is not as the center of anything but as a hyphen between the landlocked or ice-bound populations of northern Europe and the maritime Latin people of the south. Beyond this north-south dualism there are the peoples of the marches, separated by national borders from their ethnic brothers. Catalans and Basques have as much in common with their Spanish counterparts as with fellow Frenchmen, as do Bretons with other Celts, Alsatians with Germans, and French inhabitants of the Jura with their Swiss neighbors. If the Versailles Treaty concept of national self-determination had existed under the *ancien regime*, France would have been balkanized.

Only a strong central authority prevented its regions from breaking away.

Thus France is not a spatial or an ethnic unit, but an historical aggregate of zones and peoples. It has fewer mountains than Switzerland, less sunshine than Italy, less coastline than Spain, less mineral wealth than Germany, and fewer maritime interests than England. But Italy is all on the same sea, Germany has only a window on the water, Spain is arid with extreme variations of climate, Switzerland is landlocked, and Britain is foggy and adrift from the Continent. French schoolchildren are taught that their country is a concentrate of the advantages of the others. It has high mountains, but 60 percent of its soil is at less than 250 meters altitude. It is washed by water. No point is more than 600 miles from the sea. Almost half its borders are coastline—Provençal coves, Normandy cliffs, Breton capes, Atlantic estuaries, and Rhone deltas. Twenty-seven thousand rivers and streams irrigate its soil; four of these are major rivers. The geography books say France has three daughters, the lazy Loire, the laughing Garonne, the well-behaved Seine; one son, the unruly Rhone; and a prodigal son, the Rhine. Despite these advantages, there are anemic regions like the southwest, which represents 25 percent of the land surface and only 10 percent of the population, and congested regions like the greater Paris area which represents 2.3 percent of the surface and 18 percent of the population.

The principal contrast in the organization of French society is between the extreme fragmentation of urban and rural life and Paris-controlled administrative centralization. One is a result of the other. A country made up of diverse regions and of peoples who have a tendency to break themselves up into ever smaller units was unified by laws and language. Paris was the trunk, and the rest of France its thousand branches.

What France is today is, to a greater extent than for most countries, a result of what France has been. The first French achievement, from the time the Gauls grew wheat and Cistercian monks cleared the forests (ashes were the first fertilizer), was a workable rural society. This was as specific to France as the network of great trading cities was to Rome and the need for an empire-conquering navy was to Great Britain. The self-sufficient farm was a goal that preceded the rise of cities whose wealth was based on trade; thus arose a mystique not so much of land as of property. Every Frenchman's dream is to own a corner of France. The furrows of the soil repeated in the lines of a peasant's face, the hedge-enclosed fields, the *chacun chez soi* mentality, all these are said to express the invincible permanence of the land. I remember a peasant near Poitiers showing me an oak about a yard away from a north-south hedge. That oak was planted as a corner alignment for the hedge, he said, but the West wind displaced the hedge, roots and all. Can you imagine the time that took? When the hedge was aligned with the oak, the Hundred Years War had not yet begun. "If you stand one hundred Frenchmen on their heads," said Kipling, "you would find the good plough mould on the boots of at least seventy-five." Today the figure would have to be cut, but it is still the highest in Western Europe. Eighteen percent of the French live off the land, compared with 8 percent of Germans.

Agricultural specialization hardly existed before the railroad. Every region grew the vine, whether the climate and soil were adapted to it or not. Today, 75 percent of the arable land is made up of farms of less than 125 acres. The typical farm remains the one that feeds the family, supplies a little wine, and sells a little wheat, a basket of eggs, and a few gallons of milk to cover other expenses. France's agriculture remains the most unproductive of the Common Market countries, although France is the most rural of those countries. The French peasant cannot penetrate the mystery of supply and demand because he does not consider himself a cog in an economic system of exchange. He grows food, and his job stops there, so he cannot understand why, as a Breton farmer put it, "when there's lots of artichokes it's not the same price, but it's the same artichokes." A favorite saying of rural areas is that "it takes a thousand years to make a peasant." Today the French are wondering how long it takes to unmake one.

With the fragmentation of farms, there was a proliferation of communes, or townships. Today there are 37,708 (compared with 1,354 townships in Great Britain), 30,000 of which have less than 2,000 inhabitants. The smallest is Castelmoron d'Albret in the Gironde, with 116 inhabitants on ten acres of rock; there is not even room for a cemetery. The largest is Arles, ten times the area of Paris, a commune which includes farmland where the famous

Crau hay is grown, the only hay which has a right to a government-controlled trademark. The least populated is the Alpine village of Saint-Cyrice, which has no inhabitants but is still listed in the dictionary of communes because the graves of its cemetery are visited each November by relatives.

A tradition of self-sufficiency exists for communes as it does for farms. Many towns manufacture a single product, a specialty associated with its name, like Dijon mustard, but often the products are uncompetitive or obsolete. In the town of Méru only 3 bone sawers are left to turn cows' tibias into dominoes. Only 150 violin makers remain in the Vosges township of Mirecourt. Saint-Rémy-sur-Durolle in the Puy-de-Dôme remains the capital of handmade penknives, and Saint-Barthélemy-d'Anjou has a virtual monopoly on *pissotières* (public urinals), which range in size from 3 places for a small school to 100 places for the Brest arsenal. Just as many of the farms, although not viable, are perpetuated by an archaic peasant class, many of these communes are not viable administrative or economic units but simply historical accretions, like Saint Martin near Tours that grew over the burial places of saints because Roman law forbade burial of martyrs in the cities.

The flight to the cities began with the building of the first railroads, when city life seemed an emancipation rather than a burden. The railroads hired rural labor, turning peasants into tracklayers. The first railroad was built in 1837, and Paris reached its first million in 1850. Nineteenth-century conscription, seven years long, accustomed peasants to the urban comforts of garrison life, while mail-order catalogs lured the girls. Cities grew out of needs. To the Gallo-Roman network (Lyons and Marseilles) were added those founded in the eleventh century, thanks to the Crusades (Le Mans, 1066; Cambrai, 1076). Taking advantage of the lord's absence, the burghers drafted their charters, emphasizing safe-conduct for visitors to encourage trade. The returning lord was presented with a *fait accompli,* and because the Crusades had impoverished him, he was eager to accept financial compensation. Cities grew also on favored sites—a bend in the river, high points. traveled roads, around a mill (Mulhouse), a monastery (Cluny), or a bridge (Brive-la-Gaillarde). They grew in the shadow of castles (Chinon and Amboise), around fairs (Beaucaire and Fréjus), near borders (Rocroi), around fortresses (Carcassonne), and on natural harbors (Le Havre, built by François Premier after the discovery of the New World, Brest, and Sète). In the nineteenth and twentieth centuries, health and leisure created thermal stations (Vichy) and resorts (Dieppe, Cannes, and Val-d'Isère). Now the first satellite cities are appearing, like Sarcelles near Paris.

In many of the old cities the divisions of time are marked like the concentric lines in the trunk of a tree. The city presses outward, breaking through its first fortifications, which become a circular boulevard. If new fortifications are built, there is soon another *extra muros* population. To the medieval cluster around the Romanesque or Gothic church are added the fine façades and large courtyards of the Renaissance, the deep perspectives and star-shaped street patterns of the seventeenth century, the equestrian statues of the eighteenth, the *beaux quartiers* of the nineteenth, and the skyscrapers, low-rent housing, and steel-and-glass designs of the twentieth.

With the cities came the roads. The history of France could be told through its roads. The preference for straight roads began when the Romans built them wide enough for a legion to march on and covered them with huge paving stones smooth enough for carriages. The Roman network spread to France for strategic reasons. Points of conquest had to be easily reached. In the twelfth century the impulse for road building was commercial and religious. Trade fairs and pilgrimages made roads the concern of burghers and monastic orders. One such order built the famous Avignon bridge in the twelfth century. The Hundred Years War interrupted public works, and by the fifteenth century the French road network was a jumble of pieces of Roman road, pilgrims' roads, tracks for migratory sheep, rural footpaths, and the private roads of lords. Still, the system was effective enough to allow the troubadours to propagate their *chansons de geste,* and contribute to spreading the French language at the expense of local dialects. The Charlemagne cycle of romances traveled by road from Paris to Spain. Architectural styles also spread, thanks to roads, as did Gothic sculpture. Half a dozen churches along the principal road to Compostela are inspired by the same architectural model, and the theme of the tonsured saint with keys and pallium is repeated from Poitiers to Bordeaux.

But the provinces of the French kingdom were crudely soldered to one another. Only after the end of the Hundred Years War against England and the dismemberment of the Burgundian state did the history of the royal road begin. The king needed roads to quell local dissidence, move his troops to borders, supply his fortresses, collect taxes, and correspond with provincial officials. The first postmaster general was named in 1479 (the actual title was Controller of the Cavaliers of the King's Stable), and by 1584 there were 292 relays. The principal user, it was felt, should pay for the building and upkeep of the roads. Sully, the minister of Henri IV, lined the royal roads with elms and walnut trees. His purpose was not landscaping but strategy. For the new heavy cannon drawn by ten or twenty horses, Sully wanted not only wider roads but a supply of hardwood in case the gun carriages broke down. Finally the mercantilist minister Colbert made the need for good roads a principle of government. He created the Ponts et Chaussées (Department of Public Works), which still has the same name and the same authority, a tribute to the permanence of some *ancien régime* institutions.

Good frontier roads linked Vauban's fortresses. But the same roads that brought the king's troops to the border also brought invaders deep into France. The roads on which taxes were collected also spread sedition. Roads both cemented national union and precipitated the fall of unpopular regimes. Uprisings and wars created needs for new roads while reducing the funds available for them. Despite these problems, the *ancien régime* bequeathed 18,000 miles of paved roads, a star-shaped network, with its center in Paris, that followed river valleys to the borders, to cities and harbors and provincial capitals. It was the finest system of roads in Europe, tangible evidence of national unity, admired by visitors. French travelers to England were baffled by the London-Dover road which grew inexplicably narrower. The roads were a godsend for the army of the First Republic, which was able to move its artillery to the border and defeat a European coalition at Valmy in 1792. But Blücher learned in 1814 what Bismarck and Hitler were also to discover, that all French roads lead to Paris.

The invention of the automobile ended the poetry of roads and the era of nonspecialized overland travel, when hansom cabs, pedestrians, and farmers taking their produce to market could use the same road without endangering one another. Hitler's Dr. Todt was the first to recognize, in 1933, the need for turnpikes. The non-specialized road had become an agent of death and obstruction, the opposite of its original function as a means of passage. But France, because of its attachment to the past, was slow to build highways. The engineers of the Ponts et Chaussées preferred to improve old roads, to enlarge them to three lanes, leaving such bottlenecks as bridges designed for sixteenth-century carriages, or twelfth-century towns virtually impassable on market days. And with the French driver, the three-lane road often turns into a game of chicken. The building of roads continues to be dictated by historical precedent rather than present need. Rigid thinking, a stubborn attachment to the lie of royal and Roman roads, and a nostalgia for the time when horse-drawn carriages shared the roads with pilgrims have given France a serious lag in the construction of superhighways. Lack of funds, protests the Ponts et Chaussées, but it has been, even more, a matter of restrictive attitude. By the end of 1968 France had slightly more than 1,000 kilometers of turnpike, fewer than Holland, one-third of Germany's total.

A Personal Inventory

So much in the French countryside tells the lesson of its origin. Place names are the fossils of geography: Nice from the Greek Nike (goddess of victory); Caen, the Norman capital from which William the Conqueror set out, from the Latin Catu-Magus (battlefield); Avallon from the Gaulish Aballo (apple); the medieval towns named for patron saints; the Norman towns ending in *bec* (stream) which recall the Northern invasions of the tenth century; and the Alsatian towns ending in *dorf,* a result of more recent German invasions. But what to make of the place names that seem borrowed from English, like Noisy, His, Condom, and Void? More incursions of Franglais?

The unmarked regional borders are revealed by a different system of enclosing the fields, or a change in the roof covering, or the position of the front door. Moving out of Paris into the leafy Île-de-France, you come to the point of origin of two styles that renewed the arts—architecture with the Gothic, and painting with Impressionism. The Île-de-France sky catches the glare like a pair of sunglasses. But Stendhal found the countryside ugly: "All you see on the horizon are great gray flat lines—an absence of fertility, trees stunted and cut for faggots . . . and that is what they call La Belle France! I am reduced to saying: She is morally beautiful, she has astonished the world with her victories; this is the country in the world where men feel the least unhappy because of their mutual action on one another."

In the Red Belt of Saint-Denis, where more Arabic is spoken than French, the first example of the Gothic, a repository of French monarchs, rises unexpectedly. Abbot Suger, the first great Gallic entrepreneur, built the church by hand in the twelfth century, and soon it was dwarfed by its imitators. Inside lie rows of curly-bearded, vacant-eyed, white-marble crowned heads; the Renaissance tombs show them both dead and revived, naked, showing their ribs and the incisions where their hearts have been cut out, lying next to their flabby-breasted queens, hands joined in prayer, and in the splendor of the afterlife.

A few miles from this Gothic apparition, a French "new city," the satellite dormitory of Sarcelles—functional and tedious Sarcelles, with its 50,000 inhabitants living a life where what is not prohibited is compulsory. Signs on the ground-floor bulletin boards: It is forbidden to beat rugs on the landing; it is forbidden to leave domestic animals to err on common property; it is forbidden to let children play in the stairwell; parents will be held responsible for supplementary cleaning costs. Culture makes a timid appearance in the names of the streets that link the austere apartment buildings; there is a Hector Berlioz (composer) street. Eighty percent of Sarcelles' inhabitants affirm that they are happy; they like the sun, the space, the air, the calm; they dislike their neighbors.

Moving north on France's only completed turnpike, Paris-Lille, across the uninterrupted northern plain, stone gives way to brick, slate to flat tile, cafés to *estaminets,* wine to beer, green knolls to coal hills, the smell of dung-filled barnyards to the soot of factory chimneys. The north and the east are rich in finds for military archeologists: pillboxes inhabited by squatters on the Franco-Belgian border; the bombed-out Gothic church of Douai still covered with the wood scaffolding of repair crews; the Maginot Line still manned by a few uniformed custodians; and the Vauban seventeenth-century fortress cities, an expression of the French genius for shutting themselves in, the network intact although it never stopped an invader—Rocroi, Phalsbourg, and Neuf-Brisach, built from 1699 to 1708, with the same pink porous sandstone used for the Strasbourg Cathedral. Neuf-Brisach is still confined within its ramparts, there are no suburbs, only the network of detached bastions in front of the ramparts and the half-moon fortifications protecting the detached bastions, at the bases of which vegetable gardens have been planted; faithful to its vocation as a fortress, the town was bombed by the Germans in 1870 and 1914, and by the Americans in 1944 because German antiaircraft batteries were stationed there.

The Argonne forest, a French Thermopylae in 1792 when General Dumouriez posted his troops along the gorges. Marshal Pétain said in the 1930's that it was impossible for German tanks to cross the Argonne; but the German general staff was not looking at the same map. Into the Lorraine, the shining baroque gates of Nancy, product of a blacksmith's skill and the whim of an exiled Polish king. The long rows of plane trees meeting overhead like a Gothic arch, their trunks painted white as though bandaged, and the cross-shaped green road signs outside towns that announce the time of daily mass. The fish-scale slate roofs of Charleville's Place Royale, its tangerine bricks and gabled windows, iron-tipped like Prussian helmets, and the Charles de Gonzague fountain where four naked boys whip dolphins. Arthur Rimbaud was born here and fled the grayness and provincial closeness.

The lush Lorraine, its half-dozen shades of green meadows and neat rows of houses separated by spaces filled with dung, log piles, and farming instruments. The Lorraine conveys a sense of permanence and authentic tradition stronger than other parts of France; it seems a fitting province for the birthplace of a national savior. The stone house in a garden at Domrémy, "part of the moral luggage of every Frenchman," says the guide. "How do you know it's really this one?" I ask. "Because it has been recognized as such," he solemnly replies. I should have asked, "What did Joan whisper to the king at Chinon?"

Into Teutonic Alsace, and Strasbourg, the first European city ever bombed, in 1870. But the glorious pink cathedral was spared. Victor Hugo in the nineteenth century climbed to the top and found his ideal panoramic vision. He could see the notched gables of Strasbourg roofs, the belfries of a hundred villages, two rivers, three chains of mountains, and enemy territory through the breaches in the Vosges. Today, after climbing the 330 steps, one surveys the mosaic of a France surprised by the twentieth century. On the horizon line, flames from gas refineries give a reddish tinge to the blue line of the Vosges. Another line closer in separates the low, slate-roofed, gable-ended Alsatian houses from an outer circle of twenty-story, reinforced-concrete, flat-roofed buildings, a radio tower, and high yellow building cranes that seem gigantic mechanical replacements for the vanished storks. The nests have been cleaned out of the chimneys to make room for television antennae. The courtyard of the Rohan Palace, across from the cathedral, has been turned into a basketball court.

Forty miles away, on the thin Ill River, France owes one of its three best restaurants outside Paris (along with Bocuse near Lyons and Roanne's Auberge des Troisgros) to industrial waste. The modest eating house that specialized in deep-fried gudgeon had to develop other dishes when the pollution of a nearby factory killed off the fish, and did so well that it received its third Michelin star in 1967. Into Mulhouse, where a high-rise city is going up outside the limits of the old medieval town. In some places, the French are adapting Marshal Lyautey's Moroccan tactic of building a modern European city distinct from the Arab medina.

Into the pine forests of the Vosges and the town of Épinal, a nineteenth-century propaganda center that published those edifying pictures for children, from Napoleon, the hero even in defeat, to good-hearted Mimi, who gives part of her lunch to the poor, saves a dog from drowning, and puts a compress on her pet parrot's leg. In these *images,* Waterloo is described as a victory: "Europe saw what the courage and discipline of the French soldier could accomplish—the French were not defeated—the day will come when soldiers will engrave on the points of their bayonets the words 'we were betrayed.' " As heralds of national achievement, the *images d'Épinal* served the same function and reached the same audience as the state-run television does today.

Into Besançon, which Victor Hugo called *"vieille ville Espagnole"* even though the Spanish occupied the city for only nine years. They have installed parking meters in the shady streets. Posters recruiting Foreign Legion volunteers now have a Polynesian background, with swaying palms and a swaying girl in a grass skirt. Down to the southeast where, adjacent to small farms where the salt chair is still placed near the kitchen stove, stand the nuclear plants of Pierrelatte and Marcoule.

The Midi begins with curtains of brightly colored linoleum strips over open doors. The togaed stone lady six miles north of Valence, who bears the inscription "Here the Midi begins," is redundant. The Midi is flagrant, in its fieldstone houses, its ocher soil, and its accent abounding in final consonants—words ending in *on* are pronounced with a *g* on the end, like Englishmen learning French and saying *maisong*. The Roman influence: Milestones which once marked every thousand double steps (about 1,500 yards) now mark kilometers; the latrine with two corrugated footholds; the utilitarian aqueduct that crosses the Gard, a tributary of the Rhone, at Remoulins; the honey-colored stones projecting from the center of the arches were destined to support scaffolding for repairs. What better sign of faith in the immortality of their empire than the thought that one day they would have to repair the Pont-du-Gard? Nîmes takes one back to the time of the Antonines, while the women of Arles are like the profiles on Parthenon bas-reliefs, grave and serene. The Cours Mirabeau in Aix-en-Provence, the most satisfying street in France, a street to be lived on, the street where Paul Cézanne and Émile Zola became friends and where the light breaks through the chestnut trees with the slanting brightness of a Cézanne landscape.

The monasteries of the southwest, the first international; for centuries you were a Benedictine first and a Frenchman second. They created the Romanesque style, local, not national, churches for parishioners and pilgrims in brown sacking, carrying their staffs, their cockleshell necklaces, their wallets and their rosaries, bound for a local saint or a renowned Christian site like Compostela, resting overnight in the church and fixing iron points, like track cleats, to the soles of their shoes to cross mountains. The mountain monasteries of the Benedictines, built in an age when safety meant remoteness. Today Mont-Louis in the Pyrenees is a military garrison, 5,000 feet high, with a climate like Archangel's. The disturbing scenes carved in the backs and armrests of the sixteenth-century choir stalls of the cathedral of Saint-Bertrand-de-Comminges: Two lunatics fighting over a stick, a monk whipping a bare-bottomed schoolboy, the serpent in the Fall ending in a woman's body, another woman with webbed feet and spread legs, manifold miniature illustrations of sin—a French Garden of Delights.

Reminders of other religions: The destroyed Albigensian fortress of Montségur, a monument to zealotry, built for the single purpose of defending the faith, and believed impregnable; assaulted and destroyed, its occupants were thrown from the parapets—the whole episode so un-French, so unreasonable. In the shadow of its ruins a wrinkled café proprietress complaining that soldiers have stolen a bottle of Pernod. "They are so unreasonable," she said, "I only charged them one franc twenty centimes for cognac instead of one franc fifty." The desert, a period in time, not a place, the period of the persecution of the Protestants; their refuge was the Cévennes mountains, the French badlands. The only area of France where Catholic priests are absent. This tradition too is kept alive, nourishing the memory of persecution; the houses with trapdoors to hide the Camisard chiefs, the synods held in caves, the women's heads shaved for attending a ceremony, the men shipped out as galley hands, the pastors put to death or sent to Vincennes tower, which still bears the graffito: "Never will I cease to magnify the Lord." Today, the Protestant minority, only 1.6 percent of the population, remains highly conscious of its traditions and achievements, and with the vitality of groups who have found survival problematic, provides more than its share of leaders, from statesmen like Couve de Murville to bankers like Schlumberger to writers like Gide. They bear the standard of the Puritan reflex in a self-indulgent nation. They secretly believe that the repression of the Reformation has kept France from being a modern and efficient nation. The Protestant president of the Court of Appeals proudly displays in his chambers the framed decree condemning his great-grandfather to the king's galleys.

Into the humped Basque country with the corn-colored Jurançon wine, each village with its *fronton* and red-shuttered, whitewashed houses with the date of construction carved over the door, and on the coast, the beach umbrellas turning in the wind like pinwheels, and the big beaded pitchers of cold rosé. The lifeguards at Biarritz wearing T-shirts marked SÛRETE NATIONALE in blue lettering, riot policemen on summer duty, the same ones who cracked students' heads open in May and June, 1968, now cheerfully joining them in volleyball, and advising seditious bathers that it is only legal to swim in the tiny strip they have marked off between two yellow flags. The road to Spain, traveled by Hannibal, Charlemagne, Philippe le Hardi, Napoleon, and fleeing RAF men during World War II, lined with cork trees, nettle trees (a flexible wood still used for making horsewhips), rosemary, and holly oaks. My grandfather knew Pyrenean peasants who remembered the road the English took in 1814 on their march on Toulouse, saying, "They paid for everything with gold pieces."

Up the coast to Bordeaux, a wine harbor for a thousand years, and its Conception Hospital where Rimbaud died. Bordeaux, where Montesquieu was more famous for his wine (the first Entre-Deux-Mers) than for his prose, and who, in keeping with a surviving tradition of the landed gentry, was given a beggar for a godfather so that he would remember that the poor were his brethren. Bordeaux, along with Lyons and Nantes and two other cities where secret fortunes have been made, as closed as the sacred enclosure of Peking. Bordeaux, sharing the slave trade with Nantes long after the Declaration of the Rights of Man was proclaimed.

Inland again, the prehistoric caves of the Dordogne, where the first men to inhabit the land of France sketched salmon in the Gorge de l'Enfer. The damp-damaged drawings, disembodied pieces of red and black, smudged like smoke stains. The Périgord, where peasants eat whole truffles baked over embers, like potatoes, for breakfast, and sleep on goosefeather mattresses. The noble lambs of the Aveyron, who give their milk for Roquefort, their skin to make Millau gloves, their bones for gelatin, and their wool for socks and sweaters.

The Auvergne, the lungs of France, breathing in both north and south, bullfighting and *framboise liqueur*. Roofs of the country houses flaring like skirts, and Sunday dances with accordion music, where the country lads try to get the girls behind a tree to "thread the wheat stalk." The black-lava churches of the Auvergne, and the angular angels with crossed wings at Notre-Dame-du-Port in Clermont-Ferrand, its healing black virgin with her ex-voto-lined altar, hundreds of marble plaques, the bricks of gratitude: Plead my case before God; I entrust my child to you; grace obtained; I will not be overwhelmed. Pascal, so French in his aversion to water, was born here; perhaps one of the ex-votos was for him. Riom, a town describing itself as always having had a vocation for justice, and which under Vichy held the mockery trials of Blum, Daladier, Reynaud, and other Third Republic leaders; its fourteenth-century Gothic virgin saved in the Revolution by the butchers' guild. The hotels where you order breakfast in your room and ten minutes later, invariably, there is a knock on the door and a voice saying, *"C'est pour le plateau, monsieur,"* as though there were only a single breakfast tray for the entire hotel and they were afraid you were going to down it with your croissants.

Into Burgundy, where the towns have a vine branch in their coats of arms, the hills entirely planted with vines, each like a head of short-cropped curly hair. Clos Vougeot is the most expensive real estate in France, $40,000 an acre. The roofs with painted tiles in patterns and one side longer than the other. They have stopped baking the slate tiles in wooden molds which made them porous so the lichen took root and gave them a mossy patina; today, steel molds; tomorrow, canned Burgundies; after tomorrow, powdered Burgundies. Each region has distinct vine-growing methods: In Alsace the vines hang like garlands from high wires strung between two poles; the Châteauneuf-du-Pape vines, as thick as olive trees, grow singly on flat pebbly soil; the Rhone and Anjou plants are tended individually, each one tied to a stake; the cheap Provençal vines look like untended shrubbery. Each region also has its own method for tying bales of hay. France can be mapped by the shapes of its hay bales.

Alesia, where the rhetorical statue of the defeated Gaul chieftain Vercingetorix was erected, a monument to the hinge date when Roman conquest of Gaul was confirmed. The French, said Count Sforza, must always invent a victory, and the Italians forget a defeat. They remember that Vercingetorix, according to legend, "fought like a centaur," and that at Waterloo the guard died but did not surrender. The hill of Alesia, where the Gauls were surrounded by better-armed and better-trained Roman legions, is today planted with barley. There is a Vercingetorix café and two museums crowded with archeological artifacts from digs begun by Napoleon III in his research for a life of Caesar, which invited flattering comparisons.

The Loire, useless but lovely, a façade river, a French theme along with façade architecture and façade drawing rooms. Anything is acceptable so long as it is well presented. Orléans and the Gothic memory of a community welded by faith, in the shadow of whose cathedral the Catholic poet Charles Péguy was born, the son of a carpenter and a chair mender, poet and victim of the mystique of the soil, killed in the first months of the First World War. Reading Péguy's litanies aloud with the twin spires of Chartres cathedral rising behind fields of ripe wheat like a fantastic clipper on the roiled sea's horizon; approaching Chartres on foot on an Easter pilgrimage, the priests having said mass in the bright, moist morning with bales of hay for altars: "Happy those who have died in a just war, happy the ripe ears and the harvested wheat."

The thousand small signs of a regulated existence rooted in the past: The Paris Communist Party tour of the Loire castles reconciles the Sans-Culottes with the surviving monuments of absolute monarchy. A Communist lady contemplates the moated serenity of Azay-le-Rideau and announces, "Something there belongs to me." Near the brooding ruins of Chinon, Richelieu, the first housing development, a town which the Cardinal commissioned in 1630 from architect Jacques Lemercier the way he commissioned portraits. It was constructed for the perspective, so that he could look out his castle window past a tree-lined carriage drive, down the main street and out past the town gate. It is perfectly symmetrical and geometric, a rectangle divided in its length by a street ending in two identical squares with identical fountains. On each side of the Grande Rue there are twenty-eight identical two-story houses, with slate roofs, oval wood doors with decorative nails, and identical ironwork on the balconies. The town is a hymn to the classical century's love of symmetry and perspective, both now spoiled by modern accretions like service stations and shop marquees. The castle was razed in a fire, but the three thousand inhabitants still live contained within the town's moat and ramparts, as though obeying an injunction from the Cardinal to remain forever in the seventeenth century.

Westward to the Mont-Saint-Michel, an island of high observance, inspirer of Henry Adams. The sea sometimes comes in at the speed of a galloping horse, and the granite church itself, on its steep pedestal, looks like the prison it became in the nineteenth century, or like an illustration for the kind of fairy tale that gives children nightmares. Driving through Normandy, an encounter with "the gods of the road." Dense crowds raising their arms in veneration as the wearer of the *maillot jaune* (golden tunic), the hero who has proved his mettle in mountain passes, pedals by, grimacing. What is sillier than a group of grown men pumping on bicycle pedals for three weeks? And yet what remains a more popular national rite than the efforts of these muscular giants of the road? There is a French fascination with the wheel that relates the national consciousness to a two-dimensional, Ptolemaic universe, whereas the sports madness of England and America is concerned with Copernican spheres, the cricket ball and the baseball. Athletes and chefs are the last emissaries of French supremacy, and compensate for inadequacies in other fields. The Olympic skiers are the French astronauts; their victories against the clock make up for the absence of a manned space program. Killy, national hero and winner of the Legion of Honor, is the French John Glenn, and his contract with Chevrolet is viewed as less than treason, a temporary aberration.

Past Dieppe, where Oscar Wilde took refuge under the pseudonym Mr. Melmoth, and into the harsh Breton peninsula, a reservoir of priests (10 percent of French missionaries), Paris prostitutes (the pimps wait for the guileless Breton country girls on the platforms of the Gare Montparnasse), and cannon fodder (10 percent of the Breton male population died in the 1914–18 war as against 3.5 percent for the population as a whole). General de Gaulle, reviewing 400 Free French troops, 100 of them from the Breton Île-de-Ré, commented, "Is Brittany, then, one-fourth of France?" The Breton farmers still take their cows and pigs to the magic fountain of Saint Nicodemus to protect them against disease. The love of gardens—Breton fishermen made lettuce grow on the coast of Newfoundland. But love of gardens is not love of nature. The Goncourt brothers said they preferred a painting of a landscape to the landscape itself. The megaliths in a meadow near Camaret-sur-Mer serving as the borders and goals of a soccer field.

Normandy and the BOF (*beurre, oeufs, fromages,* or butter, eggs, and cheese). The farmers who always complain except in wartime when the black market makes them rich, and who sit around figuring that since there is a European war every twenty years or so, they are about due. Echiré butter, the best in the world, only 1,500 pounds a day is made; the Aga Kahn used to have it flown to him daily. And the Bayeux tapestry, the first comic strip, a 210-foot-long roll of unbleached linen on which the French version of the conquest of England was woven in the eleventh century. A triumph of the juridical French mind, an illustrated legal brief arguing William's right to conquer England because he had been betrayed by Harold, and one of the first efforts to present history, not only as epic, but as the case for the prosecution.

The Present Dead

Every French commune has a church, a café, and a *monument aux morts.* This last venerable institution resembles the practice of certain primitive societies who believe that the spirit of their dead is still among them and who periodically set out food and clothing to keep them placated. In the French vision, the *monuments aux morts* are a compensatory offering for defeat. The custom began after the rout of 1870 and spread after the First World War which, although an Allied victory, was a French defeat if measured in terms of population loss and weakened economy. With 1,400,000 dead, one French citizen out of 25, France was the *grande mutilée* of World War I. Without outside help, the hereditary enemy would once again have overrun the sacred soil of the *patrie.* The *monument aux morts,* usually granted a town's most prominent site, is a reminder of death and defeat, a morbid form of insistence on the number of times France has been bled. Their posturing *poilus* and false heroics evoke much of what is archaic and negative in France. In their families, the French are discreet and unsentimental about death, but on a national level, death for the *patrie* serves as a pretext for the worst kind of maudlin rhetoric, and propagates the myth that French wars are virtuous. The monument in the village of Les Eyzies says: "To all those who died for civilization."

Today their theme, revenge on Germany, is no longer relevant. And yet they are so much a part of the French consciousness that the commune of St. Nicolas-en-Forêt in the Moselle, created in 1958 as a dormitory city for the employees of a machine-tool factory, insisted on its *monument aux morts*. It is one of the two monuments to the dead in France with no names on it, the other being in the fortunate commune of Thiberville in the Eure, which did not suffer a single casualty in 1870, 1914, or 1940. Most of the monuments one sees, in a square next to the church or on the town's main thoroughfare, were cast in the Vaucouleurs foundry, and there is an uninspired, highly conventional Vaucouleurs style: the helmeted hero, the *poilu* sighting his rifle, waving at lagging comrades, falling with a flag draped over him, standing at attention, or shaking his fist in an easterly direction.

Normandy favors winged victories, the Midi specializes in weeping Mariannes, and towns with modest budgets can afford no better than a scroll with a list of names. The monuments of the northeast are the most *revanchard;* they were often installed when the nation was bent on recovery of the Alsace and Lorraine. At Mars-la-Tour, three kilometers from the lost Lorraine, an 1873 monument shows France in the guise of a noble lady posing a crown of laurel on the head of an expiring soldier, whose rifle is being picked up by two children leaning against an arch labeled "Hope." A few pacifist monuments erected by Socialist mayors created national scandals. One was put up in 1923 in the town of Gy-L'évêque, with the inscription "War on war." The mayor was tried and sentenced to a heavy fine, and gendarmes uprooted the offending stele.

Famous sculptors like Bourdelle and Maillol were commissioned for funeral monuments, but Maillol scandalized the population of Banyuls-sur-Mer with a naked soldier wearing a helmet. These monuments present France as a country which has been in more or less continuous warfare throughout its history. The one at Bouvines, site of a famous thirteenth-century battle that saved the French monarchy, proudly bears the dates 1214–1914, and Sedan has three separate monuments, one for each war. The pink sandstone lion at Belfort, which looks as if it were made out of huge children's blocks, marks the spot where French troops held out in 1870 for 23 days after the armistice was signed—a futile, sacrificial form of stubbornness. An old woman expressed to her grandson the *monument aux morts* mentality that it is every Frenchman's responsibility to be killed or captured by the enemy: "Remember your father, who was gassed at Verdun, and your older brother, who was taken prisoner in Germany."

The most grandiose example of the exaltation of death in battle is the area around Verdun, a national park of mourning, where picnics, music, games, and other activities usually associated with the verdant outdoors are forbidden by a 1965 law. In the words of the official brochure, the zone is maintained as "an immense natural cemetery which holds the remains of 200,000 solders." Near Verdun, there are five ghost communes, wiped out in 1916, but still kept officially alive to perpetuate their memory. Verdun was a senseless carnage, but its memory is transfigured into a ritual sacrifice to the nation. The ossuary, a church like an elongated pillbox which has sprouted a cement blossom on a long ungraceful stem, overlooks a field with a single crop: wooden crosses painted white. One is left saddened that a nation must continue to celebrate its military blunders simply because they were blunders of magnitude.

As Georges Duhamel said, "There is no poetry of hell, no transfiguring indulgence of hell." Today there is a break in the morbidity. It has little left to feed on. The *monuments aux morts* are shards of a French past abolished by the French present. A generation has come of age that learned even of the colonial wars secondhand. And there are, to my knowledge, no *monuments aux morts* for the colonial wars, which is one way of saying that there was nothing exalting about them. Perhaps the time has come when the French dead will finally be laid to rest.

Common Attitudes

Crossing dissimilar regions, one becomes aware that beyond regional customs there are common attitudes, an elusive but tangible Frenchness. Some of these attitudes are changing, and everywhere one feels the demands of the present scraping at an encrusted way of life. How do the French reconcile traditional values with belief in progress, that two-edged invention of the Encyclopédistes? After teaching at Nanterre in 1967, H. Stuart Hughes wrote about *triste Paris,* complaining that there were hardly any buses with platforms left. How to change and remain the same?

How does one reconcile the gloomy silence of the badly lit provincial towns after nine with the myth of sinful night life? Ninety-eight percent of France goes to bed early. Daniel Defoe called the French "a people of dancers," but polls show that 74 percent of them never dance. How does one explain the greater attention paid to widows' weeds than wedding gowns, the mask of secretiveness that falls over the cook's face when you ask her for a recipe?

The traveler finds signs and attitudes presenting themselves to his scrutiny like landscapes: the demeaning national emblem, the noisy, self-satisfied barnyard strutter, peremptory and unproductive. The meaning of fraternity: it no more means that a Frenchman will love you like a brother than a crucifix over a bed means that the person who occupies it is a good Catholic. It is a decorative virtue. In its highest social form, fraternity is the Frenchman's inalienable right not to dislike you. French vivacity—the same play takes two hours in Paris and three hours in Berlin. French belief in their own humanitarianism: "The French would not do what the Germans did."—"What about torture in Algeria?"—"That's not the same."— "Why not?"—"I don't know." The fondness for writing anonymous letters, so common that a name had to be devised for their authors: *Corbeau* (crow). In occupied France the German Kommandantur received cartloads it threw away unread. Liberation was the occasion for another flood of *corbeau* mail. Voltaire, the shopkeeper's philosopher: Don't ask for too much, mind your own business, find contentment in smallness, avoid quixotic pursuits. The rationale of the shopkeeper: I am my own boss, no one's beast of burden, and I see the money coming in. French distaste for the mediocrity of the shopkeeper mentality: Saint Exupéry saying that we are living in a time when the cathedrals have been taken over by the little old ladies who rent the chairs. The need to *rouspéter,* which Larousse defines as "choleric resistance." Obstinacy in sterile discussion. The Frenchman is defined more in opposition to than in agreement with his society.

Monsieur le Curé extracting from his cassock grayish lumps of sugar to give children, like a trainer rewarding an obedient horse. The church has been recognized by nearly every regime as an institution of public utility, even though the French as a people can best be qualified as moderately agnostic. Anticlericalism has lost its relevance since the 1905 separation of church and state. Gone are the days when the *instituteur* started his first-grade class by asking the pupils to recite the Our Father: Our Father who art in heaven—*What do you mean, "in heaven," I just saw him in a café.* Give us this day our daily bread. *Don't you get your bread from the baker like everyone else?* ... and so on. What religion has done for France is to help make manual labor respectable. "To work like a Benedictine" is a common expression. And was not Christ a carpenter?

The majestic *caissières:* "The handsomest woman I had ever seen give change for a five-franc piece," wrote Henry James. The conviction that civil service is a sanctuary. The domino-playing farmer adding water to his *pastis* and confiding: "My daughter married a customs official." The fragile step of the *petite vieille,* bent over the cobblestones, on her way to the post office to collect a money order, and tipping the employee the way you tip a roulette-table croupier, a propitiatory offering to the temple of the state. The houses where you still find the *certificats d'études* (grade-school diplomas) framed in the living room, next to the brownish photograph of *grand-père* in his stiff *poilu*'s greatcoat. The Café du Commerce, where the cracker-barrel types confront the past and the future, triannual rotations of crops, and astronauts. For the café is the showroom of progress, first in the village with central heating and television, unique possessor of an espresso machine. Hidden peasant wealth: Jean-Jacques Rousseau in the eighteenth century accepting rural hospitality; the larder is bare, but pink hams, wine jugs, and fresh bread are miraculously produced from a trapdoor. The 1968 peasant deliberating whether to buy a television set; he can easily afford it but doesn't like the ostentation of the antenna showing (in other countries there are houses with antennae and no sets).

The dozens of towns with municipal swimming pools built over the last ten years (the results are reflected in the improvement of French Olympic swimming teams), but the sacred noonday lunch closes them at the time you most want to swim, just as the sacred August vacation closes the provincial museums when there are the most tourists to visit them. The provincial houses, secretive as harems, a high stone wall around the garden, closed shutters, dust sheets over the furniture, a forlorn cracked porcelain cupid over the mantelpiece. The veneration of family furniture and family paintings, no matter how awful. There is no adequate translation for the French word *foyer*. It is more than a home; it is every Frenchman's private and seldom accessible *patrie*. The passion for the *vue imprenable,* the view that can't be taken from you, like an apartment on the Bois de Boulogne. The carriage gateway, still a status symbol. The importance of measuring time: the floor-to-ceiling wall clocks with bucolic scenes painted on the pendulums. The dream of "my interior," a house big enough to receive a few guests, small enough so as not to encourage them to stay. As opposed to the American open house, the French saying, *on ne donne pas la clef de sa maison* (one does not give the key to one's house).

In the eighteenth century, when the middle class became homeowners, they grew *frileux* (sensitive to chills) and obsessed with "keeping in the heat." The fear of drafts persists: Today vacationing campers tell one another as they raise the tent flaps, "attention to the current of air." The concern for health: *la santé avant tout.* The reluctance to admit sicknesses: "I am not sick, just a little tired." The other face of wine drinking is the cult of mineral water and the *tisane* (infusion).

The unsentimental attitude toward death. Gertrude Stein's story about the daughter of the café owner who had a lump of sugar ready each day for her favorite dog. One day she was told the dog was dead. She had a good cry, and then ate the lump of sugar. The indifference toward inedible animals: A police van roars up to a dead dog lying on the sidewalk of the rue St. Anne in Paris, and a passerby remarks: "And to say that they call a police *secours* van for a dog." (Inference: If a human being were lying there, no help would come.) A policeman puts on gloves to pick up the dog and throw him into the van, but his superior says "Just take it by the leash." Fondness for household pets is associated with misanthropy. (Pascal: The more I see of mankind, the more I like my dog.) Love of nature is utilitarian; the only forests left untouched are either state property or kept for riding to hounds. Nature is loved if it produces vineyards rather than leprechauns. The French garden is barbered nature. One exception: the mystical soil of the *patrie,* the veneration for sites where famous battles were fought.

The isolation of villages that are not on a main road or a direct railroad line, which creates a feeling of remoteness from centers of activity and decision. There were, before the Germans invaded the unoccupied zone in 1942, villages which had heard of the war only from hearsay, just as it took the Bolshevik Revolution five years to reach the borders of Russia. But no matter how isolated, no French town wants to be found guilty of disregarding culture. A town of 11,000 inhabitants, like Digne in the Haute Provence, which cannot be reached without changing trains twice, keeps up an active intellectual life as therapy for its end-of-the-world complex. There is a Catholic center for French intellectuals, which in a typical year gave conferences on Galileo, Marx, the Human Condition, and Growing Old; a Society of Natural History of the Haute Provence; a Society of Doctors of the Low Alps; a Club of Music Lovers; a Literary Society of Haute Provence; and a Provençal Language Association. There is an amateur theater troupe, called the Troubadours of Joy, and 40 percent of the inhabitants subscribe to the circulating library (the books most in demand are translations of Frank Slaughter and Erskine Caldwell).

Health and cleanliness: never a French priority. Public baths were reputed to be temples of sodomy. A real nobleman, it was said, had sourish armpits and smoking feet. Madame de Sévigné wrote candidly, "The marquis' hands were almost as filthy as my feet." Napoleon did not take baths or brush his teeth, but was rubbed down with cologne every day. Chamber pots were emptied out of windows until a Paris police prefect imposed the use of garbage pails which bear his name, *poubelles.* "The staff lavatory," wrote George Orwell about a Paris restaurant kitchen in the nineteen thirties, "was worthy of Central Asia." Thirty years later, the proprietor of a restaurant with two stars in the Michelin told me it was pointless to try to get rid of rats. He knew, for he had put ground glass in the ratholes and the rats had found it delicious. Negligence accounted for the high rate of venereal disease in the nineteenth century; Gustave Flaubert, Guy de Maupassant, Léon Gambetta, and Stendhal were among the foremost exponents of French syphillization. Every age has its favorite illness. Today it is the liver, but under Louis XIV it was the fistula; 1686 was the year of the king's operation, and it was fashionable to be able to say, "I had mine out too." It took two wars and the highest mortality rate of any army before French doctors learned to drain a wound.

It took a century for French surgeons to wash their hands before examining a patient. Pasteur said to Claude Bernard, one of the founders of experimental medicine: "Nothing of mine will remain." "You are mistaken," Bernard replied. "This morning my surgeon Gosselin came by to probe my poor bladder. A young intern named Guyon, one of your disciples, was with him. Gosselin washed his hands after examining me, Guyon before. That, Pasteur, is what will remain." While the putrid outhouse is still a part of the French rural scene, the statistics for families with private baths is rising. The French have, in the second half of the twentieth century, understood that culture is not only a great literature but a lack of hostility toward bathtubs.

But in the most modern apartment buildings, the French still insist on separating the toilet from the bathroom. I have never really understood why evacuation should enjoy the privilege of an individual room; perhaps to the Frenchman the toilet is a throne, as it was to French kings who received ambassadors on their *chaise percée*.

Is poor hygiene one of the aspects of individualism—affirming one's personality by not washing one's feet? But the French are also a nation of sheep, they queue up as much as the British, they blindly follow fads and fashions, and they hold predigested opinions to a greater extent than other Western nations because they are brainwashed by government-operated television. Individualism first takes the obvious form of the yeoman tradition of contesting authority. It is a polite word for selfishness and a conception of freedom which has nothing to do with the American Four Freedoms. The essential French freedoms are the freedom to judge the judges, to mock institutions, to keep one's hat on when the "Marseillaise" is playing, and to dispense with God. On another level, it is an acquired reflex to think for oneself.

In their homes and their education, the French are conditioned to think, and individualism becomes a Cartesian attitude of systematic doubt, intellectual curiosity, and not accepting as correct what is evidently wrong. Joseph Prudhomme's statement, "That is my opinion, and what is more, I share it," is still a valid stereotype. A publisher who deals with printers in France and Germany told me that if something was printed backward you could run hundreds of thousands of copies on the German presses before the error was discovered, but in France some obscure workman would spot it at once, debate the origin of the error with his colleagues, and discuss the responsibilities involved. The time lost would work out about even in both cases. This is not an age for individualism, however; and the most celebrated French trait has a margin of operation which today seems restricted to parlor eccentrics, odd political groups like the Party of the Discontented, or to profitable anarchy like tax evasion. The days of France as a nation "divided into fifty million inhabitants" has given way to the crushing popularity of the party in power, almost as effective if less spurious than the one-party system of Democratic republics.

The habit of thinking for oneself is part of every parent's repertory. A child is punished "to teach him how to think." There are many ways to Paradise. The parent's duty is to teach the child the French "way" so that he will not go astray. This starts at birth, with the absence of toilet training; the *petites coliques* are considered normal. A healthy child, French parents believe, should not cry; contentment is passive. If he cries, it must be that he is being stuck by an open safety pin in his diapers.

In the schools, decorated with bas-reliefs of François Rude's "La Marseillaise," the children work out the same *règle de trois* problems as their grandparents: Two trains traveling at the speeds of 62 and 84 miles per hour leave two cities 861 miles apart, at the same time. How long will it take them to meet? And on the frontispiece of the schoolbooks on *morale,* an ant carries a crumb of bread five times its size. Education is important because it is a useful weapon. French mothers warn their children in innumerable small ways that life outside the family circle is menacing. Because of this insistence on the domesticated child, there are, as someone has said, no young men in France, only elderly schoolboys.

Life will divide these elderly schoolboys into a group of initiates who have always done the right thing and a group of outcasts. A Sorbonne professor told me he knew, just by entering his colleagues' apartments, which of them had slipped up and lost the chance to become full professors. Their apartments smelled of persecuted heresy. In every aspect of French life there is a Masonic division between the initiated and the uninitiated, from the few favored customers for whom the restaurant owner saves his hidden store of wine to someone who has been "recommended" and gets special treatment in government offices. The attitude immediately changes from peevish indifference to conspiratorial warmth. Belonging is everything, the barriers of suspicion fall and one is allowed into the magic circle, protected from a hostile world.

France is a nation which operates largely on multiple circuits of favoritism—the Resistance, political parties, professions, old school tie, social background, clubs, geographical origin, kinship, and many others. No night of August 4 can ever banish the era of privileges; wherever there is a queue, there is someone being let in the back way. Even in a place which should normally be impervious to privilege, like the Bibliothèque Nationale, there are special arrangements because there are not enough seats. A line forms around eleven o'clock on most mornings, and those waiting pull a numbered ticket from a machine just like the ones at Paris bus stops. Users of the library often wait an hour or more, although a glance shows that some seats are vacant, but these are reserved for privileged persons who sometimes never show up. I have had the same experience at snack-bar counters, where there was only one stool vacant and the counterman announced that it was reserved. First come first served is not a French notion. Or is it? After all, we owe the queue to the French, and the queue is the recognition of the rights of those who arrive first.

The Immovable Indigestion

(With apologies to Ernest Hemingway, who carried with him memories of the twenties and, one would like to imagine, a bronze paperweight of Gustave Eiffel's 300-yard-high flagpole, the frilled pink garter of a Moulin Rouge chorus girl, the collected works of Eugène Sue, a Monet painting of the Gare Saint-Lazare in the rain, a recipe for *Entrecôte Bercy*, and a second paperweight—a paving stone.) Paris, alas, is not only the expatriate's dream, where good Americans go when they die. It is the glory and misfortune of France, the circle of selfishness, the magnet that draws the iron filings, the grafted heart that beats at the expense of the rest of the organism. It is the antidote to the complexity of the French nation and its lack of geographical definition. The guilt of regions is held together by the binding agent of Paris. Diversity finds its solution in a capital that crowns all the rest. As a result, Paris suffers from gigantism, but also from particularism. Too often, that is, Parisian attitudes are taken for French attitudes.

Much of French history is simply Paris history presented as a *fait accompli* to the provinces. Perhaps the most original aspect of the May-June, 1968, uprising was that the provinces were for once given a chance, through the electoral process, to repudiate a Paris-sparked insurrection; more than to backlash, the triumph of Gaullism was due to the long-awaited vengeance of the ignored provinces on Paris the almighty and its garrulous, insular, smug inhabitants.

What is Paris? Two banks of the Seine, 32 bridges, 75 museums, 250 movie houses, 800 traffic-light crossings, 19 swimming pools, 17 sports stadiums, 80 miles of subway built in 1900, 250 miles of laundered building frontage, a tower visited by 1,800,000 persons annually, 85,000 trees, 567 *vespasiennes* (street urinals named after the Roman emperor who was the first to charge admission to public latrines), one fortune-teller for every 200 inhabitants, and 900 statues, including those of 50 poets, 37 writers, 13 chemists, 12 politicians, 5 kings, 5 revolutionary leaders, 3 victims of religious zeal, 3 mathematicians, and 2 gardeners. Paris also has 20 cemeteries—a petrified city of the dead within the city of light—with thousands of miniature stone mansions with ironwork padlocked gates and the inscription "Perpetual concession." Thanks to these substantial tombs, the Frenchman takes his sense of property with him.

The greater Paris region today covers the department of the Seine, plus most of Seine-et-Oise and Seine-et-Marne. A population roughly the same as Australia's lives on a surface about three times the size of Staten Island. This population includes 25 percent of the nation's civil servants, 42 percent of its students, 20 percent of its factory workers, 28 percent of its doctors, 61 percent of its artists, 62 percent of its men of letters, 25 percent of its factories employing more than 25 persons, 33 percent of its stores employing more than 10 persons, and 65 percent of its company and bank headquarters. It consumes 300 liters of water per person per day, twice the national average, 38 percent of the nation's gas, and 20 percent of its gasoline; it enjoys 5.25 square yards of greenery per person (the bulk of it provided by a former royal forest donated to the city and rechristened the Bois de Boulogne), compared to 50 square yards per person for Washington, D.C., and 9 for London. Since it is France's brain, scepter, wallet, hive, beacon, and crowded attic, Paris is prone to self-congratulation. As one of its bards wrote: "On these 15,000 acres more has been thought, spoken, and written than anywhere else in the world. Here are the accumulated stratifications of wit, reasoning, and good taste. Here is the planet's freest, most elegant, and least hypocritical crossroads."

Other countries of France's importance have at least two cities with more than 1,000,000 inhabitants—Berlin and Munich, Rome and Milan, London and Manchester, Tokyo and Osaka, Madrid and Barcelona—but Paris dwarfs all other French cities, and monopolizes with cumbersome versatility the multiple functions of cities. It is not just a diplomatic capital like Rome, or a business capital like Milan, or an intellectual capital like New York, or an historic capital like London, or a tourist capital like Athens, or a hippie capital like Amsterdam, or an academic capital like Oxford or Cambridge, but all of these. It is a prism of unrelated activities. The French believe the attraction of the capital is so great that it once helped keep colonies calm. When Rudyard Kipling visited Algiers in 1921, he was surprised to find French Islam calm while the rest of the Middle East was in an uproar. The mayor told him: "Paris is the trump of our diplomacy. If a local chief becomes excited, dissatisfied, or wants to play the prophet, there is always the solution of a trip to Paris. Paris turns wolves into sheep." The capital remains a trump with which to impress visiting dignitaries.

Paris is also the strategic symbol of France. Its occupation means French defeat, just as its liberation means French victory. The famous photograph of the fat Parisian watching the *Wehrmacht* parade down the Champs-Élysées as his eyes well with tears summed up a nation's shame, just as General de Gaulle's loping stride down the same thoroughfare four years later was sufficient proof of triumph. It is inconceivable that the French would continue fighting on their own territory after Paris has been occupied, as the Russians did after Napoleon occupied Moscow in 1812.

The provincial inferiority complex goes back to the Middle

Ages; the thirteenth-century coauthor of the *Roman de la Rose,* Jean de Meun, asked that "my rude, ill-bred, and savage language be excused, for I was not born in Paris and have none of its graces." The word "province" connotes all that is backward and unfashionable, a connotation enshrined by dictionaries (the 1900 Larousse defined "provincial" as gauche and lacking in distinction) and newspapers, which continue to gather the humdrum events outside the capital under the rubric "Province." It has always been taken for granted that excellence in all fields is Parisian. Almost every provincial town has a shop called *au petit Paris.* François Villon praised the capital's food (*il n'est bon bec que de Paris*); Honoré de Balzac said that "in Paris there are several kinds of women, but in the provinces there is only one kind and that poor creature is the provincial woman." Victor Hugo's genius was considered so Parisian that the towers of Notre Dame were said to form the first letter of his last name.

Paris the religious center begins with the conversion of the Frankish king Clovis, who made it a Christian capital. Five ecumenical councils were held there from 552 to 614. So many churches, monasteries, and convents were built that the suppression of the monastic orders in 1789 turned over to the state one-eighth of the capital's surface. Equally ancient is its role as political capital. Vauban called it "the abbreviation of France." Louis XIV, while fleeing the dangers and temptations of Paris for the antiseptic splendor of Versailles, nonetheless decreed as he departed that "Paris is the capital of all our states ... and must serve as an example to all the other cities of our kingdom." The position of Paris as administrative center was not due to Napoleon but to Philippe-Auguste, in 1194. After his defeat at Fréteval by Richard the Lion-Hearted, his archives were destroyed, and he decided to keep duplicates of royal acts in the Paris Palace of Justice, an embryonic bureaucracy which finds a distant echo today when a subprefect in the Alps must ask Paris for permission to fix the town-hall roof after a heavy snowfall. Government buildings began to rise, were populated with civil servants, and could not be moved with the court to Versailles.

Early on, economic life was governed by the rulings of the Paris magistrates, such as the 1667 decree on the provisioning of Paris that was valid for the entire kingdom. The concentration of high finance came about because kings needed credit. *Ancien régime* bankers and General Farmers (who purchased contracts to collect indirect taxes) formed a Paris-based, precapitalistic financial oligarchy. The influence of Paris as a consumer was felt in the provinces. Traffic on the Seine was one-way; the barges arrived laden with grain and dairy products and left empty. In the eighteenth century the Auvergne could find no market for its Cantal and Saint-Nectaire cheeses, which were considered too pungent by Parisians, who preferred to import Dutch Edam. In the nineteenth century, Paris controlled the French economy through credit and investment. Eighty percent of the first railroad bonds were snapped up by Parisians. Provincial capital was drained by higher interest rates, taxes, and networks of middlemen and distributors who favored Paris. The railways were built to link Paris with its provincial prefectures; the anxieties of an unstable regime had priority over the economic necessity of joining remote regions. The capital became, and remains, the financial hub, the commercial pivot, and the principal consumer market.

Its importance as a university center originated with licenses the king gave the clergy in the twelfth century to teach theology and canon law on the left bank. The medieval Sorbonne was run by religious orders and attracted students from all of Europe. Teaching was dogmatic and based on the famous *explication de texte,* in which no opinion or judgment is formed. Even then it led to parrotry. Students complained about the dry scholastic methods, although the friezes of Notre Dame show them sitting obediently at the feet of their teachers. The Jesuits in the seventeenth and eighteen centuries imposed a moral interpretation of history; it was not so much the date of the fall of Carthage that mattered as the personal conduct of Hannibal and Scipio. After Napoleon placed the university under government control, many traditions of the old Sorbonne were maintained. There was a faculty of theology until 1886. Today some doctoral theses are still written in Latin.

Paris' reputation as a taste maker came about thanks to the public buildings associated with different regimes, the attraction of artists to the capital, and the concentration there of the mass media. Louis XV, Louis XVI, Régence, these are not national but Parisian styles, sometimes created by a single monument. Under the Second Empire, the architect Jean-Louis Garnier showed the Empress Eugénie his designs for the Paris Opéra. She made a face and said, "What is it? It's not Louis Fifteen, or Louis Sixteen." "It is Napoleon Three," Garnier said grandly, and so it became. Society has always meant Paris society, because the old and distinguished provincial families of Lyons, Bordeaux, Poitiers, Nantes, Bourges, Clermont-Ferrand and other wealthy cities loathe publicity. A tiny group, at first the court and then an achievement elite, has represented France because this group is the most productive, fashion conscious, and boisterous.

The *Belle Époque* was not a period of national life, but a passing Parisian phase, with its buildings, furniture, and subway stations that look as though they had been designed by an entomologist—the Maxim's dragonfly style and the butterfly-wing chairs and lampshades. France in that period is remembered less for its diplomacy or economic growth than for the fatuity of the Parisian upper crust (*gratin*) at a time when idleness was respectable and American heiresses came to pluck the often indigestible fruit from ducal family trees.

The aristocracy fulfilled a Parisian need for disinterested extravagance and sureness of taste. The comtesse Greffulhe had the dresses of her children's nurses made in Cluny lace. My grandmother, the duchesse de Gramont, bought live trout from Fouquet's restaurant on the Champs-Élysées to feed the seals at the Jardin des Plantes. Robert de Montesquiou made pederasty fashionable. This handful of spendthrifts and dandies with famous names represented *le monde*—quite literally, the world. Marcel Proust, who could sometimes be glimpsed at the Ritz eating chocolate ice cream "Vendôme columns," appropriated the Paris of the Faubourg and the *gratin,* just as the Impressionists a generation earlier had appropriated Paris light, and as Victor Hugo appropriated the capital's shifting population "which did not know by lunchtime how it was going to afford dinner," and called it *les misérables.*

Proust's Faubourg was the fragile, sovereign-deprived heir of the royal court, which became mixed with other elements to form the Tout-Paris, the Estates General of Paris social groups, a composite whose spine is wealth, whose heart is talent, and whose face is glamor. Above all, a set of people easy to catalog: a few cabinet ministers, couturiers, actors, artists, famous fortunes, parvenus, a smattering of Académiciens, the police prefect, one or two of the better con men, and glamorous ladies with mysterious sources of income. If this band of tireless parasites is the champagne of the capital, much of it is flat. It lacks the antimercantilism of the Faubourg. Tout-Paris is utilitarian, balls are given for charity organizations rather than *pour le plaisir*, fashion boutiques and art galleries are inaugurated, a book or a discothèque is launched; the last remaining four thousand Parisians who do not spend their evenings watching television form a self-serving claque.

The illusion that what is Parisian is French holds true for a gallery of social types: Hugo invented Gavroche, the street urchin who summed up French history with this quatrain:

> *Je suis tombé par terre,*
> *C'est la faute à Voltaire.*
> *Le nez dans le ruisseau,*
> *C'est la faute à Rousseau.*

Gavroche joined such familiar Paris figures as the *monsieur bien* (gentleman), *the voyou* (delinquent), the *ti-ti* (Paris cockney), and the changing faces of the Parisienne, from the *midinette* (working girl) and the *boutiquière* (tradeswoman: her appearance conforms to her profession. One of novelist Jean Dutourd's characters says "you smell of cheese, little mother; if you're not in the butter and egg business, I'm pope") to the sinning duchesses of the *seizième arrondissement,* who receive a better grade of absolution in the confessional booths of Saint Honoré d'Eylau and Saint Pierre de Chaillot.

No skeptic has ever questioned the gender of Paris. Bismarck, fixing the capital's contribution to the 1870 war damages, said: "This young lady is rich enough and well enough provided for to pay the ransom." Paul Verlaine felt uneasy "in her powdered arms." The English archeologist Sir Arthur Evans, finding a saucy profile on a Cretan fragment, dubbed it "La Parisienne." "Beautiful flowers that grow from the manure of Paris," Hugo called the women of the city. "Parisienne" is not a geographic designation but an accolade which denotes something special and authentic, a sum of worldly wisdom and natural elegance defying accurate definition, so that the French, skirting mystery as closely as they dare, call it *je ne sais quoi*. The sovereign women of Paris as opposed to the gray masculinity of the provinces: The famous courtesans of the *ancien régime,* like Ninon de Lenclos; the guiding spirits of salons, from Madame du Deffand to Madame Verdurin; the alcove empresses of the Second Empire; the *grandes horizontales* of the Third Republic, Cora Pearl, Cléo de Mérode; the revolving-door mistresses of the Fourth Republic; and the half-dozen influential women who blossomed under the Fifth despite the vigilance of Madame de Gaulle. Further down the social ladder, the little dressmakers who call themselves Madame Rose, after Marie Antoinette's dressmaker Rose Bertin; and the resourceful prostitutes of the Halles, who have so generously contributed to the foreigner's notion of Paris as a city of perdition, from Hogarth's engravings to the special *art nouveau* love seat made for Edward VII at the Chabanais brothel. The Paris prostitute's unrivaled lexicon of sex: The rose leaf, the little Shanghai streetcar, the checkered handkerchief, Napoleon on the ramparts, the lilac branch in the wheatfield, the police commissioner's shaving brush. When the Halles, the stomach of Paris, was moved to a new site near Orly Airport, the groin of Paris also had to be relocated. Paris manages to be at the same time naughtier and less permissive than cities like London and New York. The air, as Henry Miller wrote, is impregnated with sexuality, but it is a lighthearted, effortless, half-mocking sexuality, the polymorphous sexuality of a child, awakened in a metro or a café, without insistence, propaganda, or surveys: "O you whom I might have loved, O you who knew it," the Parisian says daily.

The second fatherland of foreigners is a Parisian rather than a French destination. "England built London for its own use," said Emerson, "but France built Paris for the world." The rush of travelers began with the opening of the Sorbonne in the thirteenth century. Foreign students appreciated, then as now, the mixture of worldliness, urban spaciousness, and liberality. They were allowed to use their own currency and celebrate their national holidays, and the temples of knowledge enjoyed extraterritoriality in time of war. Artists came to bask in a European center of culture, with mixed results. The Swedish portraitist Anders Zorn said a trip to Paris "always produces the same effect as spilling a little oil on a lamp about to die out." But Oliver Goldsmith, penurious in 1755, found that "the people of Paris love those who have money far more than those who have wit. I, having neither, you may imagine that I was not well received."

Those with established reputations were warmly welcomed. David Garrick in 1765 told a rapturous Paris gathering how he imitated Lear's madness: He thought of a friend who had gone mad after seeing his young son fall out of a window. He liked to go riding in the Bois de Boulogne and to imitate a drunk on horseback. August Strindberg called Paris "the marketplace and workshop for struggling minds," and wrote *Plea for a Madman* in French.

The capital has always been diverse enough to sustain contradictory opinions, and the eighteenth-century English traveler John Moore praised the hospitality of the Parisians; even the beggars, he said, are polite. Poor Mozart was bilked in Paris. Living with his mother in a room so narrow a harpsichord would not fit between their beds, he was forced to give lessons. The comte de Guines ordered a concerto for flute and harp and never paid for it. The impresario Noverre commissioned ballet music and signed his own name to the score. Then Mozart lost his mother to the Paris winter. His friend Grimm bought him a seat on a carriage to Strasbourg; Paris clearly did not suit him. Nor did it suit the Swedish queen Christina, who was exiled by Mazarin after he had her lover Morraldeschi murdered. "What," she said, "they don't mind having two thousand Germans in Paris and they banish an old ally like me!"

Germans began arriving with the Nemeitz guide to Paris in 1718. Swarms of English came too, between wars. Never was an enemy capital so relentlessly visited. For generations of Englishmen, "a weekend on the Continent" was a euphemism for wenching in Paris. Milton warned about "the monsieurs of Paris who take our hopeful youth into their slight and prodigal custodies and send them over back again transformed into mimics, apes, and kickshows." Travelers were upset by the Revolution because it altered their image of the witty, amiable, sprightly capital. They worried over the vanished Bastille and a people who destroyed their monuments. From his semiretirement in Bohemia as librarian to Count Waldstein, Casanova regretted the passing of an age in which "they did not know how to overdo . . . there was, it is true, the drawback of witnessing acts of odious despotism. That was the despotism of a king. Since, the French have known the despotism of the people. Is it any less odious?" In 1803, when the peace was broken, about 5,000 English tourists were arrested by Napoleon and either sent to detention camps or placed in forced residence. The archeologist James Forbes, arrested as he descended from his *berline* to start a Paris holiday, was generously allowed to detour through the Touraine on his way to a camp in Verdun. In the nineteenth and twentieth centuries Parisians have had to put up with Germans arriving as soldiers and returning as tourists. The lip-smacking manner the Germans adopt when recalling the pleasures of Paris under the Occupation is a form of tribute its citizens could do without.

Devaluation brought in as many foreign visitors as the Occupation. The devaluation of the Germinal franc and a strong dollar made the Paris of the twenties and thirties a fief of American expatriates; Montparnasse was the hospitable soil where transplanted genius flourished. The period has been abundantly chronicled, but the magic of those years has never been satisfactorily explained. For twenty years Paris cornered the world's talent and kept it on permanent exhibit. Since the postwar Regency period of Saint-Germain-des-Prés, Paris has slowed down. Its youth looks to London for its clothes and its fun. Art and literature are fragmented; they have no geographical center.

Paris is still a residence for foreign artists, but it is no longer the subject of their work. The expatriate islands today seem to float like air plants above the city. James Jones and his wife, Gloria, who looks like a Valkyrie and talks like a mafiosi, preside with boundless hospitality over a salon in the Île Saint-Louis that has a pulpit for a bar (it reverts to its original function for itinerant preachers like James Baldwin) and specializes in all-night poker games. It seems a distant but plugged-in New York suburb, impervious to Paris, a haven for those fleeing the problems of their own land. Another resident American writer, Mary McCarthy, although distressed by the sanitary habits of the French, respects an intellectual life that takes itself seriously. After a false start during which she complained that the French were hard to know, she formed a cosmopolitan salon in the tradition of Madame du Deffand, where the polite ruthlessness of the French intellect blends with that characteristic American trait, the enthusiastic acquisition of any subject from the seeding of French lilacs to the bombing of Hanoi, as if these were all equally digestible meals. Miss McCarthy is terribly earnest about assimilating everything French (her cuisine is *cordon bleu* in character but served with proper American I'm-not-quite-sure-how-this-is-going-to-come-out humility) and clarifying false notions of America by identifying as closely as possible with French erudition and elegance. The McCarthy *académie* of French journalists and writers is a platform for the anti-Americanism fashionable among left-wing intellectuals, whose discussions range from the CIA's murder of Kennedy to America as a country careening toward disaster. One is never quite sure who is using whom. The French are epic in their condemnations, and their sense of cultural superiority is apt to subdue. The blessings of expatriate life may be turning sour, and in any case, jet travel has abolished its traditional meaning.

More important than Paris as a foreign capital is Paris as the place where French history has been made. Paris has been at the origin of both order and disorder through centralization and uprisings. No successful revolution ever began in the provinces, but Parisians have been overthrowing regimes ever since the merchants' provost of Paris Etienne Marcel threw the dauphin out of the capital in the fourteenth century. Marcel was assassinated and became a Paris martyr, with the honors attached to that title: a statue, a street, and a metro station. The 1789 Revolution was a Paris disturbance that started with a neighborhood riot in the faubourgs Saint-Antoine and Saint-Marcel and which became known as the Storming of the Bastille. The Sans-Culottes were Paris shopkeepers, artisans, and unemployed workers. In 1830, three days of Paris street fighting, again in July, were enough to overthrow the restored monarchy of Charles X. Charles de Rémusat, Minister of the Interior under the July Monarchy, said: "We did not know the population of Paris, we did not know what it was capable of." He had occasion to see it in action again in 1848, when several days of February rioting overthrew Louis-Philippe; not a shot was fired in the rest of France in defense of the regime. The cry "To the barricades" is specifically Parisian, as are the tactics of blocking streets with sawed-off trees, piles of paving stones, and, since the invention of the internal combustion engine, parked cars. The unruly character attributed to the French, their irreverence and contestation of authority, is predominantly Parisian. Of the three principal movements in the 1789 Revolution, the Girondins represented the provinces and a federalist program, the Jacobins advocated a strong central power that would unite France against foreign enemies, and the Hébertistes were the ungovernable Parisians, railing against authority in the form of king and church. The Hébertistes were named after their leader, instigator of the September Massacres and publisher of the newspaper *Père Duchesne,* which was published in a daily state of rage. Louis Jacob Hébert had great influence in the Paris Commune, which in 1792 closed the city's churches to prevent midnight mass from being said, and thereafter began hounding priests. Robespierre suppressed the irreligious, insurrectional Hébertistes and opened the churches to celebrate the cult of the Supreme Being. Hébert's execution alienated the Parisian Sans-Culotte militants and brought into the open the contradiction between the Parisian ground swell for a popular democracy and Robespierre's Jacobin dictatorship. The Terror, too, started as a Parisian phenomenon, and then spread to the provinces to repress centers of counterrevolution, which explains why only 15 percent of its death sentences were pronounced in Paris, as against 52 percent in the royalist west.

The Paris Commune of 1871, which Marx called the French civil war, was a clear-cut conflict between the revolutionary aims of the capital and the more prosaic aspirations of the rest of France. The historical personality of Paris, its radicalism, its contradictory taste for freedom and violence, the important role played by women, and its virulent anticlericalism, all were present. The Commune lasted only 73 days, but that was long enough to create another Parisian myth, like the myth of depravity or the myth that Paris is the summary of France: the myth of popular democracy and proletarian government. The Red flag flew, the revolutionary calendar was revived, 25 members of the working class were part of a regularly elected government; it was a renaissance of Hébertisme to which were grafted the social theories of the radical Blanqui and the first Marxists. Marx interpreted the

Commune as a struggle between working-class Paris and bourgeois France. It was a brief attempt at nonbureaucratic government, with its volunteer army, its foreign policy exemplified by the looting of American ambassador Washburne's home, and its mixture of the visionary and the improvised. Recalling the *tricoteuses* of 1789 were the *petroleuses* (incendiaries) of 1871: the 120 ladies who held a barricade on Place Blanche against the troops of Adolphe Thiers, fighting to the last woman, and the famous Louise Michel, who fired at the troops from behind the tombstones of Montmartre Cemetery and was eventually deported.

It was like the Revolution of 1789, a time of brief democratic idylls, setting fire to the guillotine in April but shooting the first 80 hostages in May. One of the first decisions made by the Commune in April, 1871, was the arrest of the liberal archbishop of Paris, Monsignor Darboy, who was among the hostages. The Commune then wrote the bloodiest page of French anticlericalism, which has also been mainly a Parisian phenomenon, propounded through the Paris-based universities and school system under the Third Republic, and lapsing into violence during the Revolution and the Commune. Dozens of priests and monks were shot, and placards were posted outside the closed churches explaining: "Because the priests are bandits and the dens where they morally assassinate the masses are the churches."

Communes were attempted in Lyons and several other provincial cities but did not take hold. The provinces gave Paris almost no help, nor did the world. Finally, the Thiers government in Versailles entered into a tacit alliance with Bismarck. Germany helped France to defeat Paris. The Commune had been made possible partly because Baron Haussman sealed the proletariat off from the bourgeoisie in the new Paris neighborhoods of the Second Empire, and it collapsed also partly because of Haussman, whose broad, straight thoroughfares eased the deployment of troops and artillery. The repression set a record: 35,000 Parisians shot and 40,000 arrested. The Commune's very existence was startling, and although short-lived, it was to serve as an example for workers' movements around the world. But above all, it was Parisian.

A pendant of the myth that France was geographically predestined as a nation, is that Paris is its capital also by divine intervention. But Paris, like the rest of France, is the creation of history, not geography; it is counter determined, not preordained. The data of the original Paris are simple: an island on a bend in a river, with a plateau on one side and a swamp (today the neighborhood called the Marais) on the other. From 100 B.C., the curly-headed Parisii, a tribe of Celtic fishermen and navigators, began to settle on the five-acre Île-de-la-Cité, one of several such islands in the area, on the mistaken notion that a river is a rampart, whereas it is a fluid thoroughfare. The settlement was called Lutetia when the Romans occupied and developed it into a modest Gallo-Roman town of 6,000 to 10,000 inhabitants, as indicated by the arenas discovered on today's rue Monge.

The fortunes of Paris depended on the fortunes of its lords after the fall of the Roman Empire. Clovis made it his capital, conquered the other Frankish tribes disputing French soil, and converted to Christianity, thereby preparing Paris for its first savior in the person of Saint Geneviève, who allegedly prevailed on Attila not to destroy the city in the sixth century. Its primacy was sealed when the newly elected Capetian dynasty quite naturally chose it as its capital in the tenth century, for the Capetians owned land in the area and controlled very little other French territory. The political context, rather than any inherent advantage of its site, made Paris an important city. It was, in fact, handicapped because it was on a fluvial invasion route; Lyons, the capital the Romans chose, was far less vulnerable. The growth of Paris was uninterrupted from then on. Paris never suffered a decline, as did Rome at the end of the Middle Ages; it was not destroyed by an earthquake, like Lisbon, or by a fire, like London, nor was it the victim of a political decision, like Moscow. The capital's luck has held up, and in August, 1944, von Choltitz refrained from using heavy artillery on the Resistance-held police prefectures across the street from Notre Dame. German planes dropped leaflets that said: "Stalin would have set fire to the four corners of the city. Because of our love for Paris, center of European culture, you will be preserved from this fate."

The story of Paris' growth is the story of the displacement of its surrounding fortifications, followed by the labors of urbanists after it became an open city. With the first walls in 1190, Philippe-Auguste spread beyond the Île-de-la-Cité to absorb a right-bank shopping center, a few churches, and much of the present Latin

Quarter on the left bank. Philippe-August also paved the first streets, dug the first sewers, and initiated the practical tradition of keeping the central market outside the walls. Charles V built new walls on the right bank in 1370, and they coincide fairly accurately with today's *grands boulevards*. Within that area stands what is supposedly the oldest house in Paris, a fourteenth-century structure with exposed beams, at 3 rue Volta. Not until the sixteenth century did Paris become France's largest city, with 400,000 inhabitants. Burgeoning Paris became a trade center, attracting job hunters and adventurers. Saint Louis made it a destination for pilgrims by displaying the supposedly authentic crown of thorns in a magnificent Gothic reliquary. Catherine de Medici built the Tuileries outside the Charles V ramparts in 1564, but had to protect them with new walls when the Wars of Religion broke out.

Kings wanted to make their capital more splendid, but were nagged by the justified fear that its growth represented a political threat. Henri II in the sixteenth century was the first king to prohibit new building in an attempt to keep the monster under control. The Huguenot Henri IV was the first to formulate the idea that control over the kingdom depended on conquest of the capital. His famous profession of conversion in 1593, "Paris is well worth a mass," is the first sign that if the provinces and Paris were placed on the scales, they would tip on the side of the latter. The next wall was built as protection from tax evaders, not foreign invaders, by the Farmers General from 1784 to 1791. The gates were points at which duty on goods entering Paris was collected. From the reign of Louis XIII to the humiliating end of the Napoleonic adventure in 1814, Paris enjoyed a period of respite from invasion that lasted nearly two centuries.

Concern for the city passed from defending generals to urbanists; houses were torn down for the sake of perspective, not because they interfered with the line of artillery fire. Gates became triumphal arches, ramparts became boulevards. The city as a work of art replaced the city as a fortress. From the time Paris became an open city, a scenic concept based on Cartesian principles of perspective and alignment governed its growth, was perpetuated in the nineteenth century by Baron Haussman, and has been inherited by present-day urbanists. Paris is the only city whose urban renewal was thought out in advance by one of Western civilization's great philosophers. According to Descartes, "The buildings that a single architect has conceived and finished are customarily more beautiful and better ordered than those which several have tried to patch up."

The city was designed to be a geometric figure, with streets distributed concentrically around squares which were settings for a monarch's equestrian statue, like Notre Dame des Victoires; the square was a demonstration of royal power, it invited the construction of fine buildings, and it was a protected open space. Regularity was enforced with controls over the height of houses, the width of streets, and the necessity of alignment and symmetry. Paris, or at least parts of it, is a designed city, which can only be fully appreciated from a bird's eye view, as from the Eiffel tower, from which one gets the sense of program from the symmetrical rectangles of blocks, the star-shaped *places,* and the long straight streets. The post of police lieutenant was created under Louis XIV to enforce the growing controls. He was, in fact, governor of Paris, invested with broad powers, but significantly his first duty was to police the city. Today the most powerful municipal official is still the police prefect, whose authority goes far beyond law and order.

Paris as Babylon, a comparison most poignantly expressed in a short story by F. Scott Fitzgerald, was already the concern of Colbert in the seventeenth century. He feared that "having attained such excessive size, the city would have the same fate as those powerful cities of antiquity which found in themselves the principle of their ruin, since it was impossible to keep order in all the parts of those great bodies."

Versailles was the last attempt to circumvent the supremacy of Paris, but it was an unsatisfactory Brazilia, still in the city's orbit, while Paris remained the restive political center. The once-brilliant provincial courts died out, and from the depths of the maligned provinces, the Bordelais Montesquieu lamented the passing of a time when "each village was a capital, while today there is only one; when each part of the state was a center of power, while today there is only one; ... to conclude a business deal, to end litigation, to obtain a favor, one must go to Paris." The capital then, however, was less of a giant than London, which had already reached a population of 1,000,000 by 1789, while that of Paris was 500,000.

Paris at the time of the Revolution contained only 2.50 percent of the total population of France. The great swell came in the nineteenth century, after the basic option for a strongly centralized state had been made by the Jacobins. The federalist Gironde had wanted the Convention to meet at Bourges, not Paris. After the division of France into 83 departments named after obscure rivers, a Girondin deputy said that Paris should represent only one eighty-third of France. But this new division of the parts reinforced the power of the center. Napoleon shifted between a mistrust of Paris so intense that he considered changing capitals, and the desire to make it "something fabulous, something colossal, something unprecedented to this day." His faith in the reproductive capacity of the capital made him say, as he was counting the heavy losses at Austerlitz, "one night of Paris will make up for this."

In contrast to the changes in political regimes, there was a remarkable continuity to the plans of the urbanists. Every regime took up the public works begun by its predecessor. The Revolution, by tearing down convents and churches, made the renovation of old neighborhoods like the Cité possible. When the mob razed the Bastille, it was carrying out a project of Louis XVI for which funds had already been earmarked. Napoleon finished other projects of Louis XVI, in linking the Tuileries to the boulevards and in piercing the rue de Rivoli. The restored king Louis XVIII banished members of Napoleon's family in 1815, but continued work on the Arch of Triumph, the Étoile, and the Madeleine church. Every regime was faithful to the principles of classical urbanism and to the capital's function as celebrant of victories. The habit grew to name streets after battles; Castiglione, Jena, Rivoli. The *colonne* Vendôme was a spiraling bas-relief of high deeds, cast from the melted-down cannons of the enemy.

Paris' population explosion came in a relatively brief period. From 1851 to 1872 the number of Parisians nearly doubled—from 1,242,000 to 2,212,000. This was the result partly of better health conditions (the cholera epidemic of 1830 had claimed 1,000 victims a day), partly of the peace and prosperity of the Second Empire, and mainly because the railroads carried the promise of

Paris to rural France. Paris grew because it was the only city in France where anyone could arrive and know he could at least survive, perhaps prosper. It was during this period that the figure of the provincial arriving to conquer Paris (Balzac's young Rastignac shaking his fist defiantly at the city) became a stereotype.

Under the Second Empire, Paris found its plastic surgeon, who lopped off the city's warts and gave it its final face. Paris today is still largely Baron Haussman's nineteenth-century capital, with a few noticeable peripheral additions, like the Maine-Montparnasse tower and the rond-point de la Défense. Haussman destroyed 20,000 houses and built twice that many. He, too, was obsessed with perspective, and designed straight streets three miles long, like the rue Lafayette. Absence of symmetry caused him genuine pain. He bulldozed through several historic neighborhoods to achieve Paris' linear order. His mania for the straight line was such that a character in a novel of the period complained that Haussman had neglected to straighten the Seine, "for there is something shocking about its irregular curb." Haussman remained seventeen years in power as Paris prefect, which enabled him to carry out most of his plans. He believed his wide boulevards had made the capital secure from insurrection. He also separated Parisians by class. The working class moved from the center to the periphery to make way for the silent, placid, tree-lined, inanimate *beaux quartiers*. Paris became a rich city surrounded by a poor city, today called the Red Belt, whereas until 1850 the working class and the bourgeoisie often occupied the same buildings. Oddly, the most forlorn surburbs have the loveliest names, like The Lilacs, and Issy of the Small Mills. Haussman thus contributed to bourgeois smugness and the proletarian feeling of shame and sequestration.

He was much criticized in his day as a megalomaniac whose toy was Paris. Hugo said he had pierced the city with streets like saber strokes. But it is precisely those streets one is grateful for today when comparing Paris traffic with the near-paralysis of Rome or London. Haussman may have made some serious mistakes, such as building the new Halles in the center, or failing to encourage the extension of the capital beyond the existing city limits, but he was single-handedly responsible for making Paris better prepared than most historic capitals for the congestion of the twentieth century.

Paris today is preoccupied with an expensive face-lifting imposed on thrifty Parisians thanks to the resurrection of an 1852 law that says the buildings must be degrimed every ten years. When the first buildings were cleaned, revealing the lovely golden texture of the unsooted stone, left-wing journals waxed lyric about the poetry of blackened façades, and denounced the removal of the patina of centuries, which was mainly automobile exhaust fumes and tugboat smoke. In the same vein, there is frequent talk about "saving Paris," as though it were gradually sinking into the waters like Venice, and there is a tendency to make the capital the scapegoat for all the nation's ailments. Paris centralization is blamed, for instance, for the orientation of the French bourgeoisie toward public service rather than business ventures. These are contradictory attitudes: If Paris is an ogre feeding on the provinces, it does not need to be saved, and if it is choking on itself, it cannot represent a threat to the rest of France.

Paris remains a vigorous, well-administered capital. The reclamation of the Halles Aux Vins (wine market) for a university building, the expressways almost flush with both sides of the Seine, the creation of a new neighborhood, thanks to the banishment of the Halles *extra muros,* and the underground parking lots indicate a city that it trying to change gracefully. The primacy of Paris remains a part of the French official mentality. In December, 1968, Foreign Minister Michel Debré went to Nantes to lay the cornerstone for one of the first foreign affairs office buildings outside Paris. He took this ceremony of administrative decentralization as an opportunity to recall the "implacable role of Paris, just and legitimate expression of national unity . . . those who want to bring down France bring down Paris. When the foreigner wants to break France he occupies Paris. The greatness of Paris is the symbol of our greatness . . . Paris is the center of national decisions. It is there that our destiny is fixed."

The government considers the supremacy of Paris a virtue, just as Jules Michelet said that centralization is a mark of evolution among animal species. The concentration of talents in the capital is seen as the condition of French *rayonnement.* Reduce

Paris to the arithmetical importance of its population, the thinking goes, and you reduce the influence of France. Paris continues to be the trump in international competition. And finally, there is the sheer centripetal force of Paris. Universities refuse to move out of the capital for fear their diplomas will be depreciated. Neither of the two top engineering schools, Central and Polytechnique, will agree to move to more spacious campuses unless the other does. Precedents are discouraging. When the National Center for Judiciary Studies, the government school that forms judges, moved from Paris to Bordeaux in 1960, it lost half its student body. The same goes for business firms. To move out of Paris is often to be penalized by being far from airports, proper telephone service, banks and government offices, the best schools, and working conditions that can attract topflight management. Paris is considered the goal of a successful career, and a job in the provinces proof of second best.

But the feeling that Paris' growth must be at the expense of the provinces is changing. Paris' actual rate of growth has slowed down: Between 1962 and 1968, of the 49 French cities with more than 100,000 inhabitants, Paris came thirty-second. The provinces cannot challenge the domination of Paris, but this does not prevent them from making France polycentric. The Fifth Republic, although attached to the glory of its capital, thinks more in terms of regions than departments. Paris is one of 20 regions, and ideally it would be *primus inter pares,* like the pope among his bishops.

There will never be a French Brazilia, despite studies to create a city of 6,000,000 inhabitants in Georges Pompidou's native Cantal, if only because no government would ever agree to move out of its comfortable Paris cocoon. But there are regions ideally suited to growth because of their European location: Grenoble is well placed as a link with other Alpine nations, just as Strasbourg's vocation is to be a Common Market regional capital. Instead of all of France moving from Parisian impulses, these regional capitals are becoming genuine spheres of influence. It may take a generation before Strasbourg, Lyons, Marseilles, or Grenoble reach 1,000,000 inhabitants, but France is on the way to becoming polycentric. It is a developing country with a saturated capital, which is giving the provincial cities their first real chance to catch up. General de Gaulle's government by plebiscite encouraged the revenge of the provinces on Paris. Good teachers are more willing today to accept chairs in provincial universities. A novelist like Le Clézio is only occasionally called eccentric because he chooses to live in Nice. Nationalized industry has built factories outside Paris, like the Renault works in Le Mans, and the Peugeot headquarters in Sochaux. The provincial press is prospering, and six non-Paris dailies have circulations of more than 300,000. There are still semideserted regions in France like the Béarn, the Drôme, the Poitou, and the Berri, where one can drive for miles without seeing a farmhouse or a village. But the opposition between "Paris and the French desert" is no longer valid, for the oases are starting to reclaim the desert.

2

➤➤➤-➤➤➤-➤➤➤-➤➤➤-➤➤➤-➤➤➤-➤➤➤-➤➤➤-➤➤➤-➤➤➤-➤➤➤-➤➤➤-➤➤➤-➤➤◄◄◄-◄◄◄-◄◄◄-◄◄◄-◄◄◄-◄◄◄-◄◄◄-◄◄◄-◄◄◄-◄◄◄-◄◄◄-◄◄◄-◄◄◄-◄◄◄

The Epic Past

HAVELOCK ELLIS believed that the adoption of the bayonet as the favorite French weapon was a sign of seriousness, precision, courage, the ability to find the sensitive spots of life and penetrate deep; it explained, he thought, the French moral spirit, the incisiveness of French prose, and the French artist's mastery of line. His was a modest English contribution to the great national monument of self-congratulation. Just as the French believe they inhabit a favored land, they view their own past as an epic unmatched in the history of Western civilization. The past is a warehouse stocked with treasures ready to be displayed whenever useful: Vercingetorix and Joan of Arc were dusted off to provide symbols of patriotism after the 1870 war. France secretes, constantly reshapes and feeds on its own past. Where it has been is, more than for other nations, the explanation of where it is going. The principle of a nation, said Ernest Renan, lies in the common possession of a rich legacy of memories. France does not have a future in the ordinary sense: It has a destiny, an extension of its epic past, rich with heroes, triumphs, and great contributions to the world. It is addicted to greatness.

Just as administrative centralization and the domination of Paris are a response to a lack of geographic and ethnic unity, the epic past is the answer to the turbulence of French history. The French need to share a romanticized vision of their past because they have suffered a number of traumas, civil wars, repeated invasion, defeat, and the loss of empire. They have fitted their territory into a mythological hexagon, and they have fitted their history into a never-ending *chanson de geste*. They have turned their defeats into victories, and their civil wars into revolutions. They have experienced every form of government, but believe in an essential French stability. Under the Third Republic alone, from 1875 to 1940, France had 102 governments against 20 for England and 14 for the United States. Roosevelt once told de Gaulle: "Can you imagine that before the war, I, as President of the United States, sometimes could not remember the name of the French Prime Minister?" Words that did not shake the general's confidence in the glorious continuity of French history, which has its accredited theorists. Valéry made a virtue of political crisis, finding "a strange stability, around which events and vicissitudes, inevitable and inseparable from all life, inner explosions, political earthquakes, and storms come from abroad, create oscillations more than once a century."

Myths shape nations; their value lies in their power to convince. Perhaps the French tend to become what they believe they are. In this mythical sense, there is an inspirational France: great civilizer and altruist, most favored nation in all things, incubator of remarkable men, teacher of Europe, guardian of universal values, and missionary to the world. Here again one finds, as in the shape of the land, traces of divine intervention. With all their faults, Péguy wrote, God loves the French the best.

The Sound of the Oliphant

At its most naïve, this vision of France lives in the popular imagery taught schoolboys. French history begins with a hero on a white horse, named Vercingetorix, chief of a Gallic tribe called the Arverni. He became leader of a coalition of tribes which rose up against Roman occupation in 52 B.C., and was captured and put to death by Caesar after the battle of Alesia. This obscure tribal chieftain won his fame thanks to a double propaganda campaign. First, Caesar's account of the Gallic Wars made Vercingetorix his principal adversary, mentioning him by name 42 times. The revolt had actually broken out among other tribes, but Caesar exaggerated the role of Vercingetorix to cover up his own mistakes and to explain the difficulties of his campaign.

Caesar's commentaries were destined to bolster his position in Rome. Like General de Gaulle, he wrote his own self-serving account of the history he made. It was convenient to make a hero of Vercingetorix, both because Caesar had brought him back to Rome as a captive, and to conceal a resistance which was more broadly based. He presented Vercingetorix as commander in chief of a united Gallic army, whereas there were, in fact, troops and officers beyond his control, and many tribes that were allies of the Romans. Vercingetorix had so little confidence in the tribes under his command that he demanded hostages from each of the cities that had joined the uprising. Caesar gives us long speeches the tribal chief supposedly made to his men, in which he admits the ingeniousness of the Roman siege and praises the quality of the Roman command, adding that "One would be wrong to think that there are only victories in war."

Thanks to Caesar's account, nineteenth-century French historians made Vercingetorix the first apostle of national unity. At a time of dismemberment, because of the loss of Alsace and Lorraine, the Arverni chief became the first authentic French patriot. He served to redeem the discredited belief that France in peril always finds a defender. He was presented as a brilliant military leader, whereas in fact he foolishly gathered his armies on the Alesia hill, a hopeless strategic position which was soon surrounded, and threw in his elite cavalry at the start of the battle, when it was uselessly destroyed. With his supply routes cut off and no help arriving, he was forced to surrender. In 1948, at the bimillennial of Alesia, Vercingetorix was officially christened "the first resistance hero of French history." General de Gaulle clearly sees Vercingetorix as an early patriot, and wrote that the reason the Gallic chieftain threw his weapons at Caesar's feet "may have been so that this desperate homage to discipline might serve as an immortal lesson for his race." Thanks to this view of the Gallic

Wars, French nationalism burst full grown, like Minerva from Jupiter's brow, one thousand years before France existed.

It was the Romans and not the Gauls who achieved the first unity of France. Alesia was not the defeat of the French nation but one of the necessary conditions for its eventual formation, for the Romans pacified Gaul and gave it many of the requirements of nationhood. Was Romanization a benefit or a catastrophe? The Romans did for Gaul what the French later did for Algeria: built roads, aqueducts, arenas, theaters, and garrison towns, which they left behind. To the Romans can be traced the French taste for grandeur. "Never do anything small," could have been said by either de Gaulle, Louis XIV, or Caesar. Centralization and an efficient bureaucracy were also imports of the Romans; they took a census, established written law, and made cadastral surveys. Control over education and culture is another Roman idea; there were official statues and monuments, and official schools. But the French have always thought of the Romans as occupiers, while feeling a strong sense of kinship for the Gauls, a people who left no literature, no language, no laws, an unmanageable pantheon of gods, and who practiced human sacrifice. The Roman arch at Orange shows them fighting, naked, their hair in a long looped knot, with drooping mustaches and long narrow shields. They were "the clumsiest flayers of cattle and burners of grass of their epoch," Rimbaud wrote, saying "I have inherited from my Gallic ancestors my whitish-blue eyes, my narrow skull, and my lack of skill in fighting. My attire seems to me as barbarous as theirs. But I don't butter my hair. To them I owe: idolatry and love of sacrilege—Oh! every vice, anger, lust—magnificent, lust—above all, mendacity and sloth."

Anchored in the French mind, however, is the vision of the heroic Gaulois that was spread in the 500 editions of one of the most influential French books ever published, the *Tour de France par Deux Enfants,* written in 1880 by a patriotic lady. It told of two orphaned children who fled German-occupied Lorraine and discovered in their travels that France had the best dairy products, paper mills, farms, foundries, and smithies, and the most great men. Each chapter begins with a moral precept, like "courage makes rich and poor equal," and "he who accomplishes a useful task must never let himself be discouraged by jealousy." It begins with an account of "our ancestors the Gaulois, who were tall and robust. . . . The armies of Caesar, made up of the world's best soldiers, took seven years to conquer our fatherland. A young Gaul, born in the Auvergne, then decided to throw the Romans out of the *patrie.*" Vercingetorix is first of a series of manufactured heroes who demonstrate the valor of Gallic blood in the face of the invader.

It took a permanent state of peril to forge the epic genius, which placed both history and literature at the service of patriotism. A minor skirmish with some Basque mountaineers became the first written French epic, the *Chanson de Roland.* On August 15, 778, the Basques attacked Charlemagne's rear guard at the Pyrenean pass of Roncevaux to avenge the French destruction of Pamplona. From this scant source material was composed the French *Iliad,* with Roland a Gallic Achilles. The Basques became Saracen invaders, which made Roland the defender of both the nation and the faith. Roland was one of the twelve peers of Charlemagne, who has been appropriated by the French even though he spoke German and made Aix-la-Chapelle his capital. Of the four thousand lines that recount his rearguard action, only one might serve as evidence of his sense of nation: *"Terre de France moult estes dous pais."*

But what France is this in the eighth century? The Frankish kingdom or the Île-de-France? In any case, it has never been proven whether the first account of the *Chanson de Roland* came from France or England. Roland is defeated not by his enemies, but by a traitor, a member of his class who denies its values and ideals, the baron Ganelon. He is first of a species of villainous Frenchmen who place their interests above those of the nation, from Philippe d'Orléans, who voted the death of his cousin Louis XVI, to Laval, who served the German occupiers. The fame of the *Chanson de Roland* spread to the point where parents stopped calling their children Ganelon because the name was synonymous with treachery. Roland died in the service of Western civilization by blowing his oliphant so hard for help that the veins in his neck burst. Better death than dishonor (*mieux veuil mourir que hontage ne vienne*). With Roland, unrequited courage and betrayal became two constants of the French epic. The ring of his oliphant echoes in the works of historians who, like

Michelet, propagated the theory that contrary to the iron law of nations, France alone does not act out of self-interest: "If one wanted to pile up what every nation has spent in blood and gold and efforts of all kinds for disinterested aims which were of benefit to the world, the French pyramid would rise to the sky."

These legendary figures from the past are also held up as evidence of a continuous French sensibility. The Gauls are described as independent, individualistic, rebellious to authority, full of initiative, but quickly discouraged. Roland is a cheerful fellow who likes a good joke, and he embodies the French ideal of prowess. He strikes such a blow with his trusty sword Durandel that he smites open a boulder. In the same period, the troubadours were examples of spiritual prowess. Skill, whether in talking or fighting, cooking or lovemaking, is always respected in France, independently of success.

The brave knight is a recurring figure, like the Herculean Grand Ferré who fought against the English in the fourteenth century and met a peculiarly French demise: An iced drink consumed while he was bathed in the sweat of battle killed him, a fate that may be linked to the French mother's cautionary "One must never take a cold drink while perspiring." The chevalier Bayard, the "knight without fear or reproach" who single-handedly defended the Garigliano bridge against 200 Spanish horsemen during François Premier's Italian campaign, is a sixteenth-century Roland. As he lay dying from a crossbow arrow in 1524, sword in hand, he reproached the connétable de Bourbon for his treason (Bourbon had quarreled with François Premier and was fighting against the French). "I am dying honorably," he said, "but I pity you who are fighting against your king and your country." The French hero, whether Vercingetorix at Alesia, Roland at Roncevaux, Napoleon at Waterloo, or General de Gaulle fleeing to London in 1940, is often a defeated soldier; American heroes, by contrast, are usually victorious soldiers like Washington, Grant, and Eisenhower.

The Sense of Mission

Another theme of the epic past was born with the Crusades: the sense of mission. The first Crusade in the eleventh century was totally French, sponsored by the French pope Urban II, organized by the French preacher Peter the Hermit, and carried out by overzealous French knights. The Saracens acknowledged French primacy by calling all infidels Franks. These founders of France's first colonial empire, the Kingdom of Jerusalem, were also apostles of prowess. Grasping, brutal, and divided they might be, but they fought bravely, died honorably, and left castles in Lebanon, which General de Gaulle found a moving expression of French *rayonnement* (radiance). Moreover, they were the first to find a virtuous pretext for imperialism. The red-badged soldiers of the cross cried *"Dieu le veut"* while plundering Jerusalem and massacring the population of Antioch.

They combined the national mystique of greatness with something larger and more universal. France was fighting for Christianity. Out of this close association between the personal motives of the French Crusaders and the defense of Christianity grew the belief that those who fought against the Holy Kingdom of France were fighting Jesus Christ himself. The Crusades helped found a double myth: that the French fight for disinterested causes and that enemies of France are enemies of Christian civilization. After the Revolution, freedom replaced Christianity as the motive of civilization; other nations had policies of conquest, only France had a civilizing mission, another idea to which Michelet gave form, while noting the odd French blend of Messianism and parochialism: "The love of conquest is the pretext of our wars, something we ourselves have not realized. Yet proselytism is the most ardent motive. The Frenchman wants to superimpose his personality on the vanquished . . . he thinks he can do nothing in the world more profitable than to give him his ideas, customs, and fashions . . . this is a sympathetic instinct for intellectual fecundation." This has ever been the attitude of French invaders, like the Napoleonic officer in Germany who could not understand why German women did not at once adopt French fashions and the French language. And it was the attitude of the French soldier who was asked during the Indochinese war what he was fighting for. "Why," he replied, as though the answer was obvious, "for human solidarity, monsieur." One can only understand how revolutionary General de Gaulle's program of decolonization was when one realizes that it canceled the myth of the French sense of mission.

Conscious national feeling was in fact nonexistent under the Crusades. France was the founder of feudal institutions and customs which made nationalism meaningless for centuries. It is another nineteenth-century reconstruction to find incipient patriotism in the opportunistic and belligerent feudal lords. The real importance of the Crusades was not in perpetuating a national pride supposedly born with Vercingetorix, but in hastening the decline of feudalism. The lord leaving for or returning from a Crusade needed money and obtained it by freeing his serfs and granting charters of freedom for towns against cash payment.

With the Capetians, the French king became more than a tribal chief and extended his real power over large areas. National feeling, as anything stronger than a fondness for the place where one was born, could hardly develop under feudalism. The patriotism of the feudal nobility is a fiction. The story of the formation of France, from Hugues Capet to Louis XIV, is the story of the struggle between the king and his rebellious nobility. If the monarchy had not won that struggle, France would have become, like Italy, a geographical expression, a network of independent provinces. But the long consolidation of France by the Capetian dynasty, viewed by nationalistic historians as a high achievement of Western civilization and the safeguard of Catholicism, with the papacy protected by the eldest daughter of the church, could be seen quite differently by an outsider. Dante held the Capetians responsible for the political and economic fragmentation of Europe. They had revolted against the Holy Roman Empire, the first united Europe. He has Hugues Capet say that he was the root of the fatal tree which darkened all the Christian earth with its shadow.

The quick ascension of the monarchy vexed France's neighbors, and for the first time the threat of an invasion against a constituted French nation was posed. In 1214 took place what might with only slight exaggeration be termed the first world war, pitting an Anglo-German coalition against the thrice-married French king, Philippe-Auguste. The English king, Jean sans Terre, fourth son of Eleanor of Aquitaine, thus named because his father had parceled out his domains among his elder brothers, landed at La Rochelle in February. The merchants of La Rochelle had commercial links with England and quickly rallied to his flag. They were the first collaborators. Twenty-six Poitevin castles were opened to welcome the English lords. Meanwhile, in the marshy northern plains between Flanders and Picardy, the German emperor, Otto of Brunswick, sought the most convenient route into France. He bragged that spies told him what was being said in the most secret French councils. In the southwest the English armies trying to make their way up the Loire were beaten back by the son of Philippe-Auguste, the future Louis VIII. On the northern front, on July 27, Otto attacked the French rear guard near the village of Bouvines, on a Sunday, despite the truce of God; this was the first German surprise attack. The Capetian cavalry showed its superior training, the result of jousts and fighting the Saracens. When Philippe-Auguste was pulled from his horse, French lords rallied to his rescue. Otto, who had dreamed that he would be king of France, divested himself of the imperial insignia which would have identified him, and fled. Four German barons were taken prisoner. The coalition had disintegrated.

France was saved from invasion, on a route which would later be lined with the cemeteries of soldiers. God was already on the side of France because Otto had been excommunicated. But it was too early to talk of popular patriotism. The eyewitness chronicle of the king's chaplain, William the Breton, mentioned the flags of cities that followed the royal standard—Beauvais, Arras, Amiens, and others—but they had joined the battle because Philippe-Auguste had promised them charters in exchange for military assistance. The French king still had to negotiate the aid of his own subjects. The Peace of Chinon was botched; England kept a foothold on the Continent, and Aquitaine became the object of a long contest which required the intervention of a female savior to settle.

The Maid of Orléans

The trial of Joan goes on. Was she a nationalist or an armed nun, a mental case or a visionary touched by grace, a martyr or a charlatan, the first lady general or, as the Soviet encyclopedia sees her, a Communist freeing her people? Three thousand books have been written about her, some of whose authors apparently hope they too will hear voices, books contesting that she was burned or laboriously claiming that she was the dauphin's half-sister and a royal princess. There has been as much controversy over her identity as over Shakespeare's, and in both cases the mystery remains unsolved. Perhaps Shaw was right when he had her say: "I shall be remembered when men have forgotten where Rouen stood." Which is not bad for someone whose presence on the world stage lasted only two years.

She has been made the symbol of French patriotism, but she was not even French. Domrémy, her birthplace, was part of the independent Duchy of Bar, itself part of the Lorraine, the last province to be attached to the kingdom, in 1776—more than three centuries after Joan's death. Nor did she consider herself French. She said the archangel Michael told her: "Go, go to France if you must." Saviors have a way of being born in the marches: Christ was born in the marches of the Roman Empire; Joan, Napoleon, and de Gaulle all came from marginal regions of France.

Did Joan save France or England? For if England had won the Hundred Years War, the risk of absorption by France would have been great. Assimilation could well have been at England's expense. The division between Norman aristocracy and Saxon lower class would have relegated the language of Milton to a rustic dialect. Joan thwarted the first project for Anglo-French federation, a tenacious historical dream, that was to be repeated by Winston Churchill in the late spring of 1940 and ferociously rejected by a French cabinet in Bordeaux, which retained its chauvinism despite the fact that it was fleeing a German advance. Joan acted primarily from religious rather than national motives. She was a throwback to the theocracy of Saint Louis, and told the dauphin Charles that once rid of the English he would be "lieutenant of the king of heaven who is king of France." The English presence troubled her archaic vision of a Christian state. The English king had not been crowned at Rheims. National rivalries were preventing the church from accomplishing its mission. As she told her judges, she did not hate the English, but they had to leave so that the dauphin could carry out the commands of God.

Some of her language did have a militant, nationalistic ring: The English "would be thrown out of France, except for those who die there, and God will give victory to the French rather than to the English." But who were the French? There were French on both sides. By the time Joan appeared, the Anglo-French conflict had become a civil war, with the Armagnacs pitted against the Burgundians, who were assisted by the English. France was divided into North and South: a strong, English-supported union north of the Loire, and a weak, indecisive Armagnac confederacy. Each side had a case, which it argued with passion. To the Armagnacs, Joan was a savior, to the Burgundians, she was a usurper of their rightful claims.

In obeying divine voices, Joan was also abetting the centralizing influence of the French monarchy against feudal values. Merely by wearing a suit of armor, she violated the laws of feudal warfare, which barred women from combat (her judges were shocked when they saw her in male attire). She further violated feudal usage and created a precedent for the way she would be treated herself when she turned over the captured Burgundian chief Franquet d'Arras for trial and execution. Her own three-month heresy trial and her death at the stake caused little public reaction. There was no rioting. She did not become an object of worship. No one had interceded in her favor. No legend rose from her ashes. To contemporaries, the judges were not English puppets but prelates with impressive reputations, who had been endorsed by the Gallican University of Paris, then unrivaled in Europe. Pierre Cauchon, bishop of Beauvais and former rector of the university, was a distinguished and highly respected theologian. The University of Paris said that he was "animated by an immense fervor of most singular charity." Once the trial was under way, however, the university accused him of dragging it out, and sent him admonishing notes: "We are particularly surprised, reverend father and lord, that the cause of this woman commonly called the Maid is taking so long, to the detriment of faith and ecclesiastical jurisdiction." This man whom history was to label a monster, in fact opposed the torture of Joan, a routine procedure in ecclesiastical trials, as "neither necessary nor expedient" because the evidence was enough to convict her. It was only twenty years later that the dauphin, now King Charles VII, reopened the case. By then, the Treaty of Arras in 1435 had brought Burgundy back into the French fold. England had made its last stand at Formigny on the Normandy coast in 1450, near the 1944 D-day landing beaches.

That same year, 1450, King Charles asked a former rector of the University of Paris, Guillaume Bouillé, to direct an inquest of Joan's trial. It would not do for history to mention that the Valois dynasty had been saved by a heretic and a witch. New evidence had to be found. Cauchon had to be presented as the villain of the trial in order to rehabilitate Joan. The biggest problem was getting the church to admit it had been mistaken. But Pope Calixtus III was so eager for the French king's help in a planned crusade that he gave his blessing to a new tribunal in 1455, and Joan was rehabilitated the following year. As Milton Waldman has written: "A whole new batch of miracles was submitted to the scrutiny of the commissioners and the legend was regilded as bright as ever—none assisting more wholeheartedly than various of the clerics who had once voted with equal enthusiasm to burn her. In the end the dead Joan was so thoroughly rehabilitated that there could never in the future be the slightest danger of confusing her with the living Joan who had sat for Cauchon."

Each generation thereafter has reinvented a Joan to suit its times. Calvin, another French hero persecuted for his convictions, discoverer of a personal God, found her tainted with idolatry. The Philosophes scorned her. The cosmopolitan and irreverent eighteenth century had no use for her blend of mysticism and nationalism. Voltaire is Joan's antithesis, whether writing Frederick II of Prussia to congratulate him on defeating the French at Rossbach, or signing his letters with the salutation, "Crush the Infamous Thing" (the church). He made Joan the heroine of a ribald comic poem. The monarchy did not lavish upon her any particular attention. The long procedure for her canonization only began in 1869. The Revolution was too anticlerical to borrow her as a symbol of nationalism.

To revive the legend, it took another English threat to France and a leader for whom religion was a political weapon. It was Napoleon who remembered Joan in 1803 by erecting a monument to her in Orléans and restoring the annual feast of May 8 in her honor. She was the ideal metaphor of patriotism: a lady warrior with a sense of mission who placed God solidly on the side of the French. But the cult of Joan did not reach full ripeness until the defeat of 1870, when she became a symbol of vengeance because she was the daughter of an amputated province, Lorraine. Patriotic France wept at the gap in the Vosges and thought of Joan. A new national holiday in her honor was decreed. Statues were inaugurated in Paris and Nancy in 1890. The process of canonization was pressed. Children's textbooks showed Joan on the cover, on horseback, sword raised. Her militant image saturated France. Michelet turned her life into a five-act Passion Play.

During the First World War she was discovered to have been a military genius. Historians compared her to Joffre and said she had established unity of command in the French army. Her offensive tactics were hailed as a model during those years of trench warfare. After the war she was appropriated by right-wing parties like the Action Française as the symbol of national renewal. It was unsuccessfully argued that she belonged to the left because she was a daughter of the people, a simple peasant girl, just as the unknown soldier belonged to the left because he was a simple *poilu*. A Sorbonne history professor named Thalamas, who said Joan suffered from hallucinations and that her rehabilitation trial was a hoax, was beaten up by right-wing hooligans. Joan provides an example of the way French history is not only reinterpreted by every generation but appropriated by political groups for partisan purposes.

The Expansion-Dissension Cycle

The Hundred Years War helped make France, just as the 1870 Prussian attack on France helped make Germany. French kings after Joan were not threatened by the claims of the English crown. France thereafter followed a pattern of continental expansion alternating with internal troubles. When their own house was in order, French kings became adventurous, until some domestic crisis brought them home. After the Italian campaigns of the Valois, the Wars of Religion provided a dismal setting for the end of their dynasty. Richelieu intervened in the Thirty Years War, but his successor, Mazarin, had the Fronde to cope with. A long period of internal order followed, lasting roughly from 1660 until the French Revolution, during which France conducted a militant foreign policy, and was involved in nearly all of Europe's wars. Came the Revolution, and after the monarchy's overthrow French expansionism was couched first in the Jacobin rhetoric of freeing the people of Europe from the yoke of tyrants, and then in the imperial vocabulary that described Napoleon as a successor of Charlemagne.

Periodic internal strife characterized the first half of the French nineteenth century, but the respite of the Second Empire brought further expansion, this time as far as Mexico. The defeat of 1870 spurred the Third Republic to seek a new colonial empire as an antidote for the loss of Alsace and Lorraine. The empire helped France absorb the shock of two world wars. In 1944, the propaganda services of the Ministry of Information drafted a report on how to build up the morale of the defeated French. The first priority was "the notion of empire." In the next twenty years the empire dissolved, and after 1962 France returned to the borders of Richelieu. With the end of colonial expansion, domestic troubles grew, culminating in the 1968 student-worker revolt and the forced resignation of de Gaulle exactly one year later, a disappointment to those who believed that France under Gaullism could find an alternative to expansion other than internal dissension.

In 1495, for the first time since the Crusades, a French king left his own soil at the head of an army. Charles VIII was the first of three successive Valois kings to be lured by a Transalpine chimera. They relentlessly sought France where France was not, and instead, brought back the Renaissance. It was the age of enthusiasm, of navigation without proper maps, and wars without proper motives. Charles VIII's incursion into Italy was a spectacular but short-lived cavalcade. It was as if the king and his knights were acting out a new *chanson de geste*. The flower of chivalry partook not of booty and rape, and helped the orphan and the widow in the best twelfth-century chivalric tradition. But the rest of the French army entered Italy as awed as the Frankish barbarians who had invaded Gallo-Roman France, and grabbed what they could. Laden with loot, Charles' troops carried a new civilization back across the Alps: Paintings, an architectural style that was to shift the French passion for building from cathedrals to castles, the boldness of the cinquecento, admiration for antiquity, enthusiasm for the discoveries of the spirit, and the worship of form. Charles occupied Naples, and earned the nickname of *Cabezzucco* (pigheaded) before returning to Amboise where he died knocking his head against a gate. The name was justified, for he had pursued the Italian campaign at the expense of the genuine interests of his crown, buying with gold the promise of nonintervention from other sovereigns.

No sooner had his cousin and heir, Louis XII, been crowned than he invaded the Duchy of Milan and succeeded in getting a European coalition formed against France. The French armies were routed from the Po valley. But they were back in 1515 when François Premier succeeded Louis XII, won the battle of Marignan against Swiss mercenaries, and was knighted by Bayard, as twentieth-century French generals have been made Foreign Legion corporals after displaying heroism in battle.

François Premier's extraterritorial ambitions were disastrous for France. Flushed with the conquest of the Milanese, he aspired to the elective crown of the German empire when it became vacant in 1519. It was the first time a French king had coveted a foreign crown. He spent a fortune buying the votes of German princes, but lost the election to the greatest of all Hapsburg emperors, Charles V. In so doing, he founded the rivalry of the French and Austrian houses. In 1525 Charles V took him prisoner near the Lombard city of Pavia, a terrible humiliation for the knights who were sworn to die protecting the king's person, as they had gathered around Philippe-Auguste when he was trampled underfoot at Bouvines. François was locked up in a tower in the Madrid Alcazar, and tried to abdicate in favor of his brother. He was only set free, after a year's captivity, upon signing the Treaty of Madrid, by which he ceded to the German emperor Burgundy, Flanders, the Artois, and his Italian conquests.

Despite his rash policies, François Premier represented the French version of the Renaissance man: courageous and intellectually curious, warrior and bibliophile, displaying prowess in mind and body. He had Baldassare Castiglione's book, *The Courtier*, translated into French. He was painted by Titian and Clouet, and brought Leonardo and Cellini to France. Cellini made for him twelve life-size statues of the Olympian divinities, which Louis XIV melted down to pay his soldiers.

The final, and perhaps major result of the Valois' Italian adventure was the Concordat of 1516, a compromise arising from François Premier's need for papal support, which governed church-state relations until 1905 and contributed to the failure of Protestantism in France, and to a form of Catholicism from which piety was often absent. The French church became Gallican and national. The king disposed of church patronage and derived his divine-right authority not from the pope but directly from God. Thus, although France supplied a leader for the Reformation in John Calvin, the son of an agent for the diocesan clergy, who was weaned on tales of indulgences and revenues of priests, the Reformation withered in the Gallican French climate. Calvin fled to Geneva, which he made the Protestant capital, while in France the Reformation became a political issue that led to the Wars of Religion, France's gravest civil conflict since the Hundred Years War. From 1559 until 1598, there were eight distinct wars, interrupted by treaties, aggravated by massacres—a muddled, chaotic period which showed that the French are never more cruel than when fighting one another.

In the complex mentality of the great feudal lords like Guise, Rohan, and Montluc, genuine religious fervor was mixed with fear of the extension of royal power. The first direct contestation of royal authority was published by the Protestants after the Saint Bartholomew's Day massacre in 1572; many Protestants were conveniently in Paris on that day for the wedding of Henri de Navarre, and an estimated 4,000 were killed, including the Protestant leader Admiral Coligny, who was defenestrated. The treatise drafted by Protestant jurists stated that the subjects of a perjured king were not bound to obey him.

The monarch's prestige was further weakened when the homosexual king Henri III was accused of not being firm enough with the Protestants. Monks preached tyrannicide, and the Dominican Jacques Clément stabbed Henri III in the underbelly; the king's person was no longer sacred, a mortal could kill and had killed him. Times of strong internal dissension are times of political assassinations, as America in the sixties has learned. Never was there such a rash of political murders in France as during the Wars of Religion. Henri III, before he was himself assassinated, lured the Protestant chief Henri de Guise to the castle of Blois and had him killed by his faithful Guard of the Forty-five. The scene every schoolboy knows shows Henri III contemplating Guise's bloody corpse and musing: "How tall he is! Taller now than when alive." Two successive kings were murdered, for after Henri III, his successor, Henri IV, was stabbed while driving in his carriage through the streets of Paris, by the former monk Ravaillac.

But although the Protestant Reformation had divided the Hapsburg Empire, the first on which the sun never set, it did not succeed in permanently dividing France. The Huguenot leader Henri de Navarre wisely converted to Catholicism to become Henri IV and promised religious freedom with the Edict of Nantes. The last armed contest between the crown and the lords was the Fronde, led by the great general Condé. When the Fronde disintegrated in 1653, Condé pursued his war against the French king at the head of a Spanish army. Belying the fond fiction of ardent national feelings, the great lords periodically tried to overthrow the monarchy until the advent of the French classical age.

The Classical Age

The classical age can best be understood in terms of what preceded it. Obsession with order followed six centuries of lawlessness and struggle in which the monarchy gained effective control of the land. There were no uprisings during the three-generation reign of Louis XIV because he suppressed them in the egg. He persecuted the Huguenots both to please his pious entourage and as a preventive political measure. The classical age, like gold, was immutable and universal. In government it continued the labor of centralization begun by the Romans, although the system was too cumbersome to be effective, and every province clung to its particular laws, customs, and weights and measures. It created a bureaucracy impervious to political change, so that many of the *ancien régime* bureaucrats kept their jobs under revolutionary and imperial governments.

Order at home allowed Louis XIV to concern himself with international affairs, exactly as General de Gaulle was able to do from the time he ended the Algerian war. With the essential difference that the France of Louis XIV was the greatst Continental power and acted as arbiter, throwing its weight now against one nation and now against another, and creating the familiar pattern of European coalitions against France, again repeated under de Gaulle over the question of British entry into the Common Market. Interference in the affairs of other countries was sometimes presented under the guise of altruism. French involvement in the declining Ottoman empire was imperialism disguised as friendship, and Turkey in the eighteenth century became the first French protectorate.

This was a French century, and French culture was as encompassing as French power. France exported thinkers, artists, chefs, and ten thousand *demoiselles* who traveled eastward to become governesses to the children of wealthy Russians. The influence of French art and literature was never again to be in such glorious ascendancy. Antoine de Rivarol in 1784 said: "The time seems to have come when we can speak of a French world just as we spoke of a Roman world." But he was wrong, for by that time, with the Revolution five years away, the French classical world was already collapsing. Nostalgia for an ideal order has since haunted French conservative thinkers, who despair at the turbulence of their country's political life while looking back to an age of stylistic and political unity.

If there is any continuity among the many regimes that succeeded the monarchy, it is in the adoption of some of the goals of the classical age: government control of education and culture, centralization, the prestige of civil service, and the formation of an apolitical bureaucracy. Nostalgia for order led Paul Valéry to defend dictatorship. Valéry's life spanned the period during which the German question was uppermost in French minds; he was born in 1871 and died in 1945. His writing shines with a lucid pessimism, a subtle distaste for change, infinite dexterity matched by infinite scruple, and a mystique based on the discrepancy between an admirable land and its less than admirable inhabitants. The secret ventures of order led him to endorse the dictatorship of Salazar: "To conceive of the idea of dictatorship, it is enough to think of the way men live and to consider that their lives must be organized according to an intelligible model . . . a dictator may feel forced to seize power, just as the spectator of a game too badly

played feels a furious desire to replace the player." This is not a
Fascist, but a Cartesian, dictatorship, of which Valéry felt he had
a past model in the classical age.

The conviction of Valéry and many other French thinkers that
there is something intrinsically superior about French culture is a
backward projection to the classical age when French power carried French civilization, just as Roman power had carried Roman
civilization, and American power today carries the American way
of life. But rather than accept the connection between national
power and the extension of a civilization, the French have been
taught to believe in the timeless supremacy of their culture. The
adoption of the language for roughly 250 years as a diplomatic
lingua franca was seen as proof of its inherent superiority. Because
Cartesian thought influenced Leibniz and Spinoza, the French
credited themselves with inventing modes of thought, and Joseph
de Maistre said: "Perhaps Europe only learns something well,
once the French have explained it." This legacy of the classical age
was cheerfully inherited by the nineteenth century. Victor Hugo
demonstrated his own parochialism rather than France's intellectual supremacy when he wrote: "There is today in the universe
only one literature that is truly alive, and that is French literature.
Everywhere an idea springs up, a French book has been sown."

Other nations have high periods—the Ming dynasty, the Italian
seicento, the Spanish Golden Age, Victorian England—but France
sees itself as perennially great. Literature and history contribute to
fostering the belief that France is in all areas privileged. Genius
is attributed exclusively to nationality rather than to the international development of ideas; one is given the impression that
French inventions are born in a vacuum, that they owe nothing
to work done elsewhere in similar fields, that Joseph Niepce, who
is credited with printing the first photograph in 1822, owes nothing to Sir John Herschel's discovery of hyposulphites three years
earlier, that Louis Blériot's cross-channel flight in 1909 was made
in ignorance of the accomplishment of the Wright brothers, or
that there would never have been pasteurization without Pasteur.

The French even founded an anthropological school on the idea
that one culture is superior to another. Lucien Lévy-Bruhl spent
his life trying to prove that the minds of members of primitive
societies are fundamentally inferior to the minds of those in more

"evolved" societies, for otherwise how could the discrepancy between the "savages" and French civilization be explained? The Frenchman abroad, with a few famous exceptions, is hypercritical as soon as he loses the familiar frame of reference of his own country, which he sincerely believes to represent the highest achievement of mankind. I was once told by Armand Bérard, the French ambassador to the Quirinale, that "Africa begins in Bologna."

The Revolution did not shake the foundations of inspirational France, but merely shifted its focus from culture to freedom. After 1789, the exportable item was no longer language or art or architecture, but emancipation. Having appropriated the ideas of the Swiss Rousseau and the precedent of the American War of Independence, France became the home of revolutionary theory and action. The classical age had spread the cultural refinement of an elite; the revolutionary era radiated the will of the people. André Siegfried believed that "there was something in us that was human, universal, and that is why, all over the world, there were people and countries who turned toward us. France's sphere of influence was unlimited."

The Rise of Patriotism

What had been human and universal was not France's sphere of influence but the tolerant cosmopolitanism of the classical age. Patriotism was not then linked to a nationalist ideology. Kings who made war were cousins, and were generous in their treatment of prisoners and the wounded. Patriotism under the *ancien régime* was not differentiated from loyalty to the king. Voltaire equated *patrie* with property, and what was the monarch but the owner by divine right of a property called the fatherland? On a personal level, Frenchmen were attached to the land they owned, or to the *pays* in the sense of a region where they were brought up, like the poet Joachim du Bellay's Anjou. "My country right or wrong" was an idea foreign to the classical age, and Montesquieu counseled "to always be true, even to one's own country. Every citizen is obliged to die for his fatherland; no one is obliged to lie for it."

France, secure in its European supremacy, could afford cosmopolitanism. It was an age for European careers; the Belgian prince de Ligne, who roamed from the court of Catherine the Great to Versailles, said he felt at home everywhere; foreigners who reached positions of power in France included the Italian Mazarin, the Scotsman John Law, the Swiss Necker, and the German maréchal de Saxe. Praise of French culture was untinged by chauvinism. The prize Rivarol won for praising French culture and language is notable because it was awarded by the Academy of Berlin.

Modern French patriotism, a product of the Revolution, was first defensive, then Messianic. A European coalition army was massed on France's borders, while Louis XVI secretly negotiated with the enemy to regain his throne. Patriotism became linked to the fear of invasion, and developed into martial hatred of the foreigner. The enemy could no longer be respected. As the "Marseillase" said, his blood was impure. France had become the depository of freedom, and its foes had to be either traitors like the *émigré* nobility or enemies of the human species like Pitt. The Revolution became saturated with patriotism. Routine tasks were carried out in the name of high principles. Patriotism became an ideology of survival which revolutionary leaders found useful to exploit. Patriotism is ardent by nature, said Robespierre. Who can love his country coolly? In the Jacobin tradition inherited by the World War II Resistance movement, patriotism requires traitors who must be purged. After the success of the nation in arms at Valmy, the patriotic ideology was reinforced with a Messianic humanitarianism. This was the first total war and the first war of liberation, pitting the people against the tyrants of Europe.

France's mission was not only to defend the Revolution against invaders but to carry it beyond French borders into the rest of Europe, thus launching a period of uninterrupted warfare which lasted from 1792 until 1815. It welded the nation in a common struggle. The nation in arms meant total involvement, like a porcupine's quills going up. "The young men will go to battle," the decree said. "The married men will forge arms and transport food, the women will make tents and garments and help in the hospitals; the children will cut old rags into strips; the old men will place themselves in public squares to inflame the courage of the warriors, incite hatred against the kings, and recommend the unity of the Republic." The citizen-soldier was one of the major legacies of the Revolution to the modern world.

Patriotism was no longer love of country, it was an aggressive passion governed by hatred of the enemy, willingness to sacrifice one's life (the *patrie* is made of the ashes of the dead), and a Manichean division of Frenchmen into heroes and traitors. Its central paradox was its ability to reconcile chauvinism, the restrictive parochial sentiment that French values are better, with humanitarianism; the patriot of 1793 was both protecting France and saving the world. Official texts referred to the rest of Europe as "the enslaved peoples of the earth." The mystique of spilled blood, the suspicion of foreign machinations (the paranoid conviction of revolutionary leaders that England was responsible for French sedition), and the need for a heroic imagery helped define this new patriotism which the story of *le petit Bara* helps illustrate. Joseph Bara was a thirteen-year-old volunteer, a model son who sent his pay to his mother, and he was captured by a royalist band in the Vendée. They offered to release him if he would only shout *"Vive le roi."* He refused and was killed while shouting *"Vive la république."* "Only the French," said Robespierre, "have thirteen-year-old heroes," neglecting to add that Bara was not killed by a foreign invader but by fellow Frenchmen. The idea that one should hate one's enemies was, however, not natural to the times. Stendhal, in Germany with Napoleon in 1809 on the Elelsberg bridge, saw "a good German, dead with his eyes open; German courage, fidelity, and kindness were printed on his face."

Napoleon was well served by the revolutionary impulse, and could present his wars of conquest as wars of liberation. He was enshrined *post factum* as a liberator by bards like Victor Hugo, the son of a Napoleonic general, who presented the campaigns as a crusade of shoeless men of the people delivering their European brethren. Napoleon lost the battle of Waterloo, but Hugo set right that injustice: "The man who won the battle of Waterloo was not Wellington at five o'clock, who despaired at four o'clock, it was not Blücher who did not even fight; the man who won the battle of Waterloo was Cambronne [the major general of the Old Guard who, according to Hugo, said *merde* when asked to surrender, although there is no evidence that he actually had such presence of mind] . . . to strike the lethal thunder down with such a word is to win. . . . He seeks a word as one seeks a sword. Foam bubbles at his mouth and the foam is that word . . . and although overwhelmed by numbers, strength, and arms, he finds in his soul an excremental expression. We will repeat: To say that, to do that, to find that, is to win." Cambronne was in fact in the last square of the Old Guard. He was left for dead and taken prisoner by the English. He was credited with saying: "The Guard dies but does not surrender," although he later denied that he had said those words.

In any case, it was a good story, like the one which has given a name to the particular French kind of jingoism, the story of Nicolas Chauvin, supposedly a Napoleonic soldier wounded seventeen times and pensioned off, who made people laugh with his extravagant patriotism. But there is no evidence in the archives of the Ministry of War that the man after whom chauvinism is named actually existed.

The Napoleonic Legend

There is no such doubt about the center of the legend, Napoleon himself. For once, reality is improbable, and the legend is true. His reign was disastrous, but it left France an inexhaustible reservoir of epic memories. Stated in its simplest terms, the legend of Napoleon is frankly unbelievable. A young Corsican arrives in France to become an officer, rough-edged and romantic, speaking a heavily accented French. He displays uncanny military skill, imposes the *coup d'état* as a form of political succession and sets out to conquer Europe. He turns the essentially conservative, sedentary French into a Europe-roaming army. He turns a nation which had just discovered freedom into a base for the greatest campaign of conquest since Alexander. He makes a people obsessively concerned with property values and inheritances live a selfless epic of personal sacrifice.

If Napoleon had not existed, it would have been impossible to invent him. He is venerated for having led his own people to be slaughtered. According to his own estimates he killed 1,700,000 Frenchmen, more than were killed in both World Wars. And yet when he came back in 1815, from the dangerous proximity of Elba, the army, that ragged, abused, illusion-nourished amalgam of the active male population, once again rallied behind him and marched on Waterloo. This must be one of the most clear-cut cases

of collective hysteria in all history. It also reveals the two conflicting aspirations of the French consciousness: to cultivate one's
garden and lock the garden gate, and to participate in a large epic.
The same people who, with the exception of General de Gaulle,
have never allowed a republican government to remain long
enough in power to do its job, gave Napoleon a second chance.
Napoleon's push into Spain, Italy, and Russia (and England had
he been able) was unprecedented and never again followed in the
national experience, whose traditional goal was perfecting the
outline of its borders and keeping off less favored neighbors.

But where Napoleon links up with French tradition is in his use
of rhetoric as a strategic weapon. A general, he said, must be a
charlatan. The most important class in Napoleonic society was the
army, and he charmed the army. He could not have demanded
what he did if the army had not been under his spell. He had a
hypnotic rapport with his troops. It is to Napoleon that we owe
the traditional review of troops with the general stopping before
each man and asking, "What's your name, soldier? Where 'ya
from, soldier?" Napoleon's genius lay partly in giving each soldier
a strong feeling of personal involvement. At the *camp de Dijon*
in 1800, he talked to soldiers in wooden shoes, with no two uniforms alike:

"Are you well-fed?"

"So-so."

"And you? I hope you will be a credit to yourself."

"Yes, General."

"You were in Italy with me."

"Yes, at Arcole. It was sizzling. Without you, we would have
been roasted like chickens."

"I promote you to sergeant."

"Vive Bonaparte."

A special tone of tough frankness united the emperor and his
troops, who were nicknamed *grognards,* or grumblers. "You must
have been hit on the head to take us over roads like this without
any bread," one told him during the Russian campaign. And
Napoleon, seeing an amputee weeping, stopped to say: "What are
you crying about, you boob? Now you only have one boot to
shine." He also knew the value of promotions and decorations.
He created the Legion of Honor, and from 1804 to 1814, he named

26 marshals and 924 generals. But above all, the special form his rhetoric took was in his bulletins to the troops. In this sense, he was the first of the great modern demagogues. He spoke to the army the way one speaks to a person, and through the army he spoke to the nation. At the same time, he slowly constructed the legend of his military infallibility. The bulletins were posted on Paris walls, declaimed in Paris theaters, hawked in French streets by the tens of thousands. Families in the warm security of their homes gathered around maps of Europe and followed the emperor's progress as they read the bulletins aloud. Their themes are a mixture of Jacobin values and respect for the traditional past. Napoleon often used the device of telling his troops that they were making history. In Egypt he compared them to Roman legions, and he presented the victory of Jena as a revenge for the *ancien régime* defeat of Rossbach. He promised historical fame, something their grandchildren would remember.

General Bernadotte, who drafted his own order of the day in August, 1809, congratulated his Saxon allies on their heroic conduct, and incurred Napoleon's wrath. He was told that only French troops should be praised. The French were by definition heroic, while the enemy was always treacherous, cowardly, and perfidious. The English soldiers were described as mercenaries, while the Prussians were full of warlike frenzy. Propaganda in the modern sense, in which one's own aggressions are presented as a struggle for peace against the relentless belligerence of a bloodthirsty enemy, was perfected in Napoleon's proclamations to the troops. He could not, however, conceal his own love of war. There was something morbid in the way he spent hours on the battlefield after the butchery of Eylau. Battle in his bulletins is always eagerly awaited. On the eve of Borodino he told his haggard troops, "Here is the battle you have so long desired." By that time, the cries of "Long live the emperor" were already mixed with cries of "Long live peace." The emperor fell into false optimism, comparing the weather to sunny days in Fontainebleau as he prepared to start his Moscow retreat in November, 1812.

The sham of government based on a personality cult became most glaring in the famous twenty-ninth bulletin, describing the Russian retreat. Thousands of horses had died, and wayward troops were decimated by "contemptible" Cossack cavalry. After

listing the disaster which no euphemism could conceal (but without mentioning the half-million dead), the bulletin ended with
the cheerful news that "His Majesty's health has never been better." The emperor's highest accolade for the suffering of his men
was: "Soldiers, I am pleased with you," which seemed to satisfy
them. French troops believed that the populations of Europe were
delighted to be occupied by them. Tolstoy's Captain Ramballe,
with Napoleon in Moscow, thought Russian women were fever-
ishly awaiting his arrival. It took the burning of Moscow and the
Spanish guerrillas to prove to the *grande armée* that it was not
wanted.

Napoleon had understood that the French nation can be led
with words, and that fine phrases blunt the sting of defeat. The
danger lies in believing that words are enough. In 1940 Premier
Paul Reynaud, who had fled from the approaching Germans to
Bordeaux with his cabinet, thought it would be enough to talk
like Danton to make victory change camp. He drafted an appeal
for help to Churchill and asked his mistress, Madame de Portes, to
read it back to him. "Not bad," he said, "if I say so myself." The
eloquence of the telegram somehow balanced the sorry events.

Patriotism, although it had been placed at the service of personal ambition, retained all its vitality after Napoleon. He left
a cult based on military campaigns, veterans, regimental flags, and
the Tricolor traveling all the way to Moscow.

The restored Bourbons banished Napoleon's relatives from
France, but preserved epic continuity by keeping alive the Legion
of Honor, and in 1840, under Louis-Philippe, bringing the emperor's ashes back from the mid-Atlantic island of Saint Helena.
Only in France does a regime extol the memory of the one it has
overthrown. The July Monarchy's bourgeois National Assembly
voted a credit of 1,000,000 francs to pay for the *retour des cendres,*
partly because of the lobbying of former *grognards.* Thousands of
subscriptions of less than 1 franc increased the subsidy and showed
the tenacity of the emperor's cult. The *Revue des Deux Mondes*
wrote: "At this hour, the only event that matters for France is that
the remains of the emperor will after twenty years cross the ocean
to repose on the banks of the Seine." The ashes returned aboard
the *Belle-Poule* to Cherbourg and Le Havre, along the Seine, and
their solemn translation to the Invalides was held on a cold De-

cember 15, before 80,000 persons, including many mutilated veterans, like the man who was heard saying, "Hey, don't step on my foot, it's the only one I've got." It was not until the twentieth century that adverse judgments on Napoleon began to appear in official French articles. A lieutenant colonel named Foch made headlines in 1903 when he accused the emperor of having exhausted the resources of the nation with his immoderate ambition.

Michelet and the Female Nation

The most popular French historians are those who place themselves squarely within the context of the epic past, like Jules Michelet, rather than those who grope with the complexities of factual evidence, like Alexis de Tocqueville. From 1833 to 1869, Michelet wrote a 23-volume history of France which covers twenty centuries. Despite its constant distortions and messy scholarship, it towers over the others because of its epic power and sustained lyrical tone. A hundred years later the French still read him as though the ink were not dry, but his influence on contemporaries has been literary rather than historical. A modern historian must dismiss much of his writing as hyperbole, but a writer like André Malraux admits to having been influenced by his style; General de Gaulle read Michelet the way a seminarian reads the New Testament.

Michelet was a historian for the future. He did not explain the past; he presented a coherent vision of it that could serve as a springboard for apostles of French grandeur. Never modest, he claimed that he had "resurrected French internal life." He was propelled by a naïve faith in a few simple ideas. He believed that the people, because they are close to nature, have infallible instincts. He was the great rehabilitator of the Revolution. Writing in the time of the Bourbon Restoration, which had discredited the men of 1789, he blackened the *ancien régime* with a crude portrait of a vicious aristocracy and a Babylonian court, and gave credence to unfounded rumors like the *pacte de famine,* which claimed that Louis XV, indifferent to the starvation of his people, was involved in grain deals. He had an anti-Cartesian faith in popular wisdom, and a romantic belief in the therapeutic value of hardship. "One must arrive in America drowning on a raft," he said. "The one who arrives by steamship with his luggage achieves nothing."

He thought he was the first historian to have interpreted France as a person with a soul, a woman with a mission to humanize the world—an idea that led to nutritive analogies. The Frenchman eats bread, bread is made from wheat, wheat is transformed silex, which explains his rocklike resistance. Alcohol and tobacco gravely weakened France and flung the wives of sailors into the arms of other men. Coffee was partly to blame for the Revolution. Never had France discussed so much as after its use spread. The Yemen bean nourished the Philosophes. Once the essential goodness of the French had been stated, France's enemies could be exposed in all their perfidy; first England, and after the 1870 war, Germany. Michelet was furious at the English for claiming victory at Waterloo. "You had the whole world with you," he wrote. "Why do you want all the glory? What means your Waterloo bridge?"

He reinvented Joan of Arc with a biography that turned her life into a five-act Mystery Play: revelation, action, tribulation, treason, and passion. He lifted material from the work of previous historians, without crediting them, but maintained their mistranslations of the Latin trial. When versions conflicted he used the one most convenient to his narrative. He suppressed while he embellished, and relied on apocryphal texts to strengthen his presentation. He rewrote the trial to make Joan's replies sound more dramatic, and turned it into an *image d'Épinal*, with English villains crucifying a plaster saint. He boasted about his method, which was a model of poor scholarship. His tomes on the Revolution may well have plagiarized Thomas Carlyle, whose own *French Revolution* was finished in 1837, ten years before Michelet's, and is strikingly similar in its appeal to the emotions, its incantatory style, lyric flights, use of hyperbole, and addresses to the reader. There is no mention of Carlyle in his diary, although he knew English. When he saw the French translation, his reaction was suspiciously violent. "This pitiful work," he wrote, "so full of false light, based on lack of study, the work of a whimsical freak."

As the great orchestrator of French myths, Michelet became a cult figure in his lifetime. He drew overflow crowds at the Collège de France, where he held the chair of history. The audience came, it was said, as though to warm themselves in front of a fire. But his courses were twice suspended because they had turned into a political forum for criticizing the July Monarchy. In 1848, shortly after the second suspension, the king was overthrown. Michelet was offered a political role, but the scholar declined. In 1851 he refused to sign an oath of allegiance to the prince-president, Louis Napoleon, and his teaching career ended, although he continued to write until his death in 1874.

What is ultimately fascinating about Michelet is not his gift as a storyteller, for he sounds best read aloud with Berlioz' "Fantastique" in the background, but the interdependence between his life and his work. With few writers can the connection be demonstrated so convincingly. He achieved complete identity between his personal obsessions and his main historical themes. He described his writing as a great sea. "I am rowing into Louis Fourteen," he said. "I am rowing vigorously into Richelieu." He believed in physical and moral preparation for writing, like a priest who must be in the state of grace to say mass. Before embarking upon his *oeuvre,* he ended what he considered a degrading liaison with the wife of a friend. Difficult passages gave him migraines, and Napoleon's *coup d'état* exhausted him to such a point that he took the mud baths at Acqui near Turin. To inspire his description of corrupt prerevolutionary France, he went into a public urinal and breathed deeply of the acrid ammonia fumes. "Having come as close as I could to the subject of my horror," he explained, he returned to the work table.

His feelings for the people could be explained on one level by his working-class origins. The son of a printer who was involved in Gracchus Babeuf's egalitarian movement, he grew up "like a blade of grass between two Paris cobblestones." When he was seventeen, he felt humiliated by the spectacle of Russian and English troops occupying Paris. But on a deeper level, his writing worked out the abiding concerns of his private existence. The extended metaphor which he used to describe France was one of sickness and health. Prerevolutionary France was sick and had regained health through the Revolution. Action was the virile principle which impregnated nature to make history. He wanted his motto to be *Penetrabit*—it will penetrate. In this identity between human life and history, blood was the essential substance. It was the source of life, the color of life, and proof of the rhythm of life through the menstrual cycle. Again and again he defines key historical figures by the quality of their blood. The thin blood of Robespierre is opposed to the carmine and generous blood of the people. The spoliation of Protestant property under Louis XIV he likened to the fleshing of the hounds in the courtyard of Versailles. No battle could be described without gory details about the casualties. When Marat's doctor found his editorials more violent than usual, he wrote, the doctor would drop by to bleed him. Michelet confessed, "I have drunk too much of the black blood of the dead."

The connection between blood and feminine France is obvious. Michelet considered woman closer to nature because her life is determined by the menstrual flow. Like the ocean, woman is elemental, and like nature, she is cyclical. Her blood flow abolishes the contrast between the fixed and the fluid. Like nature, she is ever changing and bound up with time, of which the menstrual cycle is a measure. Michelet developed a cult of woman as the existential symbol of the organization of the universe, and, by extension, of France, the most perfect nation. "Always remember, Frenchmen," he wrote in his biography of Joan, "that our nation was born of a woman's heart, of her tenderness and her fears, of the blood she shed for us." His concept of the people was another natural extension of this feminine mystique. Like woman, the people were in a natural state of instinct and wisdom. By reducing life to its basic principles, they were close to truth and goodness. They were close to the land and the elements, and transmitted their wisdom like the apostles, thanks to an oral tradition.

Michelet's intimate diaries, perhaps the most startling confession in French literature, reveal the connection between his view of woman and his private life. Widowed in 1839, he began eight years later to receive fan mail from a French teacher in Austria who was thirty years his junior, Athénais Mialaret. They were married in 1849, when he was fifty-one and she was twenty-three. Sex was connected with the progress of his work, as his scribbled notes reveal: "At 5.30 came into her bed: without preparation, she opened, she made possible the difficult joy—I took the spark from her and finished my first chapter on Richelieu." His wife was frail and often ailing, which led to complaints that "the only difficulty is a wife who is nervous and unapproachable—why don't you sleep with Ernestine [the maid]—each time it is a diplomatic negotiation." When rebuffed, he had fantastic dreams: A lion with six cubs; Catherine the Great and her seraglio; "two women in heat and smelling them—an unknown woman who put both her breasts in my mouth and told me to suck them"; vast subterranean prisons like a Piranesi etching; and his wife changing into a little boy in underpants.

But more than with sex, he was obsessed by the natural functions of his wife, her digestion and menstruation, He had to watch, as though watching the tides or the seasons, the intimate cycle that was analogous to the earth cycle. He attended her "pure morning ablutions," and wrote that "what passes through her sacred body, what she brings forth enriched . . . is not indifferent . . . it is received with the respect of love." He worried over her digestion as over the coups that overthrew French governments. "Only four times in a month," he wrote. "There is a great internal irritation; the suffering of the tiny gate where everything ends is only a sign. . . . One is day by day dependent on this little mystery of nature." It became a part of Madame Michelet's conjugal duties to comply with her husband's impassioned voyeurism. At the seaside, "I sat below her as she did me the favor of adding a few little drops to the sea, in all decency." Walking on a hill, "I was filled with desire, I had hoped she would be alone on the heights and I had sat lower down, to pay my devotions to the dear fountain of love. She told me sweetly: I refuse you nothing. But don't you see those people. I said, what a strange thing this life of desire is."

Menstruation, however, was the time when woman was herself, and he noted the number of days left in her cycle, growing expectant at the promise of "the monthly crisis, the flux that raises and stimulates, the languishing reflux." If she was late, it disturbed the cadence of his work; when the period came, he was transported, and wrote: "Her period came this morning, without relieving her though, abundant and of a fine color . . . I was so happy I wanted to kiss the blood." Michelet's humorless sexual mysticism is easy to ridicule, but it is also admirable in its total earnestness, and in its strength of emotion, which clearly served as a driving force in his work. He is too devout to be salacious. If there is a pathology in his obsession, it is not the pathology of the sensation seeker but of the communicant at the rail. In much the same way, his *History of France* should be read as a religious text which conforms to the epic past. It found its most passionate worshipers after the war of 1870.

The Mystique of Revenge

Revolutionary and Napoleonic patriotism had been tied to conquest, but after the war of 1870, patriotism became identified with loss and revenge. A new mystique grew out of defeat by the Germans and the amputation of Alsace and Lorraine. French wars are usually begun in a spirit of high optimism, and in 1870 the prosperous Second Empire was convinced that no one would dare fire a shot in Europe without French permission. When war became inevitable, Paris bookstores advertised French-German dictionaries for the victorious soldiers who would soon be in Berlin. The popular song of the period was "O William, oh, you fat papa, your nose is going to be rubbed in your own *caca*." Everyone was yelling *à Berlin*, and Nicolas Chauvin was revived to reply to the spoilsports who were asking, "And what if we are not ready?" with the rejoinder, "Sir, the French are always ready." The feeling of 1870 was a combination of expectancy and optimism.

But after this inflated talk of an invincible army and an administration that was the envy of Europe, defeat was swift and brutal. So brutal that Gustave Flaubert thought he was witnessing the end of the Latin world. God, this time, was on the side of the Germans. Bismarck wrote his wife: "May God help us; His arm is not flesh. I am confident in Him when I see this dissipated people across from us. We too are sinners but not in such a Babylonian manner, and we do not defy God." The 1870 war was the first anti-French crusade, with the Iron Chancellor its Lutheran Peter the Hermit. At a time when England was at the height of its imperialism, and a victorious Germany nourished doctrines of pan-Germanism, France became absorbed in the desperate nationalism of a defeated country. The theme of *revanche*, revenge, salvaged what was left of national pride. France between 1870 and 1914 lived with its eyes fixed on the blue line of the Vosges.

As after every French defeat, a scapegoat had to be found. Like Ganelon who betrayed Roland, like the connétable de Bourbon who betrayed Bayard, like General Dumouriez who went over to the émigré army during the Revolution, like General Grouchy who failed to arrive in time to save Napoleon at Waterloo, Bazaine had faltered, and he joined the gallery of famous traitors. In charge of the defense of Metz, Marshal Bazaine had capitulated and was convicted of treason. Like the *mot de Cambronne* fabricated by Hugo, it was the literary account of Bazaine's treason that prevailed over fact. Alphonse Daudet has a French schoolteacher tell his pupils: "Bazaine, instead of carrying out his duties as a chief, was playing billiards while the battle of Saint-Privat raged."

Underpopulation and lack of proper schooling were seen as the major causes of the 1870 debacle. German victory was attributed to the *famille nombreuse* and the Prussian schoolteacher. A French general was conveniently found who did not know whether the Rhine flowed north-south or south-north. An increase in the birthrate and militant teachers were to be the remedies.

Patriotism became part of the school program, a cure for the sick French soul. The motto of the teacher's league was "for the *patrie*, by the book and by the sword." The mythology of *revanche* was summed up in the new geography books, in which the former Alsace-Lorraine border of the map of France had become a dotted line. There could be no more compelling reminder of a schoolboy's mission than that dotted line.

In French homes patriotic works like the anthology entitled *Vive la France* were held together by bookends which represented pilloried traitors like Ganelon. French history was disinfected of its German influences. The Franks became Belgians and the mantle of hereditary enemy passed from England to Germany. The theme of *revanche* was illogically linked to the old notion that France is the only nation whose sons selflessly spill their blood for humanity. Paul Déroulède founded the jingoistic League of Patriots, and the veterans of 1870 held boisterous meetings at which they sang his martial songs: "Up there, in the forest on the hill, we are watching for them, we are waiting for them."

The Lorrainese writer Maurice Barrès popularized the idea that patriotism is a religion that requires martyrs. "I have transferred my piety from heaven to the land of my ancestors," he wrote. Barrès wrote from an attitude of permanent mourning; he spent hours visiting the graves of the war dead. He could not recover from the shock of German unity. He had seen a convoy of French prisoners being herded to Germany, and he wrote: "I love France, not for its charm and history; I might on those grounds prefer Italy, but for those anonymous individuals I saw humiliated and lined up like animals on the side of a snow-covered road, while fur-wrapped brutes laughed and offended their human dignity." Barrès' nationalism was pessimistic and perfumed with the smell of corpses. Haunted by the spectacle of French greatness coming undone like a loosely sewn garment, he wrote *A Novel of National Energy,* in which seven young Lorrainers swear to redeem their country's destiny.

Not since Napoleon had the army been so popular. The historian Michelet talked of the "holy bayonet," and the poet Péguy of the glory of war. Verlaine was the first, in a patriotic poem, to call the Germans Boches. A man who dies young for his country, it is said, will have known only life's roses and leave no orphans. Jingoism was common to both the left and the right until the Dreyfus case separated those who wanted to protect the army by covering up an injustice from those who called for the acquittal of the falsely accused captain. Thereafter, the French right appropriated the Jacobin notion that France was made up of patriots and traitors. Charles Maurras, the founder of the Action Française, divided the nation into France and anti-France.

Few were the men who dared swim against the patriotic tide. In an 1891 article in the *Mercure de France,* the essayist Remy de Gourmont wrote: "Personally, I would not give, in exchange of those forgotten lands, either the little finger of my right hand, for I need it to hold my hand steady when I write, or the little finger of my left hand, for I need it to flick the ash from my cigarette." Indignation reached such a pitch that he was fired from his librarian's job at the Bibliothèque Nationale. The old French anarchist strain, however, could not be stifled and was grafted onto the internationalism of the Socialist movement. The Socialists and their great leader Jean Jaurès were ardently antimilitaristic. They told their rank and file: "Fire at your officers, not at your comrades on the other side." They insulted officers in the street, called them vampires, called the army a school of vice, and suggested that the Tricolor be planted in a dung heap.

The right wing branded all social agitation betrayal. With the paranoid streak that has always characterized French extremists, they believed that every workers' strike had been ordered by Germany. But nationalism, which had lost some of its thrust after the Dreyfus case and the dismal failure of General Boulanger, spread once more after the Kaiser's visit to Tangier. At a Paris exhibit of primitive painting, the van Eycks' Ghent reredos was claimed as a product of French art. After an antimilitarist play by Henri Bernstein was forced to close down in 1911, the London *Daily Mail* wrote: "Patriotism and militarism remain the dominant characteristics of the French people." Beatification of Joan of Arc in 1909 was a sign that God was once again on the French side.

The War to End Wars

After the 1911 Agadir incident in which the German cruiser *Panther* appeared in Moroccan waters while French troops were putting down a local revolt, there was a fusion of right-wing, anti-Dreyfusard nationalism and left-wing, Republican nationalism; together, they were increasingly self-assertive and jingoistic. Jules Cambon, the French ambassador in Berlin, who was in Paris when the Agadir crisis broke, called on the German ambassador von Schoen to tell him that his country's behavior was a *cochonnerie* (foul trick). Von Schoen complained about Cambon's undiplomatic language to the Quai d'Orsay. Hundreds of old soldiers began to volunteer for active service. "I am told I am too old for a command," wrote General de Negrier. "I simply ask to be sent to the front, to show the young soldiers of France that an old division commander, Grande Croix de la Légion d'honneur, knows how to die."

From 1912, France was convinced that war was inevitable and expected it just as happily as it had done in 1870. Military bands played marches through the streets of Paris at the slightest opportunity. A line from a successful play said: "War is not stupid, cruel, or hateful. It is merely sport for real." The campaign to revive three-year conscription succeeded in 1913, when the bill was passed by a vote of 337 to 223. Guglielmo Ferrero was shocked when he attended a meeting of Socialist railway workers who voted for a general strike but agreed to call it off if a war was declared. There were minor anti-German incidents in 1913. Two parties of

German tourists were molested, and the police failed to intervene. In July, 1914, a royalist fanatic named Villain assassinated Jean Jaurès, who had long warned that the narrow system of European alliances would lead to war. Jaurès was France's first and last Socialist of international stature, with the possible exception of Léon Blum. His death was tragic not only because he was a great man but because after the war the vacuum he left was filled by men like Marcel Déat and Jacques Doriot who disassociated the party from democracy and tried to present Fascism as the true shape of French Socialism. When France went to war, it was with a physical sense of release. For forty-four years the French had clamored for it, desired it, hoped for it. The *poilus* boarded the military trains marked *à Berlin,* like jolly vacationers. "Finally the happy day is here," wrote Barrès.

On August 1, 1914, the white mobilization posters went up on the walls of city halls and post offices. The day before, the Saint-Cyr class of 1914 had held its graduation ceremonies, and a cadet named Gaston Voizard called for a collective oath that "when we charge it will be in full dress, white gloves and Cassowary [the plumed hat of Saint-Cyr cadet officers]." Voizard was killed less than a year later. The locomotives of troop trains whistled cheerfully, women cried, and men laughed as they set out for what they called "a stroll to the heart of Prussia." It would not take long. Soon the Germans would surrender and every French soldier would be kissed by a grateful Alsatian girl.

This was the last great epic in which France was undivided. The army of the Republic was starting on its last crusade against the Austro-Hungarian Empire. It was also going to wrest Alsace and Lorraine from the barbarian Huns. It was the last example of Jacobin patriotism adopted by the entire nation, before the rise of ideologies which were not France's own. Pre-1914 France was an exporter of ideologies, but the important twentieth-century ideologies originated elsewhere. There was something cleansing about this war—it would redeem the mistakes of 1870. Indeed, the army seemed frozen in time, with the same horizon-blue and madder-red uniforms, the same tactics, and even some of the same weapons as in 1870—spears were distributed to the light cavalry. It was also the last hurrah of the nation in arms. The *poilus* of 1914 went to the front like the volunteers who had left for Valmy in August, 1792, with the secret hope that after one decisive battle the war would be over. It was with the victory of Valmy in mind that the French high command mobilized 2,000,000 men for a swift victory. The nation was psychologically and materially unprepared for a war of attrition.

The belief that the patriotic French reservist would fight better than the German professional soldier was another myth of the nation in arms which contributed to French optimism. Before the war had begun, sixty-two-year-old marshal Jacques-Césaire Joffre had confidently announced: "We will have the war, I will fight the war, and I will win the war. I have always succeeded in what I undertook." The final aspect of the nation in arms which was nightmarishly repeated in World War I was the mystique of no retreat. "Stand and die rather than go back," ordered Joffre. Sustained confidence in the tactic of throwing in more and more troops into great battles helps explain why France had the highest losses of the war. Economy of life was not one of the principles of the high command, which seemed to be imbued with the Barrèsian notion that war is sacrificial.

The French epic concept of the war soon proved tragically mistaken. It was not to be a quick war but a long one which would test less the bravery than the endurance of the nation. It was not the struggle of Western civilization against barbarians but the collision of two potent nationalisms. A writer from the prosperous German nation said that "the force to create confers the right to destroy." And Romain Rolland replied: "Are you the sons of Goethe or those of Attila?" They were neither; they were the sons of Nietzsche, responding to the jingoism of French *revanche* with their own mystical concept of a great European destiny. Henri Bergson argued at the Academy of Sciences that France's struggle was that of civilization against barbarism, but that did not help the men in the trenches, one of whom, a second lieutenant of the Thirty-third Infantry Regiment, wounded at Dinant, wrote: "It appeared in the wink of an eye that all the virtue in the world could not prevail against superior firepower." His name was Charles de Gaulle.

After the short-lived delirium of French troops entering Alsace came the anticlimax of a German advance. There was to be no Valmy. Instead, France would become the battlefield where nearly

eight million *poilus* would fight for four years. The slogan
changed from the offensive *on les aura* (we will get them) to the
defensive *ils ne passeront pas* (they shall not pass). False hopes and
optimism were manufactured by officials on the home front. It
seemed from newspaper accounts that the Russians were always
five days from Berlin, until they dropped out of the war in 1917.
German soldiers were so badly fed, it was said, that a prisoner had
been taken by showing him a slice of bread and butter. An amputee had enlisted in the air force. The wounded were refusing
evacuation. The *débrouillard* (resourceful) *poilus* were using oil
from sardine cans to fire their 75 mm cannons, the "incom-
parable 75's" which had been expected to carry the day. *Le
Temps* wrote that "as weapons are perfected, losses diminish." In
fact, losses sustained by the "stand and die" tactics caused the
gravest crisis ever to break out in the French army. It was only
after Verdun, the ten-month war within a war, and after the
bloody Nivelle offensive of 1917 that the patriotism of the *poilu*
cracked and he went on what was less a mutiny than a sit-down
strike. Verdun was the apotheosis of the sacrificial principle. It was
France's "moral boulevard," which had to be defended to the last
man, and the avowed German goal in attacking the fortified zone
of Verdun was to provoke heavy French losses. It was axiomatic
that every conquered position had to be retaken, and Fleury
changed hands sixteen times in less than a month. Verdun was
a separate, contained epic, a hell that was later turned into a
grace. It was worse than Dresden and Hiroshima, worse than
Stalingrad, because it seemed endless. If all the men who died
there were to stand up, there would not be room for them.

It was Marshal Pétain who won Verdun, replacing Joffre and
his sacrificial strategy with the sensible ideas that "it is not bayonets that win battles, but firepower," and that a strategic advantage may be gained even though a few inches of ground are lost.
It was also Pétain, who, after the Nivelle offensive broke against
the Hindenberg Line in 1917, quelled the mutinies that broke out
in frontline regiments from April, 1917, to October of the same year.
There were 250 instances of collective refusals to fight. The disciplinary problem was partly due to a dearth of noncoms in frontline regiments, and to the convicts who had been let out of French
jails to join the ranks. Men sent to the line refused to go. At

Coeuvres, 400 infantrymen ordered to follow up an attack of Moroccan shock troops hid in the woods instead. The French general staff blamed pacifists and agitators for subverting the *poilu.* Generals could not admit that the men were protesting against established military tactics of useless attacks with high casualty rates. There were no agitators, only soldiers paralyzed by fear. Pétain's great achievement, greater than winning Verdun, because if the mutinies had spread the war would have been lost, was to regain the confidence of the troops with a mixture of the carrot and the stick. He visited the disrupted regiments, granted leaves, rotated troops, improved living conditions, and promised lower casualty rates. He also announced that mutineers would be shot: 629 were sentenced to death *pour l'exemple,* but only 75 were actually shot.

By 1917 the frontline French soldier no longer hated his German enemy. The lassitude of war and the proximity of the trenches made the soldiers find more in common with each other than with their respective commanders. The last axiom of Jacobin patriotism, that the enemy is an ogre who must be hated, evaporated in dialogues across the trenches, like the following:

"Guten tag, Fritz."

"Bonjour, monsieur."

"Kalt."

"Ja, pas chaud." (Yes, not warm.)

"Et tes officiers?" (Where are your officers?)

"Quand il fait froid, officier pas la." (They're not around when it's cold.)

"Böser Krieg." (Lousy war.)

"Et pas finie." (And not over.)

The trench was a Franco-German community with its particular habits, exchanges, risks, and social types. On either side the men realized that their officers, pound for pound, weighed in not much differently from themselves. The men of both armies sometimes washed in the same stream, and gave right-of-way to unarmed enemy detachments out for water or wood. Then fighting would resume across the 100-yard no-man's-land. Plunderers left the trenches to loot the bodies of the dead, and others, if they ever existed, like Lew Ayres in *All Quiet on the Western Front,* went chasing after butterflies. And the men on the burying squads risked their lives for a shovelful of dirt, with the officers telling them. "It's got to be a perfect rectangle."

When victory came, however, it was a genuine victory for the entire nation, in the sense that France had contributed the most and lost the most, and that the principal battles had been fought on French soil. And yet, for those very reasons, it was not a healthy victory. France had displayed a national cohesion and a spirit of sacrifice it would never show again, but was exhausted by the effort. Patriotism would thenceforth be tinged with the fear that the cost is too great. Moreover, now that Alsace and Lorraine had been recovered, there was no great issue to unite national feeling. In the National Assembly, the words "I was in the war, monsieur" became one of the tactics of partisan politics. The Popular Front and the Action Française each claimed to represent authentic patriotism. Léon Blum gave a traditional definition of the *patrie* as "faith in a few great ideas which France has spread through the world." But when he appointed Jean Zay as his Minister of Education, there was an uproar because at the age of twenty Zay had published a poem with the line: "Fifteen hundred thousand of them died for that filthy bitch." The *chambre bleu horizon,* which included a high percentage of veterans, represented postwar chauvinism, but there were many dissenting voices. Historians blamed the general staff for the 1914–18 butchery. A young poet named Louis Aragon praised the mutineers of 1917.

France was no longer the repository of mankind's ideals. The "Internationale" replaced the "Marseillaise" as the song that stirred the disinherited masses and the intellectuals. The government was made the scapegoat for the financial loss involved in Russian and Balkan bonds. The franc was devalued. The depression, when it hit France, was bad enough to fan dissatisfaction but not bad enough to lead to economic reforms. The hopes of the Popular Front were unfulfilled. France ceased to have a decisive influence in world affairs, relied on the League of Nations, refused to intervene in either Spain or the Rhineland, and backed disarmament at a time when its own security was threatened. Aristide Briand wanted to be known as the apostle of peace, a role modern statesmen have learned to leave to the pope. Nostalgia for the epic past and former grandeur led to self-deception, quixotic behavior, and the resurgence of the right. The Third Republic could develop neither a policy to keep the peace nor a strategy of defense in case of war.

Right-wing thinkers trained their antirepublican nationalism on their own government rather than on the rising Fascist states with which they sympathized. The metaphor of France as a spent organism, biologically incapable of submitting to a new struggle, was adopted by the right. The specter of 1914–18 was also a powerful deterrent for the timid middle class. In 1928 a bill was passed reducing military service to one year, with the slogan "France must remain strong"—the opposite of what the bill would accomplish. Daladier was acclaimed for placating Hitler at Munich. The fervor of the *instituteur* teaching revenge on Germany was no longer relevant. There was, on the contrary, a tendency to pretend that Hitler did not exist. The costly victory of one war created a state of mind which prepared the nation for defeat in the next. Patriotism in the old sense was reawakened only with the presence of *feldgrau* uniforms in Paris.

But which patriotism? The patriotism of Pétain or the patriotism of de Gaulle? World War II for the French was a civil war. De Gaulle fought Vichy more than he did the Germans. Patriotic Frenchmen could with clear consciences follow either de Gaulle or Pétain; there were sound patriotic reasons to do both. National unity was lost in the complexity of post-World-War-I Europe. Just as the *revanchard* nationalist is a symbol for France between 1870 and 1914, the post-1914 symbol is the *girouette* (weather vane), the political, military, or literary figure who changes camps to survive. In a nation which is itself habitually changing regimes, the *girouette* is the India-rubber man, the political survivor. Changing allegiance is one of the forms the life instinct has taken in France ever since Gallic tribes sided with the Romans. Every regime has had its *girouettes*.

Choosing the wrong side could be fatal. In 1815, Marshal Ney was sent to stop Napoleon in the Provence and instead joined him; after Waterloo, he was shot. Men like Talleyrand and Fouché were able to serve their country in half a dozen regimes, thanks to highly developed gifts for duplicity. But to accuse a French politician of inconsistency is like blaming a chameleon for changing color. In the French political landscape, inconsistency is necessary and even normal. It is too easy to condemn such men or expose their turnabouts; they are not traitors, but carriers of the instability of French political life. It is pathetic to see great and famous men scrambling to change sides before their lack of foresight gets them into trouble. In 1940 there was ample confusion about where patriotism lay. For most of the nation, there was no clear cause. There was an old and famous general, the victor of Verdun, who said patriotism lay in saving French blood and preventing the destruction of the nation, and there was a middle-aged, almost unknown general, who became the improbable custodian of Jacobin patriotism. Fortunate are those Frenchmen who can say they heard his message from the start. More common were those who changed their minds at appropriate times. The novelist François Mauriac praised Pétain in 1940 as the savior of France, and remained pro-Pétain until the meeting with Hitler at Montoire in 1942. He dedicated a copy of one of his novels to a German officer. After the British shelled French ships at Mers-el-Kebir, he wrote: "For how many years now will Mr. Winston Churchill have against him a unanimous France?" This did not prevent him from becoming, after 1944, de Gaulle's most zealous bard, even comparing the general to Christ: "The source of everything is that de Gaulle believed and knew he was de Gaulle . . . only one time in the history of the world has a man said he was the Messiah without being locked up in the madhouse. He was believed by his friends and by his foes."

These are exercises in literary versatility. Paul Claudel wrote an ode to Pétain in 1940 and an ode to de Gaulle in 1944. Consistency was difficult in France after 1918. The only ones whose consistency could be proven were either shot or decorated in 1944. The degrees of collaboration are subtle. Was Sartre guilty of misconduct for staging plays during the Occupation which had to be approved by the German authorities and which were attended by the *Wehrmacht?*

De Gaulle admired the right-wing writers Barrès and Valéry, but he was not contaminated by the defeatism of the French right between the wars. In London, he appropriated the epic past, its language and its historic goals. To the complacent servility of Vichy, he opposed the Jacobin vocabulary: The French Republic does not treat with the enemy on its own territory. The sacrificial aspect was also present. When someone asked him, "Have you made a pact with victory?" he replied, "No, we have made a pact with death." The Resistance was mystical, not rational; it was based on faith in the destiny of France, not the present situation which seemed hopeless, but the conviction that the *patrie* in danger has always been saved.

The Resistance was without precedent in French history. The nature of de Gaulle's struggle was entirely new. Never had France fought the occupant of its territory from outside its territory. The lessons of the nation in arms were no longer relevant. The precedent here was the Spanish resistance of 1810 to the armies of Napoleon. De Gaulle claimed to represent eternal France, but there was no more eternal France. Not only was France divided into collaborators and Resistance fighters, but each group was riddled with subdivisions. The Resistance succeeded as an insurrection against a foreign invader, but it failed as a political movement. It tried to formulate a doctrine of national reconstruction, but it was only an active minority which could not impose itself on the nation. The divisions did not heal; they simply shifted to other problems, like the future of the French empire.

After the disunity of World War II came the disunity of colonialism. Was it patriotic to keep France's colonies or to jettison them? Where was the national destiny? The French were told at first that it was their duty to defend Algeria, and then that it was their duty to abandon it. The epic past no longer served as a guideline to postwar problems. There was a time when crisis had united the nation, but now crisis divided it. There was a time when nationalism was meaningful, but now the problems of France were part of the problems of Europe. A student riot in one country meant that other countries could expect the fallout. A financial crisis in one country was equally contagious. Such problems could only be solved on a European level. The same man whose whole career had been based on an intense nationalism and a belief in the French vocation for greatness presided over the disintegration of the French empire which was the condition of that greatness.

The empire had saved France in 1940 by providing a territorial base, soldiers, and a claim to being a world power. But the war also undermined many of the assumptions which made colonialism possible. The war made the empire more valuable, and weakened it. As soon as peace came, France began to lose it, and

with it, its claim as a power of the first rank. Joseph de Maistre
had said that the need to influence others was the most prominent
trait of the national character. But inspirational France was buried
in 1918. France has not been able to resolve the problems of its
own contemporary society, much less influence others. Malraux
said in 1958 that France was aimless because it had lost its role
as arbiter of justice to the Soviet Union and as symbol of power
to the United States. There were no more continents to civilize,
no more lessons for the world. France was a country in search of
a mission.

The key to understanding a modern French leader like Charles
de Gaulle is to see him as the point of intersection of two contradictory forces: de Gaulle was both agent of French modernization
and the guardian of an outworn ideology of French mission and
French grandeur. He was placed in the impossible position of a
modern pope who must achieve the *aggiornamento* of the church
without diluting Catholic doctrine. In this sense, the epic past
continued to shape the French present while impeding the French
future. The archaic side of de Gaulle was to continue to identify
French interests with some great human ideal, to continue to believe in a French civilizing mission at a historical moment when
France no longer had either an ideology to justify such a mission
or the power to accomplish it. De Gaulle expressed his belief that
France offers a model of civilization in his first published work,
Discord Among the Enemy, in which he repeats that familiar set
piece, the French garden, as analogous to the French mind: "In
the French garden," he writes, "no tree tries to smother the others
with its shadow. The flower beds find a reason for being geometrically designed, the pond has no ambitions of becoming a
waterfall, the statues make no claims to monopolize our admiration. Sometimes a noble melancholy emerges. Perhaps it is derived
from the feeling that each isolated element could have shone more
brightly. But that would have been to the detriment of the whole,
and the strollers can only express praise for the rule which im-
prints upon the garden its magnificent harmony."

Armed with this feeling of superiority, he continued to postu-
late, as he did successfully in 1940, that since France had always
been great it must continue to be great. The sheer power of his
character and the strength of his leadership created the illusion

that the epic past continued. For de Gaulle was able to mitigate the sense of humiliation felt by the French after 1940. French troops fought at Monte Cassino, marched into the Lorraine, occupied Strasbourg, and again took custody of the empire. When he left the government in 1946, France was soon beset with fresh humiliations. Fourth Republic governments had to give in on German rearmament because they needed military and economic help. France was incapable of resuming its rank, as the failure of the Suez expedition and the government's inability to deal with the colonial question showed. The era of gunboat diplomacy on the part of the nineteenth-century great powers was over. But when de Gaulle returned in 1958 and freed France from the Algerian albatross he was able to satisfy the French addiction for greatness with the first vigorous foreign policy France has had since Napoleon. It did not matter that de Gaulle's policy represented the illusion rather than the substance of power, it satisfied what Montesquieu called "this general passion which the French nation has for glory."

From 1962, the end of the Algerian war, until de Gaulle's defeat in the April, 1969, referendum, France basked in a warm glow of self-congratulation. The general adopted the Coué method, which consists in telling oneself "Yes, I am healthy and I do feel better." Couve de Murville, as Foreign Minister, said on television in November, 1967: "France's world position today has not been matched for generations. Today we enjoy an authority and a consideration we have rarely had in the past." The worker-student revolt of 1968 may have reminded Couve de Murville of François Guizot's words to Lord Aberdeen not long after the 1848 Revolution ended his political career: "You may count on the fact that foreign policy does not concern the French at all and will not be the cause of any important event... the only governments that are taken seriously are those that accomplish something in terms of domestic affairs."

Sometimes French self-congratulation is comic, as when the Gemini capsule went into space and a Paris newspaper headlined: "Gemini is partly French." (Collins, one of the astronauts, was raised in France.) More often, it is complacent. Gaullist France had a tendency to hide its own failings by displaying the faults of others, as when French television showed rioting American cities but passed over the student riots in its own streets. This form of patriotism came close to Dr. Johnson's last refuge of the scoundrel. The habit of self-praise also makes the French hypersensitive to criticism from abroad. In 1966 the *Corriere della Sera* published a supplement on France in which it said in the lead article: "France is no longer the mirror of freedom for the world. It is no longer the mirror of democracy, of intelligence, of art, good taste, literature, military glory, theater or fashion. It is not even the mirror of anticonformity." *Le Monde* took umbrage at this diagnosis and reported that the entire supplement had been dictated by anti-Gaullism. The supplement was described not as an impartial critique but as a deliberate and malicious attempt to strain Franco-Italian relations, as though the only basis for frendship must be lack of criticism.

When I was covering the Bizerte crisis in 1961 for the New York *Herald Tribune,* I described atrocities I had seen committed on Tunisian civilians by French paratroopers. Michel Debré, then Premier, asked his press secretary whether I was a French national. On being told that I was, he said: "Tell that fellow that he is a very poor advocate of France." I wondered about the fragility of a regime that could only tolerate advocates. The border between criticism and lack of patriotism is blurred. It is considered disloyal to bare French failings to the outside world. When Luigi Barzini wrote *The Italians,* the book was judged by Italian critics on its own merits, not as an act of treachery. But Armand Bérard, then French ambassador to the Quirinale, was shocked. "How could Barzini have written a book like that about his own country?" he wondered. "I would be ashamed to have written a similar book about France." This kind of thinking maintains the French in an attitude of false smugness about their achievements and self-indulgence about their faults, until a crisis like the student revolt or the shakiness of the franc brings the regime more in line with reality.

At its most harmless, latter-day chauvinism is merely archaic, a nostalgic attachment to times when French civilization exercised its authority over Europe. This is a sure crowd-pleaser. When I was following the election campaign of Minister of Justice René Capitant in June, 1968, I was not surprised to hear him say that France had always led the way in social progress and would continue to do so with the participation of workers in the management of their firms. Nor was I surprised to hear a working-class voice pipe up in the back of the room: "That's because all over the world they come to borrow our ideas." Every national achievement is linked to this stubborn concept of civilization. When the sailor Tabarly wins a cup, when the French skiing team carries the day, when a French engineer is chosen to build a Bolivian dam, when the Iraqi air force buys Mystère jets, these isolated accomplishments are trumpeted as proof of a general, unblemished pattern of excellence, manifestations of French superiority, like a Racine play or a Pasteur vaccination.

On a more serious level, major policy decisions sometimes seem dictated by chauvinistic preoccupations. The essential contradiction of the *force de frappe* lies in the sacrifice asked of the French people to achieve it and its ineffectiveness in the international arsenal of weapons. La Fontaine wrote a fable about the frog that wanted to be an ox. France is in the reverse situation— a former ox having trouble scaling down its ambitions to match its capacities. It is the specter of lost grandeur that makes France so touchy about minor points in international conferences. At the March 12, 1968, Paris Conference for Economic Cooperation and Scientific Development, France refused to ratify the official communiqué because of the phrase: "Europe's political division is an obstacle to its scientific development."

On November 11, 1968, during the fiftieth anniversary of the 1918 armistice, a television journalist interviewed a number of persons for a program called *Contact*. Amid the chorus of praise for the great day, one young man said: "The war was started for economic reasons, it had no meaning, and thus November eleven is for me not a time to rejoice but a time of mourning." What would normally be called balanced reporting, the high clergy of French television decided was close to treason, and it was soon announced that the journalist's contract would not be renewed and that the program would be absorbed by the regular news broadcasts. Meanwhile, General de Gaulle presided at elaborate ceremonies for the anniversary of a conflict half of which he spent as a prisoner of war in Germany. He paid homage to the eight World War I marshals at the Invalides as blue velvet batons sprinkled with gold stars were set before their cenotaphs. That night, in a ceremony that seemed inspired by the Druids, a great flame was lit in Compiègne Forest, where the Germans signed the cease-fire, using the same bowl that was built to house the Olympic flame the previous winter at Grenoble. De Gaulle celebrated "the flame of national pride," the same flame which he said must inspire France's eternal soul in the future.

The continuous exaltation of past battles makes something sacred out of war. It makes one wonder whether war has not gratified some of the indispensable needs of French society by arousing national feeling, reinforcing national cohesion, stimulating the social body, pushing the economy to new records, and giving each Frenchman a chance to show his loyalty and channel his aggressiveness. The generation of young Frenchmen who have now come of age are the first in this century with no war to fight, and they will not buy this cant. During the May-June riots, it was alleged that some students had spat on the grave of the unknown soldier. "They were not spitting on this anonymous victim of war," wrote Jean-Jacques Servan-Schreiber, "but on the monstrous stupidity of the system of national sovereignty, which secretes war. They were rejecting the curbing of human will before historical fatality, the respect of death in the name of life. This was the first real homage made to the unknown soldier." Such was not the opinion of several deputies who expressed their shock at the "profanation" and asked for a full investigation.

It is a healthy sign that the latter-day chauvinism is becoming suspect. It is a healthy sign that a Frenchman, the ethnologist Claude Lévi-Strauss, has discredited the theory that the primitive mind is inferior, which was such comforting proof of the superiority of French culture. Also, in contrast to the tendency to turn French history into an epic, he sees all history as myth; that is, every generation reinterprets the past to comply with the needs of the present, as Michelet's praise of the French Revolution was an oblique attack on the Bourbon Restoration. What is needed today for France is a history of history, a systematic analysis of the way historians have been influenced by the political context and intellectual assumptions of their own time. The epic past is the French placenta, hospitable and nourishing, but also a hermetic breeder of misconceptions, and it needs to be discarded with other relics like the *monuments aux morts,* Third Republic rhetoric, and the French civilizing mission.

Perhaps France's contemporary mission is to be a laboratory for the problems that plague modern society. Marx noted in the nineteenth century that events in France were rich in instruction for the rest of the world. France in ferment may provide new approaches to social organization, just as the Commune enlightened the theoreticians of proletarian revolution. For eleven years France had a chief of state who tried to reconcile the epic past with France's reduced role as a world power, and who was able, by the sheer force of his character, to keep the notion of grandeur alive. Finally, it was not the foreign policies to which he devoted so much of his reign that brought him down, but the sort of banal domestic problems which he contemptuously called housekeeping. The general responded to the revolutionary crisis in May, 1968, with a novel plan for a third course between Communism and capitalism, between the stifling bureaucratic Socialism of the Eastern bloc and the numbing and neurotic power of American society. But a year later, asking his people for a vote of confidence like an aging husband compelled to seek daily reassurances of love from his young wife, he was removed from office before he could test what he presented as a new form of social organization. The French will always surprise you, the general was fond of saying, and in April, 1969, they surprised him. They showed they were able to reject a political system which relied heavily on personal demagoguery and the appeal of shopworn myths to keep in power a man who represented himself as the latest incarnation of the French savior. De Gaulle was a transitional figure whose real merit lay in restoring to the French a feeling of self-respect; he did not save the patient, but he cauterized the wounds. The patient, having regained his health, dispensed with the services of his doctor in a burst of sane and hearty ingratitude. Rejection of de Gaulle meant, among other things, rejection of the epic past and showed that France may at long last have recovered from the traumas inflicted by its history.

3

❯❯❯❯❯❯❯❯❯❯❯❯❯❯❯❯❯❯❯❯❯❯❯❯❯❯❯❯❯❯❯❯❯❯❯❯❯❮❮❮❮❮❮❮❮❮❮❮❮❮❮❮❮❮❮❮❮❮❮❮❮❮❮❮❮❮❮❮❮❮❮

Traumas

THE epic past is an antidote for the traumas that humiliate and divide the nation. These are to France what a sense of sin is to the individual: the brooding reminders of a flawed nature. The Revolution of 1789 inspired Europe, but failed in France. A glorious military tradition guaranteed a period of French supremacy, but since 1870 France has experienced repeated military defeat. Colonialism was a condition of power, but France never had an authentic colonial vocation. A colonial crisis ended the Fourth Republic and brought General de Gaulle to power, after which the general was forced to liquidate what was left of the French empire.

Revolution

There has never been a French Revolution. There has never been a forcible overthrow of an existing French political system in which the new regime succeeded in maintaining itself or the values for which it fought. Revolutions were always confiscated, their principles denied or diluted. They were always the agents through which an authoritarian, centralizing regime seized power. Despite its overthrow of the monarchy, the Revolution of 1789 is closer to the Fronde and the Wars of Religion than to the Bolshevik Revolution of 1917. It was a French civil war rather than an authentic revolution. After the lyric illusion came the cynicism of strong men. Napoleon said after the 18 Brumaire coup in 1799 and his nomination as consul: "Well, now the Revolution is over, and without too much trouble, I may well boast of that. And do you know why? Because it did not displace any interests, while awakening many." Because the first revolution was botched, there had to be others; the same principles were fought for by different generations, as if a revolutionary chromosome had been transmitted. The revolutions of 1830 and 1848 were, if not parodies, at least imitations of 1789, setting a pattern in which governments were often overthrown but social change was slow. There has been more continuity despite revolution than change through revolution. Nearly two hundred years after 1789, in the student-worker uprising of the spring of 1968, the rioters were asking for the same broad mandate as the men of 1789: some form of participation in the control of the levers of society.

The regimes that took over reinforced the traditional aims of the ones that had been overthrown, as though revolutions were merely the normal process of political change. What they did accomplish was to cleave the nation, making France a country in a permanently latent state of civil war. The last civil war was World War II, in which two military men embodying different concepts of the nation fought within the framework of the Allied struggle against the Axis. The fight against the Germans lasted six weeks; the fight between Frenchmen lasted four years. The result of civil war is that most unpleasant of French words, *épuration* (purge). In the Jacobin tradition, traitors must be punished, a healthy bleeding must be administered the nation. From the Jacobins wiping out the Gironde and being themselves wiped out by the Thermidorians, to the thousands of executed Communards, to the Resistance *épuration* of collaborators, the process is invariably the same.

In France, wars are greater agents of social change than revolutions. Mandatory public education was the result of the defeat of 1870. The option of the Third Republic to seek an empire in

North Africa and Indochina was another result of the Franco-Prussian War, a compensation for wounded national pride and the loss of two provinces. It was thanks to World War I that France got the income tax, which was voted in 1917 to defray war costs, and that women were emancipated from the legal status of minors decreed by the Napoleonic Code. With the men on the front, they had assumed new responsibilities. French social legislation, based on welfare payments to large families, is equally the result of wars which drew attention to the danger of underpopulation. After World War II, the triumphant return of General de Gaulle gave France's first postwar government the authority to nationalize large sectors of the economy and to grant women the vote. The biggest change in higher education since Napoleon, came on the heels of the Liberation when de Gaulle decided to open a free university for high civil service jobs, the École Nationale d'Administration. The Liberation also transformed the French press, for Paris newspapers which had continued to publish under the Occupation were turned over to new teams created under the Resistance. Thanks to this measure, France's first genuinely independent newspaper, *Le Monde,* was founded.

De Gaulle himself recognized that in France wars are the real revolutions. In November, 1968, on the fiftieth anniversary of the 1918 armistice, he said that World War I was "a colossal revolution," after which "our society was no longer the same, not only in its borders but in its doctrine, in its family, and in its economic wealth." Wars alter the class structure. World War I laid to rest the officer caste and its mystique of a knightly death, for officers died in such numbers that they had to be replaced by noncoms (34,500 officers were killed, including 4,000 Saint-Cyriens). World War II served to discredit the *patronat* (employers), many of whom had collaborated with the Germans. In 1944 de Gaulle met a delegation of *patrons* and said acidly, "I did not see any of you gentlemen in London."

1789

The Declaration of the Rights of Man was voted in August, 1789, by the Estates General, which had turned itself into an assembly, as the preamble to the first written French constitution. Many of its seventeen articles were subsequently violated by the practice of revolution. Article 1 said that men are born and remain free and equal before the law, but this was violated by property qualifications for voters. Article 3 said that the principle of all sovereignty resides essentially in the nation, and this too was violated by the concept of "passive citizens" who could not vote, and by the Jacobin dictatorship. Article 7 said that no one may be accused, arrested, or detained, except in cases determined by the law, but soon suspects were arrested and detained without due process. Article 10 said that no one may be interfered with on account of his opinions, not even on the subject of religion, but soon the clergy was interfered with, press censorship was laid down, and the mildest form of opposition was punished as treason. Article 17 said that property rights are sacred, and this was violated by the appropriation of property belonging to the church, to émigré nobles, and in 1794, to those suspected of treason.

In five years the Revolution went through three constitutions. During that time France was never governed constitutionally, but by coups which gave power to ever more marginal groups. The constitutions were abstract and philosophical, while governments had to fall back on expediency and violence. The Rousseau-inspired Jacobin text of 1793 gave power to the people, it abolished voter qualifications in favor of direct universal suffrage, and it recognized a general will which cannot be transmitted to elected representatives. It was a visionary document dashed off in six days by Hérault de Sechelles after the victory of the radical Montagne over the moderate Gironde in the Convention, but it was, once drafted, immediately set aside. The threat of invasion and internal dissension made it impossible to enact, and in its place France was governed at first by committees and then by the personal dictatorship of Robespierre. When the Thermidorians overthrew Robespierre they needed a new constitution to legalize the principles of their conservative reaction, and drafted the constitution of 1795, antithetical to the Jacobin constitution of 1793. There was a return to property qualifications for voters. As the president of the Convention, Boissy d'Anglas, put it: "We must be governed by the best men and the best men are the most educated men and those most interested in enforcing law," that is, property owners. Not even the motto of the Republic could be enforced, for it mixed a right, equality, with an ideal, freedom, and a feeling, fraternity.

Every French regime has treated its constitution as a dispensable scrap of paper. Several of General de Gaulle's referendums (including the one that prompted his resignation) were declared unconstitutional by the French administrative Supreme Court, the Conseil d'État, but the general overruled the decisions. The belief that constitutions are ideal documents is also dangerous because it overlooks that they are, in fact, drafted to meet the needs of a specific class at a specific historical moment.

Electoral qualifications are in this sense particularly striking. To elect the 749 Conventionnels in 1792, a voter had to be the resident of a commune for at least a year (which was tantamount to a property qualification), he had to swear a loyalty oath "to maintain liberty and equality and to die defending it," and servants were prohibited from voting on the grounds that they were too closely associated with the old order. The Conventionnels were elected by one-tenth of 7,000,000 eligible voters in a France of 25,000,000 inhabitants, the rest having abstained through protest or fear. All those elected came from the bourgeoisie, except one gunsmith and one wool carder. The Revolution's belief that property is necessary for a just appreciation of the general interest, flowered after the Bourbon Restoration of 1815, when the franchise was limited to between 1 and 3 percent of the population.

The 1789 Revolution exported universal suffrage to the rest of Europe, but France itself did not enjoy universal suffrage until 1848, and then used it to vote in another Gallic Caesar, Napoleon III. Gracchus Babeuf, who died on the guillotine because he was the Revolution's only genuine egalitarian, saw its purpose as *"ôte-toi de là que je m'y mette."* (Get out of there so I can take your place.)

The regime that had made property sacred infracted its own principles with the nationalization of émigré property in 1792. The Constituent Assembly started up what de Tocqueville called the machine to chop up land. Émigré property was sold in small lots. The Republic was one and indivisible, but property was increasingly divisible. This was the extent of the Revolution's agrarian reform. The rural code of September, 1791, even maintained the *ancien régime* common pasture rights to placate non-property-owning peasants.

The Revolution was to have been for all mankind, and France was to become the *patrie* of all persecuted lovers of freedom. Article 120 of the 1793 constitution said: "The French people grant asylum to foreigners banished from their country in the cause of freedom." Which is how Tom Paine wound up in a French jail. Paine, who was one of three foreigners invited to sit in the Convention, along with the Cleves-born Anacharsis Clootz, Orator of the Human Race, and another German named Dentzel, voted against the death of Louis XVI, who had come to the assistance of the United States during the War of Independence. The Convention decided that "no foreigner could be admitted to represent the French people." Paine and the two others, who had symbolized the universality of the Rights of Man, were barred from attending. A few days later Paine, who had been denounced by Robespierre and Marat, was arrested. A petition in his favor signed by eighteen American notables residing in Paris had no effect. It took the personal intervention of Ambassador James Monroe to obtain his release.

The vocation of giving lessons to the rest of the world is an ungrateful one. Along with a universality that soured into chauvinism, the Revolution enacted antislavery measures that did not apply to France's own Caribbean colonies. Slavery had flourished since the seventeenth century in France, and there was no incompatibility between the ideas of the Enlightenment and the business of slaves. Montesquieu said that "although slavery is against the laws of nature, in some countries it is founded on natural reasons," those reasons being sound economic ones, for "without slavery, sugar would be too expensive." Accordingly, Montesquieu bought shares in the Compagnie des Indes, which then held the slave-trade monopoly, and said of the slaves that "their noses are so flat it is almost impossible to feel sorry for them."

The robe nobility who read Voltaire and Rousseau financed slave ships out of Nantes and Bordeaux, explaining that this was progress, for the slaves "are happier in the Caribbean than they would be in Africa," while if they were freed "they would go back to their old ways of ancestral indolence." The Encyclopédie itself accepted slavery as a necessary evil in its article entitled "Colonies." A Société des Amis des Noirs was founded to abolish slavery, but on March 8, 1790, none of its members sitting in the Constituent Assembly protested the decree that nothing should be done to interfere with colonial trade. The colonial lobby, headed by the Lameth brothers, one of whom was a deputy, boasted that they had maintained slavery in France's Caribbean colonies. It was only after the success of Toussaint l'Ouverture's uprising in Santo Domingo and a revolt in Martinique that the Convention proclaimed the abolition of slavery on February 4, 1794. Article 15 of the new Declaration of Rights in the 1795 Thermidorian constitution said: "Each man may rent his time and his services, but no man can sell himself or be sold; his person is not an alienable property." This turned out to be impractical. The unstated axiom of the Revolution was that it is difficult to abolish what is profitable, and slavery was profitable.

War with England superseded revolutionary principle, and in 1802 Napoleon restored slavery. His spokesman in the Tribunate took up the old arguments that slavery was part of an enlightened philosophy. "This is but a necessary evil," he said, "and if as magistrates we were to shed tears over the slave trade, we would be like a general, who on the eve of a battle, weeps for those who are going to be killed." England, meanwhile, abolished its slave trade in 1807. Napoleon, although the heir of the Revolution, had no egalitarian pretensions. Not only did he prohibit the entry into France of blacks, mulattoes, and other people of color, but he ordered officials in France and the colonies to refuse to celebrate mixed marriages. Slavery was not definitely abolished until the revolution of 1848, which paid so many of the overdue bills of 1789.

The classic illustration of the way bourgeois liberalism was turned into the defense of class interests is provided by the Le Chapelier law of June 14, 1791, which even the most radical mem bers of the Assembly approved. The guilds were suppressed as infamous holdovers of the *ancien régime* that hindered the freedom of work, since each guild kept its membership low and jealously guarded its profession as if it were an exclusive privilege. But this unfettering of the right to work was coupled with a prohibition to associate. Despite their abuses, the guilds had been the workers' only protection. The Le Chapelier law, hurriedly voted after a carpenters' strike, prohibited strikes and associations between citizens exercising the same profession. Collective bargaining and workers' petitions were also forbidden.

Work contracts would be concluded between two free and independent persons, the worker and the employer. This may have been valid in an artisanal age, when small family firms hired one or two assistants, but at the dawn of the industrial age, when the medieval personal link between worker and employer was already giving way to the soot of factories and the exploitation of cheap labor, it was a mandate to put down the working class. What was presented as equality between the employer and the worker became the free fox in the free hen house. Workers were forbidden, in the language of the law, from "debating on their so-called common interests." In the name of individual freedom, they were prohibited from discussing with each other salaries and working conditions. France has still not caught up with the backwardness of its labor legislation. The right to conduct union activities on the job was granted, not in 1789, but in the fall of 1968. The Le Chapelier law gave a veneer of legality to selfish antiproletarian measures. Robespierre froze wages. Hébert was dismissed from the Commune because he was too friendly with the working class.

Thus did the pact between employers and the regime in power begin and continue. When the silk workers of Lyons revolted in 1831, 20,000 of Louis-Philippe's soldiers marched in to put down the strikers. Under the Second Empire, strikes at the huge iron foundry of Le Creusot again brought in the troops. Under the Third Republic, the great pro-labor republican leader Georges Clemenceau became a strikebreaker. In 1908 he ordered the dragoons to break up barricades erected in a Paris suburb by construction workers, and three demonstrators were killed. In 1948, Minister of the Interior Jules Moch called out the tanks to put down a miners' strike. In 1968, riot troops fought the Renault workers at Flins and one worker was killed. Whatever the regime in power calls itself, Empire or Republic, it fears strikers as the harbingers of national catastrophe. It was only in 1884 that the Third Republic Minister of the Interior Waldeck-Rousseau pushed through a law making unions legal. But just as France has never been able to achieve orderly political succession, it has never been able to institutionalize labor-management relations, so that in both areas crisis becomes the norm.

As the era of freedom led to the oppression of the working class, the era of justice led to the extraordinary tribunal. Instead of the separation of powers which inspired the American Revolution, legislative and judiciary powers were confused when the Convention tried the king in 1793, naming the judges and constituting itself as the jury. After that came the committees of surveillance and the absence of due process. Habeas corpus did not have to be suspended for it never existed and still does not. Certain categories of persons were declared automatic outlaws. The Jacobins justified this return to the arbitrary arrests and sealed letters of the *ancien régime* as measures of exception to save France from its enemies without and within. The immunity of deputies was suspended to facilitate the purge of one faction by the other. The Committee of Public Safety, originally one of the Convention's 21 committees, invested with limited police powers, became the country's executive. Robespierre gave France the model for laws of exception adopted by subsequent regimes. The tradition of suspending justice in emergencies is embodied in the celebrated Article 16 of the Gaullist constitution, which gives the president the right to rule by decree. Indictments under the Terror became so vague that no one was safe. The laws of Prairial (June 10, 1794) suppressed the accused's right of defense and accepted "moral evidence," which could be anything from a concierge's tittle-tattle to the spite of a disappointed mistress.

That was a time when a man felt a permanent chill in the back of his neck. Military tribunals were set up in the provinces, and 178 of these primitive courts put to death an estimated 17,000 persons, 2,625 of them in Paris. The high accuser of the Paris tribunal, Fouquier-Tinville, a man who clearly enjoyed his work, chose jurors for their compliance, marking next to the name of each the degree of fanaticism that he could count on—*F* meant *faible* (weak). He would tell the process servers "You're behind, I need two hundred or two hundred and fifty every ten days." When he was put on trial, he used the same argument as the Nazi war criminals at Nuremberg: "All I did was obey orders." With the Revolution came the idea that bureaucracy absolves. An agent of the state can always invoke the protection of the administrative umbrella.

Again, after the 73-day reign of the Paris Commune in 1871, the capital was isolated and the Communards were defeated. Seventeen thousand Communards were killed in the repression. Exactly 36,309 prisoners, captured mainly during May, were tried before military courts whose task was not to judge but to punish. It was the record *épuration* of French history. Because there was not enough room in Paris prisons, the Communards were expedited to disease-ridden prison ships. The 26 martial courts did not finish their work until 1873.

During World War II, both Pétain and de Gaulle had recourse to special justice. Vichy in 1940 ordered the internment of "dangerous individuals." With a stroke of the pen, it deprived 421 native-born Frenchmen and 15,154 naturalized Frenchmen of their nationality. General de Gaulle was sentenced to death in absentia on August 2, 1940, by a jury of seven generals. After the Allied landing in North Africa, de Gaulle created a high court in October, 1943, to try collaborators. The high court reopened in Paris in November, 1944, following criticism in the National Assembly that nothing was being done to punish traitors. Extraordinary figures deserved extraordinary justice.

The tradition of special jail conditions for political prisoners was recalled by the lawyers of Vichy leaders. Had not André Chenier been allowed to compose admirable verses while in prison? Had not Charlotte Corday sat for her portrait? The high court judged important collaborators until 1949, although its composition was changed three or four times. In its original form, the jurors were picked from the National Assembly, just as the jurors of revolutionary tribunals were picked from the Convention. As the Communist leader Jacques Duclos said: "We are in the presence of crimes which cannot be judged unless one's heart is full of hatred."

The best known of those sentenced to death by the high court was Pierre Laval, who declined to comply with the custom of a noble death. He had fled to Spain and was extradited in May, 1945. On the day of his execution, his lawyer went to fetch him at 8:30 A.M. in Paris' Fresnes prison. The attorney general, Mornet, came into his cell and said: "Monsieur Laval, have courage."

Laval was lying face down on his cot. His left arm fell from under the covers and an empty glass ampul dropped from his hand. Mornet sniffed it and called for a stomach pump. Laval had embroidered sheets and white wool blankets on his bed, milk, gingerbread, two cartons of Chesterfields, a pound of sugar and a hot plate in his cell. A specialist, Professor Leuret, arrived and pumped his stomach. When he pricked Laval's left sole with a straight pin, his big toe twitched.

"We've got him," said Professor Leuret.

Coming to, Laval muttered, "glass, glass."

Someone brought him a glass of water. He pushed it away and blurted: "Not French bullets." He asked for a pistol to shoot himself.

One of his lawyers said: "This is intolerable, tie him to a stretcher and take him out and shoot him." The firing squad was summoned to Fresnes.

Laval dressed with deliberate slowness and had finished by 11:20. "Come on, come on, hurry up," a prison official kept repeating. A car drove him to the ditches where executions take place.

Laval emerged from the car, composed, smoking, and asked, "Where are the gentlemen of the high court?"

Some of the judges came up and he told them: "This is a dreary piece of work you have been asked to do, but I don't hold it against you." He asked for permission not to be tied to the stake, but it was refused. As the orders were given to the firing squad, he tried to shout *"Vive la France"* but could not get the words out. A trembling hand administered the unnecessary *coup de grâce*.

Such events did not help resolve the internal French struggle. This is why General de Gaulle encouraged Marshal Pétain to seek asylum in Switzerland, to avoid having to put him on trial. But the old marshal returned to be tried by the high court in October, 1944. The judges deliberated seven hours and pronounced the death sentence, with the stipulation that it should not be carried out against the eighty-nine-year-old victor of Verdun. This was the sentence it had been charged to render by the de Gaulle government, another example of a court working closely with the regime in a political trial. The trial revealed more about the state of France than about the motives of Marshal Pétain, who had lapsed into silence. It showed to what extent the country had been contaminated by the Occupation. Mornet, the attorney general, had served as vice-president of the Commission of De-naturalization which had revoked the French passports of more than 7,000 Jews. The most spectacular turnabout was that of the magistrates, impersonal agents of injustice, who one year sent Resistance fighters and the next year collaborators to the gallows. The witnesses who came to the stand were less concerned with helping the maréchal than with justifying their own behavior. They were the generals who had always obeyed orders, the econo-mists whose job it was to maintain the French franc, the adminis-trators who had to keep the trains moving and the schools open—this was not treason, they argued, it was maintenance.

It was a time that required more, not less, than justice. A Solomon-like subtlety was needed to decide who was guilty—the Resistance fighter who had killed a German sentry and provoked the execution of ten innocent hostages or the Vichy minister who was able to save several hundred Frenchmen from being sent to German labor camps. But the old Jacobin reflex divided the na-tion into condemning and condemned. According to official French government sources, the number of summary executions reported to the *gendarmerie* at the moment of the Liberation was 14,468. If one assumes that as many French-style lynchings and vendettas went unreported, the total comes close to 30,000.

Committees of *épuration* formed all over France and took it upon themselves to chastise traitors. In Paris, the committee of actors remembered that the playwright and wit Sacha Guitry had once been invited to dinner with Goering. He was arrested in his pajamas on August 23, 1944. One of the men said upon seeing him, "There's the bastard."

"Have we been introduced?" Guitry replied.

He was kept in jail sixty days. One of his cellmates was a man who kept asking why he had been jailed. "Because the concierge of your building denounced you," the man was told.

"But I am the concierge of my building," he said.

A commission of inquiry told Guitry: "We are going to have to indict you."

"But what for?"

"That's what we are asking ourselves, probably commerce with the enemy."

"What commerce would I have with the Germans?"

"None, we agree. Plotting against the safety of the state is no more credible. That leaves intelligence with the enemy."

"I don't think I ever lacked intelligence, even with the enemy."

"All right! Intelligence with the enemy. In any case, you know why you are here."

"Yes, I know, because of forty years of theatrical success."

"No, because you had dinner with Goering."

"Yes, I had dinner with Goering. I also had lunch with the king of England, and tomorrow I may have lunch with Roosevelt. What I can promise you is that I will never have lunch with a judge."

Guitry was finally released, furious that while searching his wallet a sealed love letter had been removed and passed around by his jailers. But others did not fare so well. Civic chambers pronounced roughly 100,000 decrees of national indignity, in itself a curious notion that "every Frenchman who, even without breaking an existing law, makes himself guilty of a characteristic antinational activity, is considered a fallen citizen." There were committees for the confiscation of illicit profits, and a supreme Court of Liberation, tailor-made for a particular form of vengeance, from which there was no appeal.

Jacques Charpentier, president of the Paris Bar Association, said of these special courts that "in general, their achievements were baneful, and their misdeeds are numberless. Their incapacity to judge fairly is obvious from the disparity of sentences from place to place and time to time. The same offense would get you twenty years of forced labor in Nîmes and two years of prison in Angers. One journalist would be sentenced to twenty years, while one of his colleagues, whose articles were just as bad, would be sentenced only to national indignity." Special justice necessarily confers an inordinate role to executive clemency. Two-thirds of the sentences pronounced by the special courts were commuted or pardoned by de Gaulle. Judge Patin, in charge of pardons at the Ministry of Justice, would present the verdicts for de Gaulle's clemency on a weekly basis.

Under the Fourth Republic there were military tribunals for the expeditious judgment of Algerian rebels. In April, 1961, a

High Military Tribunal was created specifically to judge the four generals and other leaders of the anti-Gaullist putsch in Algiers. Its members were named by decree, the accused were arraigned by decree, and the politically inspired verdicts could not be appealed. At the end of 1962, France's highest administrative court, the Conseil d'État, voided the ordinance that had created this high court on the grounds that its procedure did not provide the necessary guarantees for defendants. Despite the Conseil d'État decision, however, the high court was kept temporarily active.

A separate Court for the Safety of the State was also set up to deal with espionage, Breton separatists, and other antistate activities. This court, too, includes a mixture of magistrates and generals, and has never been known to depart from strict obedience to the government. In 1968 it sat to judge 14 workers and students charged with throwing Molotov cocktails at police stations and university buildings in Bordeaux, thereby raising to the level of a plot against the state what just as easily might have been written off as the understandable agitation of French youth. The tendency to create special courts for special crimes and to distinguish between normal and exceptional justice thus remains an essential French concept.

Not only were the leaders of the 1789 Revolution incapable of enforcing the goals of a new society—justice, equality, agrarian reform, and universal suffrage—but in many other respects they carried on the program of the *ancien régime*. They suppressed local particularisms, which the monarchy had vainly tried to do, and standardized weights, measures, laws, and local jurisdictions. They broke up the provinces which were based on natural divisions and created 83 departments based on administrative divisions. They placed in the hands of the state what had been the responsibility of other groups. The registry office for births, marriages, and deaths passed from church to state. Marriage became a contract that could be broken through divorce. They followed the tradition of Colbert with economic planning. Requisitioning, price-freezing, and control of profits made a shambles of free enterprise. The administrative personnel of the *ancien régime* was largely maintained, except for suppressed offices like the salt tax. There was also continuity in the army—60 percent of Napoleon's officers had served in the *ancien régime*.

The option for a strongly centralized rather than a federal state was the outcome of the struggle between two factions in the Convention, the federalist Gironde and the Paris-dominated Montagne, so-called because it sat on the high benches. The Gironde states' righters were the natural heirs of the feudal nobility which had sought to limit the authority of the king, just as the Montagne descended from Richelieu, who wanted France to be one and indivisible. This was in fact the first article of the Montagne-inspired constitution of 1793: The Republic is one and indivisible, an announcement which makes no sense except in terms of what was perhaps the essential conflict in the shaping of modern France, for the victory of the Montagne meant that all government decisions would thenceforth be made in Paris. Absolute monarchs formulated a theory of the centralized state, the Montagne dispensed with the monarch but kept the theory, and Napoleon created the institutions to implement the theory. No regime has ever dared backtrack until the Fifth Republic's timid and unsuccessful experiment in regionalism. The 180 Girondins were provincials, hostile to Paris, named after the southwest Gironde department. The Montagne accused them of wanting to break up France into little republics, American-style. The Gironde accused Danton of misappropriating secret funds, and Robespierre of encouraging a personality cult, but it gradually lost ground: "Yes, we are moderates . . . our moderation saved the Republic from civil war."

Admission of moderation was suicide. In June, 1793, troops loyal to the Paris Commune and the Montagne circled the Convention building, and under this threat the Convention decreed the arrest of 29 Girondin deputies and barred the rest. The Gironde perished, and with it the hope of authentic regional government in France. The arrests sparked revolts in 60 out of 83 French departments, which were swiftly suppressed. With the Girondins gone, the Montagne imposed a provisional dictatorship in the name of democracy which ended with a conservative reaction. Jacobin government was based, like divine right monarchy, on the theory that the people want the good but do not always know where it lies, and must be led. Control of public opinion, censorship, and *épuration* were instruments of guidance.

There was equally a continuity of style from the *ancien régime* to Jacobin dictatorship. The Committee of Public Safety commissioned Republican dramas as Louis XIV had commissioned *divertissements*. Art was once again at the service of the state. A flow of revolutionary masterpieces was predicted, but it was staunched with the execution of the finest poet of the time, André Chénier. The Committee of Public Safety wanted an official historiographer just as kings had, and called on "citizens who cultivate letters ... to give to history the firm and continuous character which is proper for the annals of a great people." The style of revolutionary art, like the style of the French classical century, was inspired by the models of antiquity.

Robespierre adapted the religious base of the *ancien régime* by founding the cult of the Supreme Being. He was a disciple of Rousseau's neo-Christianity, and firmly believed that religion was good for the people. In a famous speech he called atheism aristocratic, and suggested that religious irreverence was a plot "of our enemies who want to make us seem odious to other peoples." He pursued revolutionary atheists, forcing Hébert to retract irreverent statements, and personally drafting the act of accusation against Chaumette, whom he charged with "trying to wipe out all idea of divinity." On November 10, 1793, the cult of the Supreme Being was celebrated in Notre Dame cathedral. In May of the following year, Robespierre published a decree stating that "the French people recognizes the existence of the Supreme Being and the immortality of the soul." The new catechism was an attempt to reconcile God and the *patrie*. It had its own sacraments: "What is baptism? It is the regeneration of the French, begun July 14, 1789, and supported by the entire nation." "What is communion? It is the association proposed to all reasonable people for the French Republic." With the demise of Robespierre, the new religion was soon forgotten, and France returned to Catholicism under Napoleon, who also recognized the utility of a state religion.

The Revolution of 1789, then, was a displacement of strong central authority from a divine-right monarch to a small group of men who claimed to hold power in the name of the people and continued to pursue many of the traditional goals of the monarchy. A new society had been announced, but this too was mainly a displacement of one privileged group, the aristocracy and the clergy, by another, the bourgeoisie. Property changed hands, and the Third Estate was freed from paying tribute to the two others.

The venality of offices ended, or rather the method of control over offices changed from outright purchase to other forms of payment. The most profound change of the Revolution, however, was the birth of a new sensibility, perceptively described by Georges Sand: "During the Terror, the men who spilled the most blood were those who had the strongest desire to lead their fellowmen to the dreamed-of golden age, and who had the greatest sympathy for human misery . . . the greater their thirst for universal happiness, the more inexorable they became." Just as the innocent return to nature of the Romantic movement found an unexpected issue in the works of the marquis de Sade, who considered himself not a pornographer but an evangelist of freedom, the pathology of the Terror was that men could kill in the name of pity, clemency, and the Romantic imagination.

Marat said that "no one hates bloodletting more than myself." The Revolution invented the sensitive killer. The Terror had to be systematic in order to be limited, said Robespierre. Crime became bureaucratic, a technique perfected in the concentration camps of World War II. The method of execution had to be swift and impersonal, and the guillotine replaced the ritualistic executions of the *ancien régime*. The optimism of the Enlightenment had become warped, too many men had to be killed to make mankind happy. Loyalty became more important than merit, as it remains today in many government cabinets. Robespierre kept a list of "patriots having more or less talent."

The Revolution perfected a human type which sees change as apocalyptic, politics in terms of plot and counterplot, and administration in terms of repression. But the Jacobins had the qualities of their defects; they were fanatic, but they were ardent; they were sectarian, but they were heroic; they were dogmatic, but they were firm; they were uncharitable, but they were not mediocre; they were sanguinary, but they were great leaders of the masses (there were only 80,000 Jacobin militants in a nation of 25,000,000). What they left in terms of the French experience was less the defense of individual freedom than the cult of service to the state, and the individual's subjection to public safety.

Finally, when we talk of the French Revolution's influence abroad, we do not mean the example of democracy, but the theory, techniques, and sensibility of revolutionaries. In this sense their action was profound, except in their own country. For in France there is always a Thermidor. Middle France, or the plain, or the Marais, or whatever it may be called at the time, reacts, in 1968 as in 1794. The Thermidor coup which overthrew Robespierre was a reaction against virtue and incorruptibility as well as against repression. It was a reaction in the name of human foibles. The experiment had lasted almost five years to the day since the Bastille had been stormed. There was a return to moderation and a program that was pragmatic rather than visionary. Troops were called out against rioting workers. Napoleon made his reputation against other Frenchmen, not foreign invaders. Finally, after four years of the Directoire and continuing instability, Napoleon staged a successful coup and kept Thermidor's promise of a stable regime. Like General de Gaulle who, in 1958, also came to power with a coup, he had a talent for creating misunderstandings about his intentions.

Carbon Copy Revolutions

The dominant feature of France's regimes from the restoration of Louis XVIII in 1815 to the abdication of Louis-Philippe in 1848 was the narrow collaboration of the king with a class. During that 32-year period, the last three kings of France governed. The first, Louis XVIII, the brother of Louis XVI, who had fought with the duke of Brunswick against the nation in arms in 1792, seemed nostalgic for the days when the church operated the schools. A law was passed making profanation of the consecrated host a crime punishable by death, a law which only had meaning retroactively, in terms of the profanations of the Revolution. Press censorship included the offense of outrage to religion and criticism of the divine right of kings. Louis XVIII also returned to the traditional foreign policy goals of the monarchy, sending an expeditionary force to Spain in 1823 to restore the Spanish Bourbons. It was as though 1789 had not taken place. Seventy thousand émigrés were back, and employed their keen medieval minds in obtaining compensation for their property losses. Stendhal's *Armance* is a study of their efforts. The Restoration developed into a confrontation between post-1789 France and the noble relics who were back in power.

Louis XVIII died in bed in 1824 and was succeeded by Charles X, who revived the coronation ceremony at Rheims and placed the landed gentry in positions of power. A 30,000,000-franc trust fund at 3 percent interest was created to pay off the émigrés. For them it was not enough and for the rest of the country it was far too much. Charles X, who had the political acumen of a moose, frittered away the foundations of the restored monarchy by becoming increasingly authoritarian and dependent on cabinets of feudal throwbacks like his good friend Jules de Polignac, who remained in power after legislative elections in 1830 had given a majority to opposition parties. On July 25 the four repressive ordinances were published, and on July 26, Charles X went hunting as Louis XVI had done on July 14, 1789.

It began with a journalist's revolution. Adolphe Thiers, one of the first French examples of a crusading editor, called on the nation to resist in *Le National*. In what was either a typical lower-the-shutters defensive reaction or a calculated move to push the crowds into the streets, manufacturers and shops closed on July 26. Suddenly unemployed, with the price of bread soaring, the Paris proletariat had good reasons for discontent, and on July 28 the barricades went up. In three days, known as the *trois glorieuses,* the insurgents took control of the capital, having lost 1,800 of their own against 200 army casualties. The bourgeoisie was waiting in the wings to confiscate the Revolution. The dissolved deputies formed a provisional government and offered the throne to the head of the Orléans branch of the Bourbon dynasty, pear-shaped Louis-Philippe, who was on call not far from Paris. Thiers described him as "a prince devoted to the cause of the Revolution." It was less a revolution than an abdication under pressure. Charles X left for exile, and the aristocracy never again regained political influence in France. The gentry went sulking back to their lands, abstaining from public life in what became known as the internal emigration.

France was now ready for the rule of bourgeois notables that had been prepared by the measures of 1789, under a king who was willing to assume the duties of chairman of the board. The aristocracy of office, which had existed since the *ancien régime,* was now made secure with more sophisticated methods. This was the golden age of bourgeois power; it began and ended on the barricades. A class succeeded in controlling national life because it held political office through restricted suffrage and wealth, passed laws which enforced and guaranteed its power, subsidized the enterprises of its members, and formulated an ideology which justified its dominance. A powerful class-conscious bourgeoisie took a century's head start on the proletariat, and keeps that head start today. Laws were, as Balzac said, spiders' webs through which the big flies pass while the little flies get stuck.

The principal instrument of power was the vote, which continued to be, in the tradition of 1789, not a right but a reward for owning property. A voter had to pay at least 200 francs a year in direct taxes. In 1846 the total French electorate was estimated at 241,000, or 2.8 percent of the total male population over twenty-one. The bourgeoisie now owned land, and 90 percent of the electorate obtained their franchise from property. Under the July Monarchy, property qualifications became a philosophy; the further one went down the social ladder, it was believed, the more one strayed from the national interest. This was the meaning of Premier François Guizot's famous phrase, "enrich yourselves." It was not an invitation to fill one's pockets, but an appeal to broaden the electorate.

The bourgeoisie found the measures taken by the Revolution of 1789 highly suitable instruments of control. With property qualifications they controlled the government and put in banker-premiers like Jacques Lafitte and Casimier Périer; with the Le Chapelier law they prevented the passage of labor legislation. Devices were found to cheat the workers, such as fines for bad workmanship, and salary deductions for the maintenance of machinery. Such measures were not based on conscious cruelty, but on a conception of freedom as "the power we have to dispose of our faculties," which included the freedom to exploit other classes. Freedom also remained the right of the individual worker to reach agreement with the individual employer, and was made synonymous with order. "The state does not limit freedom," said Guizot, "but guarantees it by maintaining order and discipline and preventing insurbordination."

A further reason for repressing the worker was the equation of indigence with delinquency. The workers were underpaid and then blamed for not saving money. The physical and social diseases of the working class were attributed to their vices and weaknesses. On the one hand the July Monarchy bourgeoisie created an ideology which made the poor necessary for a balanced society. (See the Pink Library books for children by the comtesse de Ségur, written during this period, which repeatedly include that set piece, "the visit to the poor.") On the other hand, the poor were blamed for their poverty. Poverty was necessary, but immoral; pauperism was defined as living beyond one's means. The bourgeoisie was able to reconcile the proletariat's misery with its own belief in progress. If the worker was poor, it was his own fault, the result of his debased nature. Working conditions were better than ever, salaries were higher than they had been in the seventeenth century.

The bourgeois ideology's triumph was child labor legislation. In a nation which congratulated itself on being the highest model of Western civilization, eight- and nine-year-old children were working in factories under shocking conditions. In 1841 a law was passed fixing the minimum age for working children at eight years, and limiting the working day to 8 hours for children between the ages of eight and twelve, and to 12 hours between the ages of twelve and sixteen. The law came nine years after the English bill regulating child labor and two years after the Prussian law fixing the minimum age for working children at nine years. The vote was 218 to 27. There were deputies who opposed even so modest a measure. One deputy named Barrois argued that the prevailing 13-hour day for eight-year-old children was "long but not tiring; they get into the habit of work, order, obedience, living on little and getting along with their coworkers."

The July Monarchy businessmen saw the child as an animated instrument of production, and were genuinely baffled that efforts should be made to curtail his productivity. Another deputy, Themistocle Lestiboudois, thought the law of 1841 most unreasonable. "Children under twelve are only allowed to work eight hours," he said, "whereas the shop as a whole works twelve hours. This distinction is unfounded and impracticable. It is unfounded because the youngest children are not given work as toilsome as the others; they are granted more or less prolonged intervals of rest." Even though it could not be applied, however, the 1841 law was an important advance, because it set a precedent for government intervention in labor-management relations.

The slave-trade lobby of the 1789 Revolution was still active. Abolition, advocated by a few enlightened political figures like the duc de Broglie, was presented as an English plot to provoke French loss of the sugar islands. The old protectionist arguments still served: Free slaves would ruin French shipping and French harbors; the blacks were better off that way.

The bourgeoisie contributed both to slowing economic growth and to spreading class consciousness. Instead of multiplying alliances with other classes, like the English bourgeoisie, it remained inflexible and narrow, caught up in the virtues of success, stocks, bank accounts, and *relations* (connections).

Thanks to the nepotism of the July Monarchy, France kept its dynasties of high civil servants. Men in their twenties were appointed prefect through the abuse of political connections. If there were only two men left in France, it was said, one would ask the other for a government job. High officials like Teste, Minister of Public Works, were involved in scandals. One of the main duties of provincial officials like mayors and prefects was to insure the election of government candidates. The July Monarchy developed the technique of using civil servants as a party machine, which remains effective in the Fifth Republic.

Nonetheless, France seemed prosperous and had few foreign entanglements. The only expansionism the sedentary bourgeois ruling class permitted was the takeover of Algeria. Louis-Philippe did not, like his forebears, pursue glory, which led Lamartine to write his famous 1839 article: "France is a bored nation," a term picked up in a front-page article in *Le Monde* a few weeks before the 1968 spring riots. Complacency in France often seems to announce revolution. Political opposition grew over the extension of the franchise, but Guizot said: "The day of universal suffrage will never come." In 1847 a proposal for electoral reform was rejected. The opposition held banquets at which orators denounced the government. Fifty-one of these banquets were held for 20,857 subscribers before the government banned them. Guizot was under attack, and Louis-Philippe agreed to get rid of him. But by that time, February, 1848, the Paris crowds had taken to the streets. As in 1789 and 1830, a political crisis was conjugated

with an economic crisis. On February 23, on the Boulevard des
Capucines, the crowd faced the army, a shot was fired, panic followed, and there were 80 dead and wounded.

Louis-Philippe did not go hunting on that day, but he ordered
the army withdrawn from Paris and abdicated in favor of his
grandson. Not a shot was fired elsewhere in France in defense of
the regime. It was an accidental revolution. Marx called it a
parody of 1789. The head of the provisional government, Lamartine, personified antibourgeois values, disinterestedness, and
romantic generosity. For the first time since 1789, France vibrated
with the rhetoric of great principles. The provisional government
carried out the work of its ancestor. Within months, universal
suffrage was declared and slavery was abolished, this time permanently. The notables were uneasy. Baron Pasquier, president of
the Chamber of Peers, left Paris for his country house in Tours.
There was a run on the Paris stock market, and a suspension of
economic activity. The Second Republic was proclaimed, and a
Constituent Assembly was elected, for the first time in French
history, by universal suffrage. It was not markedly different from
one that limited suffrage might have elected. The conservative
provinces had reacted against radical Paris. Among those elected
were 190 former deputies, 100 former mayors, and 150 former
municipal councillors.

The first genuine election in French history showed the basically conservative nature of the electorate. The bourgeoisie understood that universal suffrage was not dangerous, and that it could
encourage the salutary tendency to conservatism, with the help of
money well spent, local influence, and a hired press. A workers'
revolt in June was suppressed by General Cavaignac. That December there were presidential elections, and among the candidates figured a historic name: Louis Napoleon Bonaparte, the
emperor's nephew. The notables were at first afraid of him because of two earlier attempts to have himself proclaimed emperor,
but he was able to win their support, and was considered "a cretin
who will be led by the nose." He was blessed with the support of
both the masses and the conservative press, and polled 5,000,000
of 7,500,000 votes cast.

The Second Empire was not officially proclaimed until December 2, 1852, but Napoleon's dictatorship began long before.

"I wish to be baptized with the water of universal suffrage," he said, "but I do not intend to live with my feet in the fount." Napoleon III in private called himself a Socialist. He had written a book called *An End to Pauperization*. But his regime was based on a pact with the notables of the July Monarchy. They would not oppose him if he kept order and allowed them to protect their class interests. He was no Louis-Philippe in that he advocated political freedom and economic free exchange. But the bourgeoisie found that they could maintain their influence despite universal suffrage, a revolution, and a new regime. It was not the perfect control that had existed between 1830 and 1848, but it was still a government in league with a class.

Napoleon III may have been a Socialist at heart, but he could not change the orientation of the regime. His reign coincided with the rise of industrial growth in France. The state was involved in huge deals like Suez. Morny, the emperor's illegitimate half-brother, made a fortune out of influence peddling. Press censorship eased and an effort was made toward education of the masses. But at the same time it was the reign of robber barons. As Madame Haussman, wife of the great Paris urbanist, was said to have remarked: "It is most odd, there is always a boulevard passing through the very spot where my husband has just bought a house." *Haute couture* became popular under the Second Empire so that the rich could be distinguished from the poor by their clothes, as they were, thanks to Haussman, by their addresses. If the July Monarchy was a small, closed corporation, the Second Empire was a corporation that had gone semipublic.

The emperor imposed free trade on the timorous bourgeoisie, who thought the 1860 treaty with England would "leave us disarmed before English competition." In fact, it shook up French industry, and showed that French products could compete. There was the same ambivalence toward the working class. The Second Empire repressed labor agitation while trying to seduce the worker. The emperor pardoned typographers sentenced to jail terms for striking in 1862. The article of the Code Civil which said "the employer is to be believed on his word" was abrogated, and an 1868 Ministry of the Interior circular invited officials to tolerate workers' associations as it did management associations. Nonetheless, when a strike broke out at the Schneider Le Creusot foundries in 1870, 4,000 soldiers were sent to quash it. And in 1854 the *livret ouvrier* which, by listing a worker's political activities could make it impossible for him to get a job, became mandatory.

The first French stock companies were founded in 1867, representing the triumph of liberal capitalism. The notables also successfully kept capital from being taxed. The regime turned universal suffrage to its own advantage. The technique of official candidates supported by prefects and mayors was perfected under the Second Empire. The government multiplied pressures to get its men elected, and successfully so. Napoleon III favored government by plebiscite, which General de Gaulle adapted into referendums. In the three plebiscites of his reign, in 1851, 1852, and 1870 he always polled between 7,000,000 and 8,000,000 votes. His regime fell not because of revolution, but invasion. Thus, the bourgeoisie which overthrew the monarchy in 1789 managed to consolidate its power amid the most diverse political regimes, realizing that political change does not matter as much as the maintenance of economic power.

After the war of 1870 and the destruction of the Commune, the most urgent duty of the Third Republic was to unite a divided France in a spirit of revenge against Germany. Bourgeois supremacy declined in this new context. The notables could not keep political power under a republic. Politics became a career, not a class preserve. There was a growing separation between wealth and office. Republican leaders like Gambetta and Jules Ferry wanted the improvement of the working class and helped the trade union movement. The notables suffered several serious defeats. In 1872 the first tax on capital was voted, and in 1893 stock market operations were taxed for the first time.

Freedom to form associations and trade unions came in the 1880's, much later than in countries like England and the United States. The isolation of the worker had contributed as much as any other single factor to the unchecked dominance of bourgeois interests. Now, the bourgeoisie was no longer a controlling class, although it kept the mentality of a controlling class. Legislation no longer exclusively served its needs. Elections no longer returned governments exclusively attuned to its interests. The bourgeoisie kept its dynasties, which continued to influence economic policies, it kept its ascendancy over high civil service, and it kept broad control over the press. It maintained itself largely because of the lack of cohesion of the middle and working classes.

No other single class in France has been able to take and hold power the way the bourgeois notables did between 1789 and 1900. The heavy cost of bourgeois power to the nation was continuous unrest because of its narrow view of the general interest and an ethic based on cupidity, just as the aristocracy's ethic had been based on vanity. The notables were defined by their absence of elevation of mind, their inability to see further than their own interests, and their attempt to freeze historical evolution into the form they had devised for it. The post-1789 ruling classes used the slogans of the Revolution, democracy and equality, while taking measures to prevent equality and democracy from being used against themselves. The French bourgeoisie kept power so long precisely because it had no social or political conscience and was ready to collaborate with any regime that did not threaten its property rights. The ideology of the *juste milieu* led them to appropriate freedom and make it mean order, and to appropriate equality and make it mean that everyone has an equal right to further his own interests. They also appropriated the eighteenth-century Enlightenment's belief in happiness, and capacity for assimilation. Man could through his own efforts improve himself. Social well-being could become a reality.

The bourgeoisie assimilated art forms, religions, and regimes. It formed a cohesive and self-perpetuating social group with its own values: the benefits of self-improvement through initiative and hard work, the quest for material goods, a liberal and tolerant attitude to whatever did not threaten it, the importance of private property, and a custodian mentality. These values tended to become known as French values, until a crisis in 1968 disclosed the existence of another France which, in the case of the students, repudiated them, and in the case of the workers, felt it had not been given its fair share of affluence. But if the events of 1968 were a revolution, they conformed to the familiar pattern of appropriation, and prepared the way for a record Gaullist electoral victory. The general showed he was neither Charles X nor Louis-Philippe.

Like the revolutions of 1830 and 1848, the events of 1968 took public opinion by surprise. No political figure or press commentator had seen the storm signals. And as in those two nineteenth-century revolutions, an active minority took to the Paris streets. The kings had gone hunting on the days they were overthrown, and General de Gaulle was pursuing the chimeras of his foreign policy in Rumania when France was paralyzed by strikes. But instead of abdicating (he considered the possibility), he made sure of the cooperation of the army and restored order, promising reforms which there was no longer the same urgency to carry out.

Previous revolutions had overthrown regimes and brought in a new form of authoritarian rule. The events of 1968 allowed de Gaulle to succeed himself. Although he emerged with what seemed a stronger popular base than before, less than a year later he was no longer in power. And yet there had been no revolution, no *coup d'état*, no fighting in the streets, none of the usual agitation which often announces in France that a regime has outlasted its welcome. De Gaulle was always at his best in times of crisis, when France was in danger and the odds seemed against him. In 1969 there was no danger, only the noncritical reforms of the regions and the Senate that were put before the people in a referendum. There was no compelling reason why the general should put his own mandate in the balance. It was an unstatesmanlike tactic because it violated the spirit of the presidential system he had tried to adapt to France. What if the American president, each time he made an important decision, threatened to leave office if a majority of the people did not approve it? One might call this government by petulance. De Gaulle was elected for a seven-year term but repeatedly jeopardized his office by throwing his personal prestige behind Fifth Republic reforms. It finally led to his defeat. At least he had the satisfaction of choosing the conditions of his departure. He was not overthrown; he dared the French to get rid of him, and they did, with their keen sense of cyclical history and their love of change for the sake of change. "The cemeteries are full of indispensable men," was a typical Parisian reaction. De Gaulle was like one of those Saint-Cyr officers who remains standing in the heat of battle when everyone else has dived for cover, and who finally gets hit. Who can guess to what extent he welcomed the repudiation of his people? It should be said to his credit that he innovated a form of peaceful political exit that was new for France. However bizarre his departure, it allowed the Fifth Republic to survive. An American friend, upon hearing of de Gaulle's resignation, asked me, "Will there be a Sixth Republic now?" The fact that de Gaulle could be succeeded in an orderly presidential election rather than through the process of revolution was in itself a denial of the French experience in which the passing of a great man means the passing of a regime and the beginning of a period of confusion and strife.

Defeat

Certain countries, like England, have been imperialistic without being militaristic. The army, and particularly the navy, made colonial expansion possible, but there was no veneration for the armed forces or the fallen in battle, and there were no military coups. Other nations, like Prussia, were militaristic without being imperialistic. Eighteenth-century Prussia exercised power disproportionate to its size because the country was run like a barracks by a sergeant-king. Nineteenth-century Prussia saw the rise of a Junker class of military nobility wielding political influence. France has been both militaristic and imperialistic. It has sought colonial and European expansion, and it has seen in its army the guarantor of cherished values: honor, courage, and freedom. But France has not been as consistently imperialistic as England, nor as consistently militaristic as Germany. There have been periods when France shed its colonies like unwanted ballast. And there have been periods when the army was unpopular, isolated from the rest of the nation, and when a military career lost its luster.

The army itself, called upon almost without interruption to defend France against invasions and to carry first the white royal standard and later the Tricolor across Europe and over the world, suffered from the need to adapt to new loyalties. It was possible for an officer who began his active service in 1785 to serve half a dozen different regimes, each one with a new ideology. The tradition of the army as the Great Silent One (*grande muette*) grew out of this dilemma, but in fact the army has been influential in national life. The nation in crisis has turned to its generals, and the army in crisis has wanted to save the nation from itself.

The nation has cheered and booed its army ever since the nobility became a warrior caste, exempted from taxation because it was expected to pay the blood tax. Nowhere else in Europe was the aristocracy's function so exclusively military. The king was a generalissimo, who fought with his troops and was captured in battle like François Premier, his sword wrenched from his hands. The rank of marshal created by the monarchy was maintained by Napoleon, who told his troops that every soldier had a potential marshal's baton in his cartridge pouch. Accounts of battle have always been popular. Voltaire's report of the battle of Fontenoy was an eighteenth-century best seller. Military episodes were the subjects of popular songs. How many thousands of French children have sung *"Malbrouk s'en va-t-en guerre"* without realizing that they were describing the campaigns of John Churchill? France seemed to thrive on the glories of warfare. The people of Paris coined the expression *bête comme la paix* (as stupid as peace).

With the Revolution, the army became identified with the nation in arms. Every fit man was a soldier. Soldiering became the concern of Everyman. For the first time there were plebeian heroes. Since the nation was the army, it was in the course of things that France should eventually be commanded by a military man.

Napoleon took what he needed from the monarchic and revolutionary experience—the *baton de maréchal* and the nation in arms. Is there a European country that has never been occupied by the conquering descendants of the Gauls? A visit to the Louvre shows that from François Premier to Napoleon, the French were not accustomed to return empty-handed from foreign wars. (Napoleon from Piacenza in 1796 to War Commissioner Lazare Carnot: "I will send along twenty paintings of the first-ranking masters, Correggio and Michelangelo.") Since 1789, France has been governed for roughly thirty-five years by military leaders: Napoleon, marshals MacMahon and Pétain, and de Gaulle, who made the uniform of a two-star general synonymous with the Fifth Republic.

After fifteen years of Napoleonic campaigns, an exhausted France became disenchanted with its army. Stendhal's hero Julien Sorel spurned a military career under the Restoration, even though he kept a portrait of Napoleon in a locket. The heroic *grognards* of the *grande armée* became pathetic *demi-soldes,* pushed back into civilian life on half pay. Alfred de Vigny saw "boredom and discontent on every military face." The bourgeois notables who governed Restoration France had no use for military epics. But under Napoleon III the army was again employed in impulsive expeditions from the Crimea to Mexico. The French "facility to engage in warfare" was noted by the military theoretician Ardant du Picq, who fought in the Crimea and was killed in combat in 1870: "An expedition is begun without sufficient motive, and the good French people, who have no idea why it was started, disapprove; but soon blood is spilled; common sense and justice dictate that spilled blood is the price the authors of this unjust undertaking must pay . . . but that is to reason without chauvinism! French blood has flowed, it becomes a matter of honor! And common sense is sacrificed to ridiculous vainglory." Under the Third Republic, the army, as in 1789, became the Republic's avenging angel—a slightly tarnished angel, after the Dreyfus case.

It is since Dreyfus was made the scapegoat for blunders in high military quarters and won redress after a civilian campaign in his favor that the French army has felt misunderstood. It continued to present itself as apolitical while in fact it was hostile to the unstable and sometimes corrupt republican regimes. This was a time when "often seen in the company of civilians" was a damning remark in an officer's dossier. In wartime the generals felt their efforts were scuttled by the politicians in Paris. In peacetime the military felt forgotten and discredited. To this attitude was added the stigma of three successive defeats at the hands of the Germans in less than a century (the French high command knew that World War I was not a military victory for the French army, for it was won with the help of English and American divisions). World War II created a crisis of obedience for the army. It was defeated in a matter of weeks. Each officer had to fall back on his conscience and decide whether by disobeying the Vichy regime he was being loyal to the values of a permanent France. The precedent was set then for disputing the right of a regime to be the authentic representative of France. The gap between the army and the nation grew after World War II when the soldiers who fought in Indochina and Algeria felt betrayed by anticolonial public opinion and regimes that did not support them.

The bitterness of the misunderstood army eventually led to an attempt by four Algiers-based generals to overthrow the de Gaulle government in 1961. From the nation in arms to the nation against the army, the French experience has come full circle. The French are capable of admiring the idea of a great army while remaining indifferent to their actual armed forces. July 14, which should be the commemoration of the Republic, has been turned into a military parade because the values of July 14 have had to be repeatedly defended by the army, just as the May Day celebration of Soviet Russia is also an occasion for the display of new weapons. The highest example of national veneration goes not to a civilian but an unknown soldier, which is not so much a glorification of the military as a way of stating that warfare has been a constant part of the French historical experience. The *force de frappe* is the most recent reminder that France has repeatedly been threatened and invaded. Strategically unsound and technically obsolete, the French *mini bombe* is consistent with a great military tradition. It is a psychological necessity for a nation whose armies once made Europe tremble.

The Crécy Syndrome

At Crécy in 1346, the French cavalry outnumbered the English, who were using longbowmen for the first time in Continental warfare. The French cavalry charged fifteen times without breaking the English ranks. Philippe de Valois had two horses shot from under him. When Philippe ordered retreat, the lords would not obey. Froissart, chronicler of the battle, writes that "those behind would not stop and kept riding forward saying they would get as far to the front as their followers, and that from mere pride and jealousy." The emphasis on personal bravery at the expense of other military virtues is a French military constant.

Even in defeat, the French could cherish the *beau geste* mentality. In 1870, when Sedan had fallen and the war was lost, William I said "What brave fellows" after Gallifet's cavalry charge (sabers against Krupp guns). After a first unsuccessful

charge, General Ducrot had asked Gallifet if he could try it
again. "As often as you like," he replied, "so long as there is one
of us left," and rallied his scattered, bloodied squadron for another hopeless try. The moving and often futile gesture is at
the heart of the French military tradition. Before every battle
there is invariably a general who announces, "My friends, today
we must learn how to die." The compulsion for gallantry helps
explain the readiness of World War I generals to throw their
troops into hopeless combat. That school of illusions, the École
Supérieure de Guerre, taught that "an energetic and courageous
infantry can march under the most lethal fire, even against well-
defended trenches, and capture them." Thus the insistence on
decorations and individual citations for heroism, some of them
inadvertently ridiculous: "Did not hesitate to capture a position
which, had it been occupied, would have been impregnable."

Faith in gallantry helps explain the anti-intellectualism of the
French army. Marshal MacMahon announced: "I will remove
from the promotion roster any officer whose name I see on the
cover of a book." General de Gaulle, whose name was often on
the cover of books, was viewed with suspicion by his peers. The
most popular twentieth-century French generals have been the
rough peasant types like Joffre, a cooper's son, or the pragmatic
aristocrats like Leclerc. Gamelin was considered too intellectual
because he read Bergson. The French general was intended to
be a leader of men, not a reader of books. As a cavalry general
said in July, 1870: "Do you want me to tell you what field topog-
raphy is? It's a peasant between two horse guards. You tell him
'now my lad, you're going to take us to such and such a spot and
we'll give you a shiny 100-sou piece, and if you're wrong we'll
split your head open with a pistol butt.'" When I served in the
French army from 1955 until 1957, the prevailing attitude of men
and officers alike was expressed in that oft-repeated phrase *faut pas
chercher à comprendre* (don't try to understand). The *faut pas
chercher à comprendre* mentality is one of resignation in the face
of forces beyond one's control. The army has its own rationale
and its own way of moving. Anti-intellectualism developed into
mistrust of politics and politicians.

Generals during World War I felt they had to fight on two
fronts, against the Germans and against the National Assembly

which was constantly investigating their operations and was partly responsible for the numerous shifts in command. In July, 1916, President Raymond Poincaré organized a visit to the Somme and Verdun fronts without consulting Joffre, the French commander in chief. Joffre, who thought the visit ill-timed, sent an ultimatum through the Minister of War that either he, Joffre, would accompany Poincaré, or else there would be no visit. Poincaré considered Joffre's letter "inadmissible interference of military power over civilian authority." After that, there was such agitation in the National Assembly that Aristide Briand, the premier, wrote Joffre in December that if he could not juggle his staff there would be a cabinet crisis. Joffre yielded, accepted the honor of marshal, and was kicked upstairs to the mythical post of Director General of the War.

A year later Poincaré again visited the front, but now Pétain was in charge. When the president had spoken, Pétain said: "Thank you for your praise; we did our best and we finally stopped the enemy—we would have done better yet if France had felt itself governed."

Poincaré, pale with anger, said: "Do you realize you are speaking to the President of the Republic?"

"It's precisely because I am talking to the President that I am saying what he should know," replied Pétain.

When Pétain came to power in 1940, he still saw France's problems as basically the fault of corrupt politicians, and organized the Riom trials of Daladier, Blum, Reynaud, and other political leaders of the thirties, throwing in a political general like Gamelin, in order to find scapegoats for French defeat.

It was also the sense of having been betrayed which made the army strongly anti-Communist. The Lenin train crossing Germany was irrefutable evidence that the Bolsheviks were working with the Huns. The French officer corps saw the 1917 defection of Russia as treason. In the first ten months of 1918, French losses were as high as in the entire year of 1916, the year of Verdun. Officers in their trenches in the first months of 1918 read reports attributing Allied defeats to German reinforcements relieved from the Russian front. They saw, in the fall of Czarist Russia, that a social order could disappear overnight, something which had never happened in France where the social order absorbed revolutions. The Dreyfus case and the Bolshevik revolution were the two events which made the French officer corps devoutly anti-Communist and wary of democracy.

The French army managed to be both anti-intellectual and doctrinaire, at once suspicious of ideas and attached to axiomatic principles. One of these axioms has been that the *arme blanche* (cold steel) is the chosen French weapon, ideal for the ardent but quickly spent French temperament, for the soldier-hero who is at his best in close combat, puncturing his adversary's stomach with a bayonet. Advocates of the *arme blanche* begin with Montaigne, who advised its use against the Huguenots in the Religious Wars, and end with Marshal Foch, who claimed in 1914 that "the bayonet assault will long remain supreme." The corollary of this passion for the bayonet is distrust of technological advances in weaponry. The French knights in the Hundred Years War were contemptuous of the English longbowmen whose arrows, they thought, could not pierce their armor. Nor did they realize that the shafts would make their horses panic and that once grounded in their 60-pound coats of armor, they would be helpless. Generals under Louis XIV vetoed manufacture of the first flintlock muskets. It was only after heavy losses at Steinkerque in 1692, to a European coalition army equipped with flintlocks, that the French adopted them. In 1868 Friedrich Krupp personally came to Paris to demonstrate his steel cannons to the French general staff. The minister of war, Marshal Edmond Leboeuf, filed away the Krupp brochure and reports, with the comment: "Nothing doing." It took six weeks in 1870 for the French army to collapse under attack from a German force equipped with Krupp cannons.

In 1911 the general in command of the French infantry wrote in a confidential note: "We have manufactured some machine guns to satisfy public opinion but it will change nothing." Officers given the first field radios threw them out, saying they could do just as well with bugles. Contempt for new weaponry reached astounding proportions in the years before World War II, and can only be explained in terms of a fear psychosis which gripped the French high command after the slaughter of 1914–18. It was as if refusal to recognize the merit of new weapons might stop technology from advancing. It was the ostrich reflex, so disastrous in 1940. "Forget about armored divisions," said a member of the general staff in 1938. "There are only two bridges in France that can support the weight of an armored division." General Weygand, who had been Foch's right arm in 1914, had a similar contempt for aviation: "To obtain victory one must control the terrain, and planes cannot control the terrain."

It was part of France's tragedy that too many World War I generals survived. Gamelin, Weygand, and Pétain were trench warfare holdovers who interpreted new situations in the light of their past experience. Weygand was able to rationalize this French handicap into an advantage: "They [the Germans] don't have many generals who fought in 1914–18," he said, "but most of our generals are old divisionaries and that is an experience which is hard to replace." The gospel of the French high command was a book by General Chauvineau, with a preface by Marshal Pétain, published in the year of the Anschluss. Of the tank, it said: "A vehicle obliged to run without stopping, like the wandering Jew, until it runs out of gas, cannot be considered dangerous," and of the airplane, "despite its wings, [it] has a tendency to fall heavily to the ground."

It is when the French military have been least doctrinal that they have been most successful. The paradox is that the French giants of warfare are outside the mainstream of French military thought. Joan of Arc won decisive victories against the English because she abandoned the doctrines of chivalric warfare and adopted what was then controversial to the French military mind: use of the terrain and positional battles. The *grande armée* had no doctrine. From the Revolution it inherited conscription of all fit men from ages eighteen to forty. The Revolution had itself inherited the never-retreat ideal of the medieval knight, and General Houchard was guillotined in 1793 for retreating at Menin. Napoleon's military genius was based on an absence of preconceptions and formalism, the ability to take advantage of the circumstances of battle to improvise a superior maneuver, and contempt for the established theorems of military art. He never wrote a treatise on war; he only described his battles after they were over in proclamations to his troops, lying about his losses. He combined brilliant organization with brilliant improvisation. Where Louis XIV took historiographers on his campaigns, Napoleon took cartographers. He fitted the definition of genius as an infinite capacity for detail. He translated captured enemy documents and was indefatigable in his pursuit of intelligence. He prepared for the Russian campaign with bridge-building teams and wagon regiments.

Napoleon invented the blitzkrieg, the swift advance and the decisive battle. He made the decisive battle the aim of war, and was a victim of his own strategy at Waterloo. It was the absence of apriorism and the use of simple common sense that established Napoleon as a military genius, but since he extemporized, he could teach and transmit nothing. He had to be there. "When I'm not there everything gets fouled up," he said. He was never a prophet in his own country. His disciples were German. General von der Goltz in 1890 said that "the principles of Napoleon still form today the basis of our doctrine," and the Panzer general Guderian admitted that he, too, was imbued with Napoleonic concepts of initiative and swift maneuvers. The political conclusions of the Napoleonic wars remained to be drawn by another German, Karl von Clausewitz, who saw that "war is a conflict between great interests, which is settled by the spilling of blood and only in that sense does it differ from other forms of conflict."

The Doctrinaire Generals

"May French military thought resist the secular attractions of a priori, the dogmatic, and the absolute," General de Gaulle wished in vain in one of his books, *Toward a Professional Army,* published in 1934. The book sold one thousand copies in France, but the German translation did considerably better. De Gaulle was criticized as a potential Fascist for advocating a professional army, and as a Jules Verne in uniform for suggesting armored divisions. His critics clung to the myth that only a militaristic nation like Prussia has a professional army, not realizing that France was never as militaristic as when it became a nation in arms, and that England has a professional army but has never been threatened by juntas.

De Gaulle lobbied for the cause of armored divisions in his own country. It is hard to imagine that the haughty officer spent hours in the badly lit waiting rooms of editorial offices waiting for military editors to grant him a few minutes of their time, or that he haunted the wings of the National Assembly and wrote toadying letters to political figures. Perhaps it was the memory of years when he had to stoop to be heard that made him so hostile to the press.

He wrote Paul Reynaud seventy letters in his long slanted hand, asking him to push the idea of an armored corps in the National Assembly. Reynaud was then Finance Minister, and when he supported de Gaulle's idea in a speech, the Minister of War, General Maurin, remarked: "So Monsieur Reynaud is now concerning himself with military matters. What would he say if I began interfering in financial problems?"

There was such animosity toward de Gaulle on the part of the general staff that he once arrived in Reynaud's office to tell him: "My career is broken."

"What do you mean, broken?"

"Yes, my name has been scratched from the promotion list for colonels, and if I miss it this time I'll never catch up."

Reynaud called Daladier, Minister of National Defense, and said: "So that's what happens, when an officer has some ideas of his own—they block his promotion."

"Well, no, it's not that," said Daladier, "but you know he was taken prisoner in the first war. He doesn't have as good a record as his comrades."

De Gaulle showed Reynaud his impressive World War I citations, and Reynaud took them to Daladier and said "read these." Daladier read them, contacted the right people, and de Gaulle was promoted, thanks to the intervention of two politicians, which did not contribute to his popularity in army circles. De Gaulle was not above flattering Reynaud, referring to his "magnificent speeches," and displaying a schoolboy devotion toward the rising political figure. But by the time Reynaud was premier and had named de Gaulle Undersecretary for War, it was already too late. The Germans were near Paris. Even so, Weygand was furious at de Gaulle's nomination.

"What have you got against him?" Reynaud asked.

"He's a child," said Weygand.

Reynaud later asked de Gaulle how old he was.

"Fifty," said de Gaulle.

"At your age," said Reynaud, "Napoleon was at Saint Helena. His career was over."

But somewhere along the line the French general staff had begun to equate age with wisdom.

Joan of Arc, Napoleon, and Charles de Gaulle are three examples of great military figures who went against the grain of the doctrinal French military mind, which is based on stubborn preconceptions. Those historians who wish to find in Vercingetorix the earliest example of French patriotism should also mention that he lost the battle of Alesia because of obsolete tactics and armaments. The Romans equipped their horses with metal protectors to guard their hooves against stake traps, but the Gauls did not show equal foresight and their cavalry was decimated. As early as Alesia, the French army was one war behind.

Repeated invasion and defeat gave the French high command a loser complex which made it adopt the tactics of the enemy once these were no longer valid. The invasion of 1814, with the Germans, Russians, and English in Paris all at the same time, led to a defensive psychology. Marshal Soult said he wanted ramparts around Paris equal to what the sea was to England and the winter was to Russia. This withdrawal psychology was forgotten in the exhilarating prospect of overrunning Prussia in 1870. But after the defeat French military strategy was a belated imitation of the German. In 1870 the Germans won with swift offensive tactics, so these were the tactics advocated by the French general staff for the pursuit of the next war. It developed that the next war was a war of attrition based on the defense of trenches. French military thought after 1918 was consequently based on the principle that a solid defensive line cannot be broken. This, again, was proved wrong in 1939, so wrong that the French began to wonder whether they were not suffering from some biological inferiority to the Germans.

The German Question

Overnight, Germany had become the hereditary enemy. The focus of French national life was the German question. History was rewritten to explain the origins of this fundamental enmity. For, in fact, the Franks were a German tribe which fixed itself in France after destroying the Burgundii and the Visigoths. There was a Franco-German kingdom until Charlemagne, having an-

nexed the Saxons and Bavarians, the north of Spain, and Italy as
far south as Rome, was crowned Holy Roman Emperor. France
was an accident of dynastic division after the death of Karl der
Grosse. But France became a nation while Germany became increasingly fragmented. Facing a united France in 1648, it numbered 343 principalities. The eighteenth century saw the rise of
Prussia, but Frederick II deepened the Austro-Prussian split by
grabbing Silesia from the Austrian empress Maria Theresa. It was
Napoleon who awakened German nationalism with his mania for
centralization. In 1806 he united the tiny states in a Confederation
of the Rhine, whose affairs were governed by a Diet sitting in
Frankfurt. The rulers of small principalities were mediatized.
Half a century later, Bismarck became the providential unifier,
by goading the French into war. "I wanted to wave a red cloth
under the noses of the Gallic bull," he said. Bismarck goes down
in French history as an unrepentant warmonger. In fact, he made
war less than Napoleon III: two brief campaigns against Austria
and Denmark and the short war of 1870 as against the goateed
emperor's Crimean, Mexican, and Italian campaigns.

De Gaulle wrote that "France was made with swordstrokes."
Why deny the same right to Germany? Bismarck was the German
Richelieu—the Germans simply had to wait longer for their greatest statesman. Napoleon III drafted the birth certificate of the
Third Reich when the white flag went up at Sedan: "Monsieur
my brother," he wrote William I, "having been unable to die in
the midst of my troops, it only remains for me to place my sword
in the hands of your majesty. I am your majesty's good brother,
Napoleon."

After 1870, Franco-German relations had the fatal character of
tragedy. Each nation saw the other as an irreconcilable enemy.
French negotiators told Bismarck what Talleyrand had told Met-
ternich, that generosity was the only basis for a lasting peace. That
might be true in stable countries, Bismarck said, but not in France,
with its kaleidoscopic governments and lack of respect for institutions. "One can rely on nothing in your country," he said, "the
French are irritable, envious, jealous, and proud to excess. It
seems to you that victory is a property reserved for you alone."
After 1870, the ownership of victory changed hands, along with
the Alsace and the Lorraine.

Intellectuals were situated by their position on the German question, as they are situated today by their position on Vietnam or Communism. There was a *défi Allemand,* far more menacing than today's *défi Américain.* Two conceptions of nationalism collided. French nationalism could not validly define itself as traditionally anti-German, for there had been no Germany prior to 1870. French nationalism had begun as loyalty to the state, and had become conservative and static. German nationalism began as loyalty to a language which predated the existence of a state. Once the German state was made, nationalism became expansionist and dynamic. France never had designs on Belgium as Germany had designs on other German-speaking populations. Both the French and the Germans displayed a doctrinaire passion for justifying their viewpoints.

The French developed conflicting theories of German barbarism and German superiority. The historian Edgar Quinet said the Romans had given their victims law, the Arabs had given the Koran, the French the Napoleonic Code, but the Germans nothing, for they were barbarians. But Zola said that "what must be confessed at the top of our voice is that in 1870 we were beaten by the scientific spirit . . . we were broken by the method of a people less brave and more ponderous than ourselves, we were crushed by masses maneuvered with logic, we were routed by the application of science to the art of war." Out of defeat came the search for a more vibrant nationalism, and the problem of reconciling the spiritual principles of the French nation with the demands of the avenging angel. Where was the authentic *patrie,* with or against General Boulanger, with or against Captain Dreyfus?

Behind the French image of a bellicose and barbaric Germany lay the fear of German energy and French impotence. Trying to breach these divisions, Péguy fell back on the mystical notion of France as the holder of a sacred flame. War against France, he said, was a crime against humanity, for "since antiquity, by divine right and right of birth, France has been the queen of nations . . . the poorest Frenchman had the clear and material impression that the Germans had, through him, violated an eternal majesty." In the light of this mystique, the next war would be a crusade.

The Revenge of 1914

The Frankfurt peace was only a truce, and Catholic, revolutionary, civilizing France would prevail over Protestant, imperialistic, barbarian Germany. "There are wars," wrote Péguy, "which come out of the very bowels of the people." From 1905, when William II arrived in Tangier, a zone of French influence, there were continual Franco-German incidents. Everyone sensed that the curtain was rising on the next act of the tragedy. The military felt prepared when Serbian nationalism served as a pretext. They put their faith in the victorious 1870 tactics of the Germans. The École de Guerre, founded in 1880, taught the art of war as a set of logical theorems leading to certainties. One of its most respected prophets, Colonel de Grandmaison, advocated a rush to the front and an irresistible bayonet attack. Every graduating class at Saint-Cyr and the École de Guerre learned Grandmaison's axiom that "there is no such thing as an excessive offensive." Heavy artillery would only slow down the lightning offensive, and when war broke out France was woefully behind in big guns.

French officers in 1914 were not equipped with helmets but wore iron skullcaps under their *képis*. Colonel Pénelon suggested the adoption of helmets to Joffre in November, 1914, but Joffre said: "My friend, we will not have time to use them. I will have destroyed the Boche in two months." Joffre threw 2,000,000 men into a Lorraine offensive destined to cut the German army in half. They left in their *tenue bleu horizon,* designed to make the charging French soldier a poor target against the blue of the sky, and in the bright red trousers that had been adopted as a way of subsidizing the production of madder in southern France, and they were cut to ribbons by the methodical Germans in their *feldgrau* uniforms. French corps commanders, with an average age of sixtyone, were more like a college of cardinals than combat leaders. Joffre reassigned 202 generals after Charleroi. He pitilessly liquidated some of his classmates and old friends. He himself put the number of generals whose careers he had broken at 140. "I'm fond of you," he would tell them, "but I'm more fond of France." The Marne was not a victory, it simply turned a fast war into a war of attrition, and destroyed the myth of German invulnerability. General von Küln said that in imperial France Joffre would have been made duc de la Marne as Ney had become prince de la Moskowa. Instead, Joffre became commander in chief. His principal quality was bovine impassivity. In the depth of crisis he lost neither his sleep nor his appetite. "I never saw a man eat so much," said General Serrigny watching him put away a bottle of Bordeaux and eight chops at one sitting. In the first five months of the war there were 300,000 French soldiers killed, including Colonel de Grandmaison who died at Soissons practicing what he had preached.

French strategy was described as plugging enemy shell holes with live soldiers until the enemy is out of ammunition. Pétain, who was horrified by the useless loss of life, drew on the lessons of nineteenth-century warfare. "To an orderly mind," he said, "one situation recalls another, which explains the battle of Champagne I fought in 1918. Do you recall? I had the front lines evacuated during the German artillery preparation. Result: They shelled empty trenches, and when they attacked, our troops were intact. Well! That was Wellington's maneuver at Torres Vedras— I had studied it with my students—I remembered it at the right moment, and that was the turning point of the war. The hardest part was making General Gouraud understand—he was a *brave* and in his eyes it was a crime to evacuate a position—I kept saying, 'but you'll regain it easily'—he shook his head: 'Retreat! And without a fight!' " The erosion of war discredited the best generals, Joffre and Foch, but permitted the rise of a French Churchill, Clemenceau. "What is my goal?" he thundered. "My goal is to win." He went to the trenches, stood on the parapet within enemy range, shook his fist, and shouted: "Pigs! Bastards! We'll get you!" And they did, with the help of Pershing and his inexperienced, optimistic, scrubbed divisions willing to fight thousands of miles away from their own soil. And then the silent figures walking through the cold misty air of Compiègne Forest from one railway car to another signified the end for now. It was too numbing to be victory. Post-1918 France was the France of President Paul Doumer, who had lost four sons to the Boches. The French in the marrow of their bones could not tolerate the idea of another war.

Between the Wars Defeatism

The peace was poisoned. As early as 1924, Hitler was obsessed with *drang nach osten* (eastward expansion) and with the idea that France wanted the left bank of the Rhine. "The mortal and implacable enemy of the German people," he wrote, "is and remains France. Whatever its regime, Bourbon or Jacobin, Napoleonic or Republican, clerical or red Bolshevist, the aim of its foreign policy will always be to take the border on the Rhine, to assure its possession of that river to crush and divide Germany." France had regained its lost provinces, however, and was now content to remain peacefully within its borders. Military doctrine was reversed to conform to the mood of the nation. Like taking two baths in the same bathwater, it was formulated in terms of trench warfare by Pétain's 1921 *Provisional Instruction for the Conduct of Great Units,* which became French army gospel: A continuous front cannot be broken; assault tanks can only be simple adjuncts of the infantry; the defensive is thriftier with soldiers' blood than the offensive.

The first two points had already been disproven by Allied tanks at Villers-Cotterêts, but it was the Germans who profited from that lesson. Because it had held in 1914, the continuous front became a doctrine. Funds were voted in 1930 to construct the Maginot Line. It was named after a World War I sergeant who had become Minister of War, a seven-foot giant who was virulent in his criticism of the high command but did not live to see his namesake breached, having died in 1932 of typhoid after eating a bad oyster. The French desperately needed to believe that if there was to be another war, they would be safe behind impregnable defenses. In 1936, nineteen German divisions entered the demilitarized Rhineland, and France, supposedly intent on capturing the left bank of the Rhine, did not budge. To venture beyond the Maginot Line was to lose its protection. Once built, it justified and encouraged a shield mentality, like that of the horsemen at Agincourt who thought their armor would protect them. Only de Gaulle lobbied against the false comfort of the military doctrines.

The defensive reflex of the generals was matched by pacifism in political circles. On the left, pacifist leaders like Léon Blum remained champions of disarmament long after Germany quit the disarmament conference in 1933. He believed in a world conscience and that France should set the example. He also believed, not in the deterrent of a well-equipped army, but in the nebulous dream of the *levée en masse,* a twentieth-century reenactment of Valmy, the idea that the worse a soldier is armed and equipped, the better he fights. In 1935, as a leader of the Socialist Party, he fought the law extending military service from one to two years. Stressing the rearmament of France rather than the disarmament of Germany, he said, played into the hands of Hitler. He denounced Colonel de Gaulle's project for an elite corps of armored divisions as a Praetorian Guard which could be used to overthrow the Republic.

When Blum came to power as head of a Popular Front government in 1936, he realized that disarmament was a failure and launched a four-year armament program. By the time the war started, France had 3,500 tanks dispersed along the front as support for infantry units, useless against Hitler's 2,500 tanks concentrated in the Ardennes. Meanwhile, the French right had evolved from hatred of Germany to neutralism, pacifism, and appeasement. *"Surtout pas de guerre,"* was the Action Française slogan. The Bolshevik peril, admiration of Fascism, and the absence of an urgent anti-German platform like the recovery of Alsace and Lorraine reversed the traditional attitude of the right, which encouraged Franco-German *rapprochement.* Fear of another war was rationalized with the theory that defeat would lead to a second Paris Commune and the Bolshevization of Europe. Professional pessimists like Alfred Fabre-Luce wrote: "Above all, let us not hope to save ourselves by war." Thierry Maulnier, who still writes editorials in *Le Figaro,* warned that "a German defeat would mean the crumbling of the authoritarian system which constitutes the main rampart to the Communist Revolution." After Munich, Pierre Flandin, Minister of Foreign Affairs, sent Hitler a telegram: "Please accept our warm congratulations for keeping the peace." France had a mutual defense treaty with Czechoslovakia, but the historian Pierre Gaxotte wrote that "Czechoslovakia is the invention of a few freemason professors . . . not worth the life of a single French soldier."

France abandoned Czechoslovakia despite Daladier's promise that "Munich would be the limit of our concessions." It was the end of the traditional trust the Balkan countries had placed in France. In December, 1938, the von Ribbentrops visited Paris and were given a reception by Premier Daladier to which the two Jewish cabinet members, Georges Mandel and Jean Zay, were not invited. Everyone else went, except the wife of one minister, who said she was dining that night at the Czech legation. Worse than appeasers, there were fifth columnists in France, with influence in the press and government circles. *Le Matin* hewed to a consistently pro-Hitler line. The Minister of Public Works, Anatole de Monzie, who was famous for saying "I prefer to receive a kick in the behind than a bullet in the head," was forced to resign on the basis of wiretaps of his conversations with the Italian embassy. France in 1939 was unprepared militarily, shot through with appeasers and Fascist sympathizers, and went to war with armistice as an already present, half-consicous aspiration.

Defeat and Civil War

In September, 1939, as the result of its military treaty with Poland, France declared war on Germany. The Polish defeat could be rationalized because the Poles had no Maginot Line and only thirty divisions to cover four hundred miles of front. The refusal to send an expeditionary force to help the Poles could be rationalized on the grounds of building up strength for the big push. Having declared war, France remained for nine months a motionless assailant waiting behind the snug security of the Maginot Line until the Germans had finished with the Poles and could find the time to attack them. "The relatively passive attitude of the French during the winter of 1939–40," wrote General Guderian, "incited us to conclude that the adversary had little inclination for war."

As in their previous wars with the Germans, the French had the same faith in a swift victory, the same slogans, like "time is on our side," the same overconfident generals and unready regiments of rheumatic reservists, and the same contempt for and misunderstanding of forces outside France. Weygand called the Red Army "a *gendarmerie* incapable of going beyond its own borders." Gamelin had the same imperturbability and hearty appetite as Joffre, and put away huge meals at Vincennes with the Germans two days away from Paris. The French in 1939 sincerely believed that theirs was the best army in the world. Gamelin was in fact the best general the Germans had. He decided to attack along the coast in the west and moved his troops into Belgium, leaving the way open for the German thrust on the Meuse, which was crossed on May 13; the French were paralyzed, with no planes or antitank guns. Colonel Poncelet retreated from the Meuse after burying the breechblocks of his abandoned artillery, and shot himself. Sedan was captured once again, and Guderian could not understand why the big guns of the Maginot Line did not catch the Germans in *enfilade*. The World War I tactic of relieving corps commanders was revived, and General Corap was replaced on May 15. Paul Reynaud and his anticlerical ministers went in great pomp to Notre Dame cathedral, in accordance with national tradition, to ask the heavens to bring forth the providential savior. But this time there was no tenacity, no eagerness to persist after the shock of the first reversals, so that the idea of armistice, unthinkable in 1914, was discussed as early as May 29, when Weygand told the Reynaud cabinet: "There may come a moment when France will find itself, despite its will, incapable of continuing an effective military struggle for the protection of its soil."

There was one French colonel who believed, like Napoleon, that "in war, apart from a few essential principles, there is no universal system but only circumstances and personalities." According to an officer who served with him in his successful tank attack at Abbeville, in May, de Gaulle at this abysmal moment already saw Allied victory as inevitable, and said, in his detached manner: "There is nothing simpler than the future of this war. There is no obsidional strategy. Apart from a few desperate sorties, an invested fortress must defend itself, that is, it must last. Hitler's Germany is invested. How long will it last—that is the question."

Such foresight was in marked contrast to the panic that June in Bordeaux, where the French government had taken refuge after burning the secret foreign office archives in the courtyard of the Ministry of Foreign Affairs. Ministers lingered over seven-course meals at the Chapon Fin. Reynaud's mistress, Madame de Portes, left secret telegrams lying in her unmade bed, and while no one showed any spirit of decision, everyone was ready with advice. Weygand said the cabinet should have stayed in Paris, like Roman senators on their curule chairs, waiting for the barbarians. Daladier said the difference between Fascism and Bolshevism was like the difference between the plague and the cholera.

On June 10, when the *drôle de guerre* was practically over, the Duce declared war on France, for he did not want Hitler to hog the glory. He ordered an all-out attack on the Alpine front on June 19, when the armistice had already been agreed to by France and Germany (it was signed on the twenty-second, with France breaking its promise to England not to make a separate peace).

The Italians bombed Bastia, Marseilles, Toulon, and Cannes, to show that they too had an air force, and the miniwar ended with a separate armistice on June 22, each side remaining in its positions. At the Fort de la Turra in the Savoie a French captain displayed familiar prowess and honor in this conversation with an Italian colonel:

"Who commands this fort?" asked the Italian.

"Me."

"Can't we come in out of this foul weather?"

"You have no right to enter a fort you did not take."

"But you're surrounded."

"I don't give a damn. What counts is that you stay out of the fort."

"Well, we've got to use the road to supply our troops. Will you fire on us?"

"My orders are to fire only if attacked."

"Can you sign this paper promising not to fire?"

"My word as a French officer should be enough."

A French soldier brings in a loaf of bread and hands it to the Italian colonel, who says:

"Oh, what fine bread."

"Baked under bombardment," says the captain.

"Do you have many wounded," asks the colonel.

"Not one!"

"And have you many mortars?"

"Mortars?"

"Yes, mortars, *che tirana bene.*"

On the stretched palm of his left hand, he makes a gesture with his right index finger, like planting cabbages in a circle. He points to the center of the circle and says:

"*La casa del colonele, cosi, cosa, boum boum.*"

"Many dead?"

The colonel nods and makes a face. "Yes, many. Who fired the mortar?"

"Him," a soldier says, pointing to the captain.

The colonel waves his hand like a mother promising a slap to a naughty child, and half smiling, pulls the captain's ear.

On July 10 the deputies of the National Assembly abdicated to Marshal Pétain. By that time, General de Gaulle was already in London and had delivered his celebrated proclamation. Pétain, the apostle of defensive strategy between the wars, became the high priest of renunciation. "France has been beaten," he told the nation. The old soldier of eighty-four still used World War I terminology: "We should not pop our heads out of the trenches too soon." A numbing sense of humiliation pervaded the nation, an awareness that this was the most tragic debacle in modern French history. For 1814 had been the defeat of a man, and 1870, to a lesser extent, had been the defeat of that man's nephew, while 1914 had exhausted the nation but ended in victory. Now the French were experiencing the closing of the cycle, the defeat of an exhausted nation. It meant the failure of the French army, with its outmoded conceptions of warfare and its incapacity to pass from a peacetime to a wartime mentality. It was the failure of the French fleet, which scuttled itself rather than fight alongside the Allies. It was the failure of French diplomacy, the swallow-tailed ambassadors who knew every detail of their country's diplomatic history since the Treaty of Westphalia but were blind to the rhythm of contemporary events. It was the failure of the French government, incapable of rising above partisan squabbles to provide national leadership. It was, in short, the bankruptcy of French intelligence, which became the captive of German method.

The feeling that a great civilization had collapsed contributed to defeatism. If it was over for France, it was felt, it must be over for everyone, which is why few qualms were expressed over signing a separate peace. In 1940 there were old men who could write in their diaries: "I will thus have seen three times how my country endures catastrophe." Three times the brisk step of the *feldgraus* had crossed the Lorraine. With unconscious cruelty, old Hindenberg had said to a French diplomat in the twenties: *"Mehrmals nach Frankreich gehen wir mit allen diesen Kriegen."* (Well, we have had to go often to France with all these wars.)

For four years there were two Frances and it was up to each individual to decide which one had the custody of the flag. The one that talked of sacrifice or the one that talked of conquest, the one that lauded the patriotism of the hearth or the one that said "France does not treat with those who occupy her territory," the one that said "Save what we can" or the one that said "Fight with what we have," the one that offered penitence or the one that promised revenge. There was an option to be taken between the resignation of Vichy and the boldness of de Gaulle, but on what grounds?

For the military, a tradition of the disobedience of great generals existed before de Gaulle. When Pétain came on an inspection tour of Morocco in the twenties, he told Marshal Lyautey: "I know how disagreeable my presence will seem, but what could I do? The government gave me an order, and I obeyed . . . all my life I have obeyed, and that is how I became marshal." "Well," replied Lyautey, "all my life I have disobeyed and that is how I became marshal."

Nothing was more mysterious than the motivation which made one man a Gaullist and another a Pétainist. On the lowest level, it was job security. The officer and the diplomat were reticent to give up a forthcoming promotion, a steady salary, the promise of a pension and the Legion of Honor to join what seemed like a hopeless adventure. When a general joined de Gaulle, one of his colleagues said: "What a fool, he was up for a third star." A fetichistic attachment to professional traditions and discipline was another motive. Admiral Esteva said that "it is impossible to loathe and detest the Germans more than I do," but, brought up in the highly formal and abstract context of naval discipline, this commander of the French Mediterranean fleet exhorted the French fighting with the Allies in North Africa to desert, and called for volunteers to fight those who would not desert. In 1940 only a handful of generals and one lone admiral, Muselier, joined de Gaulle in London. Only a handful of diplomats left the security of their embassies to rally to Free France and its little-known leader.

Capitulation muddled French minds. Patriots who professed hatred of the Germans ended up putting on the German uniform and fighting on the Eastern front against Bolshevism, freemasonry, Jewry, all the occult forces which they felt had conspired to bring France down; the presence of the Germans in Paris was only a by-product of French doom. In Marcel Aymé's *Le Chemin des Ecoliers,* a flag-waver who later joins the Eastern front brigade describes his feelings: "Defeated, by God. We, the French, have come to this. I can't believe it. Misery, when I think of France, it takes me back to the time when I was a kid in grade school, drawing her in my exercise book. Dressed like a lady, with her delicate shape, her cute little snout facing the sea, her blue rivers like a maiden's veins, her prefectures, and her railway lines leaving Paris like a star. But solid, too, don't kid yourself, steady on her feet. Remember Alsace-Lorraine, she carried it on her back like a soldier's knapsack. In my day, Alsace-Lorraine was a dotted line. The bastards had robbed it."

The defeat of 1940 divided the French in their families and friendships as no issue had done since the Dreyfus case. One of de Gaulle's best friends at Saint-Cyr was General Bridoux, who became Vichy Minister of War, was sentenced to death in absentia in 1945, and wound up a military adviser to Franco. I know of two brothers, one who joined de Gaulle, the other who volunteered for the French Legion that fought with the Germans on the Russian front, who pledged not to fire at one another should they meet in battle. There were journalists who wrote for the Vichy press because they said they had to keep their by-lines before their readers. There was the political rubbish of the Third Republic, men like Jacques Doriot, former Communist turned Fascist after he was expelled from the party, mayor of Saint-Denis who was removed from office in 1937 and who took his revenge on a system which had frustrated him by working with the Germans and organizing the French anti-Bolshevist legion. But there were also men who worked for the Vichy government in the sincere conviction that they, too, were part of the Resistance. Their form of resistance was saving hostages or forced laborers, and they felt as useful as the men in London. And then there was the great half-hearted majority, the wait-and-seers whose main concern was three meals a day.

The Occupation was a shameful parenthesis of French life; it reeked with much that was corrupt and opportunistic. The blond, efficient SS in black uniforms with the death's head insignia were reminders of France's humiliation. The French suffered from such an intense sense of guilt that they felt obliged to act out, as though in some penitential charade, the opinion the Germans had of them as a futile, frivolous people. In the first year of the Occupation Hitler seemed to be making good his promise that he could turn France into a vast Coney Island. Black marketeers and German officers sat congenially in the shadow of the naked ladies at the Moulin Rouge. Couturiers continued to turn out their collections. The traditional itinerary of revolutions, from the Bastille to the Madeleine, became a course for roller-skating races. The Resistance did not yet exist.

The French accepted the Vichy myth of "life as usual." People said: "the *fridolins* (Germans) are not so bad; they are going to put order into things. They've only been here a short time and they've already settled in—not bad for provincials. Of course we have to get our food on the black market, but we tell ourselves, what's sold on the black market at least the Germans won't requisition." It was a time for valued peasant friendships. Laval returned to Paris in 1942 with his briefcase stuffed with butter and eggs. It was the golden age of rural France, for Vichy had fallen back on the traditional values of attachment to the land and peasant hard work and thrift. Thanks to the combination of Vichy propaganda and the black market, never had the French peasant felt so sought after.

The country put its trust in the octogenarian Pétain with his drooping white mustache, his stoop, and his close-set vacant eyes, his reassuring newsreel speeches in a faltering voice, where even on camera he could not keep himself from playing with his blotter, putting his hand in it and making it jump. But the real symbol of France under the Occupation was the blind Minister for Prisoners, Scapini, with a black monocle over one eye, reading a speech urging collaboration while his fingers lightly brushed the braille text. The reasons were always valid—we must collaborate so that we can get our prisoners back. But one and a half million prisoners did not come back. And Laval, with his greasy voice and heavy-lidded courtesan's eyes, patiently explained that the occupation of the free zone after the Allied landing in Algiers in 1942 was in reality a way of giving the French greater freedom because no more *Ausweise* (permits to pass between the zones) would be needed. Fanatics filled up the Palais des Sports for Fascist rallies and mouthed the old nationalistic slogans as if France had not been trampled underfoot, and kept saying that England was the enemy when the daily list of hostages was being published in neat black-framed quadrangles in the collaborationist press. And then the ordinance of May 29, 1942: "It is a six-pointed star with the dimensions of the palm of a hand and a black edge. It is made of yellow cloth and bears in black lettering the inscription JEW. It must be worn from the age of six, visibly on the left side of the chest, solidly sewn to the clothing." Four hundred thousand of these badges were manufactured and became an article of clothing listed in the textile ration books.

Occupation was a lasting shame but also a highly varied and complicated matter. In the free zone Germans were seldom seen, while Alsace and Lorraine were once again annexed. The most important border in France was the demarcation line between the occupied and the free zones, which figured prominently in the maps of France printed on the silk handkerchiefs of English aviators. In Alsace and Lorraine, German efforts to eradicate all signs of Frenchness reached a thoroughness of lunatic proportions. The Gestapo searched houses in Strasbourg for mementoes of France like souvenir Eiffel towers or postcards of the Invalides. French inscriptions were removed from the mortuary crowns in cemeteries. Labels were changed on hot and cold water faucets, spice boxes, sugar and flour jars. The Place de Broglie in Strasbourg became Adolf Hitler Platz. Statues of Lafayette, Ney, and Kléber were dynamited. There was an Office for the Purge of Commemorative Monuments. Inscriptions on the monuments for the dead were replaced by *Gefallen für Deutschland*. The *beret basque* was banned, and prison sentences were given to those who insisted upon wearing it. Police arrested civilians who spoke French in the street "in a provocative manner." French-sounding family names had to be changed, Bernard to Bernhardt, Claude to Klaus,

Dupont to Brückner. Married couples had to fill out a certificate of Aryanism and were given free copies of *Mein Kampf*.

Schoolboys learned to walk in step, give the Hitler salute, and sing patriotic German songs. The French were up against a sense of mission and civilizing influence as strong as their own, stronger because it was successful and commanded perfect obedience. Albert Camus tells of a truckload of Resistance men on the way to be executed, with a German priest in the back of the truck to give them solace. Conversations turning on the afterlife are not much help when you are about to die. A sixteen-year-old, picked up by mistake, jumped out in the dark dawn. The priest banged his fist against the window of the cab and shouted *"Achtung, achtung."* In Germany, said Camus, even God is mobilized.

When we speak of Vichy and Free France we tend to think of two united and opposed camps. In fact both were fragmented. World War II allegiances in France cut across party and class lines, across the traditional division of left and right. True, the bulk of the trade movement was for the Resistance, and most of big business was to some degree collaborationist. But some union leaders joined Vichy and some businessmen were Resistance heroes. The businessmen were drawn to Vichy by fear, uncertainty, and the slogan, "work as usual." They accepted the Vichy line that France was being punished for its sins as long as they were allowed to keep their factories open. The ideal of the French *patronat* was a neutral leader, neither pro-German nor pro-English, who would just keep the economy going. At the Liberation, several thousand *patrons* were prohibited from reopening their factories, which made possible the nationalization of key industries. Management emerged from World War II with a badly flawed image, and it has been common to say since then that the French do not like their industry.

Among high civil servants there was a more even split between those who felt it was their duty to serve Vichy and those, like the great Resistance hero Jean Moulin, who refused from the start to work with the Germans. It is understandable that a certain type of French mind, taught to idealize order, would collaborate. A man like Jean Bichelonne, who graduated at the top of his class in Polytechnique, became one of Laval's key counselors out of a misguided notion that he would be allowed to reform the French economy. He signed decrees sending thousands of young Frenchmen to forced labor camps, and left with the German troops in 1944, still believing in an eventual German victory. The attitude of the Communist Party was dictated by the Nazi-Soviet pact. In November, 1940, the Communist daily, *l'Humanité,* now being published clandestinely, wrote that "our party is adamant against attempts to renew the slaughter of Frenchmen, either under the Cross of Lorraine or under the swastika." *L'Humanité* then obtained permission from the Kommandantur to publish in the open, and denounced de Gaulle's June 18 appeal as coming from a mercenary in the pay of London. When Hitler invaded Russia the Communist position was of course reversed.

The Vichy government had a minister of the army with no army, a minister of the navy with no navy, a minister of foreign affairs with no foreign policy, and a minister of education whose personnel subverted his directives. The Vichy government pretended to be a real government, independent of German influence, concerned only with the revival of France. Vichy passed some sensible economic and social policies, like the law making it easier to recognize children born out of wedlock. It encouraged the consolidation of farmland by exempting it from inheritance taxes as long as the land was not fragmented. But fundamentally, the Vichy government was founded on the illusion that fair arrangements could be worked out with the Germans. Pétain went to Montoire to see Hitler and was photographed shaking hands with him as a sign of mutual good faith. Dissension grew in the Vichy camp, and in December, 1940, Pétain staged a minor coup by getting rid of Laval. Hitler took this as a personal insult, and under German influence Pétain had to take Laval back. Laval said he would accept office to save France from having a gauleiter. In June, 1942, Laval said in a speech that he desired German victory. He explained this phrase by saying: "It's not the French I have to please to protect France, it's Hitler." But the policy of pleasing Hitler failed after the Allied landing in Algiers, when the free zone was invested and the fiction of a free and independent Vichy government was laid to rest. It had been a convenient pretext for the exploitation of French human and national resources.

The most violent collaborators, however, were not in Vichy but in Paris. They had left the free zone to work more closely with the Germans, and accused Vichy of being too soft. There was the former Communist Marcel Déat, who created a neo-Fascist political party; the beetle-browed, simian Joseph Darnand, a war hero of 1914 and 1940 who became head of the *milice;* Jacques Doriot, who founded yet another party; Jean Luchaire, editor of a pro-Nazi newspaper, who became the leader of the new Tout-Paris; and Robert Brasillach, who said he had come to Fascism by way of poetry. These and other leaders of collaboration represented many hues of French political thought and many different personal backgrounds. All they had in common was a strong dislike of the Third Republic, which had jailed some of them and frustrated the personal ambitions of others. They saw the Occupation as a French internal problem, another form of cabinet crisis, and they were eager to denounce the guilt of those who did not think as they did. They felt they were using the Germans rather than vice versa. There were a half-dozen different parties, all at daggers drawn, jockeying for leadership.

The collaborators in Paris never managed to achieve political unity. Only when it came to attacking the Republic or de Gaulle was there any agreement. It was, in fact, the collaborationist press which helped make an unknown de Gaulle famous by attacking him with such persistence. Collaborationist leaders ceaselessly vied for influence and even initiated plots against one another. After 1943 Laval had to accept some of the most extreme into his government. Déat entered the government in March, 1944, and announced in June that the Normandy landings were a civil war between the Resistance and the collaboration. The outcome of that civil war sent some high-ranking collaborators like Déat and Doriot fleeing, while Darnand, Luchaire, and Brasillach were caught, tried, and shot.

Only one top collaborator was a victim of the Resistance: the former deputy from Bordeaux, Philippe Henriot, a one-time Catholic liberal turned right-wing demagogue, who had in 1944 become Minister of Information in the last Laval government. The supreme command of the French Forces of the Interior decided to kidnap Henriot. In March, 1944, three groups, two of 6 men, and one of 5, drove to his residence at the ministry on the rue Solferino at 5:25 A.M. Two policemen were standing on the corner. Michel, leader of the first group, walked up to them with his gun and said: "Resistance, don't raise your hands, give us your weapons and follow."

Closer to the ministry they crossed another police round and disarmed them. They knocked on the door of the ministry.

A voice said: "Who's there?"

"The guards of *monsieur le ministre.*"

The concierge opened the door a crack and they pushed in, leaving the gendarmes in the concierge's loge under guard. The Resistance teams cut the telephone wires, and occupied the ministry. They moved silently over the thick carpets, crossed two offices, reached a closed door and knocked.

"*Milice,* special brigade. Terrorists are trying to kidnap the minister, he must come downstairs so we can protect him."

A woman's voice said, "Don't open, those are your assassins."

Henriot's voice said, "But who are you, what do you want?"

Michel slipped a *milice* calling card under the door. It opened. Henriot was in a corner of the room, dressed in white pajamas. Three men entered with submachine guns.

"Ah, there you are, of course," said Henriot.

Michel said to Henriot's wife, "No harm will come to you."

Henriot, a powerful man, grabbed the muzzles of two submachine guns and almost succeeded in disarming the two men. A short burst felled him. The group had entered the ministry at 5:40 and left it at 5:53. On the way out a gendarme called out: "Give us back our weapons or we'll be courtmartialed."

"You will be, anyway," replied one of the group, "you'd better come with us."

Michel went back to his home in the suburbs, and at 8 A.M. his mother turned on the radio and said, "They say Henriot's been killed."

"Is that so?"

Despite such coups, German army documents released by the State Department show that French resistance was never a military factor to be reckoned with. The Germans rated French resistance much lower than that in Yugoslavia or occupied Russia. The French Resistance was fragmented into many autonomous groups like Combat, Ceux de la Libération, Ceux de la Résistance, and the powerful Communist groups that only came into play after the end of the Nazi-Soviet pact. It was slow to organize. The first German soldier was shot on August 21, 1941, by a volunteer named Ouzoulias, who later became Colonel Fabien; he killed a *Kriegsmarine* noncom named Mozer on the metro quai of the Barbés-Rochechouart station. Three hostages were shot in reprisal. There were many misunderstandings, mutual suspicions, and animosities between north and south zones, and groups of different political coloring. The Resistance only attracted a mass following when it became an alternative to forced labor. Many of those destined for the camps preferred to take to the Maquis. Efforts to place it under unified Gaullist command did not succeed until a National Council of Resistance was formed in 1943. Thereafter, the problem was Communist influence, and when de Gaulle came to power in 1944 he had to accept several Communists in his cabinet and pardon Communist Party leader Maurice Thorez, who was accused of desertion, as a recognition of Communist accomplishments in the Resistance.

Those whom the maréchal had called bad Frenchmen were now the victors. In one of those swift reversals which recur in French history, the maréchal went on trial, and the general who had been condemned to death in absentia in 1940 governed the country. De Gaulle represented an antidote to defeat and humiliation. He had not hesitated. He had fought. He had been decisive. He had imposed himself as the representative of France against the misgivings of the Allies. When it was suggested to Stalin at Yalta in February, 1945, that France should share in the occupation of Berlin, he replied with cynical logic: "France? But France is an enemy power." The French could see in de Gaulle the symbol of their eternal values, while Pétain had merely been the feeble curator of the nation's household goods.

But too many had chosen the wrong side, like the writer Robert Brasillach, who was mesmerized by the spectacle of German strength, and liked to "chat with young German officers attached to all that their vocation brought them that was unexpected and magnificent." In 1944, with the Allies near Paris, he obtained false papers and went into hiding after a good-bye dinner at the German Institute. From his garret hideaway he heard the rooftop fighting of the liberation of Paris and a bourgeois neighbor telling his maid, "You can go get the bread now, Marie, they've stopped shooting." After his mother and sister were arrested, he went to the police prefecture to turn himself in. An inspector received him and Brasillach said:

"I suppose I am wanted."

"Go to your neighborhood commissariat. I have no order to arrest you."

"I came here directly to save time."

"You should have gone to the judiciary police."

"I don't know where it is. It's not easy to get arrested, is it?"

"I'll call for an officer. I must say that I don't approve of the arrest of Madame, your mother. By the way, what year were you in at school?" (When one Frenchman says "school" to another it has to mean Normale Supérieure, a school with the prestige of Oxford.)

"1928."

"Me too."

"But I don't recognize you."

"We must have changed. I recognize you. I was a science major, you were a literature major. That's why it bothered me when I was shown your calling card. I wish you had gone somewhere else."

The police officer arrived.

"Should we put handcuffs on him?"

"That won't be necessary," said the inspector.

Brasillach was tried and shot. He said he felt like the victim of a new Terror. The wave of repressions could not be stopped. It was too obviously a question of one team replacing another, of partisan justice, and looting in the name of requisition. By 1946, 131 generals had been sanctioned for their conduct during the war, from revocation without a pension to accelerated retirement. More than 700 officers had been removed from active service, and there was a flourishing traffic in Resistance certificates after Circular 1010 came out: "All officers who remianed in metropolitan France must ask for their reintegration into the army." Newspapers which had kept appearing under the Occupation received new managements and new names. France thus entered the difficult postwar years divided. The Resistance illusion of a nation united collapsed when de Gaulle went into semiretirement in 1946, and colonialism brought the divisions into the open once again.

Colonialism

France is the only country which has conquered and lost two separate colonial empires. Under the monarchy, the French empire consisted of Canada, most of the United States, and a large portion of India; that empire was frittered away by defeat and treaty until Napoleon sold the last piece with the Louisiana Purchase. France after Napoleon became accustomed to living without colonies. But with the advent of the Third Republic it claimed another empire in Africa and Asia, the last important piece of which was lost with Algerian independence in 1962. There are few parts of the world that France has not at some point owned: Canada, three-quarters of the United States, the Caribbean, Brazil, West Africa, the Middle East under the Crusades, Madagascar, Egypt under Napoleon, North Africa, and a large piece of Southeast Asia. It was all lost, including the five Indian commercial counters whose sonorous syllables were learned by heart by French schoolboys: Pondicherry, Chandernagore, Karikal, Mahé, Yanam.

The special character of French colonialism is that it was not a consistent imperialist policy such as England had, nor even a systematic commercial exploitation on the Spanish, Portuguese, and Dutch models. It was, rather, based on considerations of prestige, reactions to European events, and the belief in a civilizing mission. Furthermore, colonialism was seldom popular in France with the government, intellectuals, and the masses. The complaint of the great French colonial figures, from Dupleix to the generals in Indochina and Algeria, was that they were not supported at home. No nation has been so indifferent to its own colonial epic.

The colonies were always at the mercy of Continental negotiations and defeats. The first mention of an overseas territory in a French treaty was at Crépy in 1544, when François Premier sacrificed his plan for an Indian expedition as part of a broad political arrangement with Charles V, and recognized the colonial supremacy of Spain. French leaders have traditionally been just as eager to jettison their colonies as they had been to acquire them. No one was more surprised than Robert Livingston, the American envoy to France, when Napoleon in 1803 agreed to sell for fifteen million dollars a huge region that was to give twenty-four states to the union. It can be doubted whether France ever had a colonial vocation. As John Quincy Adams rightly remarked, France "may well conquer colonies but how can she possibly keep them?" The French instinct has been more for conquest and exploration than for settlement. History books resound with great names like Cartier and Champlain, but the settlers had to be put manacled on boats bound for the New World. There were no disinherited younger sons of France, there was no pilgrim mentality, and the one attempt to settle a Huguenot colony in the Western hemisphere ended disastrously. Colonies were never vital to France's survival, as they were to England's, and were thus viewed as the hobby of kings, and later, as an antidote for French defeat, the loss of two provinces, and underpopulation.

There is no French Kipling or Gunga Din, but there is a roster of anticolonialist French writers: Voltaire ridiculing Canada as "a few acres of snow," André Gide in 1927 denouncing the exploitation of the black man by a colonial system, and Sartre condemning torture in Algeria and the whole mistaken concept of colonialism. Colonial wars, although supported by lobbies and active minorities, were called dirty wars by public opinion. The 1961 generals' putsch in Algeria was an admission that colonialism had no popular support in France. The generals were trying to impose a French Algeria on a nation that did not want it. The first Algerian expedition, in 1830, did not prevent a revolution from toppling Charles X, nor did General Bugeaud's exploits there eighteen years later help Louis-Philippe remain on the throne.

Another special aspect of French colonialism since the Revolution has been its presentation as a gift from the mother of freedom. The assumption of any colonizing power is that it is bringing a better way of life to a backward people. If Cortez had not dispossessed Montezuma of his empire, this line of thinking runs, the Mexicans would still be helping the sun to rise with human sacrifices. Colonialism everywhere has been based on the questionable assumption that Western society is superior to that of so-called primitive peoples. But the French went even further in selling colonialism as a chance to share in the principles of 1789.

Charles Péguy wrote: "When the French say they are carving out a colonial empire, don't believe them. They are propagating freedom." And a geography textbook says: "Wise minds recognize that among all nations the French are those who try hardest to understand and love the inhabitants of their vast overseas territories." The historian Guglielmo Ferrero said that English colonialism was *à la* Sancho Panza, efficient and practical, while French colonialism was *à la* Don Quixote, idealistic, dreamlike, and grandiose. This may be true insofar as France's motives go, but the French *colon* mentality, although less cruel than the Spanish and less straitlaced than the English, was based not on the motto of the French Republic but on the avowed aim of "making the *burnous* sweat."

Republican colonialism was less tolerant than the colonialism of kings. In Algeria under the Bourbon Restoration, the natives were allowed to keep their personality and traditions. Abd-el-Kader fought the French and was defeated, but he was recognized as a brave man, and made dey. Under the Third Republic the idea arose that Algeria was a part of France. It was divided into three departments, and made an administrative extension of the *metropole,* to make up for the lost departments of Alsace and Lorraine. Within ten years, 220,000 dispossessed families from those lost provinces settled there and in turn dispossessed the Kabyles of their most fertile lands in the Mitidja plain. Their combination of racism, brutality, expropriation, and nationalistic fervor was couched in Republican rhetoric. Teachers explained the rights of man to men who had no rights, and the sons of serfs learned the motto: Equality, liberty, and fraternity. The contradiction implicit in such attitudes was recognized in 1932 by Paul Reynaud when he visited Indochina as Colonial Minister, and attended classes at an Annamese *lycée* in Saigon. "What are you learning in history?" he asked.

"The Revolution."

"What is that?"

"One makes a revolution to have freedom and equality and to throw out the privileged classes."

The French liked to assert that their administration was just, but there were two justices, as was known by the Indochinese planter who boasted that he had beaten eleven Annamese servants to death and never been tried, and by the native civil servants on lower pay scales and the Algerian inhabitants of French departments who were long denied French citizenship. The English never pretended that India was an extension of John Bull's island. In English colonialism tea was always more important than sympathy. They sent planters, businessmen, and soldiers to India, but the French arrived with civil servants to relegate local usages to folklore. School inspectors arrived in Madagascar before any schools had been built, and the Court of Appeals was created before it had been decided whether to apply French or tribal law.

French ambition seems always to have oscillated between the crusade and the plot of land, high adventure and the hearthstone. The golden age of French colonialism came early, in the eleventh century when the Normans built castles in Apulia and lorded over the Kingdom of Cyprus and the Kingdom of the Two Sicilies. The conquest of England was the only example of French colonialism in which assimilation took place. The Crusades, essentially a French affair, helped exhaust the nation's colonial potential, and ended dismally, with the Crusaders leaving ruins behind and bringing back new vegetables like the artichoke, spices, new words like "caravan" and "arsenal," and having learned to make better ships, to study geography, and that there were other religions on the planet. But in the race for the New World the French were left at the post. François Premier was less interested in the promise of faraway gold than in looting the Duchy of Milan. Urged by his chaplain, the abbot of Mont-Saint-Michel, he finally granted subsidies for an expedition "charged with discovering in the newfound lands certain islands and countries where, it is said, there is a great quantity of gold." He put a seafaring native of Saint-Malo named Jacques Cartier in charge. Cartier set out in 1534, went up the Saint Lawrence, reached Newfoundland, and was kind to the natives. In his travels he saw many marvels, such as a people who do not eat because they have no anus. But he found neither gold nor precious stones nor Northwest Passage, and the king lost interest.

In the second half of the sixteenth century France was too absorbed in the Wars of Religion to play a major role in the New World, which was divided by Spain and Portugal. A convoy of Huguenots was sent to Brazil in 1555 under the chevalier de

Villegagnon, who shut himself up on an offshore island instead of settling the mainland. Five years later the Portuguese took the island. The French government was indifferent to the loss, and forfeited the chance to colonize Brazil. Another detachment of Huguenots founded a settlement called Fort Caroline in Florida in 1566. The Spanish destroyed it and massacred most of the settlers, but as heretics, not as Frenchmen. Three French punitive expeditions to Florida failed.

The utility of colonial expansion remained unclear to the French. Sully, the great minister of Henri IV, said that "one never gains much wealth from territories situated below forty degrees in latitude." Cardinal Richelieu was the first French statesman to have a consistent colonial policy. He wanted to fight the Spanish and the Austrians abroad as well as at home. His ally was the queen mother, who, as he wrote in his memoirs, "constantly told the king that since he was the foremost sovereign he had to prevent the king of Spain from extending his power." Since there were new Spains there had to be new Frances. Richelieu built up the navy, founded colonial companies, subsidized explorers, and shipped settlers to the new lands, as well as ladies of middling virtue for them to marry. It was thanks to the policies of Richelieu and his eventual successor under Louis XIV, Colbert, that France was able to compete in the Western hemisphere. Champlain founded Quebec in 1608, and Robert Cavelier de La Salle took Louisiana in 1682. Colbert saw the colonies as a way to enrich France. They could furnish spices, sugar, and other goods. Seven thousand settlers were recruited for Canada.

Like Richelieu, Colbert favored mixed marriages with Indian women. The French were ambivalent in their attitude toward the natives. In the Caribbean, slaves were necessary and it was therefore impossible to found colonies on humanitarian principles. But in North America, they considered the Indians as equals and tried to convert them. French colonialism under the *ancien régime* had an altruistic, evangelical side. Louis XIV founded a convent for the education of Canadians. Louis Hébert, the first French settler to die in Canada, said in his will: "I crossed the seas to save the savages rather than for any personal profit. They are reasonable creatures like us and can love the same God if they are informed about him." Colbert directed his colonial administrators "to attract the savages among the French, which can be done with marriages and the education of children."

France in the eighteenth century lost the war with England for empire. Embroiled in European warfare, the French monarchy was unwilling to divert troops and resources to the faraway struggle for its sparsely settled Canadian empire. The marquis d'Argenson, Minister of Foreign Affairs under Louis XV, said he would willingly trade France's colonies for the head of a pin. In India, Dupleix had a plan for French supremacy, but in 1752 Silhouette, the Royal Commissioner for the India Company, ordered Dupleix to restrict himself to keeping a few commercial counters. "The idea of imposing our law on all of India with a handful of men is folly," he said. The colonial leaders were sabotaged at home. To the French, the battles with England in North America and India were remote, marginal episodes of the dynastic quarrels being waged on the customary battlefields of Flanders by the usual protagonists. France lightheartedly relinquished its empire with a stroke of the pen. The Treaty of Paris in 1763 ended the Seven Years War, the war for empire; France abandoned Canada, the left bank of the Mississippi, and India, except for the five commercial counters. The French Foreign Minister, Choiseul, called the Treaty of Paris "a good joke we have played on the English," because France had kept the sugar islands. "Don't count on me for furs this winter," he wrote Voltaire. "You are hereby notified to address yourself to England."

Post-Revolution Expansion

The men of the Revolution inherited the colonial blind spot of the *ancien régime* ministers. Danton said to Robespierre: "It's too bad we can't propose to give our colonies to the Americans, it would be a good way to become their allies." Like the *ancien régime,* the foreign policy of the Revolution was Europe-orientated.

Bonaparte saw colonies as a way of getting rid of dissatisfied Frenchmen. "If there are still men tormented by the desire to hate their countrymen and embittered by the memory of former posts, immense regions await them," he said. The end of the Napoleonic adventure left France nearly barren of colonies, with the exception of trading posts in Senegal and India, the Caribbean islands of Guadeloupe and Martinique, Guiana in South America, the island of Réunion in the Indian Ocean, and the islands of Saint Pierre and Miquelon off Newfoundland.

The Bourbon Restoration's colonial involvement was accidental. France had coral fishing concessions in Algeria, for which the dey was paid 60,000 francs a year. The dey's demands for more money and his harassments (much as the current Algerian government is making ever increasing demands for French oil rights) encouraged French intervention in 1830 with 37,000 men and 103 ships. The Minister of War, Bourmont, was pleased with the result: "Twenty days sufficed," he said, "to destroy a state whose existence had been a nuisance to Europe for three centuries." Less than a month after laying the cornerstone for France's North African empire, the regime of Charles X was the victim of revolution. The French did not know what to do with Algeria. They could not leave it to the pirates. They had to administer it. Under the July Monarchy, Premier Guizot placed General Bugeaud, a former Napoleonic corporal, at the head of France's first colonial army. After a bloody war against the Arab leader, Abd-el-Kader, during which the French committed their first atrocity in North Africa, asphyxiating 600 men, women, and children who had taken refuge in a cave, Algeria became solidly French. By 1847 there were already more than 100,000 European settlers there.

With the conquest of Algeria came the idea that colonies should be administered by military men, as if they were some sort of distant garrison. The close ties between colonialism and the French army date from Bugeaud's expedition. Until 1870, Algeria was under the jurisdiction of the Ministry of War. The army had a new role, that of colonial administrator. Under the Second Empire, another soldier, the engineer-captain Faidherbe, colonized Senegal and established an intelligent pattern of indirect rule and pacification. But like other French chiefs of state, Napoleon III was inconsistent in his colonial policies. He supported prestige expeditions such as Faidherbe's, the annexation of Cochin China in 1862, the establishment of a French protectorate in Cambodia, and the conquest of New Caledonia, but he was hostile to Algeria, which he called a ball and chain around France's feet. The settlement of Algeria was halted, and in 1863 he reminded the governor general that "Algeria is not a colony, properly speaking, but an Arab kingdom."

The Birth of French Imperialism

The Franco-Prussian war was more important than any other single factor in turning French colonial indifference into imperialism. One century after the British, the French discovered the meaning of empire. Gone were the fears of cost and catastrophe, the notion that colonies were the hobbies of sovereigns, and the lack of interest in remote regions of the world. There were never more ardent advocates of colonial expansion than the laic, civilian, pipe-and-slippers leaders of the Third Republic. France's territory had been amputated, and that loss could be made up through colonial acquisition. France's military might had been humbled, but conquest in Africa and the Far East would bring renewed luster to the army. France was written off as a second-rate power, but an empire would remind the world that it was still a great nation. Moreover, French colonial expansion was encouraged by Bismarck. It was part of his concept of a Pax Germanica to keep France isolated on the Continent and embroiled in far-flung lands. He told the French ambassador in Berlin: "I see that the Tunisian pear is ripe and it is time for you to pick it. I think the French people need something to lift their pride, and I sincerely hope that success in the Mediterranean will do the trick. The more successful you are in that direction the less you will hold grievances against us." Bismarck supported French claims in Tunisia against the Italians, of whom he said: "They had an appetite before they had teeth," and he encouraged Premier Jules Ferry to pursue his Far East expeditions. In 1881 the Tunisian bey signed the Treaty of Bardo, establishing a French protectorate. A few years later, the Tonkin was occupied. The sailor Savorgnan de Brazza single-handedly pacified French Equatorial Africa. A former post-office clerk named Émile Pavie occupied Laos. In less than thirty years, France was once again at the head of a vast colonial empire. In 1884, at the Berlin Conference, France, Germany, and England divided the world into spheres of colonial influence.

The architect of France's colonial policy was Jules Ferry. It was under his impulse as Premier in 1880 that France carried out its Tunisian campaign, and it was when he was Foreign Minister three years later that the Tonkin was conquered. How this liberal Republican, who also associated his name with free and compulsory education, could become the principal advocate of the exploitation of other peoples is one of the paradoxes of French colonialism. He was often under attack by the parliamentary opposition for betraying the principles of 1789. "That," he would reply, "is nothing but political metaphysics." With Ferry, France for the first time made empire its first concern. He said colonies would compensate for France's inability to expand on the Continent, and provide an antidote for underpopulation. Ferry developed a colonial mystique: The colonies were also French soil, and the French were spreading the heady values of their civilization among backward peoples. France was disinterested. It had no white Rajas or Teutonic traveling salesmen; it did not invest capital, it injected ideals; it did not build factories, it exported textbooks; it did not teach the natives skills but patriotism. And in doing so, it resumed its rank as a leading power; such was the reward of altruistic humanitarianism.

During a heated debate in July, 1885, in the Chamber of Deputies, Ferry said: "Gentlemen ... it must be openly stated that the superior races have rights in relation to the inferior races ... I repeat that they have rights because they have obligations—the obligation to civilize all inferior races." Shouts came from the opposition benches: "You dare say that in the country where the Rights of Man was proclaimed ... this is the justification of the slave trade ..." Ferry replied that the Declaration of the Rights of Man had not been drafted for the Blacks of Equatorial Africa. Despite all the reasons in favor of empire, the nation was never unanimous in its support, and it was finally a colonial crisis that brought about Ferry's unmerited disgrace. In 1885 General de Negrier abandoned an advance post called Lang-Son in Tonkin. That minor incident was blown out of proportion into a crushing colonial defeat. Ferry was derisively called *Le Tonkinois*. Clemenceau, one of the most vocal enemies of colonialism, said Ferry should be tried for high treason, and forced his resignation as Foreign Minister. He died three years later, another example of France's ingratitude toward its empire builders.

Ferry was dead, but imperialism remained popular. Geographical societies promoted the empire, subsidized explorers, and gave prizes for essays about colonies. The economist Paul Leroy-Beaulieu sold the Third Republic on the idea that colonies were a source of wealth in his 1870 pamphlet, *Colonialization Among Modern Peoples*. He introduced the profit motive. But the most passionate advocates of empire did not come from the business community, which remained hesitant to invest in such risky ventures, but from the academic community. A colonial school trained overseas administrators. Colonial legislation became a mandatory course in law school. In 1900, Minister of Foreign Affairs Theophile Delcassé wondered "whether the history of colonialism furnishes another example of such prodigious and swift expansion."

No one questioned the thesis that a superior society was magnanimously sharing its benefits with backward peoples. French *colons* could exploit Indochina and North Africa while they said: "Look what we are doing for them—we are discovering riches they did not even know they had, we are educating them, we are giving them orderly government, and we are building them hospitals and railroads." Even the French Socialist Party and its leader Jean Jaurès were taken in by the euphoria of do-gooder imperialism. They did not notice that the first independence movements were making their appearance.

With the coming of World War I, the civilizing mission became a recruiting mission. In 1912 the natives of North Africa, who were denied French citizenship, were nonetheless impressed into compulsory military service. It was not presented as an obligation to be butchered, but as a chance to share in a glorious military tradition. The French empire was founded as much on cant as on force of arms. Colonial troops were a precious human reservoir. Seven hundred thousand brown, black, and yellow men fought for their forcibly adopted homeland and were often sent to the front lines. The Germans came to fear what they called the black tide. As a member of the government put it in 1918: "Today we can ask ourselves with some anguish what would have become of us if we had not had this enormous reservoir from which we so lavishly drew."

After the war, the colonial peoples watched the imperial powers at Versailles invoke principles of self-determination which they knew would be denied them. The bravery of Algerian troops induced the French to grant them citizenship and the right to attain the rank of officer. But the colonial question grew more complex with the appearance of a new social type, the settler. At first the colonies had attracted misfits, men who felt frustrated by the conventions and regulations of their own society, rather than pioneers. The colonial officers were also a special breed. Lyautey in Madagascar in 1898 described his daily duties as waging war against disease and illiteracy, planting trees, building roads, founding schools, and his reward as seeing African villages destroy their parapets because they felt safe. With Lyautey, the army's colonial vocation was born and found an exemplary model. Instead of the officer who felt protected by the army's regulations, the officer for whom discipline was an excuse never to take an initiative, the officer who knew his horses better than his men, the new species was part political leader and part social worker, and sometimes wielded great power. Lyautey was the undisputed ruler of Morocco for seventeen years. A new army spirit based on independence from civilian authority was born with these colonial potentates. The colonies attracted some of the ablest officers after World War I. Marshal Juin volunteered for Morocco, saying he had no stomach for occupation duties in the Rhineland.

But the time of the generals who ruled colonies like fiefs gave way to the time of the second-generation settler, the *pied-noir,* who was not out for adventure, but to consolidate the advantages of the colonial way of life. By 1911, half a million Europeans in Algeria had been born there. They created a new landscape, were proud of their accomplishments, contemptuous of the local population, and bent on maintaining their supremacy. The Algerian *pied-noir,* with all his courage, hard work, and freedom from the restrictive habits of metropolitan France, founded his way of life on the simple-minded assumption that Algeria was an integral part of France, but that it would not do to make the Moslem population equal citizens. A lexicon of maxims and clichés justified *pied-noir* society, on the order of "You have to make these people happy in spite of themselves; we have done so much for them; we give them much more than we get; they believe in us; they would be lost without the French presence; you have to help them develop slowly—you give them a pair of shoes and you find them barefoot the next day; giving them independence would be like giving a car to someone who can't drive; the Arab laborer who thinks he is rich with a bicycle is far happier than the intellectual who becomes a renegade and a *déclassé.*" In Algeria, the only colony where France was able to install more than a million settlers, the cant of civilizing influence was used with great effectiveness to preserve the privileges of the European minority.

Lulled by the illusion of their unselfish motives, the French were slower than other colonial powers to adopt a policy of gradual disengagement. The British were applying indirect rule in Africa in the nineteen thirties. Ceylon became autonomous in 1931, and the British India Act was applied in 1935. At about the same time, the Third Republic enjoyed its first genuine left-wing government, with the Popular Front, which was incapable of adopting a liberal colonial policy. On that issue, Premier Léon Blum said, it was "urgent to wait." After World War II, when the manpower of the colonies was once again put to good use and future nationalist leaders like the Algerian Ahmed Ben Bella won the highest military decorations for their heroism in fighting for France, a French commonwealth conference called in 1944 at Brazzaville made it clear, in the words of the Gaullist official René Pleven, that "the civilizing mission accomplished by France in its colonies makes any idea of autonomy or evolution outside the French bloc impossible; there can be no eventual, or even distant conception of self-government."

The End of Empire

England and Holland were able to achieve decolonization without protracted wars, army uprisings, or government overthrows. But in France, it could only come through crisis. It caused the fall of the Fourth Republic, the coming to power of General de Gaulle, and the third great crisis in the army after the Dreyfus case and the Vichy-de Gaulle choice of 1940. Decolonization was more painful for France for three principal reasons: First, because republican governments had for three quarters of a century rationalized imperialism in terms of France's great humanist vocation. It was painful to unlearn what had been taught for so long, to realize that the Arabs and Negroes did not love the French and want them to stay, that the Gaulois were not their ancestors, and that they would not be satisfied with reading about revolution in French history textbooks. It was painful for a nation accustomed to connecting power with empire to face its loss. Politicians had stressed too often that the colonies were the essential condition of France's rank among nations. Second, there was the problem of the settlers. Algeria was the French Palestine. The metropolitan French had reason to feel guilty about the million settlers, just as a New York Jew might feel guilty about not helping Israel. The presence of the *pieds-noirs* lent credence to the thesis that Algeria really was three French departments. Finally, the history of decolonization became one with the history of the army sent out to fight colonial wars, which were lost as much on the home front as on the battlefield. Again, as after the Dreyfus case, the army became separated from the nation, with its own ideology and its own policies.

In Indochina the army equated its colonial struggle with a crusade against international Communism. It could claim that it was saving Western civilization. But the war was so unpopular at home that conscripts were never sent to fight in this crusade. The army with some justification blamed its reversals on the indecisive and corrupt governments of the Fourth Republic. It felt humiliated by the 1948 decision that Indochina citations were no longer to appear in the *Journal Officiel,* and by the 1951 ordinance that blood collected by the Office of Social Hygiene should no longer serve for the wounded of the Expeditionary Force. The army quite naturally moved closer to the right-wing minority and the lobbies that supported colonialism, and felt betrayed by the anticolonial majority of the nation. The antimilitary campaign of the intellectual establishment included personal attacks on famous generals, like the line in the Prévert poem—"those who are satisfied with ancillary masculine loves," a dig at General de Lattre. When Indochina was lost, an embittered army was given another mission in Algeria. The split grew between a nation weary of war, governments seeking peaceful solutions, and the army determined to get over its "loser's complex" and win this most salvageable of colonial wars.

Far from being converted to decolonization by the independence granted Morocco in 1956, the army in Algeria found new reasons to hang on. Algeria was like France, with its sleepy provincial garrison life. The *pied-noir* population showered the army with support and admiration. The generals, betrayed in Paris, felt understood in Algeria. A new kind of soldier was born, full of missionary zeal, addicted to psychological warfare, by turn torturer and social worker (paratroop commanders like General Massu and Colonel Godard adopted Moslem children); these soldiers believed in the loudspeaker as a weapon, and their ability to convince convinced mainly themselves. The fellaghas were called Viets. Much was made of the connection between the nationalist struggle and the Communist theory of revolutionary war. Again in Algeria, the French army felt it was fighting a worldwide conspiracy. A French general in Algiers had a map in his office with red arrows leaving Russia and arriving in North Africa. Self-determination was explained away as a Communist trick. The old anti-Bolshevik reflex that had its origin when Russia sought a separate peace in 1917 was again exploited.

All the fine traditions were out the window. The Saint-Cyrien who had died nobly in World War I as he charged the Germans in white gloves now had to apply electrodes to the genitals of Arab prisoners to make them talk. The military conscience was torn between disgust and the urge to get the dirty job done. The failure of the 1956 Suez operation was seen as a victory of Arab nationalism supported by international Communism, which must not be allowed to spread to Algeria. The army began to interfere in government policy. In 1956 two colonels thought up a plot to kidnap five Algerian nationalist leaders in mid-flight from Morocco to Tunis, by ordering the French pilot to land in Algeria. The plan was carried out with a go-ahead from the Socialist Secretary of State for War, Max Lejeune. It strained French relations with Tunisia and Morocco at a time when Premier Guy Mollet was doing his best to appease those countries because of the forthcoming Anglo-French expedition in Suez. The situation of the army, subjected to the whims of indecisive governments, was reversed; now the government was subjected to the whims of the army. A year later, the bombardment of the Tunisian village of Sakkiet, which killed 69 adults and a child, was decided on without informing Premier Felix Gaillard, Minister of Defense

Jacques Chaban-Delmas, or the head of the Tunisian Affairs Department, Christian Pineau. I remember the criticism lavished on the government by instructors when I was at officers' training school in Saint-Maixent in 1956. We were harangued about the government's incapacity, and on one occasion a paratroop captain told his assembled company of officers-to-be: "We don't even have to take power, we just have to pick it up." In 1958 the army leaders in Algeria did just that. On May 13 the coup took place which put General de Gaulle in power. The army thus helped bring back to power a man who, they thought, would preserve Algeria, but who was in fact the only man capable of putting an end to France's colonial involvements.

The army's sense of unity as it rallied behind de Gaulle in 1958 soon gave way to the awareness that it had been tricked as the general proceeded toward the liquidation of the remainder of France's empire. De Gaulle realized that Algeria demoralized and divided the nation, as Vietnam was later to do to America. He saw that implicit in colonial war was civil war. But de Gaulle himself provided a precedent for military disobedience in the name of higher values. The army was again split between loyal and dissident officers, but this time the loyal officers were Gaullist. The others refused to accept government policy. When they could not impose their views legally, they made an amateurish and unrealistic attempt to overthrow the government, with the Algiers putsch of 1961. The nation in arms again saved France, but this time by refusing to fight. The half a million conscripts in Algeria, informed over their transistor radios of the threat to the Republic, refused to be a party to the putsch. They stayed in their barracks. The professional soldiers too were divided. As in 1940, old friends and comrades in arms, members of the same class at Saint-Cyr, took different roads. General Maurice Challe, former head of the air force, commanding officer of the highly successful 1959 Jumelle operation, which convinced him that military victory in Algeria was within the army's grasp, became one of the four leaders of the putsch. His classmate and friend General de Pouilly, who commanded French troops in Oran, withheld his support. He convinced his own officers not to join the putsch and tried to convince Challe to give it up.

Many officers sympathetic to the aims and frustrations of the "lost soldiers" also knew that a military coup could not succeed in France. But for the leaders there was no turning back. Some of them, like General Salan and a dozen of the colonels who had masterminded the coup, went underground. Respected officers with long and distinguished careers voluntarily became outlaws to remain consistent with a certain conception of loyalty. For such men, the formalism and rigidity of the French military mind could not adjust to changing reality. The officers who became leaders of the terrorist Secret Army justified their conduct with rhetoric. They had given their word they would stay in Algeria, and they could not go back on it. The sanctity of oaths was invoked against political reality. They saw themselves as the "real" army, the army that had been fighting for twenty years on the battlefields of three continents. The "other" army was to them made up of armchair generals and devious politicians. They presented their senseless murders of police officials and officers loyal to the government as the "execution of traitors," whereas they were the ones who had betrayed their government.

They found a surprising number of fellow travelers in army and government circles. The crisis over Algeria penetrated civilian life and brought into confrontation two groups with opposing ideas of the state going back to the Dreyfus case: Those who dreamed of order at the expense of justice saw the army as custodian of the nation's ideals, and clung to myths of French imperialism, against those who favored a Republican government, with an army at the service of the state, and who realized that colonies were anachronisms. The French Algeria right also assimilated the second generation of the Vichy right of 1940, with its persisting hatred of de Gaulle, its nostalgia for the Middle Ages, and its dream of a return to the corporate state. Colonel Bastien-Thiéry, who organized the 1962 assassination attempt against de Gaulle, was the son-in-law of the first Vichy government's Secretary for Youth. He represented a certain fossilized, doctrinal right, ready to ally itself with Algerian ultras, leftover Poujadistes, or embryonic Fascists.

In 1962, with Algerian independence, France lost its second colonial empire and found itself virtually contained within the borders of the hexagon for the first time since the seventeenth century. As always, it kept a couple of sugar islands, Guadeloupe in the Caribbean and Réunion in the Indian Ocean, both of which are still French departments. Far from being abandoned, 800,000 *pieds-noirs* arrived in France in the biggest migration the country has ever absorbed. That they were so smoothly assimilated is a tribute to French tolerance and the resilience of the economy.

Residual Colonialism

Although practically without colonies, France still suffers today from what might be called residual colonialism. Having freed France from its empire, General de Gaulle was free to proclaim self-determination for the people of French Canada. But in the spring of 1968, nineteen nationalists from Guadeloupe went on trial in Paris for sedition. While General de Gaulle was calling for an independent Quebec, these coffee-colored nationalists were being tried by the exceptional tribunal which deals with crimes against the safety of the state for wanting an independent Guadeloupe. The trial was fascinating because it showed that no matter how scattered the crumbs of an empire, the debasing colonial mentality persists. The defendants described themselves as second-class citizens—native civil servants were on a lower pay scale and native conscripts were classified as "overseas French." Something close to a slave economy still existed, with 49 percent of the arable land in the hands of 0.4 percent of property owners. The bells on the plantation that summoned the rural laborers to work had been installed before 1848, in the days of slavery.

The court, although not known for its leniency, appears to have been sensitive to the contradiction between residual colonialism and a militant foreign policy supporting the self-determination of French Canadians, for thirteen of the Guadeloupian defendants were acquitted and six were given suspended sentences. The defense argued that since the 1961 referendum recognized the independence of the Algerian departments, the French constitution proclaims the right of self-determination for all peoples. It would be inconsistent and unfair to deny to the Guadeloupians what had been granted to the Algerians and was being asked for French Canadians.

Residual colonialism is also apparent in the African intervention force under Admiral Rivière which rushes in to bolster pro-

French regimes as it has done in Gabon, and in the military repression of nationalist demonstrations in 1967 in France's East African enclave of Djibouti. Residual colonialism accounts for the French support of Biafra, and of the Arabs in the Middle East. France continues to want to play a role in those parts of the world where it once had colonies, in a transitional fade-out from empire to noncolonial power. It was interesting to see a former colonial power, which for centuries ignored ethnic divisions to carve up Africa into arbitrary administrative units, defending the right to self-determination of the Ibo tribe.

The end of the Algerian war, however, was as important a date for France as the end of World War II. It ended a nightmarish period when parked cars in Paris streets were booby-trapped, when panicking demonstrators were crushed to death against the ironwork grills of a closed metro station, when little girls were blinded by plastic bombs intended for cabinet ministers, and when the chief of state himself was repeatedly ambushed and escaped with his life, thanks to what the Arabs call *baraka* (luck that borders on grace) and the skillful driving of his chauffeur. The Algerian war was a virus destroying the nation's healthy cells, not only dividing its army and its population, but diverting resources and absorbing the government's full energy. France in that period corresponded to Yeats' description of the world before the Second Coming, when "The best lack all conviction, while the worst are full of passionate intensity." Six years later, the last soldiers of the Secret Army organization were amnestied. The best known, returning from exile or released from prison, turned from the sword to the pen, rewriting history with the rhetorical passion that comes from an unquenchable sense of outrage. "Forget the divisive past" was de Gaulle's leitmotif as generals Salan and Jouhaud were freed, as flowers were placed on the grave of Marshal Pétain, and as the writer Paul Morand, banned from the Académie Française because he had served as Vichy ambassador to Bern, was allowed at last to join the Immortals in 1968.

Along with its colonies, France lost its hereditary enemy. It is ironic that a general who was wounded and captured by the Germans in the First World War and who became the symbol of anti-German resistance in the second should have been the one to preside over the burial of Franco-German hatred. Right after the war, General de Gaulle wanted a separate Rhineland as a buffer for France. But when the German state was restored, he quickly recovered from disillusion, and said: "Anyone with common sense can see that the Germans are where they are, at the center of our continent." In 1962 the German flag floated over Paris, and Adenauer was received like an old friend. Adenauer was not exaggerating when he called the signature of the Franco-German pact of January 22, 1963, a miracle. It was, of course, not a matter of sentiment. The *rapprochement* of a France thrice invaded in less than a century by a more powerful Germany followed the conviction that a divided Germany was no longer a threat, subject to revision as West Germany grew more powerful and assertive in European affairs. Also, the change in generations favored new bonds. The young French, from fifteen to twenty-five, have a better opinion of the Germans than their parents, even though Germany is for the French still only the sixth-favored foreign nation, after England, the United States, Holland, Spain, and Italy. But as de Gaulle pointed out: "History will without a doubt hold as one of the principal human events the change which, in the last two decades, brought the German and the French people first to renounce their ancient enmity, and then to join, side by side, in international organizations destined either for security, like the Atlantic Alliance, or for economic progress, like the Common Market."

The Army Today

With the end of colonial wars, for the first time since 1939, the French army is a peacetime army, neither girding against invasion nor fighting in rice paddies or djebels. It is not being asked to make the sacrifices that could fuel another revolt against civilian authority, although it still feels isolated from the nation. The officers at the École de Guerre in Paris arrive there each day in civilian clothes. They keep their uniforms in their lockers. They are not ashamed of what they are, but they fear "an incident" if they were to wear their uniforms on the metro or bus, or in the street. Their vague discontent has little to feed on. The heroes of colonial wars, like generals Massu and Bigeard, are outside France: the one in Germany, the other in Africa at the head of an intervention regiment. There is no longer the feeling that the army's efforts are being betrayed by incapable governments, for there is nothing to betray. There is no military-industrial complex in France, no hawkish Pentagon lobby that threatens to embark the nation on renewed military adventures. Significantly, when the franc was threatened in the fall of 1968 and cuts had to be made in the 1969 budget, it was the defense budget that suffered, as one of the least essential. The French were thereby acknowledging that the *force de frappe* is a luxury that becomes expendable in a time of domestic crisis. Certain programs, like the navy's antiaircraft missile Mandragore, were scrapped.

General de Gaulle's books on the army, which were ridiculed between the wars, are now required reading in French military schools. A general speaking at the commencement exercises of the École de Guerre in 1968 said of de Gaulle's book *Le Fil de l'Épée:* "I don't hesitate to say it; this is the most important text in the French language, second only to the Holy Gospels in importance. It ranks with the *Imitation of Christ.*" Other generals have found ways to supplement the low peacetime scales of French army pay, like the one who is on the payroll of the Central Intelligence Agency. The French army is less militant and more domesticated today than at any other time in this century. Gone are the dreams of *revanche* and empire.

The substitute for an epic military tradition is the *force de frappe*. It is important for army psychology, an antidote for the "loser's complex" of an army which either could not or was not allowed to win its wars. It is one of those reassuring conditions of French power, like imperialism in 1870 and a fragmented Germany prior to that. De Gaulle liked to say that countries that do not have the bomb, like Sweden, are eunuchs. It is proof of a nation's virility, and the price of admission to the *"club des grands."* Without it, France would be an underdeveloped nation. With it, France is in the exclusive company of Russia, China, England, and the United States. The *force de frappe* could be considered worthwhile for these side effects alone, although in its principal, strategic function its usefulness is questionable. It is a divisive factor in domestic politics. None of the other nuclear powers have a parliamentary opposition clamoring that its nuclear program be scrapped. No serious critic of the American administration suggests that the United States unilaterally get rid of nuclear armaments. But the French left has made this one of its major policies, complaining that the funds spent on the minibomb slow down social progress. Alone among the nuclear powers, the future of France's atomic program is in doubt.

Conservative estimates place the French three years behind in their nuclear program. As a deputy said during the National Assembly debate on the 1969 budget, "We are like a racing driver who starts the twenty-four-hour le Mans race with a tiny car and falls farther behind with each lap." In 1968, nine years after the first Sahara explosion, the French had 36 Mirage IV bombers with a combined nuclear payload equal to one Minuteman II intercontinental missile, without mentioning the added disadvantage that to reach Russia the Mirages would have to refuel in mid-flight somewhere over Poland. The French nuclear submarine is obsolete before it has been launched. The French badly underestimated the technical problems of the *force de frappe* and overestimated their ability to finance it. The tardiness of the program has led some military leaders to wish they could obtain American nuclear warheads. They have become partisans of narrower military cooperation with the United States. Their realistic military view is a reversal of Gaullist dogma on an independent force of dissuasion.

The policy that France will respond with its atomic weapons if attacked, thereby inviting the destruction of its own country, is not easy to live with. In reality, the underlying assumptions of this policy are that the French, although independent of NATO, will continue to benefit from the American nuclear umbrella, and that in any case, tensions with the Soviet Union are lessening so that military force will not have to be used in Europe. For, despite the *tout azimuth* strategy (that is, a nuclear force ready to strike in all directions), French strategy has been shaped with a Soviet attack in mind. In war games the enemy is called the "red party." French military strategists stress knowledge of Soviet weaponry and military organization. In French barracks there are posters of Russian tanks with the caption, "Know your enemy."

In case the atomic deterrent should not deter and a conflict erupts, French strategy is based on the kind of war France would like to, and is able to, fight. This strategy, elaborated by men like Colonel Robert Aublet, director of first-year instruction at the French war college, is designed for a war with limited use of nuclear force that would allow ground forces to enter into play, a halfway house between atomic and conventional warfare.

In map exercises, the French operate on the assumption of a two-week land war which would conclude with each side left incapable of maintaining operations above the division level. In this so-called flexible response, French ground units would interpenetrate with enemy units, making it impossible for the enemy to use its atomic weapons. The infantry, still the traditional queen of battles, would accomplish its mission of frustrating an enemy attack.

Like Louis XIV in the privacy of his study planning a campaign in Flanders with his secretary of war, French nuclear strategists disregard the kind of war the Soviets would actually fight, for Soviet military doctrine calls for the immediate and unrestricted use of nuclear weapons, which would achieve Soviet objectives before French ground forces could even mobilize. But since the French have no effective riposte to unrestricted nuclear warfare, and since in a conventional war they would be crushed by the superior Red Army, they have evolved this highly qualified strategy of combined nuclear and ground action which corresponds to no foreseeable real situation, except perhaps another war with Germany.

The final deficiency of French strategy is that the army, destined to play a key role with tactical nuclear weapons, is still burdened with conventional, often archaic equipment. The army has been neglected because the priority has gone to building up the deterrent *force de frappe*. The army comprises 57 percent of the total strength of the armed forces but receives only 25 percent of the budget. It has only one armored and three mechanized divisions, and many armored units are equipped with the 20-year-old M-47 Patton tank. It is deficient in heavy artillery. It has Honest John ramps and rockets, but it no longer has access to American warheads. Its ability to contribute to the deterrence and destruction of any nuclear-armed invading force is more than doubtful. It is armed for a conventional war like World War II. It still hearkens back to the nation in arms, with its National Guard type of organization called the Défense Operationnelle du Territoire, which would call up a million men in case of mobilization. The army is thus given a strategic role based on the unlikely event of an enemy ground attack, which it could not oppose in any case because it has no tactical atomic weapons and is not expected to have any until the mid-1970's, unless the program is further curtailed. The French are still one war behind, still interpreting nuclear strategy in the light of past military history in Europe.

The first lesson of nuclear warfare is that no chief of state can unilaterally impose strategic principles, especially if his army is the weaker in weaponry. But the French cling to an illusory strategy of interpenetration of ground forces, and of firing atomic weapons they do not have at terrain features to wipe out enemy regiments. The weakness of the strategy is covered up by self-serving patriotic declarations about French military independence. France's quixotic military course is based on the assumption that the *force de frappe* exists not to be used. A detailed comparison of France and Japan would be enlightening. Which is the real world power? Japan, which has no *force de frappe,* no army to speak of, no world diplomacy or pronouncements on international politics outside its Asian sphere of influence, but which is the world's third industrial power and a potential rival of both the United States and China—or France, with its atom bomb, its diplomatic incursions in Africa, North America, and the Middle East, its cultural imperialism with the propagation of the French language and its fifty thousand schoolteachers serving outside France, and its slow population and economic growth which makes even its European supremacy questionable?

4

The Ship of State

ROBESPIERRE founded the religion of the Supreme Being, but
did not guess that the deity was the state. Wars end and
revolutions fail, but the armature of the state remains and is fortified. In France the state existed before the nation. A strong central
authority was in place before the population defined itself as
French. In Germany and Italy the process was reversed: The
people thought of themselves as Germans and Italians but were
not to have a central government until the nineteenth century.
The epic past is Immortal France, but the state is Indestructible
France. Political instability does not weaken the state, it strength-
ens it. With every new regime, more care is given to the institutions that guarantee central authority. Regimes do not begin their
lives with political measures but with administrative reforms. The
state proposes a bureaucratic model for society, hierarchical, impersonal, and based on regulations.

In a manner unique in the Western world, the French state took
over the essential sectors of society. It took over all of higher education and most of secondary and primary education. It took over
radio and television to control public opinion. It took over culture

to shape public opinion. It took over urban planning to control the way French towns look. And it took over an important part of the economy to make it conform to national goals. The extent to which the state saturates national life can be shown by the need to create a separate administrative justice, with its own courts and its own statutes, which rules on cases opposing the individual and the state. The number of cases these courts try supports the theory that the central characteristic of French life is the struggle of the individual against the state.

French political practice does not resist, but encourages, *étatisme,* either by creating a vacuum of authority which leaves government policy up to civil servants, or by using the state apparatus to stifle political life, as the Fifth Republic has done. The French state is a benevolent Big Brother, which guarantees the basic freedoms because they are not a threat to its pervasiveness. French individualism is a defense against the state's repeated incursions in everyday life, while the stress on personal relations is a reaction against an anonymous administration that governs by remote control. When reforms result from political turmoil, like the education reform of 1968, they are kept within the boundaries of state control.

The French Establishment

The 1958 constitution states that the right to confer an academic degree is a state monopoly. The French mind cannot conceive of a university that is free from the tutelage of the state. Minister of Education Edgar Faure's 1968 reform, for all its merit in giving the students a say in their curriculum and the appointment of their teachers, does not dispute the merits of state monopoly. Even as far as it goes, it is an attempt to square the circle, since it must reconcile general affirmations of autonomy with the control powers of the state. The only authentic university reform would be the endowment of a private university completely independent of the state. This has never been attempted, for French higher education passed directly from the hands of the clergy to those of the state. Another condition for French university reform is the student-teacher ratio, a concept which is nonexistent in the present system.

How can there be improvements when classes continue to be crowded with two hundred and three hundred students?

France since the Third Republic has offered its citizens two kinds of education: free grade schools and high schools adequate for those seeking a modest place in society (school is compulsory up to the age of fourteen); and a university education destined to form an intellectual and power elite rather than cultured but nonspecialized men and women, on the Anglo-Saxon model. The prestige schools in the United States and England are not those that train for a government or a military career. In France the three top universities are run by the state and for the state. The students at these schools are already salaried civil servants.

Polytechnique is run by the Ministry of Defense, and its director is a general. It is credited with being the best engineering school, and owes its prestige to its distinguished alumni, including eight Marshals of France. Its 250 students wear uniforms and graduate after two years with a commission, which they often resign to enter public service or private business. Polytechnique traditionally controls key jobs like the directorship of the nationalized railroads.

The École Normale Supérieure is a teachers' college that prepares for the *agrégation,* the competitive examination to teach in *lycées* and universities. But it is really a seminary for intellectuals, philosophers like Jean-Paul Sartre, ministers like Georges Pompidou, and political thinkers like Raymond Aron. A graduate of Normale is by definition a member of the intellectual elite, even though he may spend the rest of his days teaching French literature in a provincial *lycée.* The number of writers and political figures it has produced is impressive. The entrance examination weeds out all but a tiny percentage of contenders.

The third *grande école* is the École Nationale d'Administration, founded in 1945 (another example of a new regime, in this case the Fourth Republic, concerning itself first with administrative reform) to recruit high civil servants for all branches of government. It has since given France 7 ministers, 3 ambassadors, 8 prefects, 30 *chefs de cabinet,* 80 members of ministerial cabinets, 135 members of the Cour des Comptes (the state's highest auditing body), 126 members of the Conseil d'État (the administrative supreme court), 154 Inspectors of Finance (the *crème de la crème*), 241 diplomats, and 833 other high civil servants.

Central to these meritocracies is admission as a rite of passage. Just as in certain primitive tribes the adolescent must kill a tiger before he can become a man, success in a competitive examination dictates the life and career of the young Frenchman. There are no alternatives. The only way to become an ambassador is to graduate from the ENA, just as the only sure way to teach in a university is to pass the *agrégation,* and the only way to obtain many top French business jobs is to graduate from Polytechnique. Failure in the examination means, to a certain extent, failure in life. A career is determined on the basis of grades obtained between the ages of eighteen and twenty-two. This is partly what the students meant when they said in 1968 that they were not revolting against French education but against French society, for promotion in that society goes through the exceedingly narrow doors of the *grande école.*

In an unpretentious house in the rue des Saint-Pères, ten men are seated around a table in the middle of which stands an odd-looking clock, with four faces like the four faces of Brahma, ticking away as menacingly as a time bomb while an ENA student is undergoing his final oral exam, the famous twenty-minute "conversation" during which the ten judges will try to confound, ridicule, and dumbfound him to test his intellectual resilience and the extent of his knowledge. Successful performance during those unforgiving minutes means high office, an embassy, a ministry, and perhaps, for one or two, a premiership.

The function of the *grande école* is like that of a gland: it secretes civil servants for the nation. What poses as a system for giving all candidates an equal chance is really a rationalization for the perpetuation of bourgeois elites. The assumptions are that the system is fair because there are no tuition fees to eliminate the poor and that competitive examinations give all candidates an equal chance. But the percentage of those admitted from working-class and peasant families is almost nonexistent. Legally, the schools are open to all, but socially they operate on the system of coopting, by which men of a certain background and training choose students with similar backgrounds who accept the same values. The lower-class sprinkling constitutes, as the philosopher Alain said, "enthroning a few kings born of the people, which helps give an air of justice to inequality." The system stresses the value of competitive examinations, which have been discarded elsewhere. At Cambridge, between 1850 and 1914, there existed a competitive system for mathematics called the Order of Merit. Graduates maintained a high professional level, but it soon became clear that the system had no intellectual value and did not favor original research. Only one kind of mind could succeed within the system, which was dropped. Rigid selectivity based on decimal-point grade differences is bound to be a hit-or-miss proposition. Napoleon's military science professor at the Brienne military school graded him as "incapable of commanding," and Charles de Gaulle graduated from the École Supérieure de Guerre in the bottom third of his class.

It is natural that civil service schools should produce brilliant civil service minds, for that is the product they manufacture, but inventive minds are produced only by default. No Polytechnicien or Normalien has ever won the Nobel Prize, except Jean-Paul Sartre in literature, and he turned it down. When Alfred Kastler won the Nobel Prize for physics in 1966, he was the first French scientist to get it since Louis de Broglie in 1929. As Balzac said: "Try to count on the fingers of your hand the number of geniuses furnished by the graduates of these schools." The idea of the *concours* was borrowed from imperial China whose Mandarins were chosen to command the armies on the basis of their ability to compose reports of future victories. The diploma from a *grande école* is called the Mandarin's button.

The *grandes écoles* are also powerful institutions for the perpetuation of a caste spirit, with its mental tics, superiority complex, complacency, prejudices, and fixed opinions. This has been the mentality of the French establishment since kings sold civil service jobs like real property. Today, offices are no longer owned, but they are still inherited. The son of a graduate of a *grande école* has a head start, and there are children who begin preparing for Polytechnique at the age of six. What the Mandarin factories primarily teach is a doctrine of service to the state, dividing France into a tiny but powerful minority with a highly developed sense of civic responsibility, since it has a vested interest in the state, and a huge majority which has little reason to have any. *Esprit de corps* takes on the restrictiveness of *ancien régime* guilds. Graduates pass at will from the directorates of public administration to nationalized and private industry. Georges Galichon went from the Conseil d'État to General de Gaulle's cabinet to president of Air France. The Polytechnicien Pierre Massé went from the Planning Commission to head the nationalized electric company, Electricité de France. Gilles Brac de la Perrière, an Inspector of Finance, went from the Planning Commission to head one of the biggest chemical companies, Phogil. There are dozens of such examples.

Relations between public administration and private industry become incestuous, since members of the same family run both. These men believe they are the agents of social redemption, and are able to impart a sense of mission to the most routine tasks, which is one reason for the uniformly high standard of their work. For they discover at an early age that they are the chosen few. The young graduate of the ENA with the sallow complexion and sunken eyes of someone who has spent too much time in study halls discovers that HE is the state when he gets off the train and finds the prefect's car waiting for him, with the chauffeur opening the door as he doffs his cap. These men become more like members of the Holy Roman Curia than corporation executives. French industry is discovering in an age of international competition that the advantages of hiring *grande école* graduates familiar with the labyrinth of government is outweighed by their incorrigible habit of applying juridical bureaucratic solutions to all the problems of business management. What France needs most today is one or two good schools of business administration.

The ENA graduate is versed in the cult of form and the balanced essay, which begins by listing one side of the problem and ends by balancing it with the other side. The students are given, as a model of administrative style, Saint-Just's order of the day to the Rhine Army: "The Republic sends its enemies, and receives from them, only lead." The perfect outline for an essay on England would be: First part: England is an island; Second part: Surrounded by water on all sides. Tautological thinking, the art of saying the same thing twice, lends itself to the formal, analytical, niggling mentality of the model civil servant.

Once he has passed the hurdle of the *examen de sortie*, comparable to the Open Ditch in the Grand National, the graduate can relax. Promotions among peers are determined strictly by seniority. He may never again have to prove his merit. This creates considerable dissatisfaction among those in the middle echelons, who know the exact point at which their own careers will be blocked by the Mandarins. The schools are firmly rooted in tradition. There is still a strong emphasis on descriptive geometry at Polytechnique, out of deference to its inventor, the nineteenth-century founder of the school, Gaspard Monge. When someone rashly suggested updating the program, he was told: "We've already done it; we've replaced fencing with swimming." Until 1918, the only foreign language taught was German, in keeping with the spirit of *revanche,* but with the result that many French generals were unable to communicate with their World War I allies. The students still religiously visit the battlefields of Verdun, Douaumont, and Hill 304.

Normale Supérieure also has its traditions: musty buildings, cobwebs, and showing off one's intellectual brilliance, like making up liturgical chants in Greek and Latin about the conjugal misfortunes of one's teachers. Precocity is admired, and it is a high though unofficial honor to be the youngest *agrégé* in France. There is no false modesty about belonging to the intellectual elite, none of the anti-intellectual façade that masks the brilliance of the best English universities. Trinity College at Oxford admits a certain number of dim students each year to avoid the charge of going intellectual, and one of the worst *faux pas* the undergraduate can make is betraying his cleverness, whereas the French are eager to display theirs. England has not developed an intellectual elite comparable to the products of the French *grandes écoles,* perhaps because the English establishment is still partly based on the accident of birth, and the English aristocracy is either genuinely anti-intellectual or maintains the pretense of being so.

The intellectual smugness of the Normalien was best expressed by alumnus and post-de Gaulle presidential candidate Georges Pompidou: "If he believes in God it is with the faith of Pascal, if he believes in science it is like Renan, if he believes in honor it is like Corneille, if he believes in love it is like Racine. He believes in France like Michelet, in freedom like Voltaire, and in equality like Rousseau . . . above all he believes in the reality of ideas. The Normalien is a Platonist." The Normalien is also quick to disparage lesser beings. But, as one of his critics has said, he is more Normal than Superior, and for the rest of his life his brains will give off the insipid odor of the classroom.

Rigid discipline and fierce competitiveness give these schools a barrackslike atmosphere in marked contrast to the relaxed environments of English campuses. Except for the politically militant minority, students have little time for extracurricular activity. This is true of the French university system in general. There are no fraternities or student bodies. In the absence of such groups, the students' solidarity is expressed as rebellion against the system, which helps explain the formation of student revolutionary movements like that of Daniel Cohn-Bendit. The nineteenth-century writer Maurice Barrès noted that already at the *lycée* level, to be a *bon camarade* is to rebel against authority. This solidarity against the forces of the state is part of a French education and is repeated at all levels of French society. At its most innocent, it is expressed in the hallowed Normale custom of the *canular*, or practical joke. Every graduating class competes for the ingenuity of its *canulars*. The class of 1927 received in great pomp a false Charles Lindbergh. Another class called the secretary of the Académie Française, Georges Duhamel, and said they were the telephone company checking his phone because it had lost some of its original musicality. Would he speak softly, loudly, sharply, slowly, close to the phone, far from the phone, standing on a chair—he hung up when they asked him to sing the "Marseillaise." The *canular* is an irreverent antidote to regimentation, conformity, and an overburdened academic program. At its least innocent, the irreverence becomes political, and we have student riots.

Although highly competitive, French higher education seems unduly abstract. Compare a French and an American law student. The French student learns broad categories of law like property, persons, family, and public law. The American uses the case method to learn about mortgages and domestic relations. At an American bar examination, the candidate is given a specific case, like a traffic accident, and is asked to advise and defend his client. A French bar examination will take an elegant, abstract case that may be full of traps for the candidate but is unlikely to turn up in a lifetime of practice, such as: "Can a mendicant friar begging according to the rules of his order be pursued for vagabondage?" Or, "You are Othello's lawyer, defend him against the charge of murdering Desdemona." The judges at the French bar examination want to see a performance. The top 200 students at the Paris law faculty are chosen each year for a training conference which specializes in the deliberation of improbable cases like the following: "Should a mother be charged with murder because for twenty years she used a thousand devices to convince her blind son that he was a great and admired writer, and the son, discovering the truth, killed himself?" The result is that the French lawyer may be brilliant but is imbued with general principles at the expense of hard legal information. With his training, according to a friend of mine who has passed both French and American bar examinations, he is practically useless in a U.S.-style law office. The harassed French lawyer, who sees five clients in the morning and pleads a case in the afternoon because he prefers working alone to joining a large office, must get his opinions out of law books on the principle that if you quote from one book it is plagiarism but if you quote from two books it is research.

Examples could be multiplied among the various disciplines to show that French higher education, the priority of priorities in a country where it is practically the only means of social promotion, is dogmatic, abstract, and inappropriate to the needs of a modern society. It took the May-June riots to shock the government into awareness of the dismal condition of its educational system and into laying to rest the outmoded principles of the imperial university. The day when a drumroll announced the time for reciting Latin verb tenses and the Minister of Education could take out his watch and proudly announce that "at this moment in every *lycée* in France every sixth-grade student is translating Vergil's *Aeneid*" is over. The mania for grading is also being replaced by more flexible methods. The French schoolboy's life was confined within the brackets of a grading system that went from 0 (nullity) to 20 (perfection). This passion for grading was reflected in the earliest classes, where six-year-old boys and girls were ranked according to academic excellence. I often wondered what the effects were on the six-year-old boy who started out life thirty-fifth in a class of 35.

Now that the Ministry of Education has strongly advised teachers to drop the system and replace it with more general evaluations of individual progress, the rule of the *fort en thème* (grind) may be coming to an end, and that will be a minor revolution of its own. It will take a generation to bury calibrated, regurgitative education. The textbooks will have to be changed—the kind that teach eight-year-olds that a tree has a trunk, that the trunk has branches, that the branches have leaves, and that the leaves have veins, all summarized in bold print at the bottom of the page for the children to memorize. Institutional reforms are only meaningful insofar as they alter social attitudes (e.g., the U.S. Supreme Court decision on school integration). As those contemporary sages the Beatles point out:

> You tell me it's the institution
> Well you know
> You better change your mind instead.

Perhaps the day will come when professors and students at the Sorbonne will no longer use different doors. Perhaps the Ministry of Education, with its 25,000 employees, will no longer feel the need to pepper the schools with an average of two circulars a day. The government has realized that in a nationalized educational system, a revolt against the university can degenerate into a revolt against the state. The huge umbrellalike apparatus is vulnerable to attacks at any one of its many points. Criticism of the school program, like criticism of television programs, becomes an attack on the government from which they originate.

The Spine of Institutions

In the American experience, institutions are regarded as antiseptic: They are not intended to improve the individual, but to provide enough social order so that he can improve himself. The American constitution was drafted to protect the individual's rights, not make him a better person. In the French experience, institutions are viewed as therapeutic: The state assumes a moral role. Public virtue becomes a model for private virtue, and the state considers itself the agent of society's progress. The Code Civil was drafted as a model for good citizens, and is based on obedience to the state. Equality is seen as equality before the state apparatus, and freedom is seen as the state's ability to regulate and adjust conflicting interests. Every law student must take a course in the history of institutions, whereby he learns that since the Romans colonized Gaul, the patient process of centralization has seldom flagged.

France is protected from itself by a cocoon of laws and regulations. Since the French have never been given the opportunity to shed this cocoon, chiefs of state justify its existence by saying that the people cannot do without it. Napoleon III expressed his regret to American ambassador Elihu Washburne that "the French people are not better fitted for more liberal institutions, and for the concessions he desired to make for them. The great trouble with the French is that they always look to the government for everything instead of depending upon themselves." What the emperor was trying to say was that they had never been allowed to look anywhere else. Administrative centralization, like language and the king's army, was one of the instruments that made the French state. In fact, centralization was the French state, which can date its existence from the birth of a class of civil servants. Centralization has meant something different for every regime. For kings it was a way of coping with rebellious feudal lords, for the Revolution it allowed an active minority to govern, for Napoleon it was a way of recruiting troops and milking the nation of its resources, for the Third and Fourth Republics it kept the country going despite a political vacuum, and for the Fifth Republic it is a way to fill the vacuum and change France. But how can France be changed unless its most constant and least challenged aspect is also changed?

Whether under Charles the Bald or Charles de Gaulle, institutions have been based on identical assumptions: That the individual exists for the state rather than the state for the individual, that legislation is a matter of reason rather than custom, and that there is no discrepancy between life as it is lived and life as it is imagined by bureaucrats. When the monarchy wanted a model for the centralized state, it passed over the experience of feudal independence and the common law of the Franks to find in Roman law a precedent that suited its needs. Rome had left a body of laws to settle any problem, a legal tradition more real than the customs of peoples, and a system of values that placed order and unity above personal welfare.

The model chosen to administer France was colonial, which helps explain why foreign visitors still have the impression that the provinces are being governed by emissaries of some distant colonial power. French kings adopted the prerogatives of Roman emperors: the right to collect taxes, raise troops, mint currency, and mete out justice. Tax evasion goes back to the Gauls, who resisted Roman taxes. A Roman tax collector named Marcus was run out of the province of Limousin by the populace. The recruitment of a standing army was also laborious, based as it was on the wiles of recruiting sergeants and plagued as it was by a high rate of desertion. Most successful of the monarchy's measures was the foundation of a professional civil service, which also became a source of revenue, through the sale of offices. This caste has managed to perpetuate itself through empires and republics, and when offices were no longer venal they could still be controlled through the connection between family background and success in competitive examinations. One of the most ancient beliefs of Frenchmen is that the best way to get ahead is to find a government job. The man who works for the state has the comfortable feeling of being at the source of power, no matter how menial his task. French civil servants should learn Parkinson's laws, particularly the one that says: "The man who is denied the possibility of making important decisions will regard as important those decisions he is allowed to make."

Families like the Nicolaï, members of the robe nobility, served kings from father to son in similar jobs for over a century. Their counterparts can be found in the Fifth Republic among the *grands commis de l'état* (high clerks of the state), as the robe nobility is known today. Cabinet ministers are descended from Philippe le Bel's Clerks of the Secret, recruited in 1309 to draft royal decrees (General de Gaulle's ministers were the atavistic descendants of these scribes). Under a strong executive, the ministerial portfolio is not radically different from the royal secretary's briefcase. The prefects of departments are the heirs of the royal Intendants established by Richelieu. The National Assembly finds a distant cousin in the Marzfeld assemblies of the Franks, which developed into assemblies of the three estates (nobility, clergy, and the rest of the nation) under the monarchy. But the absence of any genuine parliamentary tradition on the English model crippled the first real parliamentary experiment under the Revolution.

The impotence of French assemblies begins in 1793, when a tiny parliamentary committee, ostensibly in charge of public safety, became the most dictatorial executive France has known. It was as if America were being governed by the Senate Judiciary Committee. This was the French parliament's original sin: it showed that unless it is driven, it drifts. The following definition of public administration, taken from the *Dictionary of Institutions,* is valid for every regime: "The administration consists in the totality of the means destined to bring the central power, with the greatest possible swiftness and certainty, to all the parts of society, and to bring back to the central power, in identical circumstances, the forces of society, either in men or in money."

Napoleon's highest priority was manpower. The prefects assumed the responsibilities of recruiting sergeants. He told them he would judge the quality of their administration by the success of conscription. As long as the essential requirements for his campaigns were met, he was willing to indulge the illusion of freedom in other matters, chiding the prefect of the Lower Rhine for attempting to make vaccination mandatory. Napoleon recruited many of his administrators from among the former civil servants of the *ancien régime.* "They are the only ones who know how to serve," he said. All prefects were picked from outside the departments they governed so that they would not be subject to local influences. Napoleon called them ministers but punished them when they took decisions on their own. He flattered Castellane, the prefect of the Lower Alps, by saying: "You are a pasha here. Once you are a hundred leagues from the capital, you have more power than I have." But in fact he controlled them severely and considered them agents of his decisions, not viceroys.

Napoleon stifled private social groups. The penal code prohibited associations of more than twenty persons without government permission. Suspicion of groups that escape its control is another constant of the state apparatus—Richelieu pressuring an informal literary group to become the Académie Française, Napoleon suppressing harmless provincial clubs, and Minister of the Interior Raymond Marcellin outlawing student groups after the 1968 riots, all proceed from the same mentality, and help explain the absence of intermediate bodies which prevents France from being an open, pluralistic society.

Napoleon accurately prophesied that his administrative reforms would last longer than his conquests. "I count more on the Code than on the greatest victories," he wrote his brother Jérôme, "to extend and affirm our power." He was right in calling his Code Civil "a mass of granite." Its 2,281 articles and countless amendments still constitute the basic French legal text. It governs relations between persons, property, and the way property may be acquired. Bourgeois, patriarchal, and counterrevolutionary in spirit, it dispersed rural property, subordinated women to men, and made the authority of the chief of family a microcosm of the authority of the chief of state. Until the article was abrogated in 1907, a son under thirty could not marry without the consent of his parents unless he advised them in three formal acts registered by the state. The Code gave a position to real property which does not correspond to its importance in a modern capitalistic society, and that is one of the reasons for the *bas-de-laine* mentality. The Code Civil took record keeping away from the church, and set up public records offices, which defined the individual's legal existence—his birth, his death, his marriage, and his children. What is not set down in the margins of the *acte d'état civil* cannot be proved real. Registration of birth is more important than birth itself.

The archetypal French joke has to do with the relations between the individual and the state. A man goes to his local *mairie* to register the birth of his son.

"Last name?" the clerk asks.

"Hugo."

"First name?"

"Victor."

"Congratulations," says the clerk, "on being the father of France's greatest poet."

The Code was praised not only for defining proper French conduct concerning persons and property, but for the quality of its language. The Code shows that French is not the language of love but of property rights, mortgages, annuities, and contracts. Many English legal terms, like tort, judge, and venue, are of French origin. The language and the use to which it was put by the state interacted. The French language helped shape and was partly shaped by juridical and legal thinking, just as English today is being changed by its use as the language of cybernetics and computer technology. The pride of the Code Civil is that precedents are not binding because it has foreseen every possible case and established detailed legal principles to cover it. This godlike foresight strongly influences French legal thinking. A French lawyer tells his client: "The case you have just described comes under Section 1356 of the Code, or Section 2121." He flips through the pages, confirming his citations, looks puzzled, and finally announces: "No, it does not come within either of those sections. I am sorry, monsieur, but I can do nothing for you. There is no law covering your case."

The Code was also meant to be an instrument of French glory. It was imposed on conquered territories like Holland and Belgium, and fifty years later was adopted by unified Italy. It turned up in countries as far-flung as Japan, where a Frenchman named Boissonade was hired to draft a suitable version, which the emperors of the Rising Sun applied from 1880 to 1896. Louisiana still owes much of its civil code to Napoleon, as Stanley Kowalski reminded his wife in *Streetcar Named Desire*. One offspring of the Code adopted in the United States is the joint tax return, based on the idea that family property should not be taxed as heavily as individual property.

Finally, the Code made the personal life of citizens a state concern by viewing marriage as a contract and celebrating a civil wedding ceremony. Napoleon personally insisted on allowing divorce by mutual agreement, for by the time the Code became law in 1804 he was already planning to replace Josephine. More than a century later, continuing the practice of passing laws for the personal convenience of statesmen, Premier Paul Reynaud had the time lapse for the final divorce decree shortened so that he could marry his mistress, Madame de Portes.

With its hive of regulations, post-Napoleonic France seemed stable because it was uniform. Every public garden posted the identical notice that "it is forbidden to light a fire under any pretext, to fire any firearm, even with blanks, to beat a drum, blow a horn, a bugle, or a trumpet, to beat rugs, pillows, or make mattresses, to take a bath, wash laundry, startle the aquatic birds, play with balls, balloons, hoops, bicycles and other games which are tolerated only for children." Revolution did not disturb the regulation of society, and *coups d'état* occurring with such frequency came to be considered the normal process for the passage of power, as in 1789, 1793, 1815, 1830, 1848, 1851, 1871, 1940, 1944, and 1958—not the least and perhaps not the last. Change through crisis becomes normal because the bureaucratic ideal is not to think in terms of change but to create an enormous and impersonal force which controls the environment. The refusal to allow for change is enshrined in the expression, *plus ça change, plus c'est la même chose.* The bureaucratic model of society, satisfied with its laws and usages, creates a situation that can only be resolved through crisis. The principal benefit of General de Gaulle's resignation in 1969 was that it allowed the passage of power without a crisis, thanks to orderly presidential elections.

From being the safeguard of changeless France, the administration became changeless France, defined by abstract uniformity, overregulation, and an anonymous, Paris-based bureacracy that swallowed crises and digested them as red tape. No one has understood the bureaucratic model of society better than Marx: "The formalism of the state which is bureaucracy is the state seen as formalism ... it becomes a real power, its own substance and content, and then it goes without saying that bureaucracy becomes a tissue of illusions. The bureaucratic mind is totally Jesuitic and theological ... the bureaucracy is the priest republic ... the aims of the state are transformed into the aims of the bureaucracy ... the examination to become civil servant is but a masonic formality, the legal recognition that civic duty is a privilege."

In few other countries are civil service careers so sought after. This is because the most prestigious schools are precisely those which train for government service; because after the battle of competitive examinations, the government provides security; because so many jobs, which in other countries would be in the private sector, are government jobs; because these jobs are the only tested way to power; because considerable prestige is attached to membership in one of the *grands corps de l'état;* because in an unstable country, the civil servants have valid reasons for considering themselves the custodians of permanent French values; because there is a tradition of civil service unrivaled except in certain long-dead oriental societies; and because working for the state is considered more patriotic and honest than a business career. Serving a variety of regimes, the civil service acquired a sense of mission and of its own importance and a passion for authority which has come to be reflected in other areas of French life: the schools, the family, and business, with its divine-right *patron*. The state also became the biggest employer; there are twice as many civil servants in France as in Great Britain. Because working for the state is selfless, the civil servant does not earn a salary; he is given a remuneration to enable him to maintain proper status.

The grand design is based on the social animal's need for order and rationality, but it is pushed to absurd lengths. The state pours out a flood of ordinances on everything from the cost of funerals to the size of coffee grains and baby bottles. There is a man in the Ministry of Agriculture who has worked out what the profit margin should be for pluckers of angora rabbits. To fix a belfry in Quimper in 1768 or a school radiator in Arles in 1968, the decision from the proper ministry in Paris was and is still needed. An office worker in the Ministry of Finance once figured out that it took seventeen steps to obtain a refill for a pastepot, from the first written request to the actual arrival of the paste. To hire a concierge for a housing development, the decision must be approved by the prefect and the treasurer of the department, formalities that cost more than the expense involved. According to a 1949 decree, the concierge must clean the courtyard each week, "devoting one minute and a half per square meter for the first forty meters and thirty seconds per square meter for the remaining surface." Centralization breeds inertia, for civil servants sometimes prefer to do without rather than plunge into the red tape. They have developed that particular French trait called *débrouillardise,* which is the art of obtaining results outside the bureaucratic system. Instead of going through the seventeen steps for a paste jar, the *débrouillard* office worker steals it from a coworker.

Just because the state is omnipresent does not mean it is efficient, and agencies often find themselves with money that has been allotted but cannot be spent. The city of Paris in 1962 was unable to spend millions of francs earmarked for new schools because the school buildings did not comply with Ministry of Education standards. The blunders of officialdom are legion, as in the case of the woman in Nîmes who received a notice from the Social Security that she was no longer eligible for payments; the reason given at the bottom of the page: Decease of recipient. As Balzac said: "The United States, Germany, and England, who have no Polytechnique school, will have railroads when our engineers are still working on the blueprints . . . in France not a single brick can be laid until ten paper pushers have written their foolish and useless reports."

The perfect bureaucracy would administer only itself, its initial and only mission would be control. The French administration still has a dual mission, that of controlling the citizens as well as itself. A prefect is like an ambassador in a foreign country, writing confidential reports to the Ministry of the Interior on the political trends in his territory and the morale of the citizens. Nowhere more strongly than in these reports does one gain the impression that the state and the individual are adversaries, and that the purpose of the state is to protect itself from the whims of its citizens. Baron Pasquier, the president of the Chamber of Peers under Louis-Philippe, said with disgust: "What do you think of a prefect who can't control public opinion in his department?" The task of a Gaullist prefect, particularly at election time, was no different. Like a Tammany ward heeler, his most urgent job was to get in the vote.

The mania for control makes the most prestigious civil service job the Inspection of Finance, which controls other civil servants. Control at all levels is an essential part of the four-tier system: the 90 departments, the 450 *arrondissements,* the 3,000 cantons, and the 38,000 communes. The Ministry of Agriculture alone has eleven inspectorates, while the Ministry of Education has five. Bureaucratic vanity and long-windedness are other essential characteristics. Go today to any ministry and be awed by the liveried ushers, their solemn mien, the pomp of the waiting room, the mysterious screens that stand everywhere, the doors that open on other doors until the inner sanctum is reached, furnished in Louis XIV or Louis XV, the minister sitting behind a Boulle desk with the uncertain air of a traveler caught in a first-class waiting room between trains. The imposing escort of bureaucratic vanity seems more real than he is.

As for verbosity, millions in paper costs could be saved by suppressing elaborate salutations on the order of "I do not doubt, sir, that you will do everything in your power to see to it that the dispositions of this letter are carried out with your customary haste and zeal. I remain sir, etc." It is not the minister who drafts these letters, for, as the saying goes, the sure sign of promotion in the civil service is that as you rise you write less and sign more.

The citizen, outnumbered and outmanned, fights a losing battle with the state apparatus. There are a few isolated heroes, like the man whose telephone was out of order and who obediently paid his "do not fold" bill, but wrinkled it; he claims that service improved. But usually to tangle with officialdom is to taste defeat, like the man who wanted to withdraw his money from his post-office savings account. He asked for his balance in writing and made out a check for the amount. The check was returned with the comment, "account overdrawn." Upon inquiry, he learned that all written requests for information are charged 10 centimes, so that he was overdrawn by 10 centimes. He made out a new check less 20 centimes to cover the cost of two written requests, and it was again returned. He again inquired and was told that all overdrawn checks are fined 2.50 francs. Such stories have no end. They confirm the impression that civil servants are indifferent to human feelings. Overcautious because they are overcontrolled, they know the joys of lack of commitment. They seem to take genuine pleasure in presenting the citizen with the hopeless intricacies of the regulations, in making him fill out the same form five times, in telling him that his dossier is incomplete, and in generally reducing him to a state of slavering paralysis.

The system, so careful about recruiting elites at the upper echelon, invites mediocrity in the middle and lower ranks. It is not uncommon in a French *mairie*, which has recently converted from the use of quill pens, to see a secretary haltingly typing out documents with two fingers; but she will never be fired because she is somebody's niece. Not only are improvisation and precipitation condemned, but the civil servant lives in a Platonic world where he dislikes to confront his construction of things with a reality that may disprove it. Alexis Leger (the poet Saint-John Perse, winner of the 1960 Nobel Prize), who was political director of the Quai d'Orsay in the late 1930's, shared the bureaucratic dislike of the awkward truth to the point of discouraging foreign ambassadors in Paris from warning their governments about the dangers of the Nazi-Soviet pact.

The ageless bureaucracy has its own devices for carrying out the decrees of Colbert, Napoleon, Vichy France, and de Gaulle, all of which have remained on the books in confusing accretion. What they have in common is the aim to limit local freedom. If the provinces lag, if they have no public libraries or parent-teacher associations, it is because they have always been placed in a subservient administrative position. The evils of local autonomy are used to explain everything from a peasant protest to the loss of Algeria. It was frequently said in the National Assembly that Algeria was lost because it was underadministered; local freedoms are equated with disorder and disintegration. The regional reforms which were voted down under de Gaulle run against a thousand years of history and administrative practice, and any decentralization is bound to be hedged against the fear of dissolution of the state apparatus. Bureaucracy, with its reluctance to delegate authority, determined the style of French colonialism, except in the cases of soldiers like Lyautey, who seized it. The archives of the colonial administration are full of open-ended correspondence between India or Indochina or Morocco and Paris over cases involving a resident French lady's virtue or a cow that has wandered into a neighbor's pasture. Bureaucracy has also partly determined labor-management relations: Because the state was so slow to give the working class the right to strike and organize, it played into the hands of the Communist Party, which took control of the labor movement after World War I.

The mania for order makes French regimes more vulnerable to disorder. The revolutions of 1830 and 1848 were Paris disorders which in another country could have been kept under manageable proportions through a wide repertoire of political processes, like light fuses which keep an overheated electric circuit from blacking out an entire house, but in the French system there are no light fuses, and public disorder is immediately escalated into a revolution. Governments are upset by strikes. Clemenceau, the strong man of the Third Republic, was upset in 1909 as the result of a post office employees' strike, and General de Gaulle, the strong man of the Fifth Republic, was almost upset by combined student-worker disorders. Finally, a society erected on a bureaucratic model, convinced that salvation lies within itself, discourages the individual from believing in his own destiny; the French stereotype is not the self-made man, but the little employee resigned to his lot. Many citizens have nowhere to turn but to the state, which traditionally saves its lowest jobs, like ushers and minor clerks, as a form of welfare for veterans and other worthies. The state reserves for itself a monopoly on progress and the general good, and does nothing to encourage intermediate bodies such as clubs, lodges, unions, foundations, lobbies, parties, all those private associations of citizens that define a pluralistic society.

It is not felt in France that the state should delegate to the private sector any public responsibilities. And yet, in 1968, Minister of Culture André Malraux asked one of his experts, Michel Pomey, to write a report on the American foundation system. Mr. Pomey concluded that foundations play an essential role in society for the safeguard of freedom. There is no mechanism in France for setting up foundations or for pressure groups to make themselves heard. Pressures remain hidden, like the payments made to friendly deputies by the French management association, or disruptive, like student riots and plant occupations. The only permanently effective pressure group is the state, which balances its aid to private industry against "suggestions" on wages and prices. Premier Michel Debré asked the National Management Association (Conseil National du Patronat Français) on March 6, 1961, to fix salary increases in private industry at 4 percent a year. What in a democratic country would be arrived at by labor-management collective bargaining is in France decreed by the state, which also sends circulars to agricultural associations telling them what the price of milk and butter should be.

Pressure groups operate more effectively against one another, with the state acting as arbiter. When the Paris Faculty of Science wanted to build new university buildings, it thought of expropriating the rambling wine market (*Halle aux Vins*) on the Seine. The wine merchants lobbied to stay where they were. But in such cases the decision goes to the group that can present itself as most virtuous. The university described a struggle between the disinterested and enlightened aims of science and those grasping enemies of knowledge and progress, the wine merchants, who were duly eased out. The weakness of French pressure groups is also caused by a tendency toward fragmentation; there are, for example, half a dozen livestock associations and dozens of educational associations, badly organized, amateurish, some of them existing in name only. Also, the pressure group's normal channel to power, the National Assembly, could not be counted on under de Gaulle, when its role was reduced to that of a chorus.

The most successful pressure group in post-World-War-II France has been the army. Its dissatisfaction over being asked to fight and lose two major colonial wars has made the government unsure of being able to count on its support. De Gaulle in June, 1968, had to fly to Germany to negotiate the support of his generals when France was paralyzed by strikes. He obtained promises of loyalty against an amnesty of the soldiers and civilians who were still jailed or exiled for their Algérie Française stand. This is France's banana-republic side—army support in times of crisis depends on collective bargaining between the generals and the chief of state. The most unsuccessful pressure group is probably the Communist Party, which has its own network of organizations, from women's clubs to rock-'n'-roll magazines, and represents a coherent body of interests, which it is unable to advance. The best the Communists can do is take credit for labor gains that are decided in conferences between the three major unions, management, and the state. But the party has always been more concerned with maintaining its hold over 20 percent of the electorate than in pressing the interests it defends.

If the Communists are an example of a political party which fails as a pressure group, Poujadism was a pressure group that failed as a political party. Initially it defended the interests of shopkeepers; its principal platform was tax evasion. Then it penetrated peasant society, and eventually cut across class lines to recruit the systematic malcontents, those who make it their vocation to "thunder against," as Flaubert said, the state, the intellectuals, the Parliament, the foreigners, the unions, and the civil servants, all those, in short, whose only basis for association is the opportunity to rail at all other associations. Poujadism represented the most visceral level of chauvinism and xenophobia; the primitive nature of its appeal cast doubt on the widespread conviction that the French as a people are intelligent. Poujade spread the time-honored Café du Commerce philosophy: "Our fathers who went to the bistro won Verdun," he said, "when Mendès-France wasn't around." "If you had one drop of Gaulois blood in your veins," Poujade told Mendès, "you would never have dared drink a glass of milk at an international gathering." Poujadism provided a forum for the beetle-browed incompetents of French society who, because they are incapable of adapting to the twentieth century, claim to represent eternal France—men like Léon Dupont, a northern landowner who calls himself "the wild boar of the Ardennes," and who published the Poujadist newspaper, *Buckshot*. He boasted that on his editorial staff there were "no half-breeds, cops, queers, thieves, or counterfeiters." He railed against conspiracies at high levels and the decadence of the French race. Intellectuals he called "masturbators of bulls" (an allusion to artificial insemination experiments), while union leaders and civil servants, he said, "are always inside the politician's pants." During its brief heyday in the mid-fifties, Poujadism showed the strange but eventually ineffective shapes French pressure groups can take.

The Lady with the Blindfold

Because the state has its finger in so many pies, the concept of public order is much broader in France than in most Western countries. France is a police state, not in a tyrannical, harshly punitive, or arbitrary manner, but in the broad mandate given to the enforcers of public order. The job of the police is not merely to enforce law and make arrests, it is to cooperate with civilian government in the regulation of society. The French state is policed in the same sense that Catherine de Medici talked about policing manners. It has broad duties of control over all citizens, not only those who break the law. Criminals are only one of its concerns. Therefore, the French police are not, like the American police, a separate subculture that identifies with the aspirations of a *déclassé*, lower middle class. They are, rather, armed bureaucrats who contribute to the national ideal of order, impersonal and ubiquitous.

There is also in the French system a close association between the police and the judiciary. Magistrates once doubled as police commissioners, and today criminal cases are investigated, before they go to trial, by an examining magistrate working closely with the police to ascertain whether the state has a strong enough case to prosecute. The French claim to an independent magistrature

is sorely tested by the frequent collusion between judge and policeman. They are both part of the state apparatus, and serve the
regime. In the political kidnaping of the Moroccan nationalist
Ben Barka, in which the French secret service was implicated, the
Paris police was ordered by the government to withhold information from the examining magistrate, who kept up the pretense of
an independent investigation although he was aware of the pressures involved.

Broad police powers go back to the appointment of a Paris police
lieutenant by Louis XIV. He was, in fact, governor of Paris, responsible for sanitation, lighting, and the other city services. His job
was more administrative than disciplinary, as is today the job of
the Paris police prefect, who is part mayor and part cop. He is still
responsible for public health, sanitary conditions in stores and
hotels, the spread of contagious diseases, the violation of slum
ordinances, and control of the capital's doctors. Two hundred
and fifty Paris detectives serve as food inspectors. These sleuths
are more like Madame Maigret than Maigret as they check
butchers' scales for honest weight, look for traces of margarine
in *croissants au beurre,* and sample the truffled *foie gras* in *char-
cuteries* to see if it is made with less expensive Moroccan white
truffles dyed black. Paris police prefects are not veteran cops but
administrators who move on to become ambassadors or the heads
of nationalized industries. The police prefect tends to have a
philosophical concept of his job; he sees it not in terms of punishing criminals but as a means of helping citizens attain a better
standard of conduct. He places himself in the French moralist
tradition. Antoine Claude, who was Paris police prefect under
five regimes in the nineteenth century, wrote: "I can only compare a police prefect to the director of a hospital—like him, he
sees of humanity but its wounds and afflictions."

The Paris prefect is a law unto himself, but the national police
is under the Ministry of the Interior. Every regime has given the
police wide powers. The Revolution developed into a struggle
between two rival police organizations, the Committee for Public
Safety and the Committee for General Security. During the Terror, the police technique of denunciation became a civic virtue.

The police became political, so that with each regime it had to
be purged. Under Napoleon, it was used to repress strikes, and

still is. The black cabinet of the *ancien régime* was kept up on a far grander scale—Napoleon once complained that in one month only twelve thousand letters had been opened and read. The modern function of the black cabinet is not opening mail but eavesdropping on telephone conversations. During the 1969 presidential election, a deputy asked the Ministry of the Interior whether wiretaps could be suspended for the duration of the campaign. He received no reply.

Special police organizations are still given overtly political jobs which entail the use of commandolike methods. As though confirming that France has a repertory of situations from which it draws repeatedly, the *barbouzes* (bearded ones, or special police) kidnaped Secret Army Organization leader Antoine Argoud in Munich in much the same way that the duc d'Enghien was kidnaped by Napoleon in Germany in 1804. The duc d'Enghien was the last prince of Condé, and was living in exile in the house of an old friend, just over the French border in Ettenheim, near the Rhine. Napoleon mistakenly suspected him of having taken part in a conspiracy, and on March 15, General Ordener and 300 dragoons crossed the Rhine, surrounded the house, and seized d'Enghien at 5 A.M. Three days later he was shot in Vincennes fortress, not for conspiracy (a charge that could not be proven), but as an émigré who had borne arms against France. Argoud was more fortunate; he was amnestied by General de Gaulle.

Different kinds of police proliferate in France. It is hard to keep straight the attributions and chains of command of security forces like the Police Judiciaire, in charge of criminal investigations, the *gendarmerie,* a kind of rural police recruited by the army but deployed by the Ministry of the Interior, and the riot police, or CRS (Compagnies Républicaines de Sécurité). Adding them up, France has roughly as many policemen per capita as the United States, 1 for 347 against 1 for 340.

The CRS are most vulnerable to press and public criticism because violence is inherent in their mission of riot repression. They are unpopular, but the livelihood of the regime depends on them, as it did in May-June, 1968. Its men are more prone to racist and other prejudices because they are sent into combat against active minorities like the Algerians and the students, rather than being used for general law enforcement. The civilian population is to them a hostile environment, and they take their revenge by beating up and humiliating many of those they arrest. The effectiveness of the 17,500 CRS (one-third of the total uniformed police force, which goes under the blanket name of Sûreté Nationale) depends on heating their tempers before they are thrown into action. Instead of being kept in their barracks until they are needed, they are sent to likely trouble spots, caged like mastiffs in their dark-blue grill-windowed vans, a captive audience for the taunts of passersby. After being told for hours that they are cuckolds and SS (a particularly infuriating jibe to those among them who were deported by the Germans), they are fighting mad by the time they are unleashed. In the street battles of 1968, each side fought the symbol of its hates, the students arbitrary police action and brutality, the CRS the youthful revolutionaries of bourgeois background who did not know what it was to work for a living. It was a special pleasure for these men of limited education and lower-class social background to take over that temple of wisdom, the Sorbonne, and clean up the mess left by the students; it gave them valid reasons for despising intellectuals.

Finally, the French police has its particular traditions. Every Minister of the Interior and every police prefect finds his own secret dossier on his desk when he takes power, as a kind of welcome mat. And more than in other Western countries, the police in France relies heavily on informers and the infiltration of what it calls *le milieu* (the criminal element). Under Louis XV, police lieutenant d'Argenson boasted about his network of informants. "I recruit them in all classes," he said, "particularly among dukes and valets." More recently, police commissioner Chenevier asked his men: "Do you have your informers? No? Then find another job, for you may succeed in it, but you will never succeed in the police." The use of *mouchards* (stool pigeons) persists. Convicts on parole, whores, and immigrants with false papers are allowed a certain leeway in exchange for information; an alliance is formed between the police and the criminal.

In France, however, the majority of blood crimes are not the work of the *milieu*. A sampling of crime newsclippings over the years shows the recurrence of child brutality and female vengeance; they seem to have some hard-to-define but privileged place in the French social fabric. Parents who beat their children to death or chain them to their beds or otherwise mistreat them are an unpleasantly common occurrence; less common, particularly in recent years, but equally surprising, is the number of cases in which spurned women disfigure their lovers by throwing vitriol at them. The most spectacular crimes are not great robberies as in England, or kidnapings, as in the United States, but crimes of passion, usually removed from the profit motive. The Frenchman seems to murder less for money than to solve an impossible personal situation. The crime of passion is the exception to the rule that the French are a reasonable people with a high degree of adaptability to social situations.

Out of the marquis de Sade's imagination might have come the case of twenty-nine-year-old Denise l'Abbé, who filled her washing machine with soapy water and drowned her two-and-a-half-year-old daughter in it, because her lover, named Algarron, a twenty-five-year-old former student of the Jesuits and second lieutenant in the artillery, had asked her to do it as a proof of love. Once caught, each tried to place the blame for this ritualistic murder committed in the name of love on the other. Another famous *crime passionnel* of the 1950's involved the parish priest of the village of Uruffe, thirty-five-year-old Guy Desnoyers. He became friendly with the eighteen-year-old daughter of a glassblower, Régine Fays, slept with her, and made her pregnant. In the eighth month of her pregnancy, in December, 1956, he took her for a drive in the country, stopped the car in a lane, and said: "I am going to give you absolution. Do you forgive me?" "I forgive you," she said, "but I don't want your absolution." When he insisted she started back on foot. He got out of the car and fired three feet away from her. She fell on her back. He knelt, performed a Cesarean with a penknife, removed the unborn child, which was alive and opened its eyes, baptized it, cut its face to disfigure it, and stabbed it in the back, being careful not to sever the umbilical cord, since according to Catholic teaching a child attached to its mother is still a soulless embryo. His defense lawyer saved him from capital punishment with a prayer of his own: "God of the faithful, tell these judges that they have no right to touch a life which belongs only to you." "What then must a man do to deserve capital punishment," the prosecution asked? Father Desnoyers was sentenced to forced labor for life, and remained the double man, priest and murderer, throughout his trial, saying: "Poor Régine, I hope she had time to prepare her soul after death."

Capital punishment exsits in France, but is used sparingly. From 1946 to 1956, 240 persons were sentenced to death, but the slanting blade of the guillotine severed the necks of only 78; the rest were pardoned. Acquittals, however, are so unusual in French criminal trials that in the summer of 1968, when a bricklayer of Polish origin was acquitted of murdering a twelve-year-old girl, it was front-page news. Thanks to the system of the examining magistrate and the court's refusal nine times out of ten to grant bail, the defendant in France is guilty until proven innocent. It is considered more useful to the state to lock up ten innocent men than to let a single guilty one go free. In every criminal case, while the suspect waits in jail, there is a long preliminary phase during which a state-appointed judge, called an examining magistrate, investigates the crime to see if there is enough evidence to support a conviction. The magistrate works closely with the police, who help him round up suspects and witnesses.

The examining magistrate's investigation can take up to two and a half years. The nature of his task commits him. If the report he sends to the public prosecutor concludes that the case should come to trial, the obvious inference is that he considers the suspect guilty beyond doubt. He is saying in effect: "After sifting all the available evidence, I for one am convinced that the man is guilty, although if he can explain his conduct to the satisfaction of a jury, they have the power to free him." Thus guilt is determined at the investigative level, not at the trial. The examining magistrate is at the same time detective, prosecutor, and judge. He can recommend that there are no grounds for prosecution if the evidence is weak or "messy," as in a recent case of a respected professor who shot himself in the nape of the neck. This is physically possible, although it is unusual that a man bent on suicide should be so acrobatic about it. The magistrate had a strong impression that the man's wife was guilty, but could find no solid evidence, and the case was dropped. Since 1897, the defense lawyer has the right to study the examining magistrate's report and find out what the evidence against his client is. Under this system, a case that reaches trial is tantamount to conviction. As a lawyer friend of mine put it, "I have never defended an innocent man in a criminal trial."

Not only are suspects found guilty before they are tried, but they often serve their sentence before they are convicted. In 1967, the prison population of France totaled 33,831. Of these, 40 percent, or 12,767, were awaiting trial. There is no law denying bail, but it is a time-honored practice that the presence of the defendant is required by the examining magistrate. There are no bondsmen and therefore no guarantees that he will not vanish, and the judges feel it is immoral to do favors for criminals—the unspoken reason is that there are heavy presumptions of guilt, although keeping a man for several years under preventive imprisonment is simply another factor that will influence the jury to believe in his guilt. The examining magistrates sometimes recommend sentences that correspond to the time the suspect has already spent in jail. He is thus tried, found guilty, and released, having served his time before he came to trial. It also happens, as in the case of the Polish bricklayer, that an innocent man spends years in jail waiting for his case to come up.

What a lawyer can do is have a felony reduced to a misdemeanor so that it will be tried more quickly in Magistrate's Court (Correctionnelle), which can give no more than a five-year sentence, instead of in Special Sessions (Assises), which involves a long investigation and a jury trial. Jean Castel, who operates a fashionable left-bank nightclub, had a rape charge reduced to simple assault in 1968 so that it could be brought before Correctionnelle rather than Assises, which criminal lawyers avoid whenever possible. Another instance of state interference is that the jury is not considered competent to deliberate alone. The nine jurors are joined by the three Assises judges who presided at the trial, and whose knowledge and experience turn the deliberations into a lecture. A defendant can be convicted by a minority of the jurors voting with the three judges. The underlying assumption is that a man cannot be judged by his peers, who must be controlled by the state apparatus. In any French criminal trial, the lawyers address not the jury but the trinity of judges who, they know, will control the fate of their client.

A final particularity of French justice is that the concept of habeas corpus does not exist. "I have never understood what it was," my lawyer friend said. Its absence means that in France suspects can be imprisoned without a writ from a judge. Under the procedure of *garde à vue* (administrative surveillance), anyone can be held without charges or even without being formally arrested, as several dozen students discovered during the 1968 spring riots. They dropped out of circulation and reappeared after a week or two, having been locked up and questioned in the meantime. *Garde à vue* arrests are leftovers from the sealed-letter method by which the monarchy locked up undesirables without a trial for indeterminate periods of time. The only thing that has changed is that they are no longer put to the torture of the wheel.

The 4,102 French magistrates are civil servants paid by the Ministry of Justice, after graduating from the state School for Judiciary Studies. Their promotion depends on the Superior Council of Magistrature, which is under the direct influence of the regime, so that one cannot really speak of an independent judiciary. The 250 or so top judgeships are government appointments which are used to reward loyal service in reaching the right verdicts at political trials. General de Gaulle could no more tolerate independent judges than he could tolerate independent television. Judges were more independent under the *ancien régime,* when Chancellor Séguier told a petitioning courtier: "The court does not do favors, it reaches verdicts." The government, in the midst of the Algerian war, could not take the risk that the High Court of Justice might acquit the Secret Army leaders on trial. The collusion between the judges and the regime leads to great caution in judicial interpretation. A magistrate will not dare contest the government's right to seize a newspaper or make administrative arrests because he knows that when his ruling reaches a court of appeals it will be upset by a loyal judge and his own career will be jeopardized. With the exception of some young judges who have formed a magistrates' union, the French judiciary seems thoroughly domesticated. It is also badly paid, which helps explain why alimonies are so much lower in France than in the United States. A judge at the summit of his career who is earning 800 dollars a month hesitates to grant the same amount in weekly alimony to the young divorcée of a pop singer.

If a citizen wants to test the constitutionality of a law, he cannot, for there is no Supreme Court in France. There is no appeal at all from Assises and only one degree of appeal from other courts. There is, however, an entirely separate court system which deals exclusively with litigation that arises between the individual and the state and with the acts of public officials who overstep their authority. These are the administrative courts, which do not have their like in England or America. In England there is no procedure that allows a civil servant to take a grievance to court if he feels he has been unfairly fired or cheated on his pension. In France the lowliest clerk can take the most trivial grievance to the highest administrative court, the Conseil d'État. Created by Napoleon, this civil service supreme court is another proof of Big Brotherism, since so much litigation in French life pits the individual against the state. No case is too trivial when it helps define the labyrinthine relationship between the public and the private person. In August, 1968, the Conseil d'État ruled that "in no case must cow dung constitute a danger for automobile drivers." The mayor of Bligny-le-Sec in the Côte d'Or was asked to pay a fine of 2,000 dollars out of the township's budget because a truck had skidded on a road made slippery by a herd of cows which had crossed it on the way to the municipal drinking trough.

Any case involving a public official or public property escapes normal jurisdiction and goes before one of the forty administrative courts, like the Court of Accounts and the Court of Budgetary Discipline, and from there, on appeal to the Conseil d'État. Largely unknown by the public, operating in a discreet and unspectacular way, ignored by the press because of the technical nature of its rulings, the Conseil d'État is nonetheless the gray eminence of the state. Created to protect the state against suits by private citizens, it has over the years increased its authority to become the guardian of public liberties. Thanks to its skillful and seemingly innocuous scrutiny of administrative practices, it has challenged regulations and government decisions, and on several occasions declared measures taken by General de Gaulle to be unconstitutional. In theory it keeps the sovereign state within the bounds of law, although in practice de Gaulle disregarded its decisions. Thus, although it was never given a mandate to do so, the Conseil d'État has filled a vacuum in the French judicial system to become a kind of Supreme Court. Any plaintiff can introduce a suit for a small fee, if he has the patience to wait, since the court's 200 members rule on 4,000 cases a year.

More than any other court, the Conseil d'État has become a

righter of wrongs because of the complex problems that arise from modern French society. In recent years it has ruled on the right to strike in government offices, it has arbitrated a dispute among different makers of Saint-Nectaire cheese, it has ruled on the legality of special lanes reserved for buses in Paris streets, and on the right of photographers to operate on the Mont-Saint-Michel (they were barred because they had become a public nuisance). A review of cases in which an individual is suing the state does not reveal any pro- or anti-state pattern of decision. A woman in Vienne collected when she sued a state-owned theater because the lights went out and she fell down the stairs. A skier at Val-d'Isère who was carried away by an avalanche sued the township for allowing the trail to be open, and the Conseil d'État awarded him 1,000 dollars (it keeps a rein on profligacy). In 1964, a government-contracted company was spreading hot tar over a road in Le Havre. A three-year-old boy fell on it and was badly burned. His father sued the public works department. The Rouen administrative tribunal ruled in favor of the parents, but the decision was reversed by the Conseil d'État, which ruled there was no negligence involved on the part of the state. The family had to pay court expenses.

The Conseil d'État is not completely divorced from politics, since its members, all graduates of the École Nationale d'Administration, advise the government on legislation and thus become a part of the interlocking directorate that connects all state agencies. But it is probably the most independent state tribunal, and it is the only one that makes its rulings according to precedent, as in English common law. Since it is also asked to rule on cases that are not covered by precedent or the Code Civil, it is able to define new legal concepts.

The Fourth Estate

Freedom of the press no more exists in France than separation of powers, for the government controls and operates the only two television channels and, to a greater or lesser extent, the national radio networks. As Ezra Pound once said, "Free speech without radio free speech is zero." Freedom of the written press is an indulgence granted by a regime which controls what it considers the essential mass media. Some form of censorship of the written or spoken word has existed in France ever since Philippe le Hardi in 1275 put booksellers under the surveillance of the university to prevent them from peddling seditious volumes. In France, censorship existed two centuries before Gutenberg. No French regime, not even the strongest ones, like the absolute monarchy or the Fifth Republic, has ever felt secure enough to allow full freedom of the press. In 1521 François Premier banned all books not approved by the faculty of theology at the Sorbonne, and subsequent monarchs enacted similar prohibitions, which by the eighteenth century only served to guarantee the wide success of censored books like Rousseau's *Social Contract*.

In 1789 the men of the Revolution retired the hundred royal censors and replaced prepublication censorship with the post-publication censorship of the guillotine. Censorship was restored by the Commune in 1792. The Commune decreed that journals running counter to its own opinions were "poisoners of public order." Under Napoleon, the mentality of editors altered from wondering what was forbidden to wondering what was allowed. The emperor suppressed sixty of the seventy-three existing sheets, and finally allowed the publication of only four, to which he gave precise instructions through his police chief Joseph Fouché: "Let the newspapers constantly attack England ... they must serve my government, I will not allow them to publish otherwise ... I will not tolerate that they go against my interests ... finally, I will allow only one newspaper." Under the Restoration, censorship was repeatedly abolished and restored. In 1817 newspapers could only appear with the permission of the king. In 1830, freedom of the press was again suspended, and Premier Polignac said: "In all times, the press has been the instrument of disorder and sedition ... no force can resist the dissolvent that is the press." In 1850 Napoleon III, fresh from being elected Prince President, pushed through urgent censorship laws which Victor Hugo summed up as "I allow you to speak but I demand that you remain silent."

Party politics and the low cost of paper transformed the French press in the nineteenth century. For the first time large-circulation newspapers were published, the *Journal à un sou*, along with a wide variety of journals of opinion. This is the double tradition

of the French press: one or two mammoth dailies and a multiple
and diverse party press, which did not appeal to the general public,
but was able to survive because each had its own small but loyal
public. In 1881 the Third Republic passed a law stating that the
press was free, and suppressed preventive censorship, but the law
was not enforced. Editors were still jailed (a three-year sentence
for the antimilitarist editor Gustave Hervé). Censorship was used
in cases involving national security. Clemenceau's World War I
articles were often banned, and when "the Tiger" came to power
in 1917, the former crusading editor told the worried censors:
"Of course I am keeping you on. You are my best gendarmes."
After the First World War, a steady flow of decrees penalized attempts to discredit the state in 1924, news intended to demoralize
the army in 1936, outrages against good morals in 1939, and
articles concerning the pardons of men sentenced to death in 1953.

Under the Fifth Republic, General de Gaulle repeatedly expressed his contempt for "scribblers," to whom he magnanimously
granted the right to "sweat gall or spit vinegar, or to distribute
milk and honey." Instead of censorship of the written press, he
used the method of severe penalties for those found guilty of insulting the chief of state, a law which was enforced 350 times. In
1963 Jean Vicari was fined 200 dollars for shouting "Hou! hou!"
as General de Gaulle drove by, and in 1968 Francois Fonvieille
Alquier was fined 300 dollars for writing, "Good people, have
you forgotten that this hand, the hand that holds the scepter, re-
linquishes it once a day to meet the wearisome demands of the
body?" Just as the regent Philippe d'Orléans locked Voltaire in
the Bastille for hinting that he had incestuous relations with his
daughter, and Napoleon had a man committed to the Charenton
insane asylum for writing a song with the line "Yes, the great Napoleon is a great chameleon," General de Gaulle was quick to
fine and imprison those who took his name in vain.

Faced with the snipping of censors and the contempt of successive regimes, the French press has had to win not only its freedom but its self-respect. It has had to wipe out the image of the
despised gazeteer, who belongs to the same species as the black-
mailer and the slanderer, like the *ancien régime* scribbler who
apologized to police lieutenant d'Argenson: "But sire, I must live."
"I don't see why," replied the lieutenant. Journalism was long

viewed as a profession without dignity or standards, the refuge of failures and hired pens. Balzac devoted hundreds of pages to discrediting those "who require no talent as long as they have no scruples . . . when a writer cannot or will not amount to anything he becomes a journalist."

Along with low professional standards, the French press became notorious for its venality. The ministerial envelope which the journalist came to collect for adjusting his editorials to the government line remained a practice throughout the Fourth Republic. The French journalist specialized in writing about either side of an issue with equal fluency. In the early twentieth century Raffalovich, the Paris envoy of the Czarist Ministry of Finance, professed himself "astounded by the incredible venality of the French press." He arranged payments to *Le Matin* for its support of Russia in the Russo-Japanese War, intended to lift the morale of French subscribers of imperial Russian bonds. He wrote his minister on March 22, 1905: "Your Excellency's preoccupations as to the distribution of funds to the French press are well founded, and I share them . . . *Le Petit Journal* and *Le Petit Parisien,* each of which collected thirty thousand a month from the Boers, want fifteen thousand from Russia. I had not realized *Le Petit Parisien* was so venal. Each day one learns to despise someone more."

The same *Le Matin* which had been paid off by the Russians hung a portrait of Hitler in its Paris lobby in 1940. Its director, Maurice Bunau-Varilla, a power in the French establishment, had tablecloths and napkins embroidered with swastikas to receive the Nazi generals and diplomats who were his guests. One of them told him: "The swastika is our flag, sir, it is not made to wipe one's mouth." In 1941 Bunau-Varilla wired Hitler that he was a benefactor of humanity. He died just in time, in 1944. The pro-Munich press of the thirties received subsidies from the Germans, and the pro-colonialist organs under the Fourth Republic were paid off by the colonial lobbies. Part of the French press has made its reputation as the amplifier of reassuring illusions, drumming into its readership slogans like the Unpassable Maginot Line, Germany Must Pay, France Is An Empire of a Hundred Million Inhabitants, and France Is Bored. Venality continues to be suspected even when it does not exist. When most Paris newspapers chided General de Gaulle in January, 1969, for cutting off the flow of weapons to Israel while keeping the money advanced, the general replied with innuendos in his Council of Ministers about "press speculators" and newspapers that were "under the influence of Israel." The French press remains vulnerable to suggestions that it obeys other than professional motives.

The long habit of censorship has made French newspaper style Sibylline and allusive. Writers and editors have handed down the habit of writing between the lines, of masking unpleasant truths in oblique periphrases and sly inferences, as if still playing an imaginary game with a censor who no longer exists. Aversion to direct statements makes editorials read like legal briefs. The newspapers have built up a Pavlovian reaction of self-censorship. Except for the organs of opinion, whether on the left like *Le Nouvel Observateur* or on the right like *Rivarol,* whose views are entirely predictable, much of the so-called *presse d'information* suffers from political conformism which often leads it to identify with the chauvinist goals and militant foreign policy of the regime. Its servility was evident in its acceptance of prearranged questions which turned de Gaulle's press conferences into a recital. Add to this the belle-lettrist tradition of composing an article the way one would begin a novel, and the inability to distinguish between fact and opinion. French reporters have an aversion to the American-style lead which compresses essential information into the first paragraph. An article on the jury verdict in an important trial will begin with the atmosphere of the courtroom, the grimace on the face of the defendant, and the sun passing behind a cloud outside. French foreign correspondents, meanwhile, write in a lucid interpretive style and are not afraid of unburdening their pet theories on the reader.

Standards of objectivity are sometimes reached by the best publications, like the daily *Le Monde* and the weekly *l'Express,* but there is still a vigorous tradition of polemical journalism quite ready to distort news to make its point. The opinion press considers that its job is to persuade rather than inform, and its articles are slanted to present a convincing point of view. As Count Hermann Keyserling once noted: "The Frenchman ingores objectivity . . . he is gifted with an extraordinary sense of logic; but the unconscious depths of his mind are in an equally extraordinary state of partiality... it is only possible to have a candid discussion with a Frenchman if one shares his basic conviction, for he is physiologically incapable of doubting his own convictions... if someone does not share them, he sees that as a temporary aberration and is perfectly ready to help him change his mind in a completely disinterested and sincere way." Not even the mass-circulation popular press bothers to check facts. In its August 8, 1963, edition, *France-Soir*, the only French daily with over a million circulation, gave a large display to the practical joke of some hospital interns, with the headline: "Graft of a dead man's leg on an arthritic patient—the operation took seven hours."

Even when the motive is not polemical, there is an indifference to facts when they get in the way of a colorful narrative. In 1953 Jean Giono, writer of pastoral novels and member of the Académie Goncourt, submitted an article on the most unforgettable character he had ever met to the *Reader's Digest*. He told of a rocky and deserted region in the Haute Provence where only wild lavender grew. There he happened on a man selecting acorns and planting them with an iron rod. His name was Elzéard Bouffier. Born in Vergons, a mountain village behind the Durance valley, he had lost his wife and only son and withdrawn into solitude. In three years he planted 100,000 oaks and beeches. A government delegation came to see this natural forest and placed it under the protection of the state. Rangers were assigned to guard it and one of them said, "Bouffier knows more about trees than I do." Bouffier died at the age of eighty-seven in a hospital in the village of Banon, Giono said.

A young researcher named Dimitri Panitza was sent to check out the story, which perfectly summed up the *Digest* credo; it had rustic strength, honesty, a strong individualistic approach to life, hope, optimism, and faith in humanity. He checked city hall records, talked to old-timers, visited Banon hospital, but could find no trace of Elzéard Bouffier. No one had ever heard of him. Nor could he find the natural forest. He talked to the mayor of Vergons, who obligingly called a meeting of forestry officials, but they professed they were baffled. Panitza called his boss in Paris and said, "I can't find a trace of either the guy or the forest."

"What kind of researcher are you?" the boss said. "I want you to keep looking."

Panitza visited Giono in the village of Manosque, after being warned by New York: "Don't be tactless, handle him with kid gloves."

"We've already checked out most of the story," he told Giono, "it hangs together beautifully. But I don't seem to be able to find the natural forest."

Giono unfolded a map of the Haute Provence, jabbed the top of a mountain with a pencil, and said: "There."

Panitza rented a car and drove up the mountain until the road ended. Then, with commendable persistence, he found a mule to take him to the top, which was rocky and deserted. Only wild lavender grew there. He went back to Giono and said: "I went where you told me but I didn't find anything."

Giono doubled over in a fit of laughter and said: "You are more of a fool than I thought you were."

The *Digest* had to kill the story. The character was unforgettable but he did not exist. Elzéard Bouffier reappeared, however, in the March 15, 1954, issue of *Vogue,* in an article entitled, "The Man Who Planted Hope."

Le Monde is the newspaper that keeps the French press respectable. Founded in 1945 with the presses, plant, and typeface of the collaborationist *Le Temps* because General de Gaulle wanted a newspaper of international prestige to support his foreign policy, it soon charted an independent course. It has remained independent, as the repeated attempts to sabotage it show. In 1951 it was saved by its editors when shareholders, alarmed at its variance from government policy, tried to force the resignation of its editor in chief, Hubert Beuve-Méry, the former Prague correspondent of *Le Temps.* In 1956, 40,000,000 dollars of right-wing financing went into founding *Le Temps de Paris,* a newspaper specifically designed to cripple *Le Monde. Le Temps de Paris* lasted 66 issues, and *Le Monde* lost 3 percent of its readership. Efforts were then made to hire away Beuve-Méry's underpaid staff. He lost about a dozen men and decided to triple salaries. *Le Monde* practices Gaullist participation in that its editors control 80 of its 200 shares, with Beuve-Méry owning 40. On domestic affairs, it is the newspaper of record. It is the only French newspaper with a distinguished foreign staff (only two other dailies, *Le Figaro* and *France-Soir,* have a permanent foreign staff, an example of the pauperism of the French press). It is open to controversy with its "Tribune Libre" columns, and it is above suspicion where venality and hidden influences are concerned, although it sometimes gives in to government pressure. It is old-fashioned in its absence of photographs and its felt-lined prose of exquisite shading which sometimes seems designed for a handful of readers at the Quai d'Orsay, but it maintains a high level of reporting and interpretation, thanks to editors like André Fontaine and Pierre Viansson-Ponté. It has an uncanny ability for uncovering the hidden currents of domestic and international events.

French newspapers sell best on Thursday, the day the Loterie Nationale results are published. Otherwise, the French are not devourers of newsprint like the English. According to UNESCO, they rank eighteenth in the number of newspaper copies read per hundred inhabitants (27), behind Iceland and Bermuda, and just ahead of Uruguay. The government can control opinion without curtailing the freedom of the written press. It has renounced direct control over the national wire service, the Agence France-Presse, whose director is appointed by an advisory board of newspaper editors and other agency clients. The government still pays for more than half its budget, however, either in direct subsidies or in leasing the service to government agencies. The AFP cannot be called an official agency, but nor can it be called independent. Some members of its staff move back and forth between journalistic and government jobs. The AFP man in Havana in 1963, Yves Daude, was working for the Ministry of Information two years earlier. Other government men connected with the Ministry of the Interior or the Premier's office, particularly during the Algerian war, used AFP jobs as covers for their real activities. The AFP thus becomes part of the loose French power directorate. Jacques Boetsch, the foreign editor of the weekly *l'Express,* recalls that when he was working for the AFP he wrote a story on the execution of Bastien-Thiéry, who had masterminded a plot to kill de Gaulle. The story said, "He died courageously."

Minutes after it was on the wire, a furious official from the Ministry of Defense called him and said: "Kill the story at once. If you don't you will be sued and you will hear from us."

"All right, sue me," Boetsch said.

He cited the incident to show how an AFP journalist could resist government pressure, but it also showed that no ministry in a free country would have ordered a genuinely independent news service to kill a story, and adopted such a peremptory tone. The Ministry of Defense man was giving orders to Boetsch as if he were a civil service underling.

Moving from the AFP to the ORTF (French radio and television) one moves from muted to flagrant government control, outright lies, omissions, trial balloons, propaganda, and daily government interference to suppress or emphasize news items. The 8,000,000 owners of French television sets are treated to a sunshine image of France as a world leader with no domestic problems, in contrast to the Vietnam war and race riots in the United States. They live in a world of bicycle racers, Olympic ski teams, pop singers, and other innocuous activities, like progress reports on the priest who survived a heart transplant, Father Boulogne. The civil servants who run radio and television assume that the French public is infantile and must be fed pap. They have turned the Coué method, which consists in repeating, "I am fine," into a means of controlling public opinion. When Alain Peyrefitte was Minister of Information he said quite candidly that the mission of television was to balance the criticism in the written press. The policy of the Minister of Information, whose office is linked to ORTF executive offices with a private telephone line, is that a television commentator must be a loyal party man first and a journalist second. The best journalists quit or are fired, and the mediocre sycophants rise to the top. The crude slant on domestic news is one reason why the May-June events of 1968 took public opinion by surprise. It was like learning that the plague has hit Camelot.

Any government agency can exercise its right to censor national television. In 1964 the Ministry of Public Health suppressed a program on nurses, saying it would hurt recruitment. The mania for control of the "little screen" places the ORTF in a state of permanent crisis. One never knows whether a program will be canceled at the last minute because it has offended some official. Before the May-June events, a liaison office existed between the government and the ORTF, called the Inter-Ministerial Service of Liaison and Information (SLII), which "oriented" the programs. Each morning at 11, two radio and two television journalists met with delegates from the ministries of finance, information, education, cultural affairs, and foreign affairs. They were told to stress inaugurations and official ceremonies. If the Breton farmers were burning tons of artichokes that day, they were told to show some Vietnam war footage in the evening news roundup. At election time, the SLII drew up a list of pro-Gaullist communities where reporters could be sent to conduct man-in-the-street interviews, and advised commentators on what news to avoid and which political figures were not to be given TV time. A commentator who had mentioned a strike in an area which de Gaulle was visiting was reprimanded. A reporter who interviewed Bourguiba was sanctioned because he asked the Tunisian president about the nationalization of French firms. When Georges Bidault returned from exile shortly before the June, 1968, National Assembly elections, he said in a press conference: "Don't vote Communist, don't vote Gaullist." Only the first half of the sentence was reproduced in the evening TV news, which reaches 12,000,000 persons; they have expert splicers at the ORTF. Programs that showed a spirit of independence and conducted honest interviews, like *Camera III,* were taken off the air. When French students rioted, the evening news showed a mass demonstration in Peking. In the government's view, the main purpose of television is to take French minds off their own problems.

The SLII was laid to rest in 1968 after its activities were publicized, but government control did not slacken. The most pathetic failure of the May-June events was the month-long strike by 92 percent of the ORTF employees. They were unable to make a dent in the government hold on the media. The only improvement was televising the National Assembly debates live, which gave the TV audience a rare, uncensored glimpse of their country's political life. Despite official promises that no sanctions would be taken against strikers, 57 striking TV journalists were fired. The 40 or so scabs on the editorial staff who kept broadcasting during the strike included 5 former press attachés of ministers, 3 former writers for the Gaullist party organ, *La Nation,* the nephew of a Minister of Information, the wife of a Gaullist deputy, and 5 journalists personally recommended by Information Minister Peyrefitte, which helps illustrate the ORTF's recruiting methods. The strikers were fired because the worst crime in French television is not incompetence but lack of docility. General de Gaulle himself repeatedly expressed his annoyance at the mediocrity of French TV, but did not make the connection between the quality of the programs and the extent of government control. In the 1969 presidential election, the two principal candidates, Georges Pompidou and Alain Poher, both pledged to loosen government control over TV and said privately they favored an independent commercial channel, on the English model, that would compete with the government channels.

The Men at the Helm

"The Republic is lucky," wrote King Louis-Philippe from exile in 1848 when he learned about the bloody repression of a workers' demonstration in June, "it can fire on the people." French republics have repeatedly shown that a regime which is founded on the will of the people has greater leverage in keeping order. The Third Republic came into existence only after having destroyed the Paris Commune and killed thousands. The Fourth Republic survived an embryonic right wing coup in 1934 by firing at the crowds massed near the Concorde bridge, and the Fifth Republic showed in 1968 that it was not prepared to submit to the law of the street. Republics have thus been less vulnerable to the kind of disorder that overthrew the monarchy. But they have not been able to govern serenely. The Third and Fourth Republics governed amid a chronic crisis of authority. The Fifth Republic has been so closely identified with one towering figure that it is questionable whether his methods of government can survive him. In neither case has a democratic form of government been allowed to develop in France, which today still ignores the experience of democracy in the Anglo-Saxon or American sense.

The republican era of French politics began in 1870, largely by accident. Bismarck allowed a provisional government to take power because he did not want to restore the Second Empire. In 1871, 758 deputies sat in Versailles, fearing Paris as the monarchy had, and remained there for eight years. They were caretakers of the state, but did not call themselves a republic. They had no constitution. The birth certificate of the Third Republic was a brief act passed by one vote, 353 to 352, on February 25, 1875. An amendment to the act said that a president of the Republic would be elected by an absolute majority in the Senate and the Chamber of Deputies. By deciding, as an afterthought, on a president, the Republic was proclaimed inferentially, for if there was a president there had to be a republic.

This child of accident survived for three quarters of a century. The shortest document lasted the longest. The first French president was Marshal MacMahon, who had monarchist views and a good military record. He was elected to keep the throne warm, but resigned in 1879 because he found it impossible to govern. The seven-year term a French president still serves was decided on in view of MacMahon's advanced age, so that he would be too old to seek a second term. He set the precedent for the executive's impotence to control the legislature. His successor, Jules Grévy, played down his office until it became emblematic. The executive had abdicated to Parliament. Thereafter, the job of president was given to the most insignificant man, the one who offended no one. When René Coty became president in the 1950's, he said he owed the job to a prostate operation which had kept him out of the heated parliamentary debate over the European Defense Community.

Bicameralism in France was not part of French historical development as it was in England, but originated as an attempt to divide the authority of the legislature because the Convention had too much power. Under the Directoire there was a Council of 500, intended to be "the imagination of the republic," while the Council of Ancients was "the reason of the republic." Under the Third Republic, both the Chamber of Deputies and the Senate were jealous of their powers. The executive was hamstrung, and the vacuum was filled by the vote of confidence, which made every government a balancing act. The Third Republic gave the nation basic freedoms—freedom of the press, freedom to associate, and the freedom of workers to organize—but these had to be curtailed in times of emergency. The system lasted because it was the one that divided France least, but it was like a car that has a brake and no accelerator. Still, it gave the country free and compulsory education, founded a colonial empire, and survived crises like Boulangisme, the Dreyfus case, World War I, and the right-wing threat of the thirties. But it caught the bad habit, inherited by the Fourth Republic, of governments absorbed by parliamentary in-fighting in order to survive. They expended their life-force upon remaining in power, like a swimmer treading water. Universal suffrage was not a threat, for the electorate was basically conservative and the vote could be controlled. The Third Republic relied more heavily on patronage, the promise of public works, decorations, and scholarships. Gerrymandering and the *scrutin* were also used to political advantage. The *scrutin,* or voting system, was changed a dozen times under the Third Republic, always with a view to weakening the opposition. In 1889 the voting system was changed specifically to prevent General Boulanger from being a candidate in more than one constituency. The Fourth Republic changed the electoral system to block Communist strength through *apparentements,* or alliances between different parties; the Ministry of the Interior decreed which parties were allowed to enter into such coalitions, which assured the victory of the center parties over the extremes. Thus, the Third and Fourth Republics were unable to govern without manipulating the electoral system.

The secret ballot has only been in use since 1913, and the voting system has always been cynically used to give an advantage to the party or coalition in power, changing from one election to another to reflect the needs of the moment: uninominal, list, ward, proportional, two-stage, coalition, the Frenchman never knows under what system he will be asked to vote next, or whether it is intended to favor rural or urban France, large or small parties, the left or the right.

Thanks to the meekness of the electorate and the juggling of the vote, the Third and Fourth Republics managed to keep in power a caste of professional politicians who became known as the *République des Camarades.* The president of the Republic was tolerated insofar as he was passive. Clemenceau in 1920 was kept from the presidency because it was feared he would continue to apply wartime authoritarianism. The middle-class doctrine of *petitesse* presented real France as made up of little farmers, little shops, little employees, little Sunday hunters, and little tax evaders. There were half a dozen newspapers with the word *petit* in the title. Members of the government were coopted from the Chamber of Deputies, which had a high percentage of lawyers, for a resounding oratorical style was the main requirement for a political career. In the Chamber of 1881 there was one peasant and one member of the working class. Republican politicians acquired special characteristics. They were interchangeable and versatile. Men of equal competence took each other's place in cabinet posts. The ritual of replacement became well established. The incoming minister says: "It will be a heavy task to replace you." The outgoing minister replies: "It is a consolation to leave these services in such capable hands." Premiers developed a technical proficiency in forming governments, knowing how to *doser* (proportion) the cabinet portfolios among the various parties, like a chef spicing a stew.

The revolving door ministries had their own peculiar form of continuity; the actors changed parts, but it was always the same cast. Men were abruptly offered cabinet posts to resolve a crisis, like a dinner guest invited at the last minute because there are thirteen at table. They maintained close ties with the business community: Industry asked for and obtained high tariffs. Legislation was passed to help the owners of railroads make enormous profits. Firms with political connections submitted low bids on public works contracts and the Chamber of Deputies closed its eyes when costs went way beyond the bid.

Regimes were tinged by scandals. In 1892 Premier Emile Loubet fell because he refused to allow the autopsy of a man connected with the Dreyfus case. The promoters of the Panama Canal handed out 29,000,000 francs to "various parliamentary commissions." So much unfavorable publicity ensued that the Chamber had to name a committee to investigate six deputies, which showed that a political body is incapable of investigating itself. The few politicians who were asked to resign were rewarded with various sinecures. The evidence in the Panama scandal had been the stubs of checks kept by the promoters. In subsequent scandals involving politicians, like the worthless bond issues floated by the well-connected con man Stavisky, there was no such telltale evidence. The lesson of Panama was: Don't use checks. Under the Fourth Republic, André Boutemy, the agent of the CNPF (national management association), set up a front on the rue Penthievre called the Center of Administrative and Economic Studies, where cash in envelopes waited for deputies;

members of different parties would pass each other on the stairs on the way up to collect. A list of 160 deputies who had accepted money from Boutemy was circulated in 1951. When an investigation was threatened, Boutemy said: "I don't remember who I got the money from but I certainly remember who I gave it to."

It was not considered unethical under the Fourth Republic for a cabinet minister to keep up his legal practice. Edgar Faure, who matches Talleyrand in political brilliance and capacity for survival, since he has occupied almost every ministerial post in both the Fourth and Fifth Republics, received fees under the Fourth from important French firms for "legal advice" when he was Minister of Finance. When a company stopped paying the fee, he called in one of its executives, and in the marvelously covert language of French officialdom, he said: "You understand, dear friend, my duties absorb all my time. I dispose of only a few moments for private business, just enough to devote myself to a few friends like [and here he named a rival firm]." He was put back on the payroll, the executive explaining: "You understand, I don't want the Ministry of Finance inspectors hounding me."

The Fifth Republic has made private practice incompatible with ministerial duties, but the notion of conflict of interests is still vague. A cabinet minister who is chairman of a board or owns stock in a company that might influence his decisions is not bound to give up either the chairmanship or the stock. If a deputy is a member of a board when he is elected he can remain on it. The private behavior of some French politicians falls into the gray area between integrity and dishonesty. The tradition that a politician should expect favors because he is able to perform them grew up with the Republic, and affects the best French political figures. When Georges Pompidou was premier in 1967, he visited the Paris art gallery l'Oeil and admired the work of an abstract painter. Next day his secretary called the gallery director, Georges Bernier, and told him: "The Prime Minister is interested in buying one of the paintings you have on exhibition." She asked about the price, and suggested that, in consideration of the purchaser, a rebate might be granted. Bernier said that Pompidou was not a starving student unable to afford his passion for art. The secretary brusquely ended the conversation. The next day a fellow art dealer called Bernier, congratulated him on his new show, and said there was a painting he was interested in. "I'll bet I know which one," Bernier said. "Let me guess."

"You're right," said the dealer.

"Of course," said Bernier, "I'll let you have it at the usual 20 percent discount on the usual understanding that it's for your private collection and not to be resold."

"Why, of course, my dear colleague," said the dealer.

"And of course," Bernier continued, "you would be willing to loan it to me when I give a retrospective for this young artist."

"Well," said the dealer, "that might be difficult in view of the fact that I'm interested in the painting for my summer home in the Midi, and it would remain down there, but maybe we can work something out."

Pompidou got his painting, and his rebate.

Never was a reform adopted so fast as the proposal to raise the deputies' salaries from 9,000 to 15,000 francs on November 22, 1906. A left-wing deputy who was absent for the vote said, "My indignation is matched only by my satisfaction." The representatives of the Republic have a tenacious habit of permissiveness about their own conduct. When he ran for President in 1969, Pompidou went on television to deny charges that because he had worked seven years for the Rothschilds' bank, he was still linked with them. But he failed to mention that the Rothschilds were his landlords. When his luxurious apartment building in the Île Saint Louis had gone cooperative a few years before, he did not have the capital to buy his apartment. It was bought by a subsidiary company of the Rothschilds, to whom Pompidou pays rent.

Political instability became a system that handicapped France in its foreign policy and domestic affairs. As Chamberlain said in 1938, "France suffers from two faults which reduce by half the value of her friendship—she cannot keep a secret more than half an hour nor a government more than nine months." The secrecy problem grew so bad under the Fourth Republic that during the Indochina war there were matters the Minister of Foreign Affairs could not discuss in the Council of Ministers because of leaks. The Republic also became accustomed to infrequent bursts of intense activity followed by a return to lethargy. The foundations for France's second colonial empire were laid by Jules Ferry when he was premier in 1880 and Foreign Minister from 1883 to 1885. The French new deal was made law by a Popular Front government that lasted only thirteen months. In that short time, the most important social legislation France had known was voted: the forty-hour week, paid vacations, and labor's right to collective bargaining. In 73 days, 133 laws were passed.

But the Republic's first genuinely left-wing government was incapable of implementing a left-wing foreign policy. Premier Léon Blum had to make the crucifying decision not to help loyalist Spain while he saw Franco being armed by Germany and Italy. He justified his position by saying that if he had intervened in Spain there would have been a civil war in France, too. Foreign policy under the Third and Fourth Republics was often dictated by the domestic situation. In 1954 Mendès-France led another active but short-lived government, which was able to end the Indochina war and enact sound economic measures before the system purged him, saying he was more surgeon than doctor.

Just as the bourgeois notables under Louis-Philippe invented an ideology suited to their interests that equated freedom with order and the right to exploit labor, the Republic found a doctrine to justify its vacillations. The philosopher Alain wrote *Elements of a Radical Doctrine,* copies of which he had sent to Radical cabinet ministers. "If there really was a radical doctrine," said one, "wouldn't we be the first to know?" It was less a doctrine than a description of political behavior under the Third Republic. Alain favored controlling those who exercise power and limiting the authority of the government. A weak executive and ministers whose authority was sapped by short-term governments were viewed as a French system of checks and balances. He expressed in the language of the Collège de France the philosophy of the disgruntled citizen: "The politicians are crooks who fill their pockets at our expense; they threaten the family through taxes and the individual through arbitrary police action. When they are interested in you it can only mean trouble, but when you want something from them you can't get it." Vacuum of authority was raised to the level of a specifically French virtue. The history of the Third Republic became to some extent the history of squabbles among a restricted group of professional politicians. André Siegfried wrote a history of the Third Republic which did not even mention World War II because he was concerned mainly with parliamentary disputes. And yet it was because of the war that the Third Republic was quietly laid to rest when Pétain took power in 1940.

The Fourth followed the Third as if there had been no wartime interruption. The example of Pétain made the politicians wary of a real presidential regime, and they continued what de Gaulle called "the shadow theater of changing cabinets." The new leadership born of the Resistance gave way to many of the familiar and reassuring faces of the Third Republic: Auriol, Ramadier, and Herriot. The Fourth Republic was an exercise in nostalgia, a wish to return to pre-World-War-II France and to deny the changes that had taken place in the world. The old-style moderate deputy still sat in the Palais Bourbon. The irrelevance of parliamentary proceedings, the empty speeches, the banging of desks, the deputies writing letters or reading newspapers while their colleagues spoke was disturbing when viewed in the light of the grave postwar problems with which these men were unable to cope. The specialists in forming cabinets, a game played for its own sake and unconnected with the needs of the nation, were back in power: The Malthusian premiers like Queuille, who was so horrified by production increases in agriculture that he suggested 10 percent of the land should lie fallow; the cross-overs from the business community like Premier René Mayer, who believed that what was good for the Algeria lobby was good for France. The Fourth Republic had to deal with the most powerful Communist Party in Europe and with decolonization, and to its credit France did not lapse into either Communism or Fascism. It isolated its Communist Party, and achieved partial decolonization in Indochina, Tunisia, and Morocco. But it clung to Algeria. As a Kabyle leader told a cabinet minister in 1957: "You opened the window on the left, you opened the window on the right, and now you're complaining about the draft. You're dumb."

The greatest achievement of the Fourth Republic, however, was to permanently discredit the traditional French parties. It was under Socialist governments that half a million French soldiers were sent to fight in Algeria and that torture became commonplace. Socialist leaders like Guy Mollet and Robert Lacoste defended French imperialism and launched the Suez expedition. Mollet justified gunboat diplomacy by saying that for him,

Nasser was like Hitler. But the Socialists were caught in the hopeless contradiction between their pacifist, cosmopolitan convictions and the nationalist bellicose policies they had to approve. As soon as they were in power they betrayed their party goals. In 1954 all the men of the traditional left, including François Mitterand, were clamoring that "France is Algeria." They were caught with outmoded principles and goals. The most powerful party of the Third Republic, the Radicals, was split in so many different directions there was nothing left of it. It clung to its philosophy of *petitesse* and its mythical heroes like Herriot. In 1954, 38 percent of the dwindling Radical rank and file still considered Germany a threat to France. But in the 1969 presidential election it was so moribund that it did not even present a candidate. The lapses and weaknesses of the Fourth Republic created an antiparliament current which was exploited first by the Poujadistes, and then more successfully by General de Gaulle. The Fourth Republic, which had begun with the sulky departure of General de Gaulle, ended thirteen years later with his return based on highly equivocal promises.

The Gaullist Era

When General de Gaulle was invested by the National Assembly in May, 1958, his first words were: "The degradation of the state." France was then known as the sick man of Europe, in danger either of a Communist takeover or a rightist coup, an unreliable ally and an unfortunate friend. Dire predictions were made. The world asked: "What will become of France?" Ten years of Gaullism kept the French people "from the morbid attraction of the abyss," as the general put it in his 1969 New Year's message. The French knew they were governed. Institutions were strengthened, some problems were solved, and others were kept under manageable proportions. Alexis de Tocqueville showed that revolution can only come when a nation has reached a certain level of prosperity and liberalism; it broke out in 1789 under the most reform-minded of the Bourbon kings. In the same manner, the 1968 worker-student uprising was the fruit of ten years of political stability. It would have been unthinkable while the Algerian war siphoned national energy. The attack against the "society of con-

sumption" came from within a French society which had for the
first time in the twentieth century become freed from colonial
and foreign entanglements long enough to pursue coherent domestic policies. To feel disinherited, one must sense an inheritance within grasp. It was only because of what the government
had done that the workers and students became conscious of what
it had failed to do. The so-called Gaullist triptych mistakenly in-
verted the order of the last two panels; it should have been: End
the Algerian war; implement domestic reforms; give France an
independent foreign policy.

De Gaulle strove to make the Fifth Republic an irreversible
departure from its predecessors, one that could not lapse back
into "the sterile games" of parliamentary instability after his
death. He tried to change not only French institutions but the
French sensibility, since he knew that the French change their
constitutions more often than their mental habits.

He transformed the office of President. Under previous republics, the President attended the funerals of foreign chiefs of state,
went hunting at Marly, pinned decorations on the chests of VIP's,
spent evenings at the Opéra, and received new year's greetings
from the diplomatic corps. The problems of the office were on the
order of: What to give the emperor of Abyssinia in exchange for
his gift of a lion? Under de Gaulle, the ceremonial function still
existed, but not as a series of empty formalities; it was part of the
panoply of a powerful executive. The constitution of the Fifth
Republic is radically different from its predecessors in the rights
it confers upon its President. He has the right to dissolve the National Assembly and to take issues directly to the people by calling for referendums. Thanks to a 1962 referendum, the President
is elected by direct universal suffrage. If the government asks for
a vote of confidence, the opposition must obtain an absolute majority in the National Assembly to overthrow it, which is tantamount to saying that the government can stay in power with a
parliamentary minority. According to the constitution's Article
16, which was personally drafted by de Gaulle in memoriam of
June, 1940, in a case of national emergency the President can
take unlimited powers and govern by decree. From 1958 to 1961,
at the height of the Algerian crisis, Article 16 was in force 25
months, turning the general into a Roman-style emperor.

Even a strong regime like the general's could not allow democracy to function normally, and granted itself privileges like control of television and escape hatches like Article 16. The other big change for the Parliament was that no cabinet minister can be a deputy, ending the National Assembly's sordid jockeying for ministerial appointments. But the ministries keep their "secret funds," another *ancièn régime* residue; their existence implies that pay-offs are still being made to press and political figures. The Ministry of Foreign Affairs spends 4,000,000 dollars a year in secret funds and the Ministry of the Interior even more. Tradition has it that each year accounts of the secret funds are presented in a closed envelope to the Premier, who throws them into the fireplace.

The Fourth Republic situation of a weak executive at the service of an all-powerful Parliament was reversed under de Gaulle. The cabinet crisis was averted. A legislature which feels the old urge to topple a government risks dissolving itself, as it did in 1962 when a motion of censure overthrew the Pompidou cabinet. The nation judges conflicts that arise between the National Assembly and the President. A motion of censure is voted, the National Assembly is dissolved, and new elections are held. If the election were to give the majority to an opposition party or coalition, it would be a disavowal of the President and would make it difficult for him to stay in power. Such a situation never arose under de Gaulle, but it could be an element of instability under another President, because, for the French, the ability to govern is still connected with a parliamentary majority and the dangers of a motion of censure. The Gaullist presidential system is weakened by an absence of separation of powers between the executive and legislative branches, each of which has constitutional weapons to penalize the action of the other. On the other hand, the nation has become accustomed to the fact that a President elected by universal suffrage is responsible for government policy.

For the first time in the French experience, the election of the President is the essential political act. This was shown in the elections of 1965 and 1969, the first authentic presidential elections ever held in France, when the candidates spoke as men who intended to govern, presenting a domestic and foreign policy program, and thereby showing that they accepted the system. A

French presidential candidate must henceforth demonstrate the will to govern instead of being a high-powered major domo whose main job is to juggle the influence of parties and form a government which will not feel committed to the voters since it was not elected by them. To the extent that a strong, elected executive has become ingrained in the French mentality, it is one of the general's irreversible achievements. As a Gaullist says: "No one would dare take away from the people the right to decide." But the dependence of the President on a parliamentary majority persists. He is elected by universal suffrage, but he may be forced to dissolve the National Assembly and call for new elections. If the voters return an opposition majority, the President would logically be expected to resign. Another problem is that since de Gaulle was a unique figure, his rule cannot serve to test the strength of Fifth Republic institutions.

Louis XIV also thought he had created a durable form of government, but it collapsed 74 years after his death. In the case of Brobdingnagian historical figures like de Gaulle, it is impossible to separate their personal aura from the merit of their methods of government. He is Charles the first and the last, the only member of a unique species, on the same order as Napoleon and Clemenceau; their like will not be seen again. The fairest thing that can be said about the Fifth Republic is that under de Gaulle it worked, but was never tested. Only de Gaulle's successors can tell us whether the system will survive its founder.

De Gaulle was served partly by traditional electoral tactics which greatly favor the party in power and partly by a special technique he used after 1940, the summons. Among electoral tactics, there is the great, centralized bureaucratic apparatus that shudders into action at election time. The promise of decorations, tax rebates, fixing traffic tickets, all the host of little favors the administration can perform remain a useful device. There was more radio and TV time for Gaullist candidates, and occasional harassment of opposition candidates. Gaullist Committees of Civic Action were formed, and were not averse to strong-arm tactics. The prefects in close elections were known to devise methods to boost Gaullist strength, like taking busloads of the faithful from one electoral district to another. Gerrymandering broke up anti-Gaullist urban districts into sections that were absorbed by conservative rural areas to create what were called "invertebrate electoral districts." Grenoble was broken up this way in 1958 to favor the Gaullists. The polling method was also a political advantage for Gaullists, and the two-round system in legislative elections provided the voter, in most cases, with a second chance to vote which increased afterthoughts and prompted him to switch his allegiance from his own party to "the party of order." Finally, the official candidates had the advantage of promising that they would get things done in Paris, were well connected in the various ministries, and could open doors that would remain closed for members of opposition parties.

The technique of the summons presented government decisions as the direct response of one individual to another. The general began his political career with the famous summons of June 18, 1940, over BBC. The response was immediate, if less than overwhelming: fishing boats left the French coast for England. After that he made good use of the direct, man-to-man appeal which cuts through the bureaucracy that separates the citizen from the chief of state. The method was simple, effective, and flexible. It made a Gaullist of every Frenchman who at some point in his life had responded to the general's summons. It bore out the general's statement that every Frenchman either has been, is, or will be a Gaullist. De Gaulle's brilliant use of the summons was based on personal stature and the magic of the word. Without falling into the excesses of parliamentary rhetoric, he was able to make moving and forceful speeches.

The referendum was another form of summons. It has been used fifteen times in French history, once under the Revolution, twice under the Napoleonic Consulate, five times under Napoleon I and Napoleon III, and eight times under the Fifth Republic. It was never used during the Third and Fourth Republics because they governed through parliamentary balance and did not need it. De Gaulle made the referendum his political style; he felt it was suited to his own prestige and to the needs of the country. He called the referendum "direct democracy," but the method involves considerable charlatanism. In the first place, the outcome can be foreordained by the phrasing of the question, as de Gaulle learned in the first referendum he organized, on the islands of Saint Pierre and Miquelon, on December 25, 1941. The people were told: "You will have to choose between the cause of Free France and collaboration with the powers who are starving, humiliating, and martyrizing our country." The ballots offered a choice: "Join Free France" or "Collaborate with the Axis powers." As Georges Bidault has pointed out, the referendum can almost always be presented as the choice between a box of chocolates and a kick in the rear. With each referendum, moreover, the voters were implicitly asked to do much more than to reply to the question on the ballot; they were asked to express their broad approval of the government and its chief. The referendum became a tactic to reinforce the prestige of the leader. The inference was that the voter would not approve it unless he approved the general's leadership. When 75 percent of the nation voted yes in a referendum, the regime scored an important public opinion victory by presenting the result as a blanket approval. The issue was forgotten, and what was remembered was that three votes out of four were for de Gaulle. The general in fact never obtained an absolute majority of the voters in any election, either presidential or legislative. In the 1965 presidential elections he won 44.6 percent of the vote, or 37.4 percent of the registered voters. In the 1968 legislative elections, his party won 46.39 percent of the vote and 38.09 percent of the registered voters, enough to give the Gaullists an absolute majority of 294 seats out of 485 in the National Assembly.

The summons was also misleading in that de Gaulle placed himself above partisan quarrels and attributed to himself the halo of a disinterested savior; whereas he was in a very real sense the leader of the Gaullist party, the Union for the Defense of the Republic, whose candidates relied on his blessing to get elected. Aware of television's influence, the general addressed the nation on the day before an election to say, "The mission that the nation has confided in me places me above party pursuits," and to add, "Vote for me; the outcome is between each of you and myself," again the mystique of the personal summons. Those who would vote against him were bad Frenchmen who wanted the decline of the nation. Since the other candidates had neither the charisma nor equal time on the government network, they were seriously handicapped. Gaullism governed as had previous French regimes, by ignoring the concept of democratic fairness.

But in April, 1969, the system backfired, and the general became its victim. He called a referendum dealing with a reform of the Senate and the regions and pledged that he would not stay in office if it were not approved by the nation. Fifty-two percent of the electorate was against it, and the Gaullist era, which began for France in June, 1940, finally came to an end. Aside from being a humiliating defeat for the general, it exposed the inadequacy of the referendum as a method of government. If de Gaulle had not put his office in the balance, the reforms would have had a better chance of passing; the French voter felt he was confusing the issue and reacted according to the time-honored maxim, "Let us not take God's children for fools." What could a voter do who was against the reforms but did not want de Gaulle to interrupt his seven-year presidential term? What could a voter do who was for the reforms but had had enough of de Gaulle? Two totally separate issues were joined in the referendum, and the French voters could well ask themselves why their President required such frequent proofs of their devotion. It was to their credit that for the first time in French history they voted against a referendum, showing up the system as fallible and archaic, a nineteenth-century Bonapartist holdover suited to a politically immature people. De Gaulle left his office through the service entrance, not as the result of a crisis or an election, but over a marginal issue whose successs he compromised by trying to force the electorate's hand. In any case, the May 1968 events, had, like the Ides of March for Caesar, been a warning that his days were numbered, and he had decided to complete the last two years of his term only if the people gave him fresh evidence of their support.

The final and perhaps most serious disadvantage of the summons was that it disqualified the intermediate groups already so weak under French *étatisme*. Like the Le Chapelier law which defined collective bargaining as an agreement between a free and independent employer and a free and independent worker, the summons was an understanding between the individual, whose only power was his single vote, and the chief of state of the most highly centralized Western nation in the world. There could be no concept of "grass roots" under de Gaulle; there could only be isolated voters who, every few years, were asked to constitute themselves into a nation and vote yes to a question put to them by a chief of state. As de Tocqueville pointed out, the mother science in democratic countries is the science of association, whereas Gaullism stifled associations. Its rise was matched by the decline of the traditional parties. The notables of the Third and Fourth Republics, with one or two exceptions, were replaced by the Gaullist mamluks (named after the Egyptian slave militias), either those with a Resistance record or others from the *grandes écoles*, chosen for their competence and loyalty. The traditional parties of the left, like the Radicals and the Socialists, became fossilized lodges incapable of large-scale action, trying desperately to latch onto movements they did not create, as François Mitterand and Pierre Mendès-France tried to take advantage of the worker-student unrest in 1968. Gaullism permanently discredited these parties.

The only genuine opposition party is the Communist Party, which claims 300,000 card-carrying members and has ambitiously tried to create its own society within French society. But the weakness of the traditional left under de Gaulle prevented it from entering into a genuine coalition with the Communists, who would eventually have absorbed them. The Communists, by isolating 20 percent of the electorate, have made the formation of a genuine Labor Party impossible in postwar France. The Communists have been able to channel discontents but not remedy them. Twenty percent of the peasants vote Communist because in France a peasant can own a small piece of land and still be part of a rural proletariat which Marx did not foresee. The Communists are glad to get their vote, but do little to help them understand the mechanisms of the market or the role of state intervention. The French Communist Party has also repeatedly shown that it combines some of the worst traits of the French personality: formalism, abstract doctrine, and ideological hairsplitting, with a total absence of revolutionary goals. Communist Party boss Maurice Thorez came back from Moscow in 1945, was pardoned for deserting, and dissolved the militias and committees of liberation that were creating an armed Communist menace. Twenty-three years later the party showed once again it had no intention of carrying out revolution; it denounced the student revolt and its leaders. The party was most useful when used by de Gaulle to scare the voters back into the sheepfold.

What was new in Gaullism was a party grown to such proportions that it threatened to split into its different factions: the right which tried to sabotage Minister of Education Edgar Faure's university reforms, and the left which had faith in the reality of participation. What will become of these Gaullist troops now that the general has departed from the scene? It will take a figure of comparable strength to keep men of such divergent views under the same banner.

The very fact that Gaullism could gather men of such different persuasion was evidence of its lack of political philosophy. Like Bismarck, de Gaulle made pragmatism the essence of his reign. He plundered ideas from both the left and the right, while relying on traditional middle France to keep him in power. There was no Gaullist doctrine, there was only a political genius for survival. He went against cherished principles in giving up Algeria and becoming an ally of Germany. Like Louis XV, he operated a *renversement des alliances* (reversal of alliances) in refusing to align French policy on the United States and switching from a pro-Israel to a pro-Arab stance in the Middle East. Here again he believed he was placing France in an irreversible situation, and told an aide: "The one who has the gall to bring the Americans back has not been born yet." But as he was the first to show, there is nothing irreversible about foreign policy shifts, and it is conceivable that his successor will repudiate Gaullist foreign policy, seek narrower ties with the United States, support Israel, and allow Great Britain to enter the Common Market.

He was a soldier, but he was twice responsible for dividing the French army, in 1940 and in 1958, and he ended a twenty-year period of uninterrupted warfare. For the first time since the peaceful Bourbon Restoration that followed the Napoleonic adventure, a French chief of state did not demand the blood sacrifice from his people. Under de Gaulle, the French could forget their humiliations and defeats and turn to the more practical matter of improving their standard of living. Again pursuing irreversible changes, de Gaulle tried to end the paternalism of the French businessman, concentrate the 38,000 communes of eternal France into viable units, and regroup small farms. But here he was handicapped by the weakness of nongovernment groups like the labor unions and agricultural associations. Participation, the magic word intended to cure centuries of poisoned labor-management relations, would have to be enacted against both labor and management; management is not against improving the lot of the worker, but is against losing the initiative to do so—the French *patron* wants the moral satisfaction of awarding benefits that do not challenge his authority. In the spring of 1969, the predominantly female labor force of a textile mill in Amiens went on strike, not for higher wages, but to demand the right to inspect salary records every three months. The French worker is still at the stage where management secretely raises the salaries of loyal employees to prevent union recruitment inside the plant.

The most important French union, the CGT (Confédération Générale des Travailleurs), which is under loose Communist tutelage, suffers from a crisis of identity. In its claim that it is apolitical, it displays an archaic attachment to the past. In May, 1968, its secretary-general Georges Séguy said: "We are faithful to the principles of the Congress of Limoges," an 1895 congress which decreed that the trade union movement would be stronger if it divorced itself from political parties. This was its original sin, and explains its isolation. It has no political base, and refuses to negotiate its support of political parties in the manner of American labor federations. The unions have been incapable of enforcing even their legal rights, like the forty-hour week and collective bargaining. Their thinking is clouded by hazy dreams of a final proletarian victory which is no longer relevant to the working man's aim of joining the affluent society. The unions do not know what to make of participation. They are not sure they want a share in management. It is a plan they did not initiate and scarcely understand. In rural France, there is peasant resistance to *remembrement*, as the regrouping of tiny farms is called. The attempt to limit the minimum size of farms by decree and to mechanize French agriculture is met by sentimental arguments on the order of: "How can a computer measure the love a peasant has for his patch of land?" The modest goal is to double, by 1985, the average size of the French farm from 42 to 84 acres.

De Gaulle wanted to shatter the structure of eternal France while remaining the heir of the epic tradition. He dreamed of a Big Four which would include France, and refused to consider that, in terms of actual power, it had become a nation of middle rank, a kind of greater Belgium. Belief in French grandeur was circuited into his chromosomes; it could not be argued or disproven. At the July 14 celebration in 1943 in Algiers, de Gaulle was sitting between the American envoy Robert Murphy and Harold MacMillan. After the troops had been reviewed, members of political parties began to speak; in the midst of a violent Communist tirade, de Gaulle turned to Murphy and said: "This is what we will have tomorrow in France when you have completely strangled us."

"But, *mon géneral,* we love France and have no intention of strangling you."

"Yes, you love France but you don't know her; for you France is the *marquise* of X and the *princesse* of Z."

"But I assure you, *mon géneral,* I know your country, I lived there for more than ten years."

"And we have been living there for two thousand years."

French grandeur was the general's only doctrine, as a visitor learned who visited him in London in the Free France days. He noticed a big ivory cane in the cloakroom. "It's a present I received in Africa," explained de Gaulle. "It's made from a single piece of ivory."

"Well, it took some elephant with some pair of tusks."

"Yes," said the general, raising his voice as though addressing the multitudes, and waving his arms, "the elephants . . . of French Equatorial Africa . . . are the BIGGEST ELEPHANTS IN THE WORLD."

Toying with the cane later, the visitor discovered that it unscrewed into two pieces.

But the great supranational political system upon which French grandeur was based no longer exists. France has shrunk to its continental size. Instead of having a sense of mission, it has become mission territory for foreign ideologies—Marxism, Maoism, Marcusianism, and American business know-how. De Gaulle kept French grandeur afloat with his prestige and rhetoric. Some of his policies could only be explained as symbols of French grandeur, which helped him impose his vision of the world in international affairs. The nuclear deterrent was important because the way France holds the sword has always been a barometer of national health; the dynamic, prosperous France of Poincaré was expressed in the offensive strategy of 1914, and the defensive Maginot Line dogma expressed the defeatism of the thirties.

The mystique of rank was used in much the same way as Louis XIV used it, accompanied by the gratuitous need to offend and humiliate. The content of policy was confused with external signs of prestige. When the Spanish ambassador's coach accidentally passed in front of the French ambassador's in a London procession in 1661, Louis XIV insisted on the Spaniard's recall and a formal apology from the king of Spain. De Gaulle was equally attentive to ceremony. He made news by attending a reception at the Soviet embassy, or by spending more time with one diplomat than with another. His slightest gestures were interpreted as policy changes. When he received diplomats at the Elysée in January, 1969, the French press noted that he greeted Israeli ambassador Walter Eytan with a forced smile while entering into a cordial conversation with Lebanese ambassador Philippe Takla. De Gaulle felt the need to transform even athletic events into symbols of French grandeur. After the French rugby team beat Cardiff, its captain received a handwritten letter from the general: "Dear sir, that was a magnificent victory, more beautiful and more complete than that of last year. It rejoiced all the French, etc." In his jealous preservation of nineteenth-century nationalism, de Gaulle was antihistorical, for the European idea spread despite him.

He entered that dimension of history where he was himself a myth. He is his own hagiographer, thanks to his *Memoirs*. It is as if Joan of Arc had written an autobiography. He cannot be adequately explained in terms of his family background and upbringing. He escapes psychological definition. Freud explained Napoleon as the second son of a large Corsican family, whose hatred of his older brother turned to love—"hundreds of thousands of persons had to pay for the fact that he spared his first enemy," and Robespierre in terms of a psychotic father who fled his family and went to live in Munich, but one seeks in vain the Freudian key to the Gaullist myth. Léon Blum came close when he said de Gaulle belonged to the same family as Clemenceau: "An often disdainful misanthropy prevents them from believing in the result of action, but nothing can keep them from action because it represents for them a vital necessity." In his refusal to relinquish power in old age, he brought to mind a passage where Caesar describes the Gallic cavalry led by a noble elder: "Because of his great age, he could hardly sit a horse, but according to the usage

of the Gauls this was no reason to deprive him of his command."
One could see him, nearing eighty, having given up the leather
belt of the warrior because of age and a fondness for heavy food,
visiting a Brittany shaken by separatist groups in January, 1969,
still declining the use of glasses despite pronounced myopia; the
schoolboys waved their paper flags and the decorated veterans tried
to stand at attention despite their rheumatism, and the general
intoned: "This province particularly dear to my heart . . ." And
one realized that the magic still worked. And then four months
later the political fickleness of the French was once again demonstrated, and the general told his friends that it was always like
that, great men are abandoned by their people, ingratitude is their
lot, and he returned to the sanctuary of Colombey to meditate
on the final vanity of any human undertaking. But Gaullism continues (if only because Pompidouism sounds ridiculous), and it
is not Bonapartism, or Orléanism, it is an invention of its own,
the rule of one man with a highly personal style, and because of
that, impossible to follow in the same manner. That is what de
Gaulle was, not an artist like Louis XIV or an engineer like
Napoleon, but an inventor.

Part II

Forms of Exchange

5

The Universal Tongue

INSTEAD of the babble of tongues predicted by the Old Testament, the number of languages is shrinking, and nearly half the world population speaks in a borrowed idiom, whether in Washington, Buenos Aires, Rio de Janeiro, or Dakar. The most tenacious form of colonialism is linguistic: 8,000,000 Belgians, 10,000,000 Canadians, 6,000,000 Pacific islanders, and 55,000,000 Africans speak, or try to speak, the language of Descartes. If the destiny of imperial powers is one day to become colonies themselves (the suggestion has already been made that Great Britain should be the fifty-first state), then perhaps France will eventually become Canada's first extraterritorial province. The French feel a mixture of pride in the wide diffusion of their language, and amusement at the way other peoples massacre their idiom. They mercilessly ridicule the sing-song Belgian and Swiss accents, the Canadian neologisms (*je vais magasiner*), and the pidgin African French of the *"moi partir toi rester"* variety. It is considered satisfying evidence of the vigor of national culture that 79,000,000 foreigners speak French, even though two-thirds of them are illiterate.

Language is both an explanation of the people who speak it and a bloodless form of conquest. The special character of French is that it was spoken by elites abroad before the French nation learned it (in 1296, the Italian Marco Polo wrote the account of his Chinese travels in French). At the same time, once the language stopped changing in the seventeenth century, an army of grammarians was recruited to defend it. French thus manages to be both universal and parochial; it is carefully tended and protected from improprieties like the most delicate orchard, and it is sent to proselytize through the world like a sturdy pilgrim. This defensive-offensive duality can best be understood if the French language is seen as one of the principal agents of the formation of the French nation.

How French Was Formed

French, of course, like Italian, Spanish, Portuguese, and Rumanian, rose from the ashes of the Roman Empire, which allowed Latin to develop freely and differently in each of the former Roman colonies. But French is the Romance language most distant from its Latin prototype. In the colony which would one day be France, the Gauls spoke one of three branches of Celtic (the other two being Gaelic and Welsh), but they were quick to grasp the advantages of learning Latin, as other colonized people later learned French. The Gauls, moreover, had no written tradition, so that only some two hundred of their words have survived in French, many of them practical words dealing with rural life, like *ruche* (beehive).

Four centuries of Roman garrisons, civil servants, and merchants made Latin stalwart enough to resist the barbarian invasions. From a language of victors, Latin became a language of the vanquished, but it survived, thanks largely to the role of the clergy as repository of culture and the written tradition. When political power is stable, language is equally stable. The anarchy that followed the decline of the Roman Empire fostered the growth of local dialects and variants in Latin speech. The church resisted assaults on Latin, but the German-speaking Franks introduced many of their own words. The church eventually bowed to usage, sensitive to the fact that many of the faithful could no longer understand Sunday sermons. Priests were told at the Council of Tours in 813 to translate their homilies into lingua romana rustica, or Old French. This is the first memorable date in the adventure that raised a crude Latin patois to the level of a national tongue. Twenty-nine years later came the first written text in French, a treaty between two Carolingian princes known as the Oath of Strasbourg. Louis the German pronounced before his troops an oath of loyalty to Charles the Bold in rustic Roman so his men could understand it.

Just as there were rival fiefs there were rival dialects, and the dominance of one over the other was a matter of political fortune rather than inherent linguistic excellence. A dozen dialects prospered under feudalism, the two most important, named after their respective ways of pronouncing the word "yes," being the northern *langue d'oïl* and the southern *langue d'oc,* which remained closer to Latin.

Francien, a subdialect of the *langue d'oil* spoken in the Île-de-France, was adopted by the Capetian kings who made Paris their capital. Hugues Capet, born in 938, was a pivotal figure, the last of the Frankish lairds, for he could speak no German, and the first French-speaking king. Francien replaced Latin in the royal entourage. It was the dialect of a tiny region, adopted by a handful of courtiers and civil servants. Its penetration elsewhere depended on the political and military fortunes of the dynasty. From the start, French was the language of a ruling class, eventually imposed on the rest of the country. By contrast, English after the Norman invasion of 1066 became the language of the lower class and prevailed against the French-speaking aristocracy. In 1362 Edward III ruled that English should be used for public trials. This was the first decisive defeat of the French language in England.

The six hundred formative years from the coronation of the first Capetian to the rule of Cardinal Richelieu could be told in terms of half a dozen dialects struggling for preponderance. The thirteenth-century Crusade against the Albigensian heretics, for instance, was less a religious struggle than France's version of a north-south civil war, and consequently a life-death battle between the *langue d'oc* and the *langue d'oil.* The repression of the Albigensians by Simon de Montfort and the annexation of the county of Toulouse by the growing Capetian land holdings ended forever any influence to which the *langue d'oc* might have pretended.

All the factors that made a genuine national dynasty of the Capetians also encouraged the standardization of language: The growing sense of nationalism that came from the Crusades and the Hundred Years War; the brilliant court life which attracted visitors from other parts of France; the roving troubadours who began to use the Île-de-France dialect to recite their *chansons de geste*. After the thirteenth century, Francien was never seriously challenged as a national tongue. Already under Philippe le Bel (crowned in 1285), official acts were being drafted in French. The administrative language was born; the character of French bureaucracy is inseparable from the structure of the language. The language was split between official and spoken French.

Racine discovered just how split it was on a trip to the southern duchy of Uzès in 1650. "Already at Lyons," he wrote, "I rarely heard the language of the country and was intelligible only to myself. My misfortune grew at Valence. As fate would have it, I asked for a chamber pot and a small stove was placed under my bed. You can imagine the results of this damned adventure when a very sleepy fellow used the stove for his night's needs. But in this part of the country things are even worse. I swear that I am as much in need of an interpreter as a Muscovite in Paris."

France had from its origins the taint of an official language, imposed by decree on diverse populations at the expense of their own dialects. With the decree of Villers-Cotterêts in 1539, François Premier ordered that all official papers be drafted in French. The development of the language continued to be closely linked to the authority of the crown. It was only after the disorders of the Wars of Religion and the repression of the seventeenth-century Fronde during the minority of Louis XIV, that France knew a long period of domestic stability which allowed the language to be weeded and sheared like the lawns and yew trees of Versailles. In 1684 Louis XIV prohibited lawyers and public officials in the recently united province of Flanders from speaking Flemish.

Other, nonhistorical factors affected the prestige of French. The Sorbonne remained the stronghold of Latin well into the eighteenth century. Descartes first wrote in Latin, out of a spirit of orthodoxy and a desire to be read by educated men. But though the educators, the clerics, the translators of learned books and the scholars of the Renaissance maintained the influence of Latin, printers began adopting French for commercial reasons: They wanted to extend their readership. Thanks to printers, written French became standardized. A single spelling had to be chosen for words that were pronounced many different ways. The logic-defying intricacies of French spelling are a sixteenth-century development whose mysterious regulations may have something to do with printers' guilds making up bizarre rules to protect their monopoly. Extra letters were introduced to make the written script appear more elegant, and it took centuries to make the silent *s* disappear from words like *beste* and *chasteau*. Other anomalies, like the silent *g* in *doigt* (finger), are even more mysterious. French spelling developed into a mass of contradictory regulations, the bane of schoolchildren and a trap for foreigners.

The year 1539 was another memorable year in the progress of French, the publication date of Du Bellay's *Defense and Illustration of the French Language,* the first of many didactic apologias. One may wonder why a language of such intrinsic merit has had so energetically to be defended. Perhaps because it was tied to the fortunes of a political regime rather than being a language which developed organically among all classes of society, like English, its gospel had to be spread by propagandists like Du Bellay, who was writing at a time when the majority of the French people still did not speak the national tongue and when formal education was in Latin. He sought to minimize the influence of Latin and prove that French was a language which stood on its own merits and reflected the personality of the French people. One of the first tasks of sixteenth-century writers, which explains their militant stand, was to justify their use of French rather than Latin.

Militancy persisted long after the struggle to impose French had been won. It took the form of an obsession with purifying the language and a presumed identity between the values of the language and the values of French civilization, both of which became models for the rest of Europe. French had a 150-year linguistic apogee which coincides with the success of absolute monarchy, roughly from the time Richelieu became cardinal in 1622 to the death of Louis XV in 1774. The language corresponded to a vision of the universe as organized and apprehensible (it postulated clarity and order as its ideals), and to a vision of the state as absolute and immutable (it needed to be constantly policed so that its rules would not be infringed). Just as Louis XIV tried to freeze political change, his army of censors and hired pens tried to freeze the language. Good usage was form control, just as in Mao's China correct thinking is content control.

It was not a time for writers, but for grammarians. Vincent Voiture, one of the *beaux esprits* who attended that headquarters of pedantry, the Hotel de Rambouillet, wrote in 1630 a defense of the conjunction *car* (for). Racine agreed to submit his tragedies to the censorship of the Jesuit grammarian Bouhours. The seventeenth-century men of letters hunted down improprieties like inquisitors. They had a dogmatic faith in the supremacy and perfectibility of their own language. Claude Vaugelas, another of those men who devoted his life to fixing good usage, believed that "there has never been a language in which one could write more purely than in our own, and which is a greater foe of ambiguity and all sorts of obscurities."

> Finally Malherbe came, and the first in France,
> Brought into his verse a just cadence.

Boileau's metered compliment defines the position of François de Malherbe (1555–1628), a law enforcement officer posing as a poet. Malherbe contributed a stultifying, arid, bureaucratic doctrine in which every rule is its own reward. Poets like Ronsard who in earlier, less constricted literary periods had not respected his still-unannounced formulas were retroactively condemned. Only the lesson in precision was useful. There is a direct line from Malherbe and his discursions on synonyms (the nuance between feeble and weak) to Flaubert's concern for the right word. But the harm done was greater, and the seventeenth century's over-refinement of language created an upper and lower French like upper and lower Latin, the one restricted to polite society and the other spoken by the Third Estate and developing independently of grammarians. A Potsdam courtier spoke better French than a Breton peasant.

Malherbe, or the spirit of Malherbe, is alive and well in the Académie Française, one of the last surviving institutions of the *ancien régime* (approving its members and pardoning criminals are the only two monarchic rights kept by the President of the Republic).

The Académie Française

The Académie was created by Richelieu as the official agency of linguistic formalism. But it began as a reaction against the female domination of the salons and the *précieuses,* a group of intellectual ladies who favored a style of speaking and writing based on periphrases, euphemisms, and fashionable words like "furiously" and "terribly." Men of letters who shrank from the mannerisms of the Hotel de Rambouillet, where feet were referred to as "the dear suffering ones," and rain as "the third element descending," began to meet at the home of Valentin Conrart, a member of the species of nonwriting writers. The atmosphere was that of an English club, informal and masculine.

Conrart and his friends made the mistake of inviting a minor dramatist named François de Boisrobert to one of their meetings. Boisrobert earned his living as literary secretary to Cardinal Richelieu and informed his patron about the Conrart salon. To Richelieu there was something vaguely seditious about a society of men of letters who met regularly without having asked his permission. What were their statutes? (They had none.) What might their influence be on public opinion? (They intended none.) Richelieu offered his protection, which it was undiplomatic to refuse. Conrart and his friends were invited to draw up statutes and become the directors of "a rich and pompous Prytaneum of *belles-lettres,*" which would adopt the name of Académie Française as "the most modest and proper to its functions."

Thus a group of friends with a literary bent who liked to spend an evening together now and then found themselves ceremoniously pressed into government service in 1635. The Académie Française grew out of the absolutist will to control and discipline language. It was part of the royal doctrine that literature must contribute to the grandeur of the state. The newly named Académiciens were put to work on a grammar and a dictionary. They were, according to their own statutes, sanitation commissioners whose task it was to "clean up the language and remove the garbage accumulated in the mouths of the common folk or in the magistrate's courts or through the abuse of the men in the pulpits who say the right things in the wrong way."

The Académie excluded women. It has remained the last French stronghold of masculine exclusiveness, with an imaginary forty-first seat which might have been attributed down the generations to lady Immortals like Mademoiselle de Scudèry, Madame de Sévigné, Georges Sand, Colette, and Louise de Vilmorin. The forty real Immortals met every Thursday in rooms prepared for them in the Louvre (tokens worth thirty sous spurred attendance) and practiced their linguistic infallibility on dictionary editions which appeared roughly every fifty years.

It also retained its clubbiness. It was less interested in men of genius than men of distinction. Corneille and Racine were elected because they wrote compliments for the king's birthday and inscriptions for commemorative medals. Molière was excluded because he was an actor, while the son of the minister Colbert was admitted by birthright. As one Immortal said in a moment of candor during his reception speech: "If to enter here, glory, genius, and the gift of creativity were required, the seats would be often vacant." The Académie never pretended to monopolize literary greatness: The list of great writers it overlooked is far more impressive than those it elected, and includes Descartes, Pascal, Diderot, Beaumarchais, Rousseau, Balzac, Stendhal, Flaubert, Zola, Proust, Gide, Camus, Sartre, Céline, Anouilh, and Malraux. These omissions, far from troubling the Académie, are seen as an advantage. "Because of our capriciousness, refusal is not taken as an affront," is the way one Immortal gracefully explained the congregation's spotty record.

Indeed, membership has less to do with writing than with social origin and professional background. The tradition is to have always on hand a sampling of dukes, generals, and high clerics. The generals were elected as proof of the Académie's patriotism, whether it was the maréchal de Villars in 1714 for his service under Louis XIV, or maréchal Foch during World War I, who dispensed with making the ceremonial visits to other members because his time was absorbed by matters at the front. Carried away by patriotic fervor, the Académie also elected Clemenceau by acclamation, even though socially he was too rough-edged and radical to fit comfortably under the cupola.

The Académie is like a family heirloom that has survived natural disasters and the attrition of time. Old-fashioned perhaps, although it tries to keep in step with the times by electing a film director like René Clair and a homosexual of the preening variety like Jean Cocteau; and sometimes frankly ridiculous, these white-haired adolescents who whisper to one another when arriving at the Thursday meetings, "class is about to begin." But nonetheless, it is a fortress of entrenched French values.

The natural disaster was the Revolution. The Convention suppressed the Académie in 1793 as "gangrened by an incurable aristocracy." One of the clerical members, the abbé Morellet, risked his life to save its archives. Another member, the writer of maxims Chamfort, contributed to its downfall in pamphlets damning its activities as futile. Its casualty list was three members guillotined and three others who committed suicide. But two years later the Académie was revived and the membership was renewed. Napoleon, faithful to his mania for putting everyone in uniform, had the painter David design one of a bilious and pedagogic green, and added a sword with a hilt richly worked with the symbols of the empire, with which the Immortals could presumably chastise those guilty of solecisms.

But what has kept the Académie going, more than the will of emperors and presidents, is simply that there are men who desperately aspire to wear its uncomfortable cocked hat and to spend their Thursday afternoons in the company of other ancients mulling over word definitions. The Académie is an elderly but still desirable lady, and Victor Hugo said, after the first of his five attempts to seduce her: "All great men have been cuckolds. Napoleon was one, and so am I." Hugo was considered a law unto himself, "a lunatic who thought he was Victor Hugo," a monster of self-importance who could tell a group of learned men after a long moment of silence, "As for me, I believe in God," as though this was the definitive remark on the subject. And yet, he repeatedly risked humiliation and sarcasm for a seat under the cupola. The critic Sainte-Beuve noted in his journal: "Hugo wants to become a member of the Académie. He is busying himself. He discusses it with you gravely. He dwells on it for hours. When he grabs an idea, all his energy pushes at it and concentrates on it, and you hear arriving from afar the heavy cavalry of his wit and the artillery of his metaphors."

Hugo's most effective weapon was outrageous flattery. He wrote the obscure historian Charles de Lacretelle: "I have just finished your two volumes, my venerable and illustrious friend. If it were not so late, I would rush to shake the noble hand which has penned these illustrious pages. There are things which transport one like the Bible and things which delight like Virgil." The Académie eventually succumbed to Hugo's siege, but other determined poets presented themselves in vain. Baudelaire patiently visited each of the forty, although the condemnation of the *Fleurs du Mal* as obscene was a heavy handicap. One crusty Immortal told him: "As for myself, sir, I have never been original." There was, and is, something suspicious to the Académie about flamboyant talent or garish behavior. It was not that Baudelaire took drugs, it was that he advertised it. Many members of the Académie were, moreover, convinced that Baudelaire was mad because he had been observed in the Louvre measuring the Greek centaur, and muttering: "There's no getting around it, he can't wipe himself." The protocol involved was so painful to Baudelaire that he contemplated suicide as an escape. Finally, although he was supported by Sainte-Beuve and the poet Alfred de Vigny, he withdrew his name and was advised not to try again. Alexandre Dumas was turned down because he was too prolific. The Académie has never liked apparent effort, and moreover, Dumas was taxed with "picking his neighbor's apples." The symbolist poet Leconte de Lisle lost out to the duc d'Audiffret, who had the advantage of never having been published. But once elected, he heard the call of the Muse, and published his uncle's memoirs. The visits which so afflicted Baudelaire are a form of final examination where the candidate must show his ability to adopt the tone of exquisite courtesy in which what is said has a contrapuntal relation to what is meant.

The special politeness of these patricians of the spirit, which damns while seeming to praise, is exercised in the speech given for new members. Thus, the Immortal who replied to Pierre Loti's *discours de réception* told that writer of exotic novels: "I would have liked to sing your praise, but you have done it far better than I could myself."

The reception speech is a tradition going back to 1640, when an otherwise unheralded fellow named Olivier Patru thanked the Académie in such eloquent terms for singling him out that it was decided all his successors should follow his example. More than three hundred years later, it is still an occasion, and the speeches are printed in full in *Le Monde*. The form, fixed by tradition, demands that the new member extol first the Académie in general and then the departed Immortal whose seat he is taking, after which one of the old boys welcomes the newcomer by summing up his life and work. A good example of this ritual was the reception in December, 1967, of Maurice Druon, a prolific author of treacly and simplistic historical novels written in collaboration with teams of researchers, and at age fifty, one of the youngest members ever admitted to the august assembly.

In his speech, Druon aptly compared the Académie to the House of Lords, since "its regulations are cursory, but its customs are ancient, subtle, and improved by usage. Although without precise powers, it has an uncontested moral authority. As in the Lords, there enter here with each generation men of every opinion and of every social and geographic origin, who have enriched the national patrimony by their works or contributed to its protection by the excellence with which they have done their jobs. Your selections maintain a wise balance between tradition and innovation. But what is a tradition if it is not the consecration of successful progress? Finally, there reigns among you a 'club' spirit, with its concern for courtesy, its sense of affinity, its tolerance for complementary particularisms, its discreet fraternity, its total solidarity, all of which was the strength of England, which I would envy if I were not certain to find it among you."

The reply by the Académie veteran Louis Pasteur Valléry-Radot, a descendant of Pasteur and a doctor by profession, was a gem of euphemism. Referring to the suicide of Druon's father, Valléry-Radot said: "Too intransigent to live our life, he left this world voluntarily." Druon's *arrivisme* became a virtue thanks to an apt quotation from Pascal (the classics can always be summoned to support any thesis): "How happy a life is when it begins with love and ends with ambition." While praising Druon's books, which the occasion demanded, Valléry-Radot could not resist quoting some of his more glaring inanities, such as: "Like nearly all those destined to the follies of passion, Mary had one eye slightly smaller than the other."

These speeches are models of what the Académie stands for: urbanity, civility, musty gentility. It may well be a conservatory of national vanity preserved as in amber or verbena sachets, but it has to its credit the secret of survival and lasting vitality. To its discredit there has been alleged a muted strain of anti-Semitism. But this was truer in the nineteenth century, when one Immortal joked about Dreyfus being the only innocent Jew, and another made the celebrated quip: "I am not an anti-Semite, but I will never prevent anyone from becoming one." No Jew became a member until the twentieth century, and today Jews are included in the Académie's particular brand of tokenism—there is always one duke, one maréchal, one cardinal, one famous doctor, one famous lawyer, one homosexual, and at least one Jew.

The Académie's function as the supreme court of linguistic litigation has declined, but it still considers itself a government agency with patriotic duties, and offers membership to those who have served the country well. In 1931 Valéry received maréchal Pétain with a speech in which patriotism blurred common sense. "You have made a great discovery," he told the victor of Verdun. "You have discovered this: that firepower kills. And such a discovery had to be made by nothing less than a man of genius." A generation later, this same man of genius and two other Immortals were excluded from the Académie, whose ways of thinking could not change with the same speed as events. Like the French army, the Académie was always a war behind. But in its own way, it tried to do the right thing. The first session after France and Germany went to war in 1939 took place on September 7. Georges Duhamel, the secretary, like a general in the trenches telling his troops that though outnumbered and out of ammunition they would fight to the last man, announced: "Gentlemen, we will continue to sit every Thursday no matter what happens." Appropriately enough, the dictionary commission that day was on the word "aggression." The retired ambassador Maurice Paléologue discussed the difference between an attack and an aggression, the latter being an unprovoked and unexpected attack. The definition finally accepted was: "Action of him who attacks." As France was overrun by the Panzers, the dictionary commission continued unperturbed to discuss matters such as whether the word *agréable* implies too much fervor in social relations.

The dictionary has become something of a joke because, in an age where everything else has speeded up, it still takes half a century to prepare a new edition. Some of its definitions are obsolete by the time they are published. But like that other ancient institution the Catholic church, the Académie feels it must proceed with stately deliberation in matters of doctrine. Words are held up for weeks while their every shading is examined. The wide professional range of the Académie membership invites the opinions of legal, scientific, medical and other experts, as the following excerpts from meetings in the 1950's prove:

> *Blanc* (white): Previous definition—"that which is the color of snow, of milk."
>
> The physicist Louis de Broglie points out that white is not a color.
>
> "In Paris," notes the poet and dramatist Paul Claudel, "milk is blue."
>
> "And in farmhouses," says the biographer of Balzac and Shelley, André Maurois, "it is yellow."
>
> "Let's leave the milk out and the snow in, which no one is contesting."
>
> "What about when snow gets dirty?"
>
> "And shouldn't we include *blanc de blanc?*" asks the literary critic and oenophile, Émile Henriot.
>
> "All right. Definition? A white wine made with white grapes."

> *Brute:* Former definition—"Animal deprived of reason."
>
> "But all animals are deprived of reason. See Descartes—the theory of the animal-machine."
>
> "My dear colleague, we are here to correct a dictionary, not to take metaphysical positions. What does Littré (a rival dictionary whose author was barred from the Académie) say?"
>
> "What animal has that is most distant from man."

Everyone shouts "too long"—"badly written"—"obscure."

"The word 'brute,' " says Jean Cocteau, "is used much more in reference to men than to animals. One says 'that toreador is a brute.' One does not say 'that bull is a brute.' "

"Because it is obvious! Let's define brute as a creature deprived of reason, which covers both human brutes and animal brutes."

"Ah! This time, my dear colleague, we are once again at the very heart of metaphysics. Creatures!—But what is there in creation? It is not the Académie's role to take a position on such questions. Adjourned to the next meeting."

In its dictionary revision, the Académie naturally reverts to precedent and logic. The question arose whether the word "Benjamin" meant the youngest or the favorite son. The duc de la Force settled the dispute by quoting Saint-Simon, who had written in his memoirs of Louis XIV: "The duc du Maine, Benjamin of Madame de Maintenon . . ." "The duc du Maine," he said, "was not the son of Madame de Maintenon, thus the meaning of favorite son is the one we should adopt." One can only admire the perenniality of certain French values when one duke uses as an example what a second duke said about a third duke.

In the previous edition, when they came to the word *vie* (life), someone suggested "state of matter characterized by activity and sensibility."

"The carrot," said Paul Valéry.

General exclamations.

"But yes, the carrot is alive, but it has no activities or sensibilities." Finally, a more logical definition was chosen: "Spontaneous activity particular to organized beings, which manifests itself in the functions of nutrition and reproduction, to which are added in man reason and free will."

If it all seems an exercise in futility, the members of the Académie have no such doubts about themselves. Membership is still the pinnacle of an orthodox literary career. The Académie has perpetuated a certain type of literary careerist who learns early how to tread water in the changing currents of polite society and win a seat on the right hand of fashionable hostesses thanks to a gift for flattery, a passion for conformity, and the knack of not making influential enemies. For every Sartre who would refuse it if it was offered, there are a dozen Druons longing to be fitted for the green uniform. And in any case, it never is offered, it has to be campaigned for like a political office. In 1967, the duc de Castries presented himself for the fourth time. A *goûter* with champagne and *petits fours* had been scheduled, without the host knowing whether it would celebrate victory or attenuate defeat. As it turned out, the Académie already had at that time its full ration of dukes. The duchesse confided to a guest: "Just think! They told him he could be sure of a seat when he had written four books and he has already published fourteen."

A duke can no longer be elected on his title alone, as was the duc de Richelieu, whose acceptance speech was ghosted, and perhaps in the Académie's perspective of change, this is a radical sign of progress. But rather than sneer at its archaism, I wonder that what was originally a group of cultivated men trying to escape the preciousness of female salons has proved so durable. It is one of the only institutions Richelieu created which has lasted, just as one day Malraux may be remembered not for his writing but for cleaning the façades of Paris buildings. To examine the Académie is like finding in a forest teeming with many varieties of vegetable and animal life the last example of some species that had been thought extinct, its physical characteristics no longer suited to the changed environment, incapable of making the mutations that guaranteed the survival of other species, but, inexplicably, in contradiction to the laws of nature, alive and healthy.

French Triumphant

Malherbe had vowed to defend until death the purity of the French language, as though it was dangerously frail, when in fact it displayed remarkable vigor. Tied to the fortunes of the monarchy, it spread through Europe with French armies, to Italy with François Premier, eastward with the Crusaders, to England with the Norman invasion, and through most of Western Europe under Louis XIV. By the sixteenth century, French grammars were as much in fashion in European courts as French whalebone corsets. Amsterdam in the seventeenth century became an important center of French-language publishing. I like to imagine that the secret reason of Louis XIV for revoking the Edict of Nantes was to send hundreds of thousands of Huguenots into English and German exile to carve out new enclaves for the language. The number of foreign writers, from Leibnitz to Gibbon, who wrote it, and the number of foreign monarchs, from Frederick II of Prussia to Catherine of Russia, who spoke it, attests to the social supremacy of French in the seventeenth and eighteenth centuries.

The odd thing is that the first international treaties drafted in French were Utrecht and Rastadt in 1713 and 1714, by which France lost Canada. French as the diplomatic language did not coincide with the height of French power, but with the start of imperial decline. Treaties drafted in French often followed French defeats, such as Aix-la-Chapelle in 1748 and the treaty of Frankfurt in 1871. Though beaten, the French drew comfort from the fact that the terms of surrender were in their own language. Czarist Russia also adopted French in its treaties with Japan in 1905 and with Great Britain in 1907. Diplomatic decline began in 1919, when the Versailles Treaty was drafted in both French and English. There are still French writers who claim that the League of Nations failed because it did not use French as its official language.

The impact of French abroad led to the birth of a mystique based on the premise that since French is spoken everywhere it is a universal language and if it is a universal language it must be inherently superior to other languages. The language was seen to possess a rich store of therapeutic virtues, and Rivarol, in his celebrated essay on the "Universality of the French Language," attributed to it the power of a pacifying Esperanto. "Social and reasonable," he wrote, "it is not the French language but the human language . . . and from now on the interests of peoples and the wills of kings will stand on a more solid basis; it will no longer be possible to use words of peace to sow the seeds of war." The idea persists that there was a beneficial period of Western civilization when all Europe spoke French, and that civilization declined when the period ended. The novelist Paul Morand wrote that "nations had in the eighteenth century adopted our language as a vehicle because it did not defend narrowly selfish interests and because it translated the thought of the most populated, richest, most powerful and most representative nation in Europe. As soon as the language was used to serve a doctrine which did not correspond to the nation's potential and was bound to go out of fashion, its use never ceased to decline."

But far from being a universal language, French was simply the lingua franca of Europe's cultural and aristocratic elite. It had not, at the height of its influence, penetrated the lower classes in its own country. French *grand siècle* literature, with its Roman and Greek models, is a class literature, written for royal performances and attended by a restricted public. French in foreign courts fulfilled the need for social differentiation. Just as the bourgeoisie in France was not allowed to wear certain kinds of silks and embroideries by which they might have been mistaken for nobles, the nobility in St. Petersburg, Potsdam, and Stockholm spoke French as one of several *cordons sanitaires* protecting it from the rest of the nation. French was not "the human language," it was an instrument of sectarianism. Extolling good usage and sealing off the language from impurity helped perpetuate a society based on inequality.

Language and Revolution

The Revolution, in language and in many other ways, continued the policies of absolute monarchy. It was the Convention, more than Louis XIV, which carried out the will of Richelieu, who wanted to eradicate the dialects still spoken in most parts of France. On this subject a royalist like Rivarol and a Conventionnel like Barère were of one mind. As Rivarol explained the growth of French: "The south of France, lacking a capital and a king, could not sustain the competition of the north, and the influence of the Francien patois increased with that of the crown. It is thus the clear and methodical genius of this jargon and its rather muted pronunciation which today dominate the French language." Barère on the benches of the Convention said: "There are no more provinces. Why then should there be thirty dialects which recall their names? Citizens, you detest political federalism. Abjure the federalism of language. Language must be one like the Republic."

Both Rivarol and Barère believed that the progress of the language was linked to the state. It did not matter whether France was a kingdom or a republic, the problem remained centralization, which would only be achieved when everyone spoke French. Language continued to be, as it had been when Du Bellay praised French to put down Latin, a vehicle of nationalism.

There were, aside from the reduction of local idioms, three main ways the Revolution affected language. First, thanks to the nation in arms and later to Napoleonic conscription, French spread to the masses. Keeping millions of soldiers under arms for twenty years bled France of a generation of young men, but the survivors left military service able to speak the national tongue. One of the privileges the nobility gave up in 1789 was its monopoly on correct French, although it did not happen overnight. The reason Bonaparte's heavy Corsican accent did not handicap his career was that most other officers spoke with accents too (maréchal Kleber, who was from Strasbourg, spoke a German patois).

Second, there was a revolt against good taste and good usage, a purposeful crudeness after the overrefinement imposed by the court, and a wealth of new terms. After a century of *style noble,* the despised popular jargon rose from the masses and found its way first into the Third Estate's written complaints addressed to the king in 1789, and then into the pamphlets of the Père Duchesne and other revolutionary journalists, to create a new style which glorified neologisms and improprieties, and was dubbed the *style sans-culotte.* In all the works of Racine and Corneille, there is probably not a single example of crudeness. Now, as if opening wells of accumulated invective, the pamphleteers called the queen a whore and the king a pimp, and sprinkled every para-graph with curses.

The violence of the language kept pace with events, just as the *style noble* had been suited to the stateliness of court life. Racine's alexandrines were written for a society where emotion must always be contained, and where tragedy is inhibited and con-trolled by a sense of decorum. The language was now enriched with words like *terrorist* and *guillotine* (named after the doctor who invented what he thought of as a painless and humanitarian method of execution), and the foundations of a political vocabu-lary were laid with the invention of prefixes like *archi, ultra,* and *anti,* and the birth of the first *isms,* such as *Jacobinism* and

Republicanism. The men of the Revolution had their own form of pedantry, which came out in the new calendar with months prettily named after the weather, like Pluviose, Ventose and Floréal. (Geared to the French climate, the calendar was another instance of the Revolution practicing nationalism while announcing itself as universal.)

Third, there was born a specific oratorical style. It turned the Revolution into a drama. Factional struggles were fought on the battlefield of eloquence. Factional leaders became captains of debating teams. Men like Robespierre and Danton could only be eliminated if they were silenced. At the Convention session at which he was arrested, Robespierre tried eleven times to speak, and when he could not, he accepted his fate and shot himself in the mouth. A good speech could save a man or a party, a bad speech could lead to the gallows. The year-long struggle between the Gironde and the Montagne was a long debate in which the losing team was guillotined. Once again, the language was appropriated to serve a patriotic ideal. But revolutionary oratory differed from the *style noble* in its emphasis on feeling over reason. The best oratory was the most passionate. The orator's ideal, as Danton said, was to make his listeners quiver. Mirabeau immediately spotted Robespierre's gifts: "That young man will go far," he said, "he believes what he says."

The speakers saw themselves as new Romans and decorated their speeches with references to antiquity. Vergniaud said: "You made me vote the king's death and now you are reproaching me for it. You are like Caligula, who debauched his sisters and then exiled them as adulteresses." The Convention swam in bombast, a style which persists to this day in the National Assembly and the overripe rhetoric used by the Fifth Republic's Ciceronian apologist, André Malraux. The following phrase of Vergniaud, with its comparison to a lost civilization, is pure Malraux: "But still we must dread that in the midst of her triumphs France may still resemble those famous Egyptian monuments which have conquered time. The passing stranger is astonished by their grandeur, but if he wishes to enter them what does he find? Inanimate ashes and the silence of tombs."

The "Marseillaise," written by a thirty-two-year-old army officer named Rouget de Lisle in 1792, is another example of the Roman influence, with its reference to cohorts and phalanxes, and its noble but gory sentiments. It must be the most bloodthirsty national anthem in existence. The word "blood" runs through it with the insistence of a litany. Before the Revolution, an enemy's blood flowed as red and fluid as one's own. Men who fought on opposite sides could still respect one another's courage. But in the Messianic élan of the Revolution, an enemy was no longer an honorable man, he was a monster come to contaminate your land with his impure blood. It has always amused me to watch otherwise mild Frenchmen, the kind who wear long underwear in June and droopy cardigan sweaters to warm their livers, grow red in the face as the veins in their necks bulge and their voices roar out about throat-cutting, outrage, parricide projects, sanguinary despots, vengeance, expiring enemies, and impure blood soaking French furrows. I have wondered whether they realized what they were singing.

In the revolutionary government of the golden tongues, Robespierre was the acknowledged master. In three years, he delivered 500 speeches. The Committee of Public Safety ruled that they should be read in the temples of the Supreme Being, the deity of his new religion. His brilliance as a speaker was noted by his teachers, the Oratorian fathers, and by his colleagues in Arras where he practiced as a lawyer. His principal contribution to the rhetoric of the Revolution is the invention of correct thinking, a political adaptation of the Catholic deposit of faith.

Robespierre was the self-appointed pontiff who enunciated dogma and excommunicated heretics. He postulated an absolute identity between his views and the will of the people, which enabled him to condemn his enemies for straying from his inflexible ideological line. To condemn Anacharsis Clootz, he said: "You were always above or below the Mountain" (the radical faction of the Convention). Repeatedly he chastised "the scoundrels who are either to one side or another of truth." Repeatedly he affirmed that he alone could "make the voice of truth ring out." Again in imitation of the clergy, he confused public and private virtue. Because he led an irreproachable private life, did not take bribes, wore clean linen, and had frugal habits, he was to be taken on faith in political matters. To question his authority was as pointless as doubting an oracle. He replied with the promise of further revelations: "I am not discouraged by those who interrupt me. I even propose to reveal other truths which will excite many other murmurs."

Officially, he was only one of the twelve members of the Committee of Public Safety, and in terms of decrees and accusations signed, far from the most active. But he governed by outflanking the opposition to adopt an ever more radical stance. He urged that the king be guillotined without a trial. No verdict was needed, he said, only a sentence. After the king came Danton's turn. Robespierre's real brilliance lay in timing, in being the first to accuse. His contribution to the Terror was the tautology of guilt: A man is guilty because he is guilty, that is reason enough, or as Robespierre put it, when public notoriety accuses a citizen, it is superfluous to seek evidence. He further announced that "there is only one crime, high treason, and only one punishment, death."

Robespierre thought he could govern by persuasion like Pericles, while in fact his power depended on summary justice. He became a victim of his own logic. The more intransigent he became the more the situation worsened, and the more the situation worsened the more traitors had to be found, until it became clear to a growing number of less dogmatic persons that their own safety depended on eliminating him. He had no mass movement and few disciples, and as the number of his enemies grew he retreated into morose detachment. He stopped attending the Convention.

He was absent forty days from Committee of Public Safety meetings. When he surfaced again at the Convention on 8 Thermidor, carrying as his only weapon a rolled paper with a prepared speech, he was prevented from speaking, and he died as the scorpion dies when its sting is removed. Jacobin rhetoric has left its mark on republican politicians. Anglo-Saxons accustomed to motions moved and seconded and proposed as subjects of debate to be voted on are baffled by the French National Assembly tradition of open-ended verbiage. Parliamentary debate is one of the few amorphous areas of French life. Under the system of interpellation, a speech by a deputy sets the topic, which may be debated for days before a question to be voted upon is formulated, and then each deputy has the right to speak on whether he thinks the question is properly put. Discussion does not necessarily lead to a decision; it is an end in itself.

Faith in the power of language commits the French to the fallacy that words are deeds. An accusation is already a verdict, a call to arms a victory, and an appeal to popular behavior an improvement in popular virtue. The illusion that words are deeds helps explain certain French attitudes in the face of crisis. In 1870, no sooner had a deputy sworn that "we cannot tolerate that Strasbourg be caught under the fire of German cannons," than it happened. Or, as a Fourth Republic orator said: "No, gentlemen, this situation cannot last. A decisive blow must be struck. I am going to write an article about it." In 1940, France's military lack of preparedness was matched by the optimism of the army's supreme commander, General Maurice Gamelin, who in March, 1940, complained to the Minister of Defense, Edouard Daladier, that the Germans were avoiding contact with the French armies. He wanted to take measures that "would precipitate events and force the Germans to put an end to their wait-and-see attitude." On March 16, he gleefully reported to Daladier: "The Germans are finally on the move." On May 10, in an order to the troops, he said: "The enemy is attacking where we expected him." A week later French resistance collapsed.

The interesting thing about Gamelin is not that he misjudged the situation, but that, on the contrary, he had a lucid vision of events. On December 16, 1939, he was visited in his Vincennes fortress headquarters by the novelist Jules Romains. Gamelin was wearing his field uniform, with a soft *kepi* and puttees, although in fact he disliked going to the front, where he might see things that interfered with his opinions. He seldom strayed from the dark, vaulted offices of the fourteenth-century fortress, where he was surrounded by fifteen loyal officers, like a chief friar in a monastery. In this atmosphere of timeless serenity, Gamelin talked for over an hour. He was charming and relaxed and reminded Romains of a country squire.

Not a single telephone call interrupted them. With his solemn, professorial air, Gamelin explained: "The whole character of this war will be profoundly new, and too few people realize this.

You know, most people think this war will be a repetition of the last. But there will be no resemblance between this war and the First World War . . . I think that a period of apparent immobility will lead suddenly to an operation in which total power will be used at once . . . it will be very swift and very horrible. When will it happen? May. Yes, May, it is almost certain." Here was the French army chief predicting the date and the outcome of the German spring offensive for which France was totally unprepared. For him, that was enough. He could go back to reading Einstein and art books. What did it matter that France did not have the planes or tanks to meet the German offensive so long as he, Gamelin, had an intellectual grasp of the situation? He lived on an abstract level, with his maps and reports. There is a family resemblance between Robespierre formulating dreams of a perfect democracy which ended in the Terror, and Gamelin postulating the theorems of a new kind of warfare which ended in French collapse. In both cases there is an ideal, self-sustaining vision of life that is removed from meddlesome reality, and an unwillingness to accept whatever interferes with this mental representation.

The Père Duchesne with his oaths and diatribes did not rub out the French of the *précieuses*. They coexisted, and the language today is an accumulation of these sometimes contradictory inheritances. The Revolution was unable to affect its deep formalism. It could not even abolish the *vous* form of address. There was a brief period of equalitarian fervor in which efforts were made to enforce the *tu* form which disregards class distinctions. Such a measure was proposed in a 1790 article in the *Mercure National*, entitled "On the Influence of Words and the Power of Usage."

It seemed reasonable to *tutoyer* everyone at a time when *Citizen* had replaced *Monsieur* and *Madame*. Orators at the Convention asked for a decree making the *tu* form mandatory. Those who persisted in using the more formal *vous* would become "suspect as adulators, guilty of supporting haughtiness, which serves as a pretext for inequality." The Committee of Public Safety used *tu* in its correspondence, but no Convention decree was ever drafted to enforce this usage. The army adopted it, and privates said *tu* to their officers. But after the Thermidor reaction, there was a return to *vous*. Defenders of the *vous* argued that social and moral inequalities are founded on nature and reason. Officers began once again to demand this sign of respect from their soldiers. Giving up the distinctions of the *vous* would have meant a mutation of the French character which the Revolution had not achieved.

Vous and *tu* are power pronouns that give away class status and reflect a society that believes in social inequality as natural and beneficial, a rigidly structured society where everyone has an appointed place and everyone also says *vous* to the powerful state as angels say *vous* to God, who says *tu* back to them, and as Corneille's nobles say *tu* to their valets. *Vous* evokes titles and inequalities, while *tu* is the egalitarian pronoun. Racine uses a change from *vous* to *tu* to mark passion or other strong emotions, and the new-wave director François Truffaut has used the same device in his films—in *Shoot the Piano Player,* the actor Charles Aznavour is being insulted by a gangster and tells him "please address me as *vous,*" and the gangster repeats the remarks using the *vous* form. In Truffaut's *Mississippi Mermaid,* Catherine Deneuve tells Jean-Paul Belmondo during a quarrel: "You were nicer to me when you said *vous.*" Perhaps the abolition of power pronouns is a condition of democracy in France. They are forgotten in certain situations, in demonstrations of students and workers, in anger, and in danger—mountain climbers above a certain altitude switch from *vous* to *tu.* The power pronouns were useful in France's colonies, establishing in everyday language the inferiority of the natives, to whom the *colons* said *tu.* Even today in North Africa many persons will expect a European to say *tu* to them and will respond with *vous. Vous* used by equals, as in the correspondence between Madame de Sévigné and her daughter, is in itself a restraint. Couples who have kept up the *vous* after ten or twenty years of marriage, not even lapsing into *tu* in the intimacy of the marriage bed, find that it is the final barrier to familiarity. The only instance in French usage when one is allowed to use both the *vous* and *tu* form toward the same person in the same sentence is during the reception of a new member at the Académie Française, if the one making the reception speech is a close friend of the new member, as in this recent case: "Lui et sa charmante femme, ta mère, étaient, vous le savez, monsieur, fort liés avec mes propres parents." (He and his charming wife, your mother, were, as you know, sir, close to my own parents.)

Language and Bureaucracy

Every French regime, although it cannot know its own life-span, can be sure that its successor will enforce linguistic centralization. Napoleon's monument to the language was the Code Civil, a treatise on civil law which elevated bureaucratic jargon to a literary style. There was something in the French language which lent itself to red tape. Stendhal read a few pages of the Code Civil every day, the way an athlete builds up his muscles with barbells. He called this "finding my tone." The tone of the Code Civil was precise and colorless, like the definition of the well-dressed man: No one can remember what he was wearing after he has left the room. Its main quality was clarity. What it had to say it said without excess, ambiguity, or imprecision. One particularly successful article, number 1101, is the definition of the contract: "A contract is a convention by which one or several persons commit themselves toward one or several other persons to give, to do, or not to do something." It must be admitted that this covers everything from Faust to white slavery.

The French civil servant today, whether he is writing a taxpayer who is late with his returns or asking his boss for a raise, can feel with considerable justification that he is the heir of pure classical French, and is, to a greater extent than the writer or the journalist, still following the seventeenth-century precept of Madame de Sévigné: "With what deference do words offer themselves to you and to the arrangement you make of them." The bureaucratic language is considered, like church liturgy, beautiful, binding, and rigorously exact. Civil servants are advised by their superiors to maintain a certain nobility of tone, to prevent their letters from being confused with commercial correspondence. They have their special form of courtesy, defined as "the art of presenting decisions which do not conform to the personal interest of those to whom they are addressed."

The shadings of introductory locutions were something I discovered as a second lieutenant in the French army, when I once made the blunder of beginning a report to a superior officer with *j'ai l'honneur de vous prier de vouloir bien* instead of *j'ai l'honneur de vous prier de bien vouloir*. As my company commander patiently explained: "The degree of insistence is marked by the place of the adverb *bien;* if it follows the verb *vouloir* it indicates an imperative request which it would be unseemly to make except of a subordinate; it does not imply the right to reply which it is essential to assume when dealing with a superior and which may be shown by placing the adverb *bien* before the word *vouloir."*

The French civil servant arranges words in formulae that cover every conceivable situation. In phrases swollen with prepositional, conjunctional, and adverbial locutions, he observes, he notes, he ascertains, he signals to the attention of, he adds, he makes more precise, he underlines, he confirms, and he reminds. He also allows himself to remark, he considers, he estimates, he cannot but specify once again, he does not doubt, he does not underestimate, nor does he ignore or lose sight of. After the initial study of a matter, its examination can be deepened, attentive, benevolent, detailed, favorable, swift, or serious, whereas a solution can be efficacious, equitable, opportune, desirable, or questionable. In support of this close-ranked verbal assault, the conditional clauses serve the function of a reserve which can be brought in to save the day: Considering on the other hand that, while not forgetting that in case of, eventually, unless, and the quintessential *en principe,* which takes away with one hand what it is offering with the other. The way bureaucracy permeates French life: Ask a man in the street his name and the chances are he will give you his last name first as though he were filling out a form.

In 1832, under the Restoration, correct spelling became mandatory for civil servants. That a general or a minister massacred spelling could be excused as an amusing eccentricity, but civil servants, as the representatives of official France, could be allowed no such diversions. There arose a caste of correct spellers, able to find their way through the labyrinth of French orthography, modern Druids to whom the secrets of the cult have been passed along with the mistletoe branch. Good spelling became a class symbol, and expressions arose like *une orthographe de cuisinière* (she spells like a cook).

As nineteenth-century governments strengthened the hold of official, correct French, the Romantic movement developed as the linguistic progeny of the Revolution. Like the pamphleteers of

1789 who used purposely coarse language to discredit *bel usage,* the Romantics announced their intention of emancipating the language. They rebelled against the conventions of seventeenth-century tragedy, the Aristotelian rules of unity (time, place, and action), and the distinction of genres (nothing comic in tragedies). They rebelled too against the periphrase. For a dramatist like Racine, it was bad taste to call a spade a spade; it had to be called a broad-bladed implement of digging. Esther is not a murderess, she is "the execrable instrument of an infamous death." A misalliance is "a fatal knot." Language is veiled and shrouded like a woman in purdah. The Romantics insisted on the use of concrete words and tried to abolish the distinction between words that could and could not be used. "A word is a living thing," pronounced Victor Hugo, who elsewhere claimed that he had "put a Phrygian bonnet on the old dictionary." But their revolt was timid. Hugo, while railing against "that aged dowager, the Académie," was already planning his campaign to storm it. The Romantics were traditional in their use of the alexandrine and polished rhymes, an attitude that was parodied in a Théophile Gautier novel: A disillusioned young poet puts a pistol in his mouth to end it all, but realizes he has left no epitaph. He puts the pistol down and begins to write:

> From the cruelties of chance, will may triumph,
> The weakest of mortals can master his fate.
> When one had courage and . . .

The poet ponders, rings for his servant, and asks for the rhyming dictionary. Alas, there is no rhyme in French for triumph, and the poet puts away his pistol. Concern with meter and rhyme, assisted by the poverty of the vocabulary, has saved his life.

The rise of nineteenth-century nationalism, itself the result of the French Revolution, meant the gradual decline of French as a universal tongue. It persisted to some extent as the language of elites. Bismarck warned his son: "When you venture forth into society, you will often find yourself in situations in which you feel uneasy and humiliated if everything that is French is not familiar to you." The Italian nationalist Cavour's diary, as well as sections of Lord Palmerston's intimate correspondence, was written in

French. But Goethe, after a visit to Strasbourg in 1820, was "repelled by rather than attracted to French language and manners ... We found their manner of living too fixed, too aristocratic, their philosophy abstruse and yet inadequate."

The penetration of French into the countryside was begun in earnest with Napoleonic conscription, although Napoleon was understanding about dialects and told his generals to "let the Alsatians speak German as long as their swordstrokes are French." Penetration continued with the laws of the Second Empire and the Third Republic setting up free and compulsory education, so that the illiteracy rate was reduced from 60 percent in 1789 to 12 percent in 1882. French evolved from the tongue of a discredited nobility to a truly national language, thanks to the schoolroom and the *instituteur* who, with the mayor and the parish priest, formed the nineteenth-century trinity. It was drummed into schoolchildren that "without education, one arrives at nothing." They were told about the little boy who could not read and who, when his father asked him for a spoonful of cough medicine, took it from the bottle labeled "poison." *"Misérable!"* said the doctor, "you have poisoned your father."

Like most aspects of French life, language becomes a political issue. The post-World-War-I resurgent right wing, led by Charles Maurras, and the Action Française hotly defended regionalism and a return to local patois. In 1924 President Herriot felt moved to denounce "the reactionaries who want to bring back patois, counting on ignorance to destroy the Republic itself." The quarrel continues today. Officials in Brittany refuse to register the birth of children who have been given Celtic names that French law does not recognize. Legal action for "nondeclaration of children" was taken against a Monsieur Manrot, who named his five children Maydon, Gwendal, Diwenska, Skeltjenn, and Brann. He appealed and won the case in 1961. But when he moved to the Morbihan department, he was refused family allocations for his numerous family. He sued, the court of appeals in Rennes ordered an inquiry, and in 1963 there was a small triumph for regional dialects when the legal existence of his oddly named children was recognized. But the use of patois continues to be discouraged, and Basque, Breton, Catalan, and other local tongues are proscribed in French schools.

The Best Language

The national language is attributed qualities linked to other aspects of national life, such as climate and geography. Language is part of the mystique of a unity in the life-style, which has its partial origin in nostalgia for absolutist France, when Le Nôtre gardens, Vauban fortresses, Racine tragedies, Philippe de Champaigne paintings, and Mansart designs all seemed to be inspired by the same golden rule of classical order. Thus, the language is said to have "the clarity without violence of the skies of Île-de-France and Touraine."

The fetish of clarity hounds every schoolboy, who is taught that "what is not clear is not French." I once had a *lycée* teacher who taught the class to admire the works of writers "who do not throw a shadow," like Marivaux and Molière, and who was fond of quoting this line of Anatole France: "French has three qualities: the first is clarity, the second is again clarity, and the third is still clarity." Clarity depends largely on the famous sequential order which took centuries to develop from the Latin order based on declensions. French is a language which can be understood as it is spoken. It unravels like a ball of wool. To each idea corresponds a phrase. German, with its verb clusters at the end of a sentence like actors taking curtain calls, offends the French sensibility, which is deaf to its secret resonances. If French is weak on music, it is strong on form. As for English, French linguists consider its inversions and flexibility a form of syntactical irresponsibility. A Dickensian sentence like "a rosy-cheeked, apple-faced lass" would have to be translated in French: "A young woman with cheeks like roses and a face like an apple." There is to the French a lack of precision in the English use of prepositional phrases like "to go out" (*sortir*), "to get down," (*descendre*), and "to go away" (*partir*).

Along with clarity, French is praised for having the regularity of a metronome. If one assumes that the perfect language would have an exact alternance of vowels and consonants (but on those grounds what is more perfect than baby talk), a study of cryptographer's charts on the regular frequency of vowels shows that French, with a regularity of 44 percent, strikes a mean between

German with 38 percent (clusters of unpronounceable, guttural consonants) and Italian with 48 percent (a spineless and vowelized Mediterranean idiom, think the French, like overcooked spaghetti). Patriotic French linguists support the conclusion of Rivarol that the French language is still the human language, a happy mean between the harsh languages of the north, products of foggy, intemperate climes, and the soft languages of the south, overripe from too much sun.

To the apologists of the French language, its genius is also seen as the genius of its people, an expression of basic traits in the French personality. The genius of certain writers does seem to lie in their ability to express the sensibility of a people. When Colette compares the bodies of two women lying in bed to two spoons that have been fitted away in the silver drawer, she combines sensual understanding with a practical, orderly, *ménagère* side, in a manner that we think of as characteristically French. The desire for clarity and order is explained as inherent in the French mind as well as in the French landscape. It corresponds to a distaste for ambiguity, a need for heightened differentiation.

Whether the French language is a product of deep French personality traits or whether the personality was shaped by the language is a chicken-egg dilemma. Inasmuch as a language is a representation of the world, the French idiom has a tendency toward the abstract and the juridical; it breaks up and classifies reality according to an ideal order which it imposes on the sensory world. It carries the rearrangement of the order of perception further than other languages. Thus the importance of arbitrary rules like gender and conjugation. There is no organic reason for the gender of words. Moon is feminine in French and masculine in German, while sun is masculine in French and feminine in German. As for verb tenses, it has always seemed to me a singular lapse that a language which has an imperfect tense and a more-than-perfect tense is missing a perfect tense. But perhaps the traps of existing tenses are sufficient. Is the imperfect of the subjunctive really necessary, with all those endings with *ass* in them, like *que je me couchasse* and *assassinassiez?* Thanks to these seldom-used inventions of grammarians, there is such a discrepancy between spoken and written French that on occasion the government has had to intervene to simplify the language. In 1900 the Ministry of Education ruled that the use of the subjunctive present after a conditional clause would be tolerated as correct usage, allowing Frenchmen to say things like "I may go to bed" without making a grammatical blunder. Other tenses like the *préterit supérieur surcomposé* died from disuse.

Molière has his characters use complicated verb tenses to reveal their characters; they say *vous mourûtes* instead of *vous êtes mort,* and with each sentence are made to appear more precious. And as if the regular verbs were not enough, there are 350 irregular verbs that mock the rules.

The preoccupation with purism and grammar and the government policy to make correct French prevail have obscured those writers who steeped their talent in the tradition of the spoken language or who broke the bonds of grammar. Villon is viewed with uneasy suspicion in the classroom, for his ballads echo the pungent imagery of Paris streets, and are filled with a realism and intensity which make Malherbe's correct lines written nearly a century later seem more like water than wine. Just as human tissue produces antibodies, the French classical movement secreted its opposites in La Fontaine and Saint-Simon. Like Villon, La Fontaine had recourse to daily life and popular language for his fables, and was credited with "rumpling the stiff classical drapery." Saint-Simon, whose memoirs are one of the five or six indestructible monuments of French prose style, could disregard the canons of his age because he was writing for posthumous publication. Expressiveness was his only rule, and the modern reader is likely to find his vividness more rewarding than the periphrases of Racine and the pedantic phraseology of Corneille—their style is modish, it was intended to please a particular court, just as a couturier's collection is designed for a small number of private customers and American buyers. The collection is outdated in a matter of months, but Racine and Corneille live on, not only because of their mastery but because their style has been handed down as the true French literary tradition. When copies of Saint-Simon's memoirs were privately circulated among fashionable Parisians before their first publication in 1788, the queen of the literary salons, Madame du Deffand, found them abominably written because they were graphic and concrete and avoided the solemn.

Saint-Simon invigorated the language with expressions like *une amitié de mie* (a friendship made of the crumb of the loaf rather than the crust), *avoir ses bucoliques* (to have one's bucolics, or frivolous pastimes), *rotir le balais* (to roast the broom, or burn the candle at both ends), *etre dans la bouteille* (to be in the bottle, or informed of a secret), *on a voulu me jeter le chat aux jambes* (they wanted to throw the cat at my legs, or to trip me up), and *il parla comme un chien qui court sur de la braise* (he spoke like a dog running over hot coals). But to a purist like Albert Dauzat, author of a respected *History of the French Language*, Saint-Simon is as bizarre as a baroque pearl, "an excitable fellow who was out of place in his century of grammarians."

Proust is even more of a problem to linguists, for it is harder to disclaim his genius. But Dauzat plunges in and calls him "one of the most artificial of our recent writers . . . complex if not confused." The Proustian sentence seems to have been invented to infuriate grammarians and shatter their dreams of sequential order. It blossoms, it spirals, it meanders, it mushrooms, it does everything but follow the linear progression so dear to Rivarol. It clings to associations and perceptions rather than to an ideal of clarity. Gide was put off at first and wrote an unfavorable report to the publisher Gallimard, who turned down *Swann's Way*. Grammarians today still tax him with gratuitous obscurantism and linguistic homicide (he "drowns" each main clause in subordinate causes). But Proust showed how flexible and rich in construction the French language can be, and produced an alternative for sequential syntax.

The Académiciens of the seventeenth century who thought they were leaving their successors a language which would no longer need to change because all its rules had been laid down, were confounded by writers like Saint-Simon and Proust, and in the twentieth century by Céline, who invented a highly sophisticated prose style by using a mixture of spoken language, slang, and telegraphic punctuation. Céline is the last Hébertiste, a direct descendant of the Père Duchèsne, to whose sense of outrage and deliberate crudeness he adds contemporary man's awareness that the cry of anguish must be its own reward since there are no alternatives to human suffering. Céline's jagged, ungrammatical style was the linguistic counterpart to the dislocation of the French psyche that followed World War I. Just as Saint-Simon chronicled absolutist decline, Céline buried nineteenth-century *douceur de vivre*. Like Saint-Simon, Céline invented words and colloquialisms and made expressiveness rather than correctness his aim.

But such writers throw shadows, their innovations are alarming, they represent a countertradition to the deep conservative longing for a fixed and immutable idiom. They break the continuity of a written style which from the sixteenth century was tended in the hothouse climate of an elitist culture. The custodians of French literature tell us to admire, not the power of Céline's prose but the matchless legato of nineteenth-century French verse, and its use of the silent *e*. The melodic line is compared in subtlety to a Debussy prelude, because its effect depends on what is left unspoken. We are given as an example of good poetry Musset's line, *"Voici la vert(e) Ecoss(e) et la brun(e) Itali(e),"* because of the music of its four silent *e*'s, and we are left to ponder whether there is any save a phonetic reason for this sudden proximity of Scotland and Italy.

Can any valid claim be made for the superiority of a language? If it were to be based on the masterpieces of literature, then English with Shakespeare, Italian with Dante, German with Goethe, Russian with Tolstoy, and Spanish with Cervantes, all come before French, which boasts no single overwhelming literary figure. The French acknowledge that their literature is a republic which has never had a monarch. The argument of universality is more historic than linguistic. French spread, as did Spanish and English, on the wings of colonial empires. It was adopted in foreign courts and by foreign writers because France was the first major European nation to be formed. Its unchallenged position of power and wealth gave its language a privileged position, which has declined since the rise of English-speaking world powers in the nineteenth and twentieth centuries. The idea that there is anything inherently superior in the French language is simply one of the more deep-rooted instances of national self-congratulation. Every language has the defects of its virtues, and the paradox of French is that in stressing clarity, it becomes ambiguous.

Sequential construction leads to sentences such as *J'ai des bonbons pour mes enfants qui sont dans ma poche* (I have candy for my children who are in my pocket). The regularity of vowel gradation, along with the habit of keeping new words out of the language, has led to ambiguities of the ear which can only be corrected by the eye. Since so many words sound the same, the only way to differentiate them is by their spelling. French is the leading manufacturer of homonyms: *Pin* (pine), *pain* (bread), *peins* (paint), *peint* (painted); *poids* (weight), *pois* (peas), and *poix* (pitch pine); *saint* (saint), *sain* (healthy), *sein* (breast), and *seing* (official signature); *louer* (to let) and *louer* (to praise); *croquer* (to sketch) and *croquer* (to crunch). Phonetic spelling in French would make the written language unintelligible. Another ambiguity lies in the frequent double meanings of short phrases which, again, can only be sorted out on the printed page: *je veux l'avoir* which, spoken, could mean either "I want to see her" or "I want to have it," and *trop peureux* which could be either "too scared" or "too happy."

The poverty of contemporary French vocabulary can be shown by comparing the Joycean vocabulary of 55,000 words with the Racinian vocabulary of 1,500 words or the 4,000 words Baudelaire used to write *Les Fleurs du Mal*. This means that a great many words are impressed into multiple duty—the highly praised Robert dictionary lists 277 meanings of the verb *faire* (make). It also means that a great many common, everyday words simply do not exist in French and must be expressed by periphrase. To sip becomes *boire à petites gorgées* (to drink in small swallows), to bake becomes *cuir au four* (to cook in an oven), and to shrug, *hausser les épaules* (to raise one's shoulders). This reinforces the tendency toward composed words (like ground-apple for potato) and word clusters (like thoracic cage for thorax).

The Racinian habit persists of refusing to call something by its direct name when a chaste periphrase can be found. At their best, these are both elegant and precise, like *le grand frisson* (the great shudder) for orgasm. But more often, they simply clutter up the language. A slum becomes an "insalubrious island" (*îlot insalubre*), gerrymandering is "active electoral geography" (*géographie electorale active*), and a false alarm is a "malevolent appeal" (*appel malveillant*). The tendency to express oneself in euphemisms is so ingrained that even the OAS killers in Algeria resorted to it, calling their systematic murders of Moslems "punctual actions." Paris prostitutes never ask for money but for their *petit cadeau* (little gift). A condom is a *petit chapeau* (little hat).

After it's over they say "Well, did that relieve you?" (*Alors, c'a t'a soulagé.*)

From the periphrase, it is easy to slip into the pleonasm, and French is stocked with unexpected hazards, involuntary errors, onerous expenses, forced constraints, exclusive monopolies, and disappointing illusions. Hard on the heels of the redundant are the truisms, which are called La Palissades after Captain de la Palisse, who was famous for stating the obvious. A song composed in his honor after he was killed at the battle of Pavia said that a quarter of an hour before his death he was still alive. A corollary of the truism is the use of conventional phrases that mean the opposite of what they say. In the Frenchman's personal strategy, *vous pouvez compter sur moi* (count on me) means forget about it, and *nous sommes parfaitement d'accord avec vous sur le principe* (in principle we are in perfect agreement) means we are poles apart.

There is also bound to be considerable ambiguity in a language which lends itself to subtle shadings the way French does. Paul Claudel was not *un admirable ambassadeur* (noteworthy in the office), but *un ambassadeur admirable* (worthy of admiration). When Musset writes *"une robe blanche et de blanches mains,"* the position of the qualifying adjective is intended to mean that whiteness is the color of the dress but an intrinsic quality of the hands; whatever the nuance, how to render it in English? And how, I wonder, does a professor of French explain to a foreigner learning the language the difference in meaning between *encore plus* (again more) and *plus encore* (more again). It is all too remote from the empirical world, an ideal construction where meaning depends more on the position of the word in the sentence than on the object to which it refers.

French is also restricted in its construction and in its inability to derive adverbs and adjectives from nouns. Poets like Mallarmé and Claudel derived some of their effects from unexpected syntax which read like literal translations from some other language, like Claudel's line *"les yeux comme pour chanter qui m'attendant"* (the eyes as if to sing which await me). But such inversions have more to do with a private esthetic than with rebellion against stiff French syntax. As for derivations, often an English word must be translated by its opposite in French; shortness equals *peu de longueur* (of little length), or by an approximation, like *admirablement* for beautifully.

Is French a Dead Language?

Written French, like Greek in the third century and Latin in imperial Rome, may be headed for the linguistic cemetery. It shows some of the symptoms of a moribund language: An inability to renew itself, a frozen syntax, and an impoverished vocabulary that seems archaic for its time. The language of businessmen is English (there are no French words for management or marketing), the language of airplane pilots is English, the language of outer space is English or Russian, and the language of modern science is English. When the prince de Broglie, 1929 Nobel Prize winner for the wave character theory of electrons, wanted to discuss nuclear physics with his cousin the duc de Broglie, also a distinguished physicist, they found it necessary to resort to English. A study should be made on the influence of language on the technological gap, taking as a starting point the way Latin impeded scientific advance when it was the language of scholars in the Middle Ages. The predominance of French seems today reduced to gastronomy—they will continue writing *hors d'oeuvres* on menus the way they write *andante* on music scores.

The French remain faithful to the classical tradition. Who else could name a rocket Bérenice, after the heroine of a Racine tragedy? They continue to set up, just as they did in the seventeenth century, agencies concerned with the defense of the language. But today, the language really needs to be defended from the inroads made by English. The twentieth-century Du Bellay is a Sorbonne professor named Etiemble, who has turned what he feels is the corruption of French by English into a full-time crusade. He relentlessly hunts down Anglicisms in the press, in political speeches, in the entertainment world, and in military jargon, and from the examples he gives, it sounds as though French has capitulated as a vehicle to describe contemporary life. He reminds his readers that the French language has always had to fight corruption, but this time, he says, it is an uphill battle: French is slowly being replaced by what he calls *sabir Atlantique*, a hodgepodge with a strong strain of English destined to become a European lingua franca.

Contagion is a symptom of weakness; French vulnerability to English is a sign of poor health, like a run-down organism. French linguists are haunted by Joseph de Maistre's observation: "National degradation is always announced by the degradation of the language." Curiously, at a time when the French educational system is being reformed to stress science and modern languages, the defense of the language is being linked to the defense of Latin, as if a dying language could be helped by a dead one. Like a twentieth-century Bossuet, the writer Roger Ikor pleads that Latin be saved. "If the famous French clarity exists," he writes, "compared to English empiricism, German mists, and Russian ardor, it is largely thanks to Latin." Nostalgic partisans of Latin recall that when the École Polytechnique was founded in 1806, one condition of admission was "a knowledge of Latin perfect enough to discuss the *De Officiis* with its author Cicero." But the last word on the subject must be given to Rimbaud who, when a fourteen-year-old schoolboy, said: "Why learn Latin, a language that no one speaks?"

Government zeal in support of the language reminds one of those energetic committees formed to save wildlife threatened with extinction, like the dodo. There is a Committee for French as the Language of Europe, a High Committee for the Defense and Expansion of the French Language, an International Association for French-speaking Parliamentarians, and many others.

Only General de Gaulle among more recent chiefs of state talked about his language in the martial terms of battles to be fought against other languages throughout the world. "Whether the French language wins or loses the battle in Canada," said the general in his first 1968 press conference, "will weigh heavily in the struggle being waged for it from one end of the world to the other." This kind of linguistic militancy is yet another sign of a country which must satisfy itself with the illusion rather than the reality of grandeur. France can no longer compete in terms of power, so it continues to compete in terms of language. One of the reasons the general kept the Common Market door shut on England was the fear that English would supplant French as the working language of the Six. One wonders what the fact that a few million Africans more or less speak a few tortured words of

French or that the Ottawa museum has a record library of 6,500 French folk songs has to do with the merits of the Fifth Republic. And yet every time the French language holds its own it is hailed in the French press as a triumph. In the spring of 1968, France and 35 other countries asked that French be used as a working language in the United Nations, along with English. The proposal was adopted by a vote of 73 to 9 with 26 abstentions. A few days later, the Canadian government agreed to make the entire country, not just the province of Quebec, bilingual. The French press rejoiced over this dual triumph. "The battle of the French language has been won," the headlines said.

In October, 1968, the first assembly of French-speaking parliaments met in Versailles, gathering members of 26 national and 6 regional assemblies, mainly from the African continent. The Assembly decided to study the launching of a communications satellite so that from time to time word from the heavens can come in French. Malraux gave the closing speech and agreed that attempting to measure the value of rival cultures is hardly a rewarding approach. But he could not resist saying that French culture had given birth to fraternity, a statement on the same level as the schoolboy dictum that the French *colon* came to Africa to help the native and not to exploit him. French culture, more accurately, has been one of the vehicles of French nationalism and French colonialism. To claim a monopoly on fraternity is cultural bigotry akin to claiming a monopoly on linguistic clarity. Malraux ties the spread of French culture to the Revolution, whereas the great period of French cultural expansion took place under the absolute monarchy; thanks to the nineteenth-century rise of European nationalisms, other cultures resisted French culture.

If there is hope for the French language, it is not behind the creaky doors of the Académie, the better-oiled ones of government agencies, or plans to put French in orbit. It is in the linguistic resourcefulness of the French people, in the expressiveness of popular French. I spent months in the Bibliothèque Nationale digesting an overdose of stilted French, with its smug use of ready-made phrases and its formal, inflated, redundant manner of getting at a subject. I repaired frequently to a café near the Halles that was patronized by men in faded blue smocks who came in for a quick *petit blanc* and by women in white from the BOF (*beurre, oeufs, fromages,* or butter, eggs, and cheese) shops. Their day-to-day phrases summed up a highly civilized philosophy of life. When one of them said, after downing his glass, *"ça ne fait pas de mal"* (it can't hurt you), he seemed to be expressing the natural prudence of a people who have learned that one way to cope with life is not to expect too much, and who approach its pleasures with a certain amount of discretion. Other oft-repeated phrases were *"ne vous compliquez pas l'existence"* (do not complicate your existence), which seemed as deserving and unattainable an ideal in present-day society as Plato's Idea of the Good, and, on leaving the establishment, *"bon courage quand même"* (well, anyhow, take courage), which hinted at a profusion of mysterious, threatening forces that are bound to strike when one is least expecting it, and against which one should take permanent courage. In the day-to-day talk of Frenchmen who are not necessarily concerned with correct grammar, there can be found a great linguistic richness. If the French language is seen as the product of a human community, it becomes a living thing involved in a process of change and evolution. But if it is seen as an inheritance from the seventeenth century, with a "DO NOT TOUCH" sign on it, then it is just a fossil. The mystique that it is a superior language can only help embalm it in textbooks. Fifty years from now French schoolchildren may be translating Montaigne into Atlantic sabir rather than Livy into French.

Little Anthology of Random Remarks

A charcutière on the storks of Strasbourg: "Ah, you know, monsieur, they are something to see. They fly in formation like airplanes. All those birds lack is the ability of speech."

A retired carpenter, talking about his son who never visits him: "Some people have a cobblestone in place of a heart. When he was a kid in the Luxembourg one day, he wanted his mother to pick up his ball. Hey, I said, she's not a beast of burden. A year ago he came when I was sitting on the edge of my bed and he said 'you certainly have got nice pajamas.' I ask you, is that a thing to say to a sick old man, to compliment him on his pajamas? Ah, it's always the same.

"They get out of the regiment and they don't know what to

do, they don't even have their elementary school certificate. So they get a job with the metro. It has to be seen—wage-earners in uniform. The punchers use both hands to remove the little confetti from your ticket. Then he wanted to get married. What a disaster! He didn't even own a bed. I said, how are you going to do it, on the floor? I always had a craft, I was above average, but today, it's credit that is ruining them all. They earn forty francs and they spend fifty."

A son talking about his father: "In France the old ones always have the last word. You have to have lost at least two wars to be an adult here. The closer you get to ninety the more chance you have of being taken seriously."

Old man: "When you get to be seventy, it gets so more members of your family are dead than alive. I've stopped counting, they all went, one after the other. It was a good thing I didn't get along with my family, they could all die, it left me neither hot nor cold, at least I was ahead that way."

On a child who isn't doing well in school: "It must be that he's growing too fast."

Café orator: "If France is on the edge of the abyss, let me tell you, it's because she's a nation of fifty million cuckolds. The cuckolds are in the majority, *voilà!* That at least is plain, clear, and easy to understand."

In the metro: "Why should it be me who has to give his seat rather than someone else? I'm tired too. My feet hurt too. I paid my seat like everyone else. That fellow across the aisle is younger than I am, why doesn't he get up . . . Oh, excuse me, madame, I hadn't noticed, please don't thank me, it's perfectly natural."

Returning lady vacationer: "Let me tell you I came back well done. It's when the sun is hiding behind clouds that he's most dangerous."

Two readers leaving the Bibliothèque Nationale: "There is no more respect for the old, it is held up to ridicule."

"It depends. There are some admirable things."

"There is truth in what you say. Not everyone is obliged to like Picasso, is it not so? Picasso, would you like me to tell you, he began as an artist, and then, he wanted to do something commercial, so he discovered Cubism."

In a café: "What's become of you?"

"I don't become, I continue."

Elderly bachelor: "No, don't give me any hard-boiled eggs, they remind me of picnics and summer camps. And no chicken, I eat too much chicken in planes. Women have a talent for wasting time. Take my maid Jeanne for example. I wanted to train her, I taught her to go out in the morning for croissants, an operation which takes me two minutes, since the bakery is fifty meters from the house. Well, she always takes between a quarter of an hour to twenty minutes, to such a degree that one day I followed her, for I could not imagine what she was up to during that quarter-hour. She left the building and hesitated a long moment between two bakeries, the one on the left and the one on the right. And yet I had told her the one on the left had the best croissants. She could not decide. Finally, she went toward the left, stopping in front of each store window, windows she passed twenty times a day, but she could not help stopping before each one. And I realized there was no mystery, that it was easy for her to waste a quarter of an hour or twenty minutes by dragging out each of her gestures and decisions."

Two fathers waiting for their children outside an elementary school and discussing the technical merits of punishment: "The slap, it vexes, it is the gesture, you understand."

"Yes, but I could not restrain myself, that is why I prefer the spanking, it relieves, it makes the anger pass."

The defender of equality: "No, monsieur, I'm not afraid to say it, I've never been a racist, never! I'm broad-minded, we're all made alike, isn't that true? All the races are equal, a Negro is the exact equal of a white—of anything—of a Frenchman if you like, why not? How can I forgive the Americans for shutting the trapdoor on the Negroes? That affair is the shame of America. Individuals like that, they disgust me, I vomit them. They've got no past, they've only got the dollar. What they want is to take Notre Dame apart stone by stone and rebuild it on the banks of the Hudson—and on top of that they have the gall to treat Negroes like dogs!"

6

❯❯❯-❯❯❯-❯❯❯-❯❯❯-❯❯❯-❯❯❯-❯❯❯-❯❯❯-❯❯❯-❯❯❯-❯❯❯-❯❯❯❝❝❝-❝❝❝-❝❝❝-❝❝❝-❝❝❝-❝❝❝-❝❝❝-❝❝❝-❝❝❝-❝❝❝-❝❝❝-❝❝❝

Thinking French

FRANCE is a Koranic nation. The Koran dictates not only the Moslem's relationship to his God, but also his social behavior. Concerning every event of his life, the Moslem can say, "It is written," because he knows there is a prescription of conduct in his sacred book governing such nonreligious aspects of life as courtesy, divorce, and inheritance. Although there is no French Koran, there is a sum of written and unwritten procedures that the Frenchman can follow in most situations, whether a *boule* breaks during a game of *pétanque* or he is looking for the proper salutation in a letter to his mother-in-law. The Frenchman lives in a climate of social certainty. The meaning of *savoir-vivre* is that there is a definite way to do even something so trivial as sitting in a chair in the Tuileries: You pay 45 centimes (about 10 cents) and you receive a ticket from a lady which informs you on the back that you can sit in the chair all day but that there is no right of transmission, as that would be prejudicial to the concessionaires; the cost of rental is due no matter how brief the time of occupation of the chair. Should you be a mutilated veteran you will be exonerated from all rental fees on presentation of your mutilated veteran's card (visible mutilation being insufficient evidence of same).

The Great Codifiers

The French live in a codified environment, where every situation is either legislated or determined by usage. Prevision and a sense of form contribute to a life-style that helps bind a people into a nation. This was so under the *ancien régime* when Louis XIV on his deathbed decreed the length of the trains the ladies of the court should wear at his funeral. It was true under the Fourth Republic, when an ordinance was passed instructing concierges on how much time they should spend sweeping courtyards. And it is true under the Fifth Republic, which has ruled that the inside of the windows in the Ministry of Finance in a wing of the Louvre are the responsibility of the resident ministry, while the outside of the windows should be washed by the Cultural Affairs ministry.

Nothing must be left to chance. Not only did Napoleon codify law with the Code Civil, but the chef Carême codified gastronomy in his twelve-volume treatise, the nineteenth-century diplomat Gobineau codified racism in an essay in which he was the first to introduce race as a factor in history, the marquis de Sade codified sex by cataloguing its variants, and Louis XIV codified slavery. No sooner was France involved in the slave trade than he had a 60-article Black Code drafted in 1685. As a result, French slaves were treated less harshly than their English and Spanish counterparts because every detail of their treatment was subject to regulations. They were to be given two and one-half pounds of cassava flour a week, two pounds of salt beef, and two suits of cloth a year. Torture, abandoning the old and infirm, separating families, and forced marriages were forbidden. Punishment was harsh but not capricious: Fleeing slaves one month absent were marked with a hot iron on the shoulder and had one ear cut off.

As Paul Valéry said: "France is the only country where considerations of pure form, a concern with form for its own sake, have kept a dominant position." These virtues of the mind, which are sought also in the organization of social life, might be called "thinking French." They can be beneficial or paralyzing. No one, it has been remarked, can carry a wrong idea further than the French. The need to bend nature to the norms of the mind can lead to sawing off the legs of the passerby to make them fit the bed, in the manner of the Greek highwayman Procrustes. But there is a reassuring continuity in French concern for form. When one compares Louis XIV's compliment upon receiving the ambassadors of Siam in 1686 with the speech General de Gaulle made in 1967 to King Mahendra of Nepal ("You reign over a Himalayan land which nature makes epic"), the similarity of style is striking. The main difference is that the Siamese envoys walked away backward, not wanting, they said, to turn their faces from the king.

Form becomes an end in itself. Seventeenth-century French dramatists conformed to the constricting Aristotelian rules of "one place, one day, one single action." Adherence to these unities became the measure of dramatic excellence. Classical tragedy is so attuned to the French mind that what is patently ridiculous, such as Hippolyte taking two pages of thumping alexandrines to expire in Racine's *Phèdre*, is seen as sublime. Corneille took the Spanish dramatist Guillén de Castro's *Cid* and taught him to speak like a gentleman. Instead of saying he is unhappy, he announces that he is "pierced to the depth of my heart by a shaft unforeseen as well as mortal." Racine and Corneille are never out of fashion. To lift civilian morale during World War I, Corneille's *Horace* (the tale of a Roman hero who kills his sister out of patriotic virtue because she is weeping for a slain enemy) ran as long as the Battle of the Marne lasted. Admiration for their classics is the French form of ancestor worship.

In contemporary France concern with form turns up in a variety of places:

In Le Corbusier's Radiant City development in Marseilles, which Lewis Mumford described as built according to arbitrary dimensions, making it impossible for the inhabitants to isolate themselves, a failure in the use of natural light, a building of inflexible dimensions not meant to be lived in.

In the teachings of Auguste Comte, the nineteenth-century positivist philosopher whose sense of formal categories made him say that psychology was part of biology. Wanting nothing to do with it, he suggested leaving psychology to Dumas *père* and *fils*.

In a time of crisis: General Maxine Weygand, who was French commander in chief in 1940, published a book to dispute what General de Gaulle had said about him in his *Memoirs*. Weygand seems less concerned with history than with protocol. He insists that he did not, on the afternoon of May 10, 1940, enter Premier Paul Reynaud's office unannounced; nor was he dismissed—"No one has ever allowed himself to dismiss me." Nor did he summon Churchill to a meeting—"I would not have permitted myself." Weygand gives the impression, at a time when French survival was at stake, that he had an overriding interest in petty disputes of rank.

Before a firing squad: Pierre Pucheu, the son of a Béarnais peasant, rose on the social ladder by becoming a teacher, a businessman, and a politician. He was active in several right-wing groups of the thirties, and in 1941 became Vichy Minister of Production. He then accepted the more compromising cabinet post of Minister of the Interior. One of his duties, after the first German soldiers were killed by the Resistance, was to help the Gestapo select hostages from Vichy internment camps.

In 1943 he resigned from the Pétain government and fled to North Africa through Spain, after General Giraud wrote him that he would be allowed to enlist as a simple Free French soldier under an assumed name. But upon arriving in Morocco he was arrested, tried for treason, and sentenced to death. Giraud could not or would not intervene. Pucheu's lawyers appealed to General de Gaulle, who said: "M. Pucheu followed policies which have failed. Today France is a boat tossed on a furious ocean. Events dictate, we follow." Events dictated that Pucheu be shot, even though de Gaulle was sensitive enough to his personal tragedy to promise his lawyers that "I will personally do everything I humanly can to assure the education of his children; I will also do everything I can so that they will not have to suffer because of the decision I may have to take."

In the cold predawn of March 20, 1944, at the abandoned Algiers race track, Pucheu was brought before the firing squad. "I will give the orders myself," he insisted. "I do not want any French soldier other than General Giraud to direct this crime. Please introduce me to the sergeant major in charge of the squad. I hope all its members are French."

The sergeant major stands at attention and Pucheu shakes his hand.

"What unit?"

"The guards."

"Monsieur, I am taking your place. It is I who will direct the squad. What are the prescribed orders?"

"Prepare yourselves—Aim—Fire!"

"Please introduce me to your men. I wish to shake their hands."

One by one, the firing squad is introduced. Pucheu removes his coat, embraces his lawyer, and says: "*Au revoir;* we will see each other again in a better world."

He stands six yards away from the squad, which is divided into two rows, the first one kneeling. His figure is lighted by the beams of automobile headlights. "Are you ready, gentlemen?"

His voice carries much further than the squad. He raises his right arm: "Fire!"

Through the smoke of the volley, the sergeant major advances to fire a pistol into his temple for the *coup de grâce* and his body gives a slight jump.

The French transform every aspect of life into a ceremony.

Politesse

France has maintained a ceremonial tradition directly derived from the usages of court life, when a breach in protocol could cost a courtier his apartment at Versailles, when royal infants were born in public, and when foreign princesses arriving to wed the French king were requested to disrobe completely at the border and change into French clothes. France has an almost Oriental sense of decorum. As a Chinese professor told Giraudoux: "Our countries were made to get along. They are the only ones which have both a *cuisine* and a *politesse*." But with the Jacobin reaction against the courtly tradition, good manners were denounced as a class weapon. There arose a countertradition of deliberate gruffness. Rudeness in the Jacobin mentality was a way for the common man to affirm his equality. If you called a man a *bougre* or a *jean-foutre* (the two most common Jacobin epithets) you showed that you were as good as he was. In contemporary France these two traditions coexist. Visitors are baffled by the tangle of perfect courtesy and incredible rudeness. This does not mean that some Frenchmen are rude and others are polite. It means that the same man who kisses a lady's hand in a drawing room will half an hour later be grossly insulting to a fellow motorist at a red light. Such inconsistency is only possible because good manners are considered a form of currency which makes it possible to obtain certain amenities in life and thus should be used thriftily and not on strangers.

The polite tradition is considered a rampart of French civilization, a code of behavior which makes life in society possible. Since the twelfth century, books on etiquette have been advising the French on how to mop up the sauce and blow their noses. In 1559 Mathurin Cordier wrote in his *Mirror of Youth for the Formation of Good Manners and Civility:* "If you blow your nose with two fingers and snot falls on the ground, place your foot over it."

Politeness in the French sense is not natural, but contrived. It is precisely because it is artificial that it is recognized as a mark of special attention. It is, as Montesquieu remarked, an embellishment. To present his hand to a lady passing from one room to another he rushes toward her as though she were in danger of falling; he runs to pick up a glove or a handkerchief with as much precipitation as if he were withdrawing it from a fire."

The French *gendarmerie's* book of etiquette, which is called *Advice from an Old to a Young Gendarme,* describes the correct way to shake a hand: "The way to shake a hand is equally a sign of good education. It must not be squeezed, or brandished, or slackly dropped. The shaking of the hand must be straightforward and without brusqueness. Too brief, it is discourteous; too prolonged, it indicates a familiarity which is permitted only among intimates." Attention must be paid this basic daily ritual of French life. The factory foreman spends ten to fifteen minutes each morning shaking the hands of all the workers in his keep. The busy waiter in a café, his hands wet from rinsing cups and saucers, extends his folded elbow like an amputee to regular customers. Ostracism in France is to spend a day without shaking anyone's hand.

Another treatise on *savoir-faire* defines manners prettily as the "fusion of the movements of the mind and the heart." Manners, it goes on, are a form of human progress; man in the twentieth century has not only reached the moon, he has advanced to the stage where spitting is considered indecent. There have, of course, been regressions, as when Edward VII made eating asparagus with one's fingers fashionable. But politeness is not restricted to table manners. There is, for instance, the politeness of the bed. On his wedding night, the husband should, like Renan, masturbate in the bathroom so as not to pester his bride. This mixture of the practical and the romantic is the mark of a people who have managed to combine the unashamed celebration of instinct with a multitude of small complicated observances.

More than the mechanical practice of etiquette, politeness in its highest form is a state of mind, a path to virtue, a philosophical system which teaches how to cushion the rude shocks of life. It permits in French society what Henry James calls "the inarticulate murmur of urbanity." At its most refined, it is a cross between Confucian politeness based on mastery over oneself and the maieutic system of Plato, in which ideas are brought out through questioning. It postulates that the oblique is better than the direct. If someone tells you what you already know, appear grateful. Never say "you misunderstood me," but "I explained myself badly." When someone asks about your health, it is to be told "I am well, thank you," and not to be given a medical bulletin. This was Swann's great mistake. Never praise too highly and never condemn outright. Do not say "de Gaulle's speech was terrible," but "too much had been expected of the speech for it to be anything but disappointing." The goal of conversation is to sustain a high level of urbanity. It is less important to be good or moral or honest than to be well brought up. This is an attempt to salvage order and cohesion in social relations, and it is also a protection against intimacy, for it encourages and maintains a minimal distance even between close friends.

The observance of the proprieties forbids the investigation of motives. As Chamfort said: "I have renounced the friendship of two men; the first because he never spoke to me of himself and the second because he never spoke to me of myself." This form of courtesy becomes second nature, remembered in the most extreme moments. The marquis de Montaignac, competing in the first French automobile race, doffed his hat while passing another car near Perigueux, sideswiped it, and landed in a ditch. His dying words: "I excuse you entirely, you are not to blame, it was I who struck you, please accept my most heartfelt apologies."

Modern life seems less and less suited to such exacting standards, and in recent years, France has singled itself out as the country where motorists are most violent to one another. The reverse of *politesse* is a rudeness that quickly escalates to violence and homicide. The same people who once considered it essential to wear hats so they could doff them, now kill one another over parking space.

The contrived courtesy of the French, except in that small portion of the population which has made a vocation of its observance (the old men with beautiful manners), breaks down more abruptly in the grind of urban life than the more natural courtesy of a people like the Italians. I remember a second-class train trip from Paris to Ancona. On the French part of the trip there were arguments about whether the window should be open or closed, a woman had a violent fit of coughing when a man lit a cigarette (although it was a smoking compartment), passengers hid behind newspapers and threw suspicious glances at each other. Once in Italy, there was sharing of food, kindness to children, amiability— I stepped on a man's foot and he said "Go ahead, I've got another." At a café in Ancona, my son Gabriel, three and a half, handed the tin foil from a chocolate bar to the waiter with a gesture of childish arrogance. The waiter took it, bowed, and folded the paper into a bird with two wide wings and a twisted head. He had, I thought, a natural elegance which made the formal proprieties of the French seem petty. In a Paris *patisserie,* Gabriel touched an éclair and a middle-aged customer said "I don't want to buy cakes that have been touched by dirty little urchins." Rudeness to children is particularly easy because children hold no rank and nothing can be gained from them.

Everyone else has a rank. I have heard the begrimed and odorous fishwives of the Halles address each other as Madame with great decorum. Everyone must say Monsieur and Madame to everyone else, which leads to bizarre street-corner arguments on the order of: "Go to hell, sir."—"And you likewise, sir." The equalitarian principles of the Revolution fight an unsuccessful battle against the tradition of a hierarchical society where every individual has his appointed niche. As the old gendarme says to the young gendarme, even though gendarmes are always being ridiculed, one should be proud of what one is, and there was even once a French general who did not hide the fact that he was the son of a gendarme.

French Communists, who are supposed to defend equalitarianism and the Communist International, revert, when their vanity is threatened, to the protocol consciousness of their own country. The Communist novelist Louis Aragon was invited to a lunch given for a Czech diplomat at the foreign ministry. He called the protocol director to complain that his wife, Elsa Triolet, also a novelist, had not been invited. "But it's a stag lunch," he was told. "You should know, sir," he replied testily, "that Elsa Triolet is not a man or a woman, but a great French writer."

Of all the external signs of prestige that help determine individual rank inside society, the most obvious are decorations, which helps explain why they are so eagerly sought.

Love of Decorations

Two distinguished gentlemen in the cloakroom of the Elysée Palace:

"What! You wear it on your overcoat?"

"The call of vanity, my dear colleague, is like the call of nature, it must be satisfied."

"That is not vanity, it is ostentation."

"But how can police and customs officials otherwise know whom they are dealing with?"

"That is secondary, what is essential is that one does not leave the Legion of Honor in a cloakroom."

There comes a time in the life of every Frenchman who has performed some small service to the state when he becomes preoccupied about the removal of his prostate and the acquisition of his Legion of Honor. The lapel of his jacket seems naked if that bit of red ribbon does not garnish it.

"What did you do to deserve it?" I asked my uncle Gratien when his turn came.

"Nothing," he replied, "but conscientiously."

Others do a great deal, not to deserve it, but to obtain it. They haunt the waiting rooms of deputies and senators, write flowery letters to influential friends, and read the *Journal Officiel* the way a gambler reads a racing sheet. So many of his constituents asked the Corsican senator Emmanuel Arène to intervene in their favor that he devised a stock evasion. He would shout indignantly: "How do you dare ask me for the Legion of Honor after what you have done!" No one ever insisted. The consistency with which the French have pursued honorific rewards is touching, and the state encourages their solicitation, since they cost nothing.

Every regime has, as one of its first tasks, set up a system of rewards. The revolutionary government itself, after abolishing the various orders of the monarchy, instituted its own. Parisians involved in the July 14 uprising wore a Victor of the Bastille pin.

Napoleon turned the Frenchman's love of decorations into a method of government. On May 4, 1802, he suggested the creation of a Legion of Honor at a meeting of the highest administrative tribunal, the Conseil d'État, whose members pointed out that the proposed Legion was nonequalitarian. "Crosses and ribbons are the baubles of the monarchy," one said. Napoleon replied: *"Eh bien,* it is with baubles that men are led. Old and corrupt nations are not governed like the virtuous peoples of antiquity. Sacrifices must be made to vanity and the joy of possession. That is one of the reasons we adopted certain monarchic forms, the return of titles, crosses, ribbons, trinkets, all proper to win the respect of the multitude. I would not say so in public ... but I do not believe the French people love liberty and equality. The French are not changed by ten years of revolution. They are what the Gauls were, proud and frivolous. They believe in one thing: Honor! This feeling must be nourished and channeled. France can expect great results from this creation, if my successors have the good sense not to spoil it." As if attentive to the emperor's words, every subsequent regime has made ample use of the Legion of Honor. It was salvaged by the restored monarchy in 1815 and handed on to the Second Empire and three Republics. France was thenceforth divided, not only into 89 departments, but also into 16 cohorts of legionnaires. From 1802 to 1814, nearly 40,000 of the enameled, ten-pointed stars of the Legion were awarded with great fanfare to military and civilians alike. Only one man, General Joseph-Victor Moreau, is on record as having made fun of the system. He gave his barber a razor of honor, his dog a collar of honor, and his cook a saucepan of honor. The Legion nonetheless was accepted as a mark of great prestige, and became an indispensable part of the Napoleonic legend. Everybody wanted one. The painter David wrote: "So you are organizing a Legion of Honor. Breathes there a man on such poor terms with glory that he does not aspire to become a part of it?"

The Legion served as a bond between the commander in chief and his men. The Napoleonic legend is incomplete without the story of the grizzled veteran who calls out while the emperor is reviewing the troops: "Followed you everywhere, wounded five times, four horses shot from under me, and I'm no further than these green kids who are still wailing for their mother's milk. Sire, let me see a bit of red ribbon." Napoleon nods. "Yes, but promises are often made and not kept," the veteran says. Napoleon unpins the Legion of Honor from his own chest, hands it to the soldier, and says: "Here's a down payment."

With the end of Empire, the Legion remained no less desirable. Under the Third Republic, well-connected political figures discovered that it had a market value, and promptly subjected it to the laws of supply and demand. The episode is remembered as the Wilson scandal, because the scheme was apparently thought up by David Wilson, the ne'er-do-well son-in-law of the French president, Jules Grévy. He paid his gambling debts with the proceeds of decoration sales. Also involved was a general at the War Ministry named Caffarel. The scandal splattered Grévy, who had to resign. It was also under the Third Republic that famous men and women began to turn it down. Maupassant said grandly that "the Legion implies a hierarchy and there is no hierarchy in the world of letters." Georges Sand refused it because she said she did not want to be mistaken for a retired camp follower.

But such cases were exceptional, and French fondness for decorations led to their proliferation, until under the Fourth Republic there were 85 different kinds. It seemed the aim of the government to create enough medals so that no Frenchman would be without one. A postman was entitled to a Postal Merit Medal, a mother with healthy children to a Health Merit Medal, and an all-around good fellow to a Social Merit Medal. If one met a diplomat with a barren lapel one could only wonder what terrible blunder he had committed. Cabinet ministers were given a certain number of Legions of Honor to hand out to their employees each year, like Christmas bonuses. It was a useful device to refuse promotions and raises. "I am so sorry I cannot grant the promotion you are soliciting," the minister says, "since I have included you in my Legion of Honor List for the year."

General de Gaulle reduced the 85 to 7: A revamped Legion of Honor, whose membership in the higher brackets is severely restricted (there are only 75 Grands Croix), while the fields of endeavor in which they can be won has been expanded—a special cabinet decision awarded a Legion of Honor to Jean-Claude Killy after his 1968 triple victory in the winter Olympics; a national Order of Merit; the Order of Companions of the Liberation, with only 1053 members; and four military decorations, the Médaille Militaire, the Croix de Guerre, the Médaille de la Résistance, and the Croix de la Valeur Militaire.

I wonder whether it would occur to anyone but the French to decorate a pigeon. At the battle of Verdun, carrier pigeon no. 787.15 flew out of the besieged Fort de Vaux with a last desperate appeal for help, completed its mission but arrived gassed and dying. Pigeon no. 787.15 was given the highest citation obtainable, which read: "Despite enormous difficulties, resulting from intense smoke and an abundant emission of gases, accomplished its mission. As the heroic defender's only remaining method of communication, transmitted the last message received from this officer. Fatally gassed, arrived dying at the dovecote."

Esprit

The accomplished Frenchman who wears the Rosette pretends not to see you in the street, but if hailed, pretends he is delighted and removes his glove to shake your hand and regale you with some example of his wit, for he is *un homme d'esprit*. The French frequently tell themselves that they are the most *spirituel* people in the world, which is like saying that no one speaks German better than the Germans. For the quality of *esprit* is a particularly French one; it is one of the ways of thinking French. It is not wit, not humor, nor intelligence, nor anything spiritual. It is, in fact, best defined by what it is not: not coarse, heavy-handed, obvious, or insistent. *Esprit* is a verbal spark, quick, bright, and ephemeral. It serves, like courtesy, to deflect the thrust of all that is unpleasant in life. It is a defense against what the society cannot accept or understand. In the work of the seventeenth- and eighteenth-century masters of aphorisms who fixed the form of French *esprit,* there is an underlying strain of pessimism and resignation. In France, says Chamfort, one must be either a forge or a hammer. They comment on those things they know they cannot change—the government, religion, and women. The last refuge against the aberrations of life, they say, is laughter. Thus, the French tradition that "one must have the laughers on one's side." "Without the government, we would run out of reasons to laugh," is something every generation says.

As for religion, it does no harm, let us accept the useful conventions of faith. This was Voltaire's attitude, as it was later Jules Renard's, who said: "There is no heaven, but we should act as though there was one to deserve." As for women, they too are necessary, and one should make the best of them, although as La Rochefoucauld observed, "There are good marriages but there are no delightful ones." Woman, like heaven, is an idea, so that Clemenceau could say: "The most beautiful moment of a love affair is the one when you are climbing the stairs"—a remark the corollary of which had been made two hundred years earlier by the prince de Ligne. When in his seventies he told a middle-aged mistress: "Madam, you are the last woman I shall ever love on the third floor." "At my age," she replied, "it is the last means I have to make a man's heart beat faster." Along with the theme of pursuit, there is a strain of misogyny. A man in mourning is asked what he has lost. "No one," he says, "I am a widower." The ladies reply in kind, as when Colette defines candor for a woman as not lying uselessly.

The man with *esprit* is the one who has the last word, and in the National Assembly there are standard repartees: "Sir, you are the basest of men."—"Sir, you are forgetting yourself." Used by the ruling authority, *esprit* can make a difficult decision more palatable. A lord whose nephew was going to be put to death asked Henri IV for mercy. "You are an uncle," he replied, "I am a king. If I excuse your request, will you excuse my refusal?"

Subtlety of observation also defines *esprit;* not the description of Pantagruel's gigantic appetite in Rabelais, but Madame de Verdurin's breakfast in Proust, reading about a drowning in the newspaper and saying "how frightening, as she dunked croissants in her café au lait and assumed an expression of bovine contentment." Rabelais is part of an alternate tradition which makes a virtue of bawdiness. Broader Gallic humor has its advocates too, who admire not only Rabelais but that archetypal French figure, the puppet Guignol. Borrowing from the Italians, a citizen of Lyons named Laurent Mourguet staged the first French puppet show in 1803, creating his own characters and scenarios. Born after the Revolution, Guignol is a child of the people and a friend of freedom. Whatever the regime, he is against it. He embodies the Frenchman's contentiousness. Under the Third Republic, he began knocking policemen about. He talks and drinks too much, lies, cannot keep a job, and makes fun of the Gaston-Alphonse brand of *politesse*. His best friend, Gnafron, says that three rivers cross Lyons: the Rhone, the Sâone, and the Beaujolais. Guignol defends the independence of the little fellow, is allergic to authority, and is always ready to help someone less well off than himself, supposing that he should ever find such a person. He has no foresight, but since he expects the worst from life he is never surprised. His native common sense makes it hard for the scheming notary to trick him. His head may be hollow, but his nose is keen. His wife Madelon is a bossy, narrow-minded, shrill-voiced, calculating shrew, but a good and thrifty housewife. To stop her nagging, he beats her with a broom, but never considers divorce. Guignol is both resigned and optimistic. When someone tells him "I live on my inherited wealth," he replies: "Do you by any chance need an associate?" He may be *Punch*'s first cousin, but his character and his very appearance, with his large nose and quick gestures, seem specifically French. Go any Thursday afternoon to the Luxembourg Gardens and watch the hundreds of children in rapt attention as Guignol in a wig and three-cornered hat is harangued by his wife, badgered for a loan by the teetering Gnafron, and chased by the gendarme Pandore, and you will realize that . . . Guignol lives!

It is Guignol's ability to laugh at misfortune which shocked an English visitor to Paris in 1814, when he heard the story of a man who had dropped a five-franc piece in the bear court at the zoo.

A destitute Napoleonic veteran crept down to retrieve it early the next morning, but was eaten by a bear. "In England," wrote the visitor, "the bear would have been shot, a deodand levied, and subscriptions raised for the man's widow. In France they caricatured the incident and called the bear by the veteran's name. Everyone was asking 'which bear is it that ate the mustache?'" What Guignol lacks and *esprit* confers is a systematic vision of life: We have been dealt a bad hand, but let's try to stay in the game. *Esprit* is also linked to formalism in its urge to define and circumscribe. Aphorisms and epigrams, the form in which French *esprit* is most at home, are dogmatic pronouncements, one-line definitions of the human condition, like "The mind is always the heart's dupe." Such statements are final, they do not invite argument or additional comment. Every famous French writer has added his page to a national anthology of *esprit* which is at the same time a treatise on *savoir-vivre:* Montaigne (the profit of one is the loss of another), Pascal (it takes little to console us, since it takes little to afflict us), Boileau (often the fear of evil leads us to worse evil), Montesquieu (when you pursue wit, you catch foolishness), Voltaire (know that the secret of art is to correct nature), Rivarol (to teach is twice to learn), Stendhal (beauty is but the promise of happiness), Lamartine (glory cannot be where virtue is not), Balzac (glory is the sun of the dead), Hugo (the best heritage is a revered name), Flaubert (I call a bourgeois whoever has base thoughts), Renan (the great general is the one who succeeds and not the one who should have succeeded). Perhaps this would be the French Koran, this sum of aphorisms and pronouncements by the country's writers.

The nineteenth-century Romantics reacted against the love of capsule definitions, like "Racine paints men as they are and Corneille as they should be," which saturate the French educational system. *Esprit* stays clear of metaphysics. It runs, as Voltaire said of his own writing, limpid but shallow.

Esprit de Système

Esprit is itself part of the larger compulsion to organize the universe; better a wrong theory than no theory. Everything must be labeled and classified. This is what one might call "the determination to shatter the charm." Mystery cannot be tolerated, it must be broken down into its components, which led Montesquieu to the paradoxical enterprise of defining good taste. He found it to include order, variety, symmetry, contrast, surprise, plus a *je ne sais quoi,* which canceled the value of his own definition. The scholar's job is to take inventory and tidy away. "Thinking French" supposes that human nature is always and everywhere the same, that there are fixed standards of truth, beauty, and justice. Racine said as much in the preface of *Iphigenia:* "Common sense and reason being identical in every century, the taste of Paris coincides with that of Athens." It also supposes that the laws of nature can be discerned by the correct application of reason. The supremacy of reason is hammered into the French consciousness at an early age. The English child is told to "be good" (stressing character), but the French child is asked to "be reasonable" (*sois raisonnable*). He will continue, as a result of his schooling, to favor theoretical hypotheses that lead to abstract conclusions.

The scientific model of "thinking French" is Urbain-Jean Leverrier, who became an astronomer after failing Polytechnique. His feat was discovering the planet Neptune on the point of his pen. Instead of exploring the heavens with a telescope, he calculated that the hitherto unexplained perturbations in the orbit of the planet Uranus had to be caused by another planet which had escaped the observations of astronomers. He computed its mass, its orbit, and its distance from the earth, and he wrote the Berlin Observatory in 1846: On such-and-such a day point your telescope in such-and-such a direction and you will see a new planet. Leverrier refused to look into a telescope at the planet he had discovered. Certainty was in his mind more than in visible phenomena. King Louis-Philippe asked to congratulate personally the man who had discovered a planet, not because he had seen it, but because he had known it was there. Leverrier modestly declined to have the planet named after him, but agreed to pose for a statue which stands in the courtyard of the Paris Observatory. Even Pasteur, whose science was based on experiments, operated from an inner certainty, and was analyzing the nature of rabies before he had ever seen the microbe under a microscope. Pasteur's dogmatism could also lead him astray, and he commented on a treatise on fermentation by the physiologist Claude Bernard:

"All this is wrong, and to prove it I will conduct an experiment the outcome of which I can predict beforehand."

The urge to classify is not limited to science. When I told French friends, who asked about the book I was working on, that it concerned France, the question invariably came: From what point of view? Political? Economic? Sociological? Psychological? Noncategorical, I would lamely reply. An ordinary conversation can make one feel like an element whose properties are being examined. Once at a dinner party I was seated next to an attractive lady philosophy professor and the following dialogue ensued.

"You seem dissatisfied," she said.

"No, I am on the contrary delighted to be chatting with you."

"Stylistic clause."

"What I don't like about Paris is that I never feel clean."

"Determinism."

"Except when I've gone to the pool, when I feel like a new man."

"Phagocytism."

"Of course, it's a very personal thing."

"Solipsism."

I began to watch what I was saying.

A garden must submit to the passage of the compass, the bevel, and the pruning shears before it can be called French, and the French mind is just as strenuously tended, leaving no idea to sprout outside a comprehensive design. Raymond Queneau's theory of literature is an example of French garden-thinking. He holds that all fiction can be reduced to the *Iliad* and the *Odyssey*. Either the character is placed in a historical context, like Achilles, and the book is about the way history interferes with character (*The Charterhouse of Parma* and *War and Peace* fall into this category), or, as in the *Odyssey*, an individual passes through various experiences and becomes a wiser man. Every autobiography is an Odyssey, as are works like *Moby Dick* and *Don Quixote*. Such inclusive categories help explain why there are no French Hamlets.

Esprit de système crops up where one least expects to find it, in the resolution on the celebrated seventeenth-century courtesan Ninon de Lenclos, for instance, who decides that since she cannot control her vices she will "endeavor to organize them." Does there exist a prettier definition of prostitution? It recognizes both the frailty of instinct and the need to control its disorders. The lady of virtue named Marthe Richard who closed the brothels in France was in fact crusading against *esprit de système,* which legalized the houses so that the needs of the male population could be channeled in a rational manner. After the houses were closed, prostitution in France became illogical, since it is legal to engage in it but illegal to solicit for it.

More recently, when French doctors began performing heart transplants, the immediate results were not medical but juridicial: The Ministry of Social Affairs decreed a new legal definition of death based on encephalograms and superseding the 1948 definition based on heart stoppage. The initial urge is always the urge to define.

When in 1791 the Academy of Sciences explained why it had proposed the metric system to replace the confusing variety of weights and measures in monarchic France, it said it wanted to pass along to posterity a system so universal that it would be impossible to guess by which nation it was commissioned and carried out. But the metric system immediately gives itself away as "thinking French." The English system of weights and measures is an historical accretion. Custom imposed the gallon, the yard, the pound, and the Winchester bushel of Henry VII's time, which apparently is still in use. The French method was to devise an abstract, ideal system, arbitrarily based on the arc of a geographic meridian. It proved so convenient that most of Europe adopted it (it was in fact the Revolution's most successful export item). The meter was defined as one ten-millionth part of a quarter of the forty-fifth meridian, which passes through Dunkirk and Barcelona. A platinum prototype was built and deposited in the National Archives. In 1960 the platinum meter's slight error in measurement was rectified by pegging the meter not to a bar of platinum but to the wave length of cadmium.

Descartes

There is something Cartesian about the origin of the meter. But what do we mean when we say the French are Cartesian?

Schoolchildren are told "Write like Descartes!" "Think like Descartes!" The tercentenary of the *Discours de la Méthode,* celebrated in 1937, was a great national occasion. It seems odd that a seventeenth-century philosopher should maintain such a hold over his countrymen. The quest for the touchstones and talismans of the French conscience still leads unerringly to Descartes. On his own terms, Descartes' system of thought was a heroic failure. He devised a method which he held to be infallible and which reduced the universe to a rational-mechanical system expressed in mathematical formulas; but nearly every conclusion he drew from this method was a scientific error. Newton read Descartes when he was twenty, Voltaire tells us, "marking the margins of the first pages, but always with the same mark, consisting in the single word, 'error'; and tired of writing 'error' on every page, he threw the book away and never read it again."

In cosmology, Descartes was a heliocentrist; he thought that the sun and the stars were fixed in the heavens, at a time when the German astronomer Johannes Kepler had already published his findings on planetary motion. In physics, his first axiom was that there is no such thing as a vacuum; he disputed Galileo's discovery that bodies of different weights fall at the same speed. In physiology, he believed that the small, dark-gray pineal gland behind the brain was the seat of the soul; the human body was, he wrote, a kind of mechanical engine, and the pineal gland was a valve that regulated the distribution of thought. His universe was classified into imaginary elements: Large terrestrial masses, small aerial balls, and a "subtle liquid" which was spread, like engine oil, through the interstices of the universe. Matter was formed from primitive chaos thanks to the intercession of special whirlwinds which created condensation by rotating around each other.

Obviously, it is not Descartes the scientist who has served as a model for French thought. It is, rather, his quest for a rational meaning of the universe, which would make man the master of nature. Descartes embarked on the highest adventure of the mind: to conquer the universe without ever leaving his study. It does not matter that his findings were inaccurate, as long as the method was convincing. Descartes is the intellectual father of French preoccupation with form. A general who devises a perfect battle plan with incomplete information about enemy capacity, and goes on to elegant defeat, is Cartesian. An engineer from the ministry of Ponts et Chaussées who designs a bridge for a town on the Drôme which he has never visited, on the basis of topographical maps, is Cartesian. When he is told that the bridge has been washed away by floods he merely says: "That is impossible."

Where does the seduction of the system lie? Perhaps in that Descartes goes the limit; he leaves nothing unexplained. Montaigne began his investigation of life with the question: "What do I know?" Descartes reaches further back, to the question: "How do I know I am?" And, from this self-inquiry, like a deepsea diver coming up with some new species of marine life, he surfaces with the *cogito*. Why "I think therefore I am" rather than "I digest therefore I am," or "I feel pain therefore I am," or as French philosophy students jocularly say, *coito ergo sum* (I copulate therefore I am)? The *cogito* serves a triple purpose: It allows Descartes to begin his inquiry with an attitude of systematic doubt which will act as a guarantee for all the wrong conclusions he presents with such blissful certainty; it postulates the superiority of mind over matter, since proof of one's existence derives from taking one's distance from the sensory world rather than immersing oneself in it. And finally it sets up his proofs of the existence of God. This is not a demonstration but an axiom, assented to as soon as it is enunciated: "I am, therefore God exists."

Descartes buttresses this self-evidence with Anselm's argument that if we can imagine a perfect being, he must exist. And he adds the ontological corollary that a perfect being is necessarily a being that exists, for existence is a necessary part of its perfection. Both these arguments are merely a roundabout way of saying what God told Moses: "I am He who Is." The Cartesian system is closed and tautological; it sets up propositions that prove each other: The discovery of man and of the universe depend on the knowledge that God exists, and the existence of God is proven by the discovered mind of man. It is like proving the properties of water by gazing at a cloud; the demonstration is missing.

God was necessary to the Cartesian system to keep it innocent of heresy. Writing in the climate of the Catholic Counterreformation, which was obsessed with defending the body of Catholic doctrine, Descartes would not risk reproof from the center of scholarship and learning that the church still was. He needed his axiomatic God just as Voltaire needed his watchmaker God. If he had not said that the world was an inert machine to which God gave life, he might have been tried in Galileo's wake. The effect Galileo's condemnation had on him is significant. Here was a respected scientist, an Italian and a friend of popes, who was brought to trial in 1634 at the age of seventy, in his own country, by a pope, and forced to abjure his theories in public. The news reached Holland, where Descartes was living. Perhaps he thought that as an unknown French writer living in a Protestant country he had to be more careful than Galileo. He considered burning his papers. He wrote a friend that the trial would reduce him to silence since, like Galileo, his philosophy accepted that the earth revolved around the sun. He never considered fighting for his ideas; the notion of struggle was foreign to his nature. He preferred to keep working within the context of Catholic orthodoxy and wrote: "I would not want for anything in the world that there would come from me a discourse which contained the slightest word of which the church could disapprove."

The *Discours de la Méthode* was published three years later. There is nothing controversial in it, and the first three copies were sent to Cardinal Richelieu, Louis XIII, and the Prince of Orange. But his treatise on the world, with its Galilean theories, was published posthumously in 1664, and was condemned by Rome. Religious piety or intellectual cowardice? This remains one of the mysteries of Descartes.

One aftereffect of Descartes' inclusion of God in his system has been a naïve form of scientific humanism. In his own time, a critic remarked that according to Descartes, an atheist could not be a good geometer. So be it, replied Descartes, for founding science on the existence of God is the only way a thinker can be sure of being right. In a more recent example, the mathematician Henri Poincaré insisted that a man who is investigating the magnificent harmony of the laws of nature will be disposed to conquer his own paltry selfish interests. Moral rearmament through trigonometry? Another result of the Cartesian system was to erect as a scientific truth what for seventeen centuries had been a religious belief: the dualism of the body and soul and the essential physiological difference between man and other animals.

Descartes had even found the glandular seat of the immaterial
soul. It took another two centuries for Darwinian thought to
invalidate his findings.

After founding his system on the purely academic device of
doubting his own existence, Descartes never doubted again. His
grandiose presumption in fitting the universe into a series of
geometric theorems can only be explained by the primitive state
of seventeenth-century science. As science advances, scientists become more humble. Einstein said that he was incapable of proving
or disproving the existence of God. Descartes, as Voltaire said,
"made a philosophy the way a good novel is made. Everything was
plausible but nothing was true."

His reply to critics was always in the form of a further self-
evidence. "The quickest way I know to reply to the reasons of the
atheists," he said, "is to find an evident demonstration which will
show everyone that God exists. Let me dare to boast that I have
found one which satisfies me entirely and which leads me to a
knowledge of God's existence more certain than the knowledge
that I have of any geometric proposition." Descartes couched
his system of the universe in irreproachable mathematical language. But it was, again ironically, in the realm of pure mathematics that he made his most lasting scientific contributions. He
devised the useful system of converting lines to numbers and
numbers to lines, that is, of algebraic notation, to solve problems
in geometry, and of using curves and coordinates. He is the father
of the company production graph and the temperature chart. But
in extending the methods of geometry to other areas, he had to
assume that every human experience, including religious experience, could be charted mathematically. After proving the
existence of God he had to become God, the all-knowing, whereas
the other great French thinker of the seventeenth century, Pascal,
who was also the more deeply religious of the two men, said that
"the last analysis of reason is to recognize that there are an infinity
of things which surpass it." This Descartes would never recognize,
and went bravely on to subject human passion to his system. The
first step was of course to draw up a list: Admiration, love, hate,
desire, joy, and sadness. Here again, the secret is supreme reason,
which leads to personal self-control just as it does to the conquest
of nature: "The man of reason substitutes for passion in the

direction of his life a rule which in old French was called a *reign.*"

Knowledge is seen as therapeutic: If an alcoholic realized what strong drink did to his liver he would never touch another drop. Whereas he often drinks precisely because he knows how damaging it is. As for generosity, Descartes said it "makes it possible for a man to esteem himself to the highest legitimate point." Because of this self-esteem, he cannot despise other men because he is aware that their faults are not bred in the bone but are a result of faulty knowledge. In one of the rare applications of his ideas, along with the dissection of animals to search for their pineal glands, Descartes in 1648 wrote his friend Constantin Huygens, military secretary of the Dutch prince Frederick-Henry, to intercede in favor of a peasant who had murdered his stepfather. He explained that the peasant's act was contrary to his character and motivated by the fact that one of his children had been gravely ill at the time. "It sometimes happens," he wrote, "that the best of men commit very grave faults, and in such cases, mercy is more useful than laws."

Like Molière's Monsieur Jourdain, who found himself effortlessly speaking in prose, the French mind seems naturally to fall into Cartesian patterns in its respect for knowledge, its belief that good conduct depends on clear thinking, its fondness for the systematic, its attraction toward what is clearly and sharply defined, and its distaste for what is murky and unintelligible. Self-esteem, the rule of reason, the conquest of nature, all these were goals of the rising eighteenth-century bourgeoisie. And even after the bourgeois revolution deteriorated into the Terror, what did Robespierre do but found a new religion based on reason? Descartes' ghost should have been included among the high priests. In the *Discours de la Méthode* there is the kernel, the twenty lines that shook French thought, the definitive lesson on how to think, or, as the subtitle says, "how to conduct one's reason and search for truth in sciences." The rules of reason resemble the instructions on a can of window cleaner or floor wax, the "four easy steps":

1. Never accept anything as true unless I know it to be so with certainty.

2. Divide each of the difficulties I am to examine in as many parts as required to solve them better.

3. Order my thoughts, beginning with the simplest objects and the easiest to know, and rising little by little, as if by degree, to more complicated matters.

4. Make everywhere such complete enumerations and such general reviews that I would be assured never to omit anything.

This is the ground plan for linear thought, whereas science's great advances are due to quantum jumps, ideas in intermittent flashes rather than following one another like soldiers on parade. It was a method for the dawn of science. The theory that the blood circulated in the body was slowly gaining ground. To believe that the earth revolved around the sun was heresy. The concept of gravity had not yet been formulated. Magnifying lenses were in use, but Descartes never managed to obtain proper ones.

There is no room for invention in the Cartesian method. It is proper to the solution of problems in Euclidian geometry, where one proceeds by supposing the problem resolved. The answer is contained in the question. Not to accept anything as true unless one is certain that it is so is a self-evident proposition. The tautological strain in Cartesian thinking finds unexpected echoes in contemporary France. General de Gaulle's speaking style rested partly on the enunciation of self-evident propositions, as when he told the heads of the Citroën auto works at the Salon de l'Automobile which he visited in October, 1968, at a time when the Fiat-Citroën merger was in the news: "What will happen will happen because it must happen." The Gaullist manner of dispensing irrefutable wisdom seemed to draw its inspiration from the Cartesian method of correct thinking. Descartes writes: "A child versed in arithmetic who has added a sum can be sure of having found, concerning that sum, all that the human spirit could find." And de Gaulle said: "Whoever they are, wherever they are, when you get down to it, men are men," or "The national discussion must for us be summed up with this question: France must be France," or "England is, in fact, insular." De Gaulle told students at the École Normale, "You are young, you are numerous," and peasants in Bordeaux, "Most of you here are rural folk." When he visited Fécamp near Le Havre, he said: "Fécamp is a sea harbor and intends to remain one."

The fetish of orderly thought is another Cartesian contribution to the French mind. The correct method is to present ideas in consecutive sections, like slices of cake. One of the more interesting thinkers in France today, however, has found the Cartesian method inadequate to his purpose. The ethnologist Claude Lévi-Strauss, in his study of the myths of South American tribes, attempts to explain a style of thought based not on logical propositions, but on the conversion of symbols and the apparently arbitrary variants of the same myth. In order to discover the common origin of hundreds of different myths, his books, he says, are like spirals; themes overlap, there are sudden reversals of direction, and the progress is slow and circular as he tries to cope with the complexity of non-Cartesian thought patterns.

In the ambition of his undertaking, however, Lévi-Strauss remains an heir of Descartes. For he is not content, like other ethnologists, to gather data about kinship in primitive societies. He seeks, on the one hand to discover laws governing primitive cultures, and on the other to make the human sciences as exact as the natural sciences. Lévi-Strauss and the structuralist method he has elaborated are a twentieth-century version of the Cartesian dream of making man the possessor of nature. His writings on the uses of structuralism constitute a twentieth-century ethnologist's *Discours de la Méthode*.

The progress of Cartesian thought and its obsession with the unimpeachable can be observed in the need of French philosophical schools, from Descartes, to the nineteenth-century positivists, to the twentieth-century structuralists, to reveal the order of nature; to discover rational principles rather than describe phenomena; to bring out an identity between the order of the reasoning mind and the order of nature.

Finally, if the French are Cartesian, is Descartes French? By birth, he was of course French, the fourth child of a prosperous family of doctors and merchants which had settled in the Loire country; by education he was French also, for he studied at the famous Jesuit college of La Fleche. But there was clearly something uncongenial to him about his own country. As soon as he came of age, he went abroad to join Maurice of Nassau's Dutch army. Thereafter, he spent all but five years of his adult life in the Low Countries. He returned intermittently to France, once to settle family affairs which gave him an independent income, and, two years before his death, on the promise of a pension. But Paris was then in the midst of the Fronde, his pension was forgotten, and Descartes once again went abroad, appalled by the confusion and superficiality that seemed to reign among his countrymen.

"What most disgusted me," he wrote, "was that no one seemed to want to know anything about me except what I looked like, so I began to believe that they wanted me in France the way they might want an elephant or a panther, because it was rare, and not because it was useful." Nor was he particularly concerned with the French language. His first published work, the *Principles of Philosophy,* was written in Latin. When he wrote the *Discours de la Méthode* in French, it was because he wanted to reach more readers. He advocated a universal language, but recognized the practical problems involved, and despaired of ever seeing one in use.

His personal life, far from being a reflection of the clarity of his writing, was secretive. There are few famous Frenchmen of whom so little is known. Long sections of his life are a total blank. Summing up a nine-year period, he writes: "and for the nine following years, I did nothing else but roll around the world, trying to be a spectator instead of an actor in all the comedies that I saw played." Franz Hals has left a portrait in which Descartes looks like a musketeer in mourning, dressed in black, with a shoulder-length black wig, a wispy mustache and goatee, and the wide-set, dull, heavy-lidded eyes of a man who has spent too much time reading by bad light. He seldom allowed himself to be caught off the philosopher's pedestal. We know that he had an affair with a Dutch girl named Helen, probably a servant, and that she gave him a daughter who died at the age of five. Descartes called her Françine and deduced that she had been conceived on October 15, 1634. We know also, that despite his treatise on how to govern the passions, he was capable of outbursts. Learning that his Dutch friend Beeckman was boasting that he had inspired one of his early works, the *Treatise on Music,* Descartes fired off an angry letter: "Let me warn you very briefly that if you say you have told someone something, even if it is true, it is nonetheless odious. Let me warn you that boasting to those who know me will greatly harm your own reputation. And let me advise you not to show my letters as proof, for it is well known that I am accustomed to obtaining information even from ants and earthworms."

It is when the founder of modern rationalism lapses into irrational behavior that he is most interesting. Why was he constantly on the move, shuttling from Amsterdam to Leyden, and from Leyden to Utrecht, and from Utrecht to Deventer, as though he were being followed? Why his obsessive secretiveness, to the point of adopting as personal mottoes Ovid's *Bene qui Latuit, Bene Vixit* (a good life is a good secret) and the even more puzzling *Larvatus Prodeo* (masked, I advance), of which he explained: "Just as actors, who wish to cover the blush that rises to their forehead, dress up for their roles, at the moment when I am about to enter the world's stage where up until now I had been a spectator, I advance masked." Does this mean that his writing conceals his real ideas? More probably, he feared the notoriety that publication might bring, and preferred not to publish rather than risk becoming a target of the church, like Galileo. Writing interfered with his goal of perfect anonymity. The reason he liked living in Amsterdam, he wrote a friend, was that "since I am the only man who is not a merchant, everyone else is so attentive to his profit that I could remain here all my life without ever being seen. Every day I go walking in the crowds with as much freedom and tranquility as you could in your lands, and I do not consider the men who pass in front of my eyes any differently than you would the trees that grow in your forests or the animals who graze there."

And why, after a lifetime of solitary independence, did he agree in 1649 to become philosopher in residence at Queen Christina's Stockholm court? Did vanity overtake him in middle age? He went despite misgivings about "the land of bears, between the boulders and the ice," and once arrived, he complained that "it seems to me that the thoughts of men freeze here in winter just like the water." The queen assigned him to work on a compliment in verse for her twenty-third birthday, and enforced a Spartan schedule: She insisted that the proper time for philosophy lessons was five in the morning. Descartes, whose health had always been frail, rose in the middle of the night to arrive shuddering at the palace and give his lesson. He had hoped to live a hundred years, but he did not survive his first Stockholm winter, and died there on February 11, 1650, at the age of fifty-three. The spectacle of the French sage being subjected to the whims of the eccentric Swedish queen might have been borrowed from Commedia dell' arte buffoonery. Descartes deserved a more dignified death.

Finally, there are two keys to Descartes: The body of his work, which continues to nourish the French intellect, and his celebrated three dreams, which Freud analyzed as the representation of an inner conflict. Again, the intrusion of the irrational in the form of dreams provides a counterbalance to his rationalism. On November 10, 1619, the twenty-three-year-old Descartes, having attended the coronation of Emperor Ferdinand III, was making his way back through Germany when he was stopped by bad weather near Frankfurt. Shut in a room all that day, "the fire seized his brain," he wrote, and he had the revelation of the unity of all the sciences. But that night he had three consecutive dreams in which appeared the obstacles to his endeavor.

In the first dream he wants to reach a church. He is walking in the street, but finds he cannot make progress unless he lists to the left (the terror of falling and not making his way). He tries to pay his compliments to an acquaintance but is driven back by a violent wind (another impediment). He is told that someone has a melon for him (Freud saw the melon as a symbol of sexual frustration). Others are present, standing straight, while he is unsteady. In the second dream he hears thunder and sees sparks of fire in the room, which awaken him (the certainty of the existence of God?). In the third dream he finds a dictionary and a book of Latin poems. Upon opening the book he finds the verse "what path shall you follow in life" as well as a series of engraved portraits. Without going into a detailed analysis of the dreams, it can be said that Descartes had, in the same day, the vision that there was a meaning of the universe to be discovered, and the vision that there were obstacles to its discovery. Awake, he saw the certainty of success, and asleep, the possibility of failure.

In Descartes' dreaming there is the glimmer of the twentieth-century existential man, who can find no finality other than himself. The symbols of the dream are sometimes menacing, sometimes gratifying, but always ambiguous. In reply to the question of the third dream, Descartes followed the rational path, and set out on an extraordinary odyssey of the intellect. His merit is based on the breadth of his quest. The inscription in the church of Saint-Germain-des-Prés, where he is buried, is fair enough: "Descartes was the first in Europe to assert and assure the rights of human reason."

The Frenchman has continued to assert those rights and there are traces of Cartesian logic in many instances of "thinking French":

The individual's belief that he is equal to his superiors and superior to his equals. The inadequacy of defining individuals by intelligence alone was brought out by the English psychologist who gave IQ tests to the Nuremberg war criminals and found that they all had high marks: Goering 138, and Schacht 143.

Method Coué thinking, named after the French psychotherapist who tried to heal the unwell by telling them to repeat "I feel fine, I feel fine." This form of autopersuasion has another use, the rationalization of failure: Napoleon saying, to explain the Moscow retreat, "Winter came eight days too soon," or the Fourth Republic president finding merit in political vacuum: "In France when there is no cabinet crisis there is no freedom."

The rationalization of prejudices: The particular form French racism takes is an attempt to reconcile the lessons of the Rights of Man and France's reputation for welcoming outsiders with prejudices born of colonialism, native suspiciousness, and the fear that black and brown men will make off with jobs and women. The Frenchman formulates his racism in sentences which also affirm his basic equalitarianism: "I'm not a racist but why is that pretty blonde going out with that dirty black?" "The Jew is like anyone else, of course, but why does he wind up so often in the gas chamber?" French towns rationalize their dislike of Algerian workers by asking them for health certificates if they want to live there. Colonialism depended on the myth of inferior races, whose members were turned into second-class citizens, but it will never occur to the average Frenchman, the one who can tell that a Negro is in the room from the smell, the one who rails against "domino couples," or the one who insists that if the Jew has been persecuted so much there must be a reason, that he is a racist.

The readiness to bow to the lessons of the past: The blind obedience to what happened last time. In 1939 French troops were issued gas masks because the general staff foresaw a repetition of trench warfare and widespread use of poison gases. Because the barbarians had been assimilated by Gallo-Roman civilization, in 1940 the men of Vichy believed they could handle Hitler. It is interesting in this sense to note the number of French leaders who have been historians: the kings dictating to their historiographers—premiers Guizot and Thiers, the Minister of Foreign Affairs and poet Lamartine, the socialist leader Jaurès; Daladier and Bidault were history professors; and General de Gaulle continued the tradition of the chief-of-state historian. The French incorrigibly think according to precedent; history is the national vice.

The compulsion for high-sounding principles. When the reporters for the Paris newspaper *Le Figaro* went on strike in May, 1969, they were not satisfied with listing their demands. They felt it necessary to explain their position on the philosophical foundations of private property.

The brilliant generalizers: French lawyers and doctors admit that there are better specialists elsewhere, but they pride themselves on turning out the most versatile specimens: the lawyer who can go from a criminal case to an inheritance dispute; the unerring diagnostician.

The ability to turn an idea into its opposite, Valéry writing: "There are people who wish to preserve their originality—in doing so they become imitators for they obey those who have made them believe in the value of originality."

The attraction of the extremes that has plagued French political life by dividing it along left-right lines. The myth is that France swings from left to right, whereas most governments have relied on the Plain, the great mass of middle-of-the-road Frenchmen who are horrified by extremes. Authentic left-wing regimes like the Commune and the Popular Front were never allowed to last. And there has been no authentic right-wing regime in the history of modern France. Those leaders who have been able to stay in power, like Napoleon III and Charles de Gaulle, escaped the dichotomy and took from the left and the right whatever they found useful. The left-right myth has impoverished French political thought. Every movement has the thinker it deserves, and the French right has Charles Maurras, the founder of the

Action Française. For Maurras, democracy was part of the Lutheran conspiracy, freedom was an illusion—for the freedom of a
madman is madness—social justice did not exist, and free speech
was a menace. France was being destroyed by half-breeds, Reds,
and Jews, and military defeat was a punishment for its degradation. There was a secret order of the world which the French
could regain by submitting to an absolute monarch. This badly
digested amalgam of Hobbes and Aristotle, this mania for order
and this apocalyptic vision of history were propounded by Maurras in twenty thousand articles and governed the thinking of the
French right for fifty years. The Maurrasian mixture of xenophobia, racism, and dictatorship persuaded a generation of French
youth that democracy was moribund. As for the French left, its
only authentic thinker has been Marx. Outside of that, one sinks
into the flaccid liberal left, tomorrow's soft center. Its members
define themselves in misty terms as men who always choose justice,
believe in man, and defend the oppressed.

This comfort-loving, carpet-slippered, salon left is typified by
men like Claude Perdriel, a manufacturer of plumbing for toilets
who dabbles in the press and publishes the liberal left's house
organ, *Le Nouvel Observateur*. Perdriel makes a point of beginning his conversations with "of course you know that I am profoundly a man of the left," a declaration of faith in a life-style that
is made up of weekends at Saint-Tropez, sports cars, an apartment
near the Champs-Élysées, beautiful ladies sympathetic to the cause,
a sovereign indifference to the working class, and sound ideological
reasons for not paying bills. Publications like *Le Nouvel Observateur* belabor the left-right thing to the point of announcing
in an article: "Finally! A left-wing dictionary." One wonders why
they have not adopted shoes with two left feet. The French
sensibility is conveniently built along left-right lines. The right
wants to be obeyed, the left wants to be understood (in fact the
men of the liberal left tremble at the implications of their own
beliefs). The right is traditional, the left is utopian. The right
wears gloves and likes to hunt, the left likes checkered tablecloths
and the Club Méditerranée. The left forms parties, the right
forms leagues. Left against right means workers' rights against
paternalism, suspicion against defense of technology, courage
against solidarity, the chevalier Bayard against Jean Jaurès. The

right prefers biological images like the root and branch, the left dynamic natural images like the avalanche. The right forms committees of retired generals and Académiciens to bring Pétain's remains back from the Île d'Yeu; the left forms committees of lady writers and popular singers to protest the censorship of an Ingmar Bergman film. Left and right are convenient stereotypes, and another example of the French urge to classify. Perhaps the 1969 presidential election, in which both major candidates claimed to represent the center, laid to rest the myth that politics in France is a matter of left versus right.

Descartes charted the French intellectual landscape but did not explain the origins of its terrain features. The need to order nature comes partly from the fear inherent in a predominantly rural society, where livelihood is uncertain and dependent on the whims of nature. A constant threat hangs over lives like a prolonged shudder of fear. The superstitions of peasants take strange shapes, a shooting star, a horse's gallop in the night, the disjointed mumbling of a village idiot. In French rural society, the Devil has always been more present than God. When sheep are taken to pasture there is always the possibility that they will eat poison grass. Fear of nature extends to fear of the outsider, he who is not from the same place as we are, *celui qui n'est pas de chez nous,* and the French insistence on caution, expressed through a repertoire of proverbs—cultivate your garden, sweep your own doorstep, everything comes to him who waits, it's no use running if you don't leave on time—which is coupled with a strong dose of fatalism, *c'est comme ça,* nothing can be done. One example of everyday secretiveness is the French preference for cards and dominoes over board games, the closed hand as opposed to the open board. Vauban in the seventeenth century mentioned "all the animosities, the inveterate hatreds which are perpetuated in peasant families." The Jacqueries, or peasant revolts, which have existed from the Dark Ages, are explosions of these hatreds and animosities in response to political and economic changes the rural folk do not understand, like the Breton peasants destroying their crops as a reaction to Common Market agricultural agreements.

Descartes also deserves credit as the founder of a caste of Brahmins, the intellectuals. Literature is to the French what the playing fields of Eton are to the English, and Descartes is the first of that breed of men of letters who have felt it was their mission to explain the world. They have always been treated like sacred cows, although often underfed ones, even by governments they were undermining. The eighteenth-century Encyclopédistes found support in unexpected quarters, from the royal censor, Malesherbes and Madame de Pompadour. Voltaire returned triumphant from exile in Ferney to take his seat in the Académie, alongside other critics of monarchic institutions, like Diderot. Whether they in fact had any influence on the events of 1789 is contingent upon the tradition they founded of writers who set themselves up as thinkers and concerned themselves with current events. Descartes established that there was nothing dishonorable in a life devoted to thought, and Voltaire converted the pure intellectual into a committed writer. Literature viewed as a struggle led to the idea that the writer has a mandate to watch over the moral and cultural values of the nation. The Cartesian credo of the supremacy of reason gave birth to a mystique that intellectuals shape history. The influential literary critic of *Le Monde*, Pierre-Henri Simon, has written in this connection that "the inspiration and the movement of history belongs to those who think, that is, to those who make the judgment of facts and the choice of acts depend on the demands of the spirit; not only the calculations of intelligence which make the end fit the means, but the deeper reasons, the evaluations of the ends themselves in the light of truth and justice." If only it were so. But this opinion is not more or less valid than saying that history belongs to unthinking brutes who bludgeon those who disagree with them into submission. But French tradition encourages the intellectual to believe that he helps shape public affairs. When a Nobel-Prize physicist speaks out on Vietnam or a novelist takes a stand on the Common Market, no one questions their qualifications, for they belong to that elite which is expected to articulate the problems of society.

It is another aspect of "thinking French," to believe in the power of ideas and in a caste that is appointed to guard them. The word "intellectual" itself was not used until the Dreyfus case, when Clemenceau published a "manifesto of intellectuals."

The writers and political figures who believed in Dreyfus' innocence began to refer to themselves as such. Zola's *J'accuse* was another tribute to the power of ideas and to the influence of the intellectuals, who were considered dangerous enough to be brought to trial and jailed. An anti-intellectual tradition was born with the nationalist, reactionary writer Barrès, who compared the teachers and the university students marching in the streets in defense of Dreyfus to the guinea pigs who were injected with rabies at the Pasteur Institute.

In the eighteenth-century climate of enlightenment, intellectuals were automatically on the side of the angels. The Encyclopédistes were manifestly the agents of truth and freedom; there were no anti-Encyclopédistes to come to the defense of *dragonnades*, the salt tax, the question, or other *ancien régime* abuses. But with the Dreyfus case, for the first time, intellectuals divided into partisan factions, each of which claimed to be speaking in the name of truth and virtue. Twenty-five members of the Académie Française were members of Déroulède's jingoistic and anti-Dreyfus League of Patriots. Barrès, for all his diatribes, was himself an influential intellectual whose mystique of the nation left its imprint on General de Gaulle. With the Dreyfus case, intellectuals divided along left-right lines. Those who asked for Dreyfus' liberation in the name of justice fought those who believed that the integrity of the army would be seriously weakened by his release. Descartes' vision of one truth foundered in the self-serving rhetoric of modern party politics. Since then, French intellectuals have combined the assumption that they are speaking in the name of universal reason with partisan pursuits. A good deal of French writing has been slanted by this approach.

In the period between the wars, two of the most popular historians were men of the right, like Jacques Bainville and Pierre Gaxotte, who proceeded to rehabilitate the *ancien régime* and discredit the Revolution. In the same period, the left could count on the allegiance of two surrealists turned Communists, the novelist Aragon and the poet Paul Eluard, while young novelists like Robert Brasillach and Drieu de la Rochelle were drawn to the Fascism of the thirties.

Intellectuals have thus tended to reflect rather than to rise above French factionalism, with the unfortunate result that despite their privileged position within French society, some of them have in our time been sentenced to prison and worse (the right-wing thinker Charles Maurras died in jail and Brasillach was shot as a collaborator). Intellectuals are able to explain away the discrepancy between lofty ideals and sectarianism by assuming that the average citizen obeys only narrow interests. Even Charles Péguy, who believed with religious fervor in the essential goodness of mankind and in the special excellence of the French, refused to consider, when anyone canceled a subscription to his *Cahiers de la Quinzaine,* that it was for intellectual reasons; according to him, a cancelation had to be the result of family influence, personal bitterness, or some obscure grudge.

The main virtue of the French tradition is that intellectuals have nonetheless been able to reverse some unjust political decisions. Ever since Voltaire took up the *affaire Calas,* and won the rehabilitation of a Huguenot who was put to death on trumped-up charges of having done away with his son, intellectuals have from time to time not spoken in vain. The campaign that led to the liberation of Dreyfus was one such instance. In a minor key, the campaign to reinstate Henri Langlois was another. Langlois, the founder and director of the French cinémathèque (film library), a private but government-endowed organization, was fired without an explanation in the spring of 1968, thanks to government pressure following a malicious whispering campaign that hinted at embezzlement. Although Langlois was an indifferent administrator who stored the priceless film library in a converted World War II bunker outside Paris, he was a close friend of France's important film directors, who marshaled the intellectual community in defense of one of their own. At stake was an issue broader than one man's job: the Gaullist tendency to interfere peremptorily in cultural affairs. Enough directors threatened to withdraw copies of their films from the cinémathèque to make the government back down, and after several months of skirmishing, Langlois was reinstated. Such victories are possible only on the domestic front. A similar campaign in favor of the captured French revolutionary Régis Debray backfired, creating the issue of foreign interference, and giving the Bolivian government a further motive for the stiff sentence it dealt on four counts: foreign gringo intellectual guerrillero.

The French intellectual community, although divided into schools like fish of similar striping, constitutes an intermittently successful pressure group. When Jean-Paul Sartre took General de Gaulle to task for refusing to allow the Bertrand Russell Vietnam tribunal to sit in Paris, the general took the trouble of repeating his refusal in a personal letter. An issue arises, committees are formed, manifestoes are produced. In 1935, it was the manifesto of the 64 for peace in Europe. Peace did not come. During the Algerian war, the manifesto of the 12 denounced torture in Algeria. Torture continued, but a bit more uneasily. General Jacques Massu, who commanded the Algiers sector, felt obliged to undergo the *gégène* (torture by electric shock) as a form of preventive expiation. When France's behavior is too flagrantly in contradiction with its traditions, the intellectuals' role is to ferment guilt feelings.

Another trait of the French intellectuals is that even when they are politically radical, they remain socially conservative. Tradition means defending the Rights of Man, but it also means suspicion of change. Victor Hugo, exiled to Jersey for his opposition to Napoleon III, was an equally impassioned foe of the railroad, of which he said: "From now on, the demon of speed controls the world." Stendhal and Alfred de Vigny also contributed to the campaign to present the railroad as a threat to the genuine values of French civilization. To the warnings of writers about "the great modern monster where ideals perish" (Alfred de Musset) were added the dire diagnoses of well-known doctors. Passing through tunnels would give you pleurisy, pregnant women would miscarry, the motion of the wagons would induce epilepsy, and the moving landscape would cause eye inflammation.

As the heir of an unparalleled classical tradition, the French intellectual feels a secret pride that while so much has changed, he is still using the instruments of Descartes and Montaigne, pen and paper. His hostility to change takes different forms. Georges Duhamel, who became secretary of the Académie Française, made a literary career out of resisting "progress." For years he wrote articles in the *Figaro* mourning patches of grass that were being replaced by superhighways, and streams diverted from their natural course by a hydroelectric plant. He saw himself as the curator of a vanishing rural France. On a higher plane, Valéry, also the heir of Descartes, found he could not come to terms with a world that eluded his Euclidian sense of form, and somberly predicted that Western civilization would be as ephemeral as that of Babylon and Nineveh. Another form of escape from the perplexities of the present was nostalgia for a world one never knew. The Catholic monarchist Bernanos longed for the pastoral utopia of the twelfth century, with its chivalric ideals, its Gothic monuments to religious observance, and the stained-glass windows peopled with happy peasants and nobles.

French writers of the thirties realized that the era of confident humanism was over, but the tradition was still too ingrained for them to shake loose. Malraux's escape was to write about revolutions in China and Spain instead of about his own country, and thereafter to pursue eternal values through art criticism. But no French novelist of stature dealt with the discrepancy between an intellectual tradition which assumed that reason correctly applied can diagnose and cure all the ills of society, and a society which was in fact disintegrating from the time of the Popular Front until the German Occupation. A writer like Céline responded to the end of humanism with a cry of despair. Sartre, who acknowledged his debt to Céline in *La Nausée,* wanted him put to death in 1945 for his anti-Semitic diatribes, which is an indication of the animosities that agitated the postwar French intellectual scene.

There are no revolutionary French intellectuals, because one way or another they are tied to the establishment. They become members of the Académie, or teachers at the Collège de France, or leaders of a philosophical school, or cabinet ministers. They acquire disciples, a comfortable apartment, and a house in the country. Ever since Richelieu founded the Académie, France has solved the problem of the alienation of intellectuals by recruiting them. They are encouraged to serve the state, and at the same time intellectual pursuits are recognized as sufficiently important to deserve the sustained attention of the state. Governments have had a house intellectual since Racine and Voltaire were royal historiographers. Chateaubriand became Minister of the Interior because the Restoration felt it needed the luster of his name. Lamartine considered himself a politician first and a poet second, an opinion that was not shared by his colleagues in the Chamber of Deputies. The Second Republic was proclaimed, thanks largely to his efforts, and he became Foreign Minister in the provisional government, followed a year later in the post by Alexis de Tocqueville. Victor Hugo also sat in the Chamber of Deputies, while Clemenceau, when he was defeated in legislative elections, started a novel. The Socialist minister Jules Guesde wrote Baudelairian verse. The historian Gabriel Hanotaux became Minister of Foreign Affairs.

Alexis Léger was the much-criticized political director of the French foreign service in the nineteen thirties and a Nobel-Prize poet under the name St. John Perse. Paul Claudel was a highly praised dramatist and poet and an average ambassador to Tokyo and the United States. Léon Blum was a drama critic and the author of a book counseling premarital sex for women, before he became Premier. Malraux gave up a long career as a writing revolutionary to become the domesticated bard of Gaullism. But the dilemma of the man of letters, accustomed to the authority of the intellect, who becomes a government official and has to face everyday reality is perhaps best illustrated by Jean Giraudoux. As a playwright, he made urbanity and wit seem unlimited natural resources. His polished versions of Greek myths were a penetrating analysis of modern society. But as Minister of Information he was a self-deluded propagandist. In 1939 he encouraged false optimism. "The Descartes line and the Wagner line will hold when the Maginot Line and the Siegfried Line will have given way," he wrote. Reality arrived in the shape of the Nazi officer who said, "When I hear the word culture I draw my revolver." Giraudoux said young Frenchmen should practice sports more. "Every hero of Racine is an athlete," he wrote. This was at the end of 1939, and it was too late for athletics. Giraudoux blamed immigrants for whatever interfered with his vision of a great classical France. Here was an important writer, bred on the humanism of French civilization, adopting a racist stance in the name of his humanist convictions. Immigrants, he wrote, were like "fleas on a dog." They are the harbingers of "expediency, clandestine action, collusion, and corruption; they are a constant menace to the spirit of precision, good faith, and perfection which were characteristic of French craftsmanship."

In every immigrant, Giraudoux saw a potential stock-kiter, abortionist, and dealer in pornographic postcards. After the debacle, he saw them as a cancer that had destroyed France. Giraudoux's attempt to reconcile events with his high vision of his own people led him to describe the exodus of Frenchmen fleeing the German advance as a collective act of heroism: "The exodus was a burst of religious feeling which was given a Biblical name ... a people well known and often jeered at for its attachment to its land, to comfort, and to a regulated life, renounced its land, its homes, its material existence, to rejoin a sacred place, which was any province that was still free." Instead of running for their lives, the French were patriotically regrouping. Giraudoux could not come to terms with defeat; it was not part of his intellectual panoply.

Whatever the merits of mixing intellectuals and politics, there can be no harm in political figures being highly cultivated men. Whatever the content of a de Gaulle press conference, his syntax is irreproachable. One way the educated Frenchman defines himself is by the extent to which he has absorbed his own culture. There will be a murmur of approval for the board chairman who quotes Pascal appropriately. Assembly debates are sprinkled with apt literary references which enhance the reputations of those who make them. Literary allusions can smooth over difficult moments. When Minister of Education Edgar Faure presented his reform program to the National Assembly in October, 1968, one of the foes within his own party was the Gaullist Secretary-General, Robert Poujade. Meeting accidentally in the lobby, Poujade said "I have a strange weakness for you." Faure, of course, recognized the line as coming from Molière's *Le Misanthrope,* and filled in the rest: "Although you are probably deceiving me with sweet words, I want to gaze all the way into your heart and see whether it will be black enough to betray me." Political differences are made less harsh when expressed within the frame of reference of a comon culture.

One of the reasons for Pompidou's popularity as a Premier was that he qualified as an intellectual. He was a graduate of a *grande école,* Normale Supérieure, he had written an essay on Racine, and he was the editor of an anthology of French poetry. It would not occur to an English or American publication to interview a Prime Minister about his tastes in art and literature, but this seems perfectly normal in France, and in September, 1966, the

Figaro Littéraire ran two full pages of Mr. Pompidou's remarks on matters intellectual and strictly nonpolitical. He had read the principal works of the *Nouveau Roman* and found them fertile in new narrative techniques. But he added that technique is never enough. He expressed his admiration for abstract art "and its refusal of the subject, which corresponds, in the first half of the twentieth century, to a weariness and a need." His definition of art: "It is not decoration, its purpose is not to increase the comfort of our daily lives—it is the archangel's sword, it must pierce us."

French culture is government-sponsored. In the recruitment of intellectuals, the proliferation of literary prizes, the French Premier's interest in Op Art, the Ministry of Culture and its encouragement of artists, in these and one hundred other ways, an official prejudice in favor of intellectuals is manifest. Authors on trial in one generation, like Flaubert and Baudelaire, find their way into textbooks by the next. Culture saturates daily life. On the body of a young soldier killed in the World War I trenches a scribbled note was found in which he asked to be buried at the feet of Lamartine. He was. Pasteur is on the 5-franc note, Voltaire on the 10-franc note, Racine on the 50-franc note, Corneille on the 100-franc note, and the minority of Frenchmen who have owned 500-franc notes (100 dollars) have looked upon the smiling countenance of Molière.

Writers whose works are forgotten are remembered in street names. When the federal treasury puts Whitman and Hawthorne on 5- and 10-dollar bills and names a Washington street after William Faulkner, the American government will have understood the advantages of culture. The French see themselves as a people selflessly concerned with cultural over material values. In 1944, Wladimir d'Ormesson, the French ambassador to the Holy See, gave Pope Pius XII a copy of Richelieu's *Instructions to Christians,* and drew his attention to the small type on the last page: "Finished printing on the presses of the national printing office, Paris, August 24, 1944." "I could make a lot of fine speeches to your Holiness about the perennial nature of French culture," he said, "but I don't think anything could match this simple inscription. Thus, on the very eve of the Liberation of Paris, while the capital, and all of France, were in chaos, without a government, without an administration, without a police, typographers in the heart of Paris were conscientiously putting the finishing touches to a spiritual essay by Cardinal Richelieu."

"That," said his visibly impressed Holiness, "is France."

D'Ormesson displayed a satisfaction with his own culture that bordered on smugness. But the French have several reasons for smugness. First, their culture's European tenure for a century and a half, and second, its power of absorption. Rousseau was Swiss, and Simenon is Belgian. Holbach, although German, is listed in encyclopedias as French, giving rise to the notion of a cultural nationality. Or, as Conrad said when he refused the attraction of French culture by writing in English, "My nationality is the language in which I write." Casanova was an Italian lecher but a French man of letters. Jose-Maria de Heredia was Cuban, but joined the Académie Française as a French symbolist poet. Another great symbolist poet, Jean Moréas, was born in Athens and Gallicized his name from Papadiamentopoulos, while the poet Apollinaire was a Roman-born bastard who was christened Wilhelm Apollinaris de Kostrowitzky.

French music owes much to an Italian, Lulli, who was Louis XIV's official composer, and to a German, Glück, who reformed French opera. French painting of the nineteenth and twentieth centuries appropriated Sisley, Van Gogh, Soutine, Modigliani, Picasso, Chagall, and Matta. As for French drama, the founders of the theater of alienation are an Irishman, Samuel Beckett, a Rumanian, Eugene Ionesco, and a Russian, Arthur Adamov.

Not only did France attract foreign artists, but the breadth of French culture seemed to represent all the trends of the human spirit. There is no single national poet, no French Goethe. The same culture that produced the tragedies of Racine produced also the popular wisdom of La Fontaine, and, in contrast to the overladen frescoes of Victor Hugo can also submit the anti-eloquence of Verlaine, the hermetic musings of Mallarmé, and the illuminations of Rimbaud. French culture is a genuine Republic of Letters, where Emma Bovary, Tartuffe, Candide, and Swann live as equable neighbors, none towering over the others like a Faust or a Hamlet.

Why should the French be interested in other cultures if their own is so varied and attractive to foreigners? What has sometimes been called intellectual protectionism is often mere lack of inter-

est which threatens to become provincial. The professor who
knows all of Racine by heart has never read Melville or Evelyn
Waugh. Important foreign scholarship about France, like Pot-
tinger's study on book publishing under the *ancien régime,* is
not even translated into French. The reason Raymond Aron's
Introduction to the Philosophy of History was greeted by French
critics in 1939 as a new and original work was because they had
never read Max Weber.

The French have had a tendency to ignore great twentieth-
century thought. Freud is a relatively recent discovery, which explains why most French psychiatric care has not advanced beyond
the orthodox Freudian stage. The literary convention of the
examen de conscience long served as a substitute for psychoanal-
ysis. This stylistic exercise combines psychological insight with
the awareness of self that the *cogito* brings. Listen to a contemporary classical voice, that of Jean Paulhan: "Toward the age of
six, I was surprised to notice that I existed. Later, I tried to know
myself. The emotion felt at the sight of a donkey being beaten
by its master long led me to believe that I was good. And yet
sometimes, I would wait for hours along a railway track for an
accident which seemed probable . . . although I like presents, I
don't like to receive them: I feel too involved. Being thus made,
it is easy to see that neither approval nor blame, love nor hate,
can ever satisfy me. Whoever finds me in the wrong attracts me.
Whoever finds me right, I feel that he has not understood me. . . .
When I realized that I was persisting in taking myself for God,
I renounced all attempts at understanding myself." Why should
a people so gifted in self-examination read Freud?

Cultural parochialism is an attitude inherited from an age
when French thought inspired the rest of the literate world, but
no one today, and certainly not the French, can pretend to such
primacy. In this sense it is encouraging to see André Malraux
adopting the line, unoriginal but provocative for France, that implicit in the idea of culture is the need to know other cultures
than one's own, and that there is no superior culture. The French,
who continued to consider themselves the cultural center of the
planet long after their cultural influence had declined, seem more
willing now to return to a long-neglected tradition of "thinking
French," the generous cosmopolitanism of Montaigne. There is

more to be learned and more to be gained from a man who traveled, not like Descartes, to make himself invisible among Dutch merchants, and "not only to bring back, as our French nobility do, how many steps there are at the Santa Rotonda or how much longer or wider is Nero's face on some old ruin than on some other medal, but rather to bring back the temperaments of these nations and their habits, and to rub and rasp our brain against that of others. . . . From frequenting the world a wonderful clarity of human judgment is acquired."

7

╼╼╼╼╼╼╼╼╼╼╼╼╼╼╼╼╼╼╼╼╼╼╼╼╼╼╼╼

Art Styles

THERE are critics whose claim to a unity of style in French art has led them to find analogies between the drawings in the Lascaux caves, a Burgundian wood carving, a Gothic angel, a Georges de la Tour Biblical scene, a Fragonard interior, a Degas dancer, and a Bernard Buffet landscape. Art interpreted in this manner serves to demonstrate the continuity of certain French traits, but not very convincingly. Changes in art styles are the result of multiple outside influences, or a reaction against a previous style. Conversely, imported artists like the Belgian Philippe de Champaigne exemplify the French classical ideal of clarity and proportion. It is rare that a style can validly be called national. The only two authentic French national styles, in the sense that an entirely new artistic concept can be traced to a geographical site, are the Gothic in architecture and Impressionism in painting. Both originated in the Île-de-France, both broke up light to create new chromatic effects, and both suffered periods of derision; the Gothic was held in contempt by the eighteenth century and the Impressionists were considered decadent by their contemporaries.

Unity of style lies not in comparing two diverse examples of

French architecture like Chartres Cathedral and the castle of Fontainebleau but in realizing that for several centuries Europe adopted a style which, as Erwin Panofsky has noted, was born in a hundred-mile radius around Paris. In contrast to the cherished notion of individualism, the only art in which French supremacy remains uncontested was esentially anonymous and collective. What made the adventure of the Gothic possible? Geometry was taught in religious schools; craft guilds were formed with high standards of excellence; cities that could lodge and finance a cathedral first drafted their charters in the middle of the eleventh century while their feudal lords were away on the Crusades. The returning Crusaders probably brought back the principle of the ribbed vault. The divorce between philosophy and the revealed truth had begun, and perhaps the cathedrals were an unconscious attempt to reconcile the divisions of faith and reason; for the mass of people, however, this was a period of high observance, and the essential artistic act was the building of a beautiful church.

Monumental art had been in eclipse since Rome fell, for the decline of an empire means the decline of its forms. The Romanesque churches had cozy, human proportions and there was nothing specifically French about them. They were a form of monastic architecture that borrowed the motifs for its carvings from such disparate sources as Byzantine manuscripts and Celtic zoomorphic figures. No single person invented the ribbed vault and the flying buttress which distributed the weight of the stone and permitted the Gothic. There are early examples of Gothic vaults and pointed arches in Romanesque churches. But it was in the Île-de-France that these technical innovations were adapted to create a new style. The Gothic developed at first for practical rather than esthetic reasons, because a stubborn abbot named Suger wanted to enlarge his abbey a few miles outside of Paris. It was a small Carolingian chapel dedicated to Saint Denis, the martyred bishop of Paris who had been tortured at the age of ninety and put to death four different ways; according to his hagiographers, he was roasted on a grill, thrown to the lions, crucified, and, finally, decapitated (as soon as his head touched the ground he picked it up and began to recite psalms). The spreading fame of the martyred saint attracted pilgrims eager to gain indulgences by seeing his relics. Abbot Suger wrote that on holy days when the relics were shown "the women were squeezed in by the mass of strong men as in a winepress . . . they cried out horribly as though in labor."

Abbot is the wrong title for Suger, who was an extraordinary entrepreneur. A canon writing his obituary said that he was "small of body and family, but although constrained by this twofold smallness he refused to be a small man." He became political adviser to two kings and regent of France while one of them was on a Crusade. Louis VI made him minister of defense, justice and foreign affairs. His own crusade consisted in enlarging and making beautiful an overcrowded chapel, and with that eminently practical motive he inspired a century of European architecture. He was "modern" in the sense that he had to argue against foes of change. Cistercian puritans objected to his plans to alter the chapel—it had been erected by King Dagobert and consecrated by Christ in person. It was, says Panofsky, "as if a President of the United States were to have had the White House rebuilt by Frank Lloyd Wright." Suger was not one of those unscrupulous monks who grew fat on a sinecure, with whom the age is identified. He had a single passion, the embellishment of his church. He became a fund-raiser and promoter whose drive made his contemporaries think he was after personal glory. But he was past the point of distinguishing his own interests from those of the abbey; his personal aspirations became fused with his task. He thought of himself as an adopted son of Saint Denis who was fulfilling a divine mission. When he talked about the abbey, he said "we."

Work began around 1130 and Suger suffered from insomnia as his mind grappled with the problems of each day's task. He dreamed that the great beams for the roof could be found in the forest of Rambouillet, but when he went there the next day the woodsmen scoffed. He went scurrying in his cassock through the thickets and did indeed find twelve beams of the needed size. He discovered a quarry near Pontoise and recruited the manpower to dig the stones out, shaping them in the quarry to save money. "Whenever the columns were hauled from the bottom of the slope with knotted ropes," he wrote, "both our own people and the pious neighbors, nobles and common folk alike, would tie their arms, chests, and shoulders to the ropes and draw the columns up like draft animals." Constantly hounding his workers and the wealthy bourgeois of the capital, attending to every detail, lifting beams and stones himself, guiding the sculptor's chisel and the master mason's callipers, Suger finished the first Gothic church in 1144. Two bays were built at the west of the old Carolingian nave, and a new façade went up. With its three portals adorned with columns and statues it became the model for the Gothic façade. Until the day of its consecration before Louis VII, five archbishops, and fifteen bishops, which assured the triumph of the Gothic in the Capetian domain, Suger was not quite sure the looming structure resting on delicate ribbed vaults would stay up. He wrote that once during a storm he greatly feared the church would collapse: "Because the arches were not supported, they shook in a terrible manner, bent this way and that, and threatened to go down in ruins." In bad weather he sat up to watch over the unfinished vaults like a worried mother over a sick child.

Suger's other innovation was the rose window. Gothic walls could neither be painted on nor left bare. The whole principle of Gothic, rooted in the earth but soaring to the sky, required some decorative solution to the problem of full walls and a necessary passage of light, which was solved by the stained-glass windows. They were translucent frescoes, with a line formed by the lead tracery that held together the bits of colored glass. The rose windows are like enormous retinas, capturing and filtering a mosaic of light which bursts in wavelike patterns in the gloomy aisles of the cathedrals.

Suger wrote that he wanted "to make what is material immaterial, so that it resides in a strange region of the universe which does not exist entirely either on earthly clay or the pureness of the sky." The Cistercians found the joyousness of stained glass too garish and used only green glass to obtain what became known as windows *en grisaille*. The great cathedrals of the Île-de-France—Chartres, Rheims, and Amiens—all finished in the twelfth and thirteenth centuries, were built on the double principle of allowing the passage of light and reducing the volume of stone; the ideal cathedral is the glass skyscraper of today. Because we do not know who their architects were, the idea has arisen that they were improvised, like Brigham Young's Mormon temple. But the Gothic cathedrals were constructed along such exacting geometric principles that five hundred years later the architect Viollet-le-Duc

showed that Saint-Sernin in Toulouse was designed according to
a system of isosceles and equilateral triangles. The cathedral was
a geometric figure, but the arch was also, as Rodin said, a pair
of hands in prayer.

The Gothic tried to combine worship with a love of nature,
represented in scenes of daily and seasonal concerns. Its capitals
are a botanical encyclopedia and a record of rural labors; they
show ploughs in the fields, Burgundian peasants pressing grapes,
and women with sweeping scythes. The floral decorations are a
precise indication of the style's life-span: early Gothic shows
flowers in bud, thirteenth-century cathedrals show them in full
bloom, and the flamboyant fourteenth-century churches favor
autumnal flowers. After Saint-Denis there was a great burst of
construction financed by the monarchy and the burghers: Noyon,
Senlis, Laon, which showed sculptures of the oxen that had hoisted
the heavy stones used to build the church, and Chartres, where
47 windows were offered by 19 guilds. Architects competed to
raise their vaults and spires ever higher, until the 153-meter-high
Beauvais spire came crashing down, Babel-like, in 1284, dragging
its flying buttresses with it.

The buttresses had both a stylistic and a structural function:
they took some of the load off the vaults and they served as a
transition between the mass of the cathedral and the space beyond. If a French unity of style is sought, it might be found in
the similar use of structural materials, with different degrees of
felicity, in the Gothic cathedrals and the Eiffel Tower. Suger was
the innovator, and can hardly be blamed for having himself represented in his church, like the donors of Flemish triptychs; his
slight figure is sculpted in the doors and columns and appears in
green vestments in one of the windows. After Saint-Denis was
finished, he induced wealthy visitors and clerics to part with the
stones in their rings for the adornment of a new altar. He hoarded
gold vessels, pearls, enamels, and richly worked textiles. He took
a childlike delight in precious stones and bright colors. He cornered visitors from the East and would not leave their side until
they had acknowledged that the treasures of Saint-Denis were the
equal of those in Santa Sofia. His own monks derided his flamboy-
ance. He was a name-dropper, a snob, and a chauvinist, who wrote
that the English "were destined by moral and natural law to be

subjected to the French." He embodied many so-called national traits, among them the ability to combine a spiritual ideal with a practical, shrewd, hard-working temperament; de Gaulle was no different when he combined political pragmatism with a mystical ideal of France. The French priest knows that the celebration of the essential mystery in the mass need not prevent him from enjoying the sacramental wine. This dualism was the essence of the Gothic: It was both a spiritual hymn and a triumph of engineering.

Suger died of malaria in 1151, but the Gothic spread, first beyond the Île-de-France and then beyond France; French masters built Gothic cathedrals as far afield as Nicosia, Uppsala, Canterbury, Prague, and Cologne (an imitation of Amiens). Every country in Europe, with the exception of Italy, wanted to defy the logic of stone and gravity as Abbot Suger had done. In France the cathedrals were not only places of worship but community centers. They served as theaters until the Passion Plays incorporated so many profane elements that they were banned from churches; balustraded galleries were added in many cathedrals for the Compostela-bound pilgrims who crossed Europe with a necklace of shells for a passport; university students who attended classes in the shadow of their fluted columns learned the seditious mystery-denying truth that no one can believe what he has not yet understood; the Estates General convened in cathedrals and voiced their complaints before the king; in Gothic France the cathedral was the site of a fragile unity between the monarchy, the church, and the people. Notre Dame was financed almost entirely by the state; it was the first national cathedral, and even today distances from Paris to the borders of France are measured from the Notre Dame parvis. The pride of the parishioner in his Gothic church was a form of naïve patriotism expressed in the words of an artisan from Le Puy: "The said city is honored to have inside its Notre Dame church, the most beautiful and holy relics in the world, specifically: the holy foreskin of our Lord, which is of his own flesh, and of which there is no other part in all the world."

The iconography illustrated the Christian mystery. Along with superstitious symbols such as griffins and gargoyles, the sculptures and bas-reliefs illustrated the faith, and already, in Chartres Cathedral, the faithful could see, not far from Adam and Eve ashamedly covering their genitals with fig leaves, Pythagoras working out his square root. Among the stylistic innovations was the column that became a statue. It was sculpted directly in the stone; there were no wax models as in Renaissance sculpture. And unlike the Greek caryatids, the sculpture was subordinated to the architectural whole. The drapery of the tunic followed the fluting of the column, the head was in its axis, the gestures of the arms were concentric. Gothic sculpture does not try to impose an emotion, it stands in tranquil objectivity, like a force of nature. A counterpoint to the lofty proportions was the wit the sculptors found to express human foibles: Pride falling from a horse, Cowardice as an armed knight fleeing before a rabbit, Cruelty as a noble lady kicking her servant in the stomach, Inconstancy as a monk throwing his habit into a thicket.

Seldom has an artistic style had such a pervasive influence on society and on the other arts. Polyphonic music developed only after the Gothic, as though it needed a cathedral to be played in; the French claim that two Notre Dame organists named Léonin and Pérotin were the first to write music for more than one voice. Also, painting, once removed from church walls, took refuge in illuminated manuscripts, which became known as the French art (see Dante's "Purgatorio"—"*Quell'arte ch'alluminar chiamata e in Parisi*"). But the world of the Gothic could only last as long as the conditions under which it developed. While the twelfth-century cathedrals promoted faith, the twelfth-century universities taught deductive reasoning, dialectics, syllogisms, the philosophical hairsplitting that became scholasticism, the positive side of which was a passion for the intelligible, whereas half the attraction of the Gothic was its mystery. When the Hundred Years War began in 1337, building on unfinished cathedrals was interrupted. Even without war, the Gothic was in decline; the names of the masters and sculptors begin to appear in fourteenth-century documents; the social condition of the masters had changed to make art an individual pursuit; piety took new forms, such as paintings offered by wealthy donors: The great collective enterprise that was the Gothic cathedral was no longer attuned to the French sensibility.

The Gothic ends with the erosion of the theocratic order, the close of the fourteenth century, the failure of the Crusades, the resurgence of heresies, cities struck with famines and plagues, and the countryside turned into a battlefield. It ended also because of social change, the rise of phenomena as varied as the art form of the portrait and the invention of mechanical clocks. In portraits an individual artist painted an individual subject; it was an art for domestic interiors, secular, commercial, and private. As for the birth of linear time, theologians had said time did not exist for God, and thus could be arbitrarily measured by man; the first cathedrals had timekeepers who divided each day into twelve equal parts despite its length, as a convenience for the community. Objective time, measured spatially by mechanical hands covering a face, is the privilege of imperfect, ephemeral creatures concerned with adapting time to their earthly obligations. Quite suddenly the frenzy of construction came to a full stop. By the time the magnificent flamboyant examples like the rose-red cathedral of Strasbourg were completed in the fifteenth century, the age was demanding an individual-oriented humanism which the Italian Renaissance supplied. Domes replaced spires, and the invention of printing made culture the purview of the educated and the Gothic form of storytelling superfluous. No more would Villon's mother say: "I am a poor old woman who knows nothing, who cannot read. But in church I see paradise painted and hell where the damned broil."

French style is usually associated with the façade architecture of the *grand siècle* and the gridiron regularity of streets and squares rather than the extravagant vertical constructions of the Gothic. This is partly because the classical French age systematically disparaged the Gothic; the very term is an insult devised by Raphael as a synonym for barbarity. In its time, the Gothic was known quite simply as French architecture. The seventeenth-century French preferred the work of Italian architects to the masterpieces of their own anonymous masters. The tradition of going to Rome to be inspired by the ruins of antiquity, which continued until 1969 with the Prix de Rome and the villa Medici, began in the seventeenth century. Thousands of Italian stonemasons and master craftsmen arrived in France to build Fontainebleu and Chambord. Seldom have a nation's intellectuals attacked a national style as ferociously as the writers and thinkers of the classical age and the Enlightenment ganged up on the Gothic. Molière called Gothic ornaments "odious monsters of ignorant centuries which the torrents of barbarism have produced." Fénelon called the flying buttress a useless frill because he did not understand its purpose. In his 1715 letter to the Académie Française, he wrote: "The inventors of the architecture that is called Gothic, and which undoubtedly originated with the Arabs... lift on very thin pillars an immense vault that rises to the skies. One would think that everything is up in the air." Jacques-Germain Soufflot, the architect of Louis XVI, conformed to the spirit of the times when he mutilated Notre Dame, breaking the windows, whitewashing the walls, uprooting the paving stones, and melting down the medieval altarpiece to make coins. In exchange, Soufflot gave France that bastard Greek temple the Pantheon, which sits on the Montagne Sainte-Geneviève like a cap on a dunce. The Gothic came back in fashion under the Second Empire, when Viollet-le-Duc restored a number of famous churches, but the French writers were still divided. Stendhal railed against "all-powerful habit, which prevents us from being sensitive to the ugliness of the Gothic." While Proust, who shared Ruskin's admiration of the great cathedrals, made pilgrimages to Chartres to hunt for one tiny but sublime stone figure which had enchanted the author of *The Seven Lamps of Architecture.*

Whatever the artistic merits of the Gothic, it was at the center of French national life, whereas nearly all French monumental architecture from the Renaissance to the Restoration was an Italian-derived imitation of antiquity. What counted in French classical architecture was the façade. Versailles and the Louvre are buildings to be looked at, not lived in, and even their decorations are not so much constructed as sketched—compare the proportions of the Louvre, its odd, decorated rivulets and its gingerbread chimneys, with the purity of line, the combination of massiveness and elegance, of the Farnese Palace. The architect Gabriel purposely designed the buildings around the Place de la Concorde like a stage set. He built the façades according to a harmonious division of verticals and horizontals before deciding what he would build behind them. Although they have a pleasing sense of proportion, they are oddly one-dimensional. Italian Renaissance architecture flowered into the baroque, but the French frowned on curvilinear façades and broken pediments. Bernini came to Paris to design the Louvre colonnade, but offended French sobriety with his flowing designs and haughty behavior. His project was rejected in favor of Perrault's uninspired but orthodox version. Until Viollet-le-Duc drew attention to the architecture of the Middle Ages, the French continued to design dull, neoclassical, columned buildings like the Madeleine church and the Palais Bourbon, where the National Assembly sits. They imagined they had captured the refinement and simplicity of the ancient Greeks.

The formal gardens of Le Nôtre have the same one-dimensional quality. Walking through them, one does not have the impression of being outdoors, but of having stepped into the annex of a drawing room. A great formal garden like Vaux le Vicomte, Le Nôtre's masterpiece, satisfies the same yearning for order that makes housewives adjust the level of wall paintings. It has been said that the Italian garden is constructed, the English garden is planted, and the French garden is sketched. The gardens of Versailles were a one-way thoroughfare, for Louis XIV decreed there was only one direction in which they could be visited, in a little book entitled *Manière de Montrer les Jardins de Versailles*. Even his vegetable garden was pruned and arranged in geometric figures.

French classical architecture was doctrinal, and as contemporary Russian painters know, doctrine can stifle art. French painting also suffered from rigid esthetic principles that were adopted by the Royal Academy when it was created in 1648. A rewarding period of French painting had followed the Gothic, in the sixteenth century. There was a Flemish love of texture and an Italian humanism in the portraits of Clouet and the miniatures of Jean Fouquet. Georges de la Tour, with his Caravaggio-like use of artificial light, was the last master of this radiant period. He was followed by the first court artist, Nicolas Poussin, who spent much of his adult life in Rome, and is buried there. His paintings were a model of the lessons to be drawn from the sculptures of antiquity, and in his religious allegories his Christs are thinly disguised Jupiters. His successor, Le Brun, who ruled over art from 1664 until 1690, dictated that the proportions of antiquity should be the canons for French artists.

Conferences were held at the Royal Academy to determine how to show passion with facial expressions. There was a theory for each feature—the eyebrows when gently raised together indicated pleasant feelings, but when pointed, sadness and pain. Admiration was to be expressed with the body held straight, arms together, hands open, and feet close together. For desire, the face was inflamed and the tongue showed on the edge of the lips. Nicolas Testelin was responsible for an illustrated dictionary of facial expressions. Poets praised painters (Molière wrote a poem on Mignard's painting of the Val de Grace cupola) and were rewarded with portraits of themselves. Art was official and supported the regime. Louis XIV ordering a *divertissement* with text by Molière and stage sets by Mignard is not very different from Malraux commissioning artists for official buildings. "Was I supposed to hold a referendum to choose a painter for the Opera ceiling?" Malraux asked when he was taxed with being autocratic.

The official style was one that seventeenth- and eighteenth-century French elitist society could support and export. It reflected a consistent way of life. Like someone who does all his shopping in the same department store, a man could wear French breeches, sit in a French chair, and eat a French sauce from a French plate. Europe succumbed to French diversification. Everything that served to decorate or refine, from a palace to a snuffbox, came from French hands for a century and a half. This was a side effect of the artistic absolutism that was enforced at home. The Academy of Painting, for instance, had a monopoly on the teaching of art. Any provincial city that wanted an art teacher had to obtain one through the Académie. Copies from antiquity sketched by art students in Paris were sent to the provinces to be recopied by students there (in the same manner that the Frick mansion is the copy of a building on the Place de la Concorde which was itself a copy by Gabriel from antiquity). Lulli had the same monopoly in music and prevented musicians and singers from appearing at court unless they obtained his permission.

Dynastic art encouraged allegory, which is an attempt to surmount time and escape reality. Louis XIV did not appreciate Jacques Callot's accurately observed engravings like "The Miseries of War." What he liked was the portrait of himself as Caesar being guided by Mars, which raised him above events. Art, in striving for timelessness to please the king, became emblematic, although within its narrow conventions a few French artists were capable of major achievements, as Watteau showed. French classicism softened, thanks to a revolution from within. Watteau, the son of a Valenciennes roof mender, became a member of the Académie but painted his contemporaries rather than copy Greek statuary. The French had rejected the baroque in the seventeenth century but in the eighteenth they devised the rococo, which was the antithesis of the French virtues of proportion and measure. Contrary to popular opinion, Madame de Pompadour discouraged the bizarreries of rococo.

With the Enlightenment came the idea that art is instructive, which is simply another kind of regimentation, and Diderot said to Greuze: *"Fais-nous de la morale."* The Encyclopédie was didactic; it included illustrations of tools with notices on how to use them. Diderot said there were two essential qualities in art—morality and perspective—and two kinds of landscape, "historical and ordinary; the first should have a convex composition to attract attention to the scene in the center, the second concave for balance." In each successive school there were painters whose genius escaped regimentation: Watteau under the absolute monarchy, and Chardin under the Encyclopédistes. Chardin, like the makers of stained glass, was concerned with the mysterious play of light as it filters through windows into gloomy interiors. The sectarian salons of the Académie, held in the Louvre's main gallery, refused his work, as a century later they were to refuse the Impressionists.

More typical of the period was the literal accuracy of the sculptor Bouchardon, who spent hours on his back between a horse's legs studying the veins in its stomach. Academic art continued to flourish after the society which had created it had died. The Revolution was incapable of devising a style, and fell back as had the monarchy on the imitation of antiquity. Sculptors like Houdon had no trouble bridging the regimes, and made busts of Buffon and Robespierre with equal facility. David, the painter of the Revolution, was as much of an artistic tyrant as Le Brun. David had been a member of the Académie Royale, made the pilgrimage to Rome, and worked with Boucher and Fragonard. He proposed that the feudal Académie be abolished, but he replaced it with his own. He organized revolutionary celebrations with the same zeal that he might have directed *fêtes galantes*. Nothing had changed. The Revolution continued to admire Roman-style sculpted busts and equestrian portraits. The conservative revolutionary instinct, when the clergy's property was seized, was to preserve the art works in the churches for provincial museums rather than destroy them. The religion of the great man remained, and there was a Robespierre cult just as there had been adoration of kings. One nail drives out the other, as Voltaire liked to say, and one sectarianism replaced the other. David was brimming over with revolutionary zeal and voted the death of the king who had encouraged his work. He set up revolutionary salons for painters with a more broadly based jury made up of shoemakers, gardeners, army commissioners, Conventionnels, magistrates, and scientists. Good painters were those who served the Revolution, just as under the *ancien régime* they had been those who catered to the monarchy. What was new, however, was the Rousseau-inspired notion that the artist carried his talent in his heart and that his subjects were "everything that lived." The canons of official beauty were shattered in 1804 when Gros painted the plague victims of Jaffa. "Be proud that you are irresistibly ugly," Victor Hugo was later to say of Delacroix's "Medea." But Gros, after daring to paint horror, repudiated his work and committed suicide.

The romantic embrace of life's full experience was delayed by the rule of Napoleon, who required a Caesar-like heroic style; It was a time for columns, trophies, arches of triumph, and decorative symbols like helmets, pennants, and swords. Style was an amalgam of barracks life, the looted museums of Italy and Egypt, and the introduction of martial metals like copper for the decoration of furniture; Empire style was a hybrid pedantry that mixed the sphynx and the Coliseum. The favorite rhyme of Empire poets was "glory" and "victory," and the favorite task of sculptors was to cast in bronze the exploits of the *grande armée*. Romantic art, in hibernation during the Empire, reappeared in 1819 when Géricault took up the expressive themes of Gros by using as a subject the shipwreck of the French ship *Méduse*, which had been sent to take possession of Senegal and foundered off the West African coast; 149 survivors took refuge on a raft, but after twelve days on the high seas, only 15 survived. The rest had drowned or been eaten by the survivors.

It was only with the Romantic movement that Shakespeare was accepted by French audiences. Voltaire had translated him and brought him to France, but was offended by his improprieties and guardroom language. The mouse the sentinels of Elsinore could not hear stirring particularly shocked him, and his final estimate was that "Shakespeare has not written two decent lines." Ladies at court who took enemas in public, with their backsides to the fireplace, objected to Shakespeare's lack of decorum in lines like "Portia is Brutus' harlot, not his wife." Shakespeare could only be appreciated under regimes which did not try to appropriate art, like the Restoration and the Second Empire. The bard enjoyed a nineteenth-century French revival, and Alexander Dumas magnanimously said that "after God, it is Shakespeare who has created the most."

Under Shakespeare's spell, Delacroix defended color against line and started an absurd quarrel with Ingres that lasted thirty years. "Nature has no line," said Delacroix, echoing Rousseau and the revolutionary tradition of true feelings. "Line is the integrity of art," replied Ingres, the heir of the classical tradition, who had studied twenty years in Rome, lived on patronage like an *ancien régime* artist thanks to his flattering portraits of Russian archdukes and fashionable bourgeois, and embodied classical modesty by telling his pupils to lower their eyes before Rubens' nudes. Ingres' line won a small triumph when the 1836 salon rejected a misty Delacroix scene based on *Hamlet*. But it suffered a setback fifty years later when Cézanne damned "the maniacs of the line." Nature for him was too complex to be linear. When he died at the age of sixty-seven, still modestly calling himself "Paul Cézanne, Pissaro's student," he said that he had only begun to understand nature. The salons were filling the role of the eighteenth-century Académie. As Stendhal wrote: "In all these contests I see aging artists gravely preoccupied with judging whether young painters have imitated their own manner of painting more or less faithfully."

When painters started taking their easels outdoors as a result of the occupation of Algeria and interest in the Arab *pittoresque*, a French art teacher named Valenciennes drafted a series of rules for landscape painting, including the hours at which each kind of *paysage* should be executed. When artists revolted against the narrow standards of the salons, they lost their patrons, became alienated from society, and created *la bohême*. Courbet still had the patronage of dukes, even though he announced Impressionism by saying that painting was concrete and a painter did not need to preach. In 1863, painters who were rejected at the annual salon set up a "Salon of the Refused," which included the work of Manet, Pissaro, and Whistler. In the catalog, Manet wrote: "If our works have a character that makes them seem like a protest, that is the result of sincerity, since the artist is only trying to render his impression."

The misunderstanding over Impressionism was so complete that French museums, well stocked in Italian art and Greek and Egyptian archeology, thanks to the rapacity of French military leaders, have to buy French Impressionist works from private collectors or show works borrowed from the Leningrad and Berlin museums. In 1897 the government turned down the Caillebotte collection because it included too many Manets, Cézannes, and Renoirs. There could be no greater contrast than that between the court influence and wealth of a Poussin and the constant struggle and poverty of a Van Gogh and a Gauguin, whom circumstances forced to be each other's patrons. Even the Impressionists, however, had a French tendency toward nomenclature, the will to exhaust a subject and abolish its mystery; Monet painted the same lagoon forty-eight times. But the Impressionists were outcasts, while the mainstream of French art, the recourse to antiquity and allegory, was represented by Puvis de Chavannes, who had the enthusiastic patronage of the state. Highly praised in his day, this contemporary of Manet decorated the Sorbonne with a series of frescoes which the rebellious students of May, 1968, left undamaged. It was odd to see them holding their insurrectional meetings on a stage in front of Calliope reading verse, while other draped muses arrived floating horizontally on thin air as they crossed fragments of Doric temples.

The Salon of the Refused became the Independents, who first showed in booths in the Tuileries; soon there were 400 Independents, presided over by Odilon Redon, and including the great names of nineteenth-century French painting. Fear of the new is by definition temporary. Rodin's "Balzac" was refused by the writers' society which commissioned it, but was later installed in a Paris square. The rebellious artists of one generation shatter auction prices in the next. The Independents controlled the market as long as Paris remained the art center of the world—until 1940. Some famous painters, like Chagall and Picasso, still live in France, and a loose collection of talents known as "the Paris school" come as close to an official line as the culturally fragmented twentieth century will support. But the traditional artistic control of the French government was revived under the Fifth Republic with the appointment of André Malraux as Minister of Culture.

With music, there was the same pattern of government support and misunderstood geniuses. The first great French composer was Jean-Baptiste Lulli, who came to France from Florence at the age of twelve and obtained the court concession in 1653. After him, François Couperin was given the sinecure of organist for the King's chapel. The first major figure of French music to be ridiculed was Berlioz, who died a poor and forgotten man. Debussy said the "Berlioz is not at all a musician. He gives the illusion of music with methods borrowed from literature and painting. In any case, I don't see anything that is French in him." For Debussy, French musical genius lay in a combination of fantasy and sensitivity. He believed so strongly in a special French musical sensibility that he signed his letters, "Claude Debussy, French composer." His contemporaries did not recognize his nationalistic gifts, however, and the premiere of *Pelléas et Mélisande* in 1902 caused a scandal, with the audience shouting, "When will they finish tuning their instruments?" A critic wrote that "M. Debussy's music is vague, floating, colorless, and lifeless . . . it contains germs, not of life and progress, but of decadence and death." Debussy's countrymen treated him almost as badly as they had Berlioz.

As the Goncourt brothers said: "We admit our complete inferiority, our musical deafness, we who like only military music." Victor Hugo, Balzac, Dumas, and Lamartine all professed their hatred of music. The authentic French musical sensibility seems attuned to accordions and kettledrums, July 14 marches, *bal musette* waltzes, and the folk songs like *"En Passant par la Lorraine"* that are so closely entwined with the nation's history.

As a famous violinist told a friend: "I wonder why France is the only civilized country in the world where I can't go in the street with my violin case without being laughed at." There was an outcry when *Tannhäuser* was first performed in 1861; Parisians preferred the only original art form bequeathed by the Second Empire, the *opéra bouffe,* which corresponded to their taste for farce and their indifference to bad music. At the same time, the French are quick to point out that their country favors the development of musical genius, and wonder what obscure fate would have befallen the Belgian César Franck, the Spaniard Manuel de Falla, and the Russian Stravinsky if they had not migrated to Paris.

In today's France, the self-perpetuating hierarchies of the academies and the salons still thrive. Government control, with its insistence on non-creative, administrative functions, is a heavy handicap to art. It is no accident that what is most fertile in French art is precisely what revolts against the bureaucracy of the Ministry of Culture. The most famous French artist and the most famous French composer are respectively Jean Dubuffet and Pierre Boulez, both of whom conduct private wars against official culture. Dubuffet made himself the apostle of anticulture and for years refused to exhibit in museums. Conversely, the French Museum of Modern Art for years refused to buy one of his paintings and today it owns only three, whereas the New York Museum of Modern Art owns more than 200 of his works. Finally, in 1961, Dubuffet agreed to an important retrospective at the Musée des Arts Décoratifs, because it is a private museum not primarily concerned with painting. When news of the planned retrospective came out, Malraux put pressure on both Dubuffet and the museum. He promised Dubuffet a Legion of Honor if he would only donate some of his works to the Museum of Modern Art. The Musée des Arts Décoratifs was threatened with eviction from its government-owned building in the Louvre. The retrospective opened as planned, and who should attend the *vernissage* but René Cassou, the curator of the Museum of Modern Art. Dubuffet greeted him by saying, "Of course this is not your kind of painting." Cassou, conscious that he was representing the government, was stung, and said in Dubuffet's earshot that he was impertinent.

A Dutch curator at the *vernissage* pointed out to Cassou that

Dubuffet had found admirers in Holland before France. "My dear friend," replied Cassou, "Monsieur Dubuffet does not want to be admired, he wants to be said *merde* to, and I say it to him; and, dear Monsieur Dubuffet, I will continue to say it to you as long as it pleases you." But several days later, Cassou wrote Dubuffet an odd letter which helps illustrate the relations between the bureaucrats of culture and the artist. He began by saying that he was the sort of man who was "capable of going to prison for worthwhile things," an allusion to his Resistance record, but that since he had to make a living, he had accepted the post of curator of the Museum of Modern Art, implying that there were a good many other things he would rather do. After continuing in the same aggressive vein and as much as saying how little he thought of Dubuffet's work, he ended the letter by urging Dubuffet to contribute to a government-sponsored show of modern French painters in Sao Paulo. Dubuffet of course refused and would not even lend photographs of his work. Shortly afterward, the same Dutch curator and Dubuffet were at a restaurant when Cassou came in. Dubuffet pretended not to notice him and said to his Dutch friend, "Don't pay attention to that fellow, he's nothing." Cassou, furious, came up to them and said: "I don't give a damn what people say about me—*I emmerde* you." And Dubuffet replied: "I know you don't give a damn, everyone knows you don't give a damn, it's notorious that you don't give a damn, it's internationally known that you don't give a damn." Such are the unusual relations that can sometimes develop between the artist and the government officials whose job it is to support culture.

Boulez, the only French composer-conductor of international stature, finds his own country so culturally stifling that he lived in comfortable exile in the West German spa of Baden-Baden until he was appointed in 1969 to be conductor of the BBC symphony in London. Although he is recognized as the first French musical genius since Debussy, Boulez' atonal compositions were long barred from the French radio. Boulez, like Dubuffet, finds the French system of government guidance in the arts withering for creativity. Both men believe that what is creative is what contests the way things are being done, whereas the purpose of the government is to protect and continue the way things are being done. Boulez agreed in 1966 to conduct *Wozzeck* in its Paris Opéra premiere and was outraged by the bureaucratic pettiness of the nationalized musical administration. It took three signatures to get a stage curtain fixed.

The Fifth Republic feels, as did the monarchy, that culture is too important to be left to artists. It must be a government department. A glance at the 1969 budget for the ministry of Cultural Affairs shows both the scope of its action and the limitation of its means. It amounts to less than one-half of 1 percent of the total budget and includes among its items the construction of art and architectural schools, thousands of scholarships, subsidies for orchestras and theater groups, the upkeep of museums and the Gobelins factory, three new Houses of Culture in Rheims, Nevers, and Rennes, the creation of regional orchestras and a ballet troupe for the cultural center of Amiens, the construction of a French Lincoln Center on the fringe of Paris, and a training center for apprentice violin makers, the French stringed instrument industry being in danger of vanishing. Most of these activities in the United States are privately endowed, supported by the box office, or subsidized by state and local government. In France no legislation exists that covers the operation of cultural foundations on a tax-exempt basis, because of the long habit of government control.

It is contrary to the whole experience of French government to hope that foundations will be allowed to exist in France without being tied by some umbilical cord to the mother-state. Malraux promised to decentralize government-controlled culture by disbanding the creaky Beaux Arts school and withdrawing state support from the famed Prix de Rome for architecture, which guaranteed its winner a lifetime of government commissions. This was simply a device for perpetuating the musty academic standards of the judges and teachers, passing along bad style from one generation to the next. The very notion of the Prix de Rome is a measure of French cultural archaism. The pilgrimage to Rome was valid in the sixteenth and seventeenth centuries, to learn the lessons of the Renaissance. Long after its usefulness had ended, the Prix de Rome persisted, when, as Malraux says, it should have been replaced by a Prix de New York or a Prix de Brasilia.

Malraux's method for bringing culture to the French provinces is to build Houses of Culture, miniature Lincoln Centers. But what he is actually doing is perpetuating French elitist culture. France is a country in which a tiny intellectual elite fosters the illusion that the general population enjoys a high cultural level, whereas, in fact, as a 1966 survey showed, France is one of the three countries in both Western and Eastern Europe in which the fewest books are read. The Houses of Culture make no compromise with the workers and peasants they should be trying to reach; like Houses of Tolerance, they cater mainly to students and pensioners. They smell of *Kulturkampf* with their will to impose the classics on the forty million Frenchmen outside Paris who inhabit the cultural desert, with their troupes playing Marivaux and Molière, their lecturers discussing "the notion of honor in Corneille," and their directors sent from Paris to teach the provincials how to appreciate fine things. The programs are administered and the budgets are made up in Paris, in exactly the same manner as the French cultural program for its former colonies. The same thing goes for provincial television: Local programs take up an hour or two a day at most, and the rest of the programing comes from Paris. Thanks to the Houses of Culture, Malraux has said, "that odious French word 'provincial' will disappear from our vocabulary." But the Houses of Culture are instead dispensing provincial culture chosen by Paris civil servants, and maintain the provinces in a kind of cultural colonialism. Malraux will have been proven right when a city like Nantes or Bordeaux produces a French equivalent of the Mersey sound and the Beatles, or when a provincial repertory company stages a production that is good enough to come to Paris, like the American repertory groups in California and Ohio that regularly bring their productions to Broadway and off-Broadway. It is no accident that the most vigorous and fertile French art form today, the film, is also the least subject to government regimentation.

Even when the nationalized cultural program attracts talented artists, they soon grow impatient with the lack of available funds, the red tape, and the climate of mediocrity generated by run-of-the-mill civil servants who worry about paper clips and pastepots. The artist in the national sector must never forget that he is first a civil servant hired to propound and defend a government policy.

Jean-Louis Barrault was fired as director of the Odéon Theater in the fall of 1968, not because of artistic failure, for the Odéon could claim to be one of the most consistently interesting theaters in Paris, and his dedication to his art was not questioned, but because as the director of a government-subsidized troupe he did not express his loyalty to the regime vigorously enough when students occupied the theater in 1968. Presumably, he should have shown a heroic Mirabeau-like defiance and shouted "I will only be removed from this stage by force of bayonets." The result of the government's cultural control is that the best men leave or are evicted, like Boulez and Barrault, while those who shine by their subservience are elevated to important posts. When the state considers that taste and style fall within its jurisdiction and links culture to the preservation of national values, it does not create, it embalms.

8

⋙⋙⋙⋙⋙⋙⋙⋙⋙⋙⋙⋙⋙⋘⋘⋘⋘⋘⋘⋘⋘⋘⋘⋘⋘⋘⋘⋘

Simple Needs and
Great Pleasures

Food

ANTHROPOLOGISTS rely on the cooking and clothing of societies
in order to define them. The kitchen utensils of Pompeii
reveal hidden corners of the Roman consciousness. An anthropolo-
gist examining the buried remains of a French kitchen centuries
from now would conclude that here was a society which applied
as much method to eating as to thinking. The national reputation
for frivolity has always astonished me because the French are one
of the rare people who take the feeding and clothing of man with
utmost seriousness. *Gourmandise* and *coquetterie* are two constants of French civilization. Out of ten shops on any Paris street,
four are devoted to filling stomachs and three to covering naked-
ness. The logic of gastronomic art is clear. Man has five senses,
and just as painting corresponds to sight, music to hearing,
gastronomy is the art that corresponds to smell and taste. It is the
most selfless art because it is by definition perishable. What the
sculptor Tinguely accomplishes with his self-destroying machines
is achieved by every great chef every time one of his dishes is

brought to the table. Its function is to be consumed. It is the most practical art because it is the only one upon which physical survival depends. And it ranks with the other arts as a means of discovery of a nation's culture. The stomach absorbs culture as much as the mind or the eye. *Beurre blanc* is one of the summits of French subtlety.

In the pursuit of this art, battles have been lost, crimes have been committed, and men have taken their own lives. A history of France could be written from the admittedly limited viewpoint of the intestinal tract. It would mention that Louis XIII on his deathbed was threading morels to have them dried, that the marquis de Sade washed down truffled sausages with a bottle of excellent claret while imprisoned in the Bastille, and that Philippe Égalité ate a dozen oysters before his appointment with the Widow, as the guillotine was known. After the battle of Dresden, Napoleon ate a stew with garlic. He had stomach spasms, thought he had been poisoned, and ordered a retreat, which led to the debacle of 1813. In the last years of his exile at Saint Helena, his French chef retired for reasons of health and the emperor, reduced to eating English cooking, died soon afterward. To the *ancien régime* banker Grimod de la Reynière, the Revolution was an unpleasant interlude when austerity had to be simulated and chefs given their notice. "If it had lasted," he wrote, "France might have lost the recipe for fricasseed chicken." Danton was a gourmet and Robespierre was not; that was the tragedy of the Revolution. Danton was guillotined, and Robespierre wanted the French to eat a dish of lentils, with love of the *Patrie* as their only seasoning.

There is in the French genius for gastronomy something of the Cartesian dream to order the universe, to refine the physical until it is trembling on the brink of the ideal. This is the essential artistic act, to magically transform raw material. There is the same mysterious gap between the musical scale and a Debussy prelude as between an egg and a soufflé. Gastronomy is also part of the humanist vision: It defines man as a superior species because he is the only animal who cooks his food and because he is capable of eating when he is not hungry. "He who invents a new dish," said Brillat-Savarin, "will have rendered humanity a greater service than the scientist who discovers a planet." A great cuisine comes from the same impulse that designs gardens in geometric patterns and distills flowers to improve the body's fragrance.

The danger is overrefinement, yew trees tortured into fanciful shapes, elderly ladies drenched in Arpège, and recipes that call attention to their own cleverness, like this one: Introduce an olive into the beak of an ortolan; place the ortolan in a clean turkey eggshell with its head emerging from the shell like a baby chicken's; place the eggshell over embers; the fat on the ortolan melts until it covers him up to his beak and perfumes him; when the fat has evaporated you replace it with Alicante wine, and after five minutes you serve it like a soft-boiled egg; do not eat the ortolan, only the olive in its beak.

The urge to refine the physical world must be accompanied by rules as strict as those of grammar. The sequence of dishes and the accompanying wines follows an order as precise as the place of words in sentences. The rational enjoyment of food induces a particular seriousness and gravity. Think of the solemn silence with which a table of Frenchmen greet the arrival of a dish in a restaurant. They might as well be in church. The famous nine-teenth-century gourmet, the duc de Luynes, who had a half-moon cut out of the edge of his dining-room table to fit his prodigious stomach, thought of himself as an ascetic because he frequently did not eat even though he was hungry. Although excessively fond of oysters, he held himself to three dozen at a sitting, believing that beyond that it became impossible to fully appreciate their flavor. "The French are one of the most ascetic races in the world," Edith Wharton noted, "and that is perhaps the reason why the meaning they give to the word 'volupté' is free from the vulgarity of our 'voluptuousness.' The latter suggests to most people a cross-legged sultan in a fat seraglio; 'volupté' means the intangible charm that imagination extracts from things tangible. It means the 'Ode to the Nightingale' and the 'Ode to a Grecian Urn.'" It can also mean the marvel that occurs when one combines the simplest ingredients, for instance: a ripe Brie, fresh bread, and a good Pommard. French judges were merciful toward the man who shot his housekeeper because she was decanting a very rare bottle with a tin funnel. It seeme a clear-cut case of *crime passionnel*.

No matter how many drugstores open in Paris, and even if the Tour d'Argent becomes one of the 300 Wimpy hamburger shops that have recently opened in France, there will always be a great cuisine as long as men are willing to die for it. The chef at the Relais de Porquerolles who shot himself in 1967 after the disgrace of losing his stars in the Michelin guide was the heir of a tradition going back to the celebrated Vatel. As commander in chief of the prince de Condé's kitchen and house staff at the castle of Chantilly, Vatel was in charge of arrangements to receive Louis XIV and a suite of several hundred in 1671. Reputed for his poise under pressure, it was his task to equal the luxury of Versailles and see to it that the lawns were mowed, the linen fresh, the curtains dusted, the furniture oiled, and the candles in their holders. He ordered the food and supervised its cooking, tasting the sauces and carving the roasts. The king arrived on the evening of April 23 and hunted by moonlight. A light supper was served in the daffodil garden. There were more guests than expected, and the roast was lacking at several tables. The harassed Vatel felt his honor was lost. The prince de Condé, noticing his agitation, had him summoned to praise him for the supper. The next day was a Friday, and a large shipment of fish was expected in the morning, but only two baskets arrived. The distraught Vatel, his mind reeling with awful visions of the King and his court sitting down to empty plates, retired to his room and stabbed himself three times. Shortly after his body was discovered the rest of the fish arrived. "Everyone said that in his own way he had a sense of honor," a court chronicler said. "He was much praised for his courage but much blamed for his act." Madame de Sévigné wrote her daughter that Vatel's death had spoiled the king's party.

The first condition for a great cuisine is in the land, and France can fortunately provide a high quality of almost everything edible, like *pré salé* lamb, Charollais beef, Normandy butter, Adour salmon, Nantes ducks, Périgord truffles, and Loire asparagus. The ingredients are plentiful and varied. Very little has to be imported (a high percentage of the snails now come from Eastern Europe, and some of the goose livers come from Israel). Good food has been available ever since the Gauls became sedentary and pastoral, sat on bales of hay and ate pike with vinegar and cumin, raised their famed Cambrésis geese, and discovered that wild asparagus tasted good. But what was the process that led from roast bear to *bécasse Montmorency?*

It was a vast cooperative effort that involved the top and bottom layers of French society, advanced in periods of prosperity, depended on foreign influences and government regulations, and found its final form in the postrevolutionary bourgeois society of the nineteenth century, which achieved a synthesis between the peasant's *marmite* and the court's *pièces montées.* Gastronomy had to lift itself from the culinary banality of the Dark Ages, when all Europe smelled of herring, and the medieval crudeness of thick soups with groats and enormous piles of meats on skewers. The rural classes relied on their regional products and invented *pot-au-feu.* Daughters learned from their mothers how to *soigner la marmite* (keep the pot simmering). The *marmite perpétuelle,* that simmers all winter, its stock getting richer and more savory, is still a feature of family life in some rural French areas.

Then there was the ability to assimilate and improve on foreign contributions. The Crusaders brought back spices and recipes for aromatic Eastern dishes. François Premier returned from his Italian campaigns to teach his chefs the intricate recipes of the Renaissance courts. Catherine de Medici brought a Florentine recipe for sherbet, which French chefs made more substantial, just as, later, Marie Antoinette, arriving from Austria, brought the recipe for a curved bun which became known as the croissant. The deposed eighteenth-century Polish king Stanislaus Leszczynski's most enduring contributions to France were the delicate wrought-iron gates of Nancy and the *Baba au Rhum.* French cooking was enriched by the campaigns and marriages of its kings. With Henri IV, who promised a *poule au pot* for every Frenchman, gastronomy entered the houses of the humble. Good cooking was no longer reserved for feast days. Meals were the high points of court life, and huge appetites became evidence of high birth. When they cut Louis XIV open to embalm his heart, they found that his stomach was twice the size of an ordinary man's. Conversation at one meal was often about other meals. Madame de Sévigné mentions the court's passion for peas, which had been imported from Italy. "We are still on the chapter of peas; the impatience to eat them, the pleasure of having eaten them, and the joy of eating them again are the three points our princes have been dwelling on in the last few days."

Gastronomy was considered a serious enough pursuit for courtiers to invent dishes. Here is the marquis de Béchamel's original recipe for the sauce that bears his name: "Put three or four dabs of butter in a saucepan, with a little parsley, some scallions and chopped shallots, salt, crushed pepper, a little nutmeg, some flour to bind the sauce; wet it with good cream, and stir over the fire until it becomes consistent." Louis XV created the asparagus omelet for Madame du Barry, and Louis XVIII invented a recipe for chops: You put three chops in the oven one on top of the other, but you only eat the one in the middle which has absorbed the juice of the two others.

Béchamel used flour to bind his sauce, but soon some unheralded genius thought of egg yolks. The use of stock was another great leap forward. And in 1788, the maréchal de Contade's chef, Close, invented the *paté de foie gras en croûte,* which one of his colleagues from Bordeaux improved by adding the truffle. Add to inventiveness a lack of squeamishness about the physical world that could find gastronomic possibilities in a creature as unappetizing as a snail. Protestant countries, with their puritanism and kindness to animals, have shown themselves incapable of developing a great cuisine. Their attitude is typified by the English lady at a dinner where tongue was being served. She said, "How can you eat that when you know it came out of some animal's mouth?" "Why, madam," said her dinner partner, "have an egg instead." A law for the protection of animals was passed in France in 1850, but it is unenforceable, and in open markets in the Loire country they still put out the eyes of rabbits with a skewer on the theory that they taste better that way.

By the eighteenth century France was exporting its chefs. La Chapelle worked for Lord Chesterfield and the Prince of Orange. Escoffier in the nineteenth century spent most of his career in London. Gastronomy had its hall of fame, its inventors like Close, and its martyrs like Vatel. It also found its great codifier in Carême, who performed a task that was to cuisine what Napoleon's Code Civil was to law, by setting down the principles of the art in 12 volumes. This is the key to the continued supremacy of French cooking. Thanks to Carême, the principles were formulated, the philosophy of gastronomy was set forth, and the standards of a great chef were defined. Just as French professors can recite entire plays by Racine, the great chefs today know their Carême by heart. Barrier, whose restaurant in Tours won a long-overdue third star in 1967, reads a few pages of Carême every night before retiring. Carême was born in 1784 in a family so poor that his father tried to give him to an orphanage, but a baker took him in as apprentice. He taught himself to read and write, and studied engravings in the Bibliothèque Nationale to reproduce them on cakes. "Pastry," he said, "is the principal branch of architecture." His fame came as chef to Talleyrand, and he was convinced that his talent in the kitchen was partly responsible for the triumphs of French diplomacy.

"Cooking has this in common with painting and music," he wrote. "The first, by the richness of its colors, produces the great paintings that seduce the sight and the imagination; the musician, by the combination of his notes, produces harmony, and the sense of hearing receives the sweetest sensations that melody can produce; our culinary combinations are of the same nature; the gourmet's palate and sense of smell receive sensations similar to those of the connoisseurs of painting and music." Carême saw himself as a missionary spreading the gospel of succulence. He traveled to Russia and England, and turned down fortunes to return to France and become the chef of the Rothschilds, who indulged his whims and left him enough time to write. Today, the king of cooks and cook of kings is more of an illustrious ancestor than an example, for most of his recipes are all-day efforts. To whip up one of the simplest of his 400 soups, turtle soup à la Washington, you prepare a turtle bouillon, sauté a salmon cutlet with salt and Cayenne pepper, add eel quenelles made with anchovy butter, mix into the boiling soup some crayfish butter, and serve. The legislator of a great culinary tradition died in 1832; his last barely audible words concerned forcemeat for a fish.

A life dedicated to the preparation of food needs to be matched by equal dedication in its consumption. Gastronomy developed a distinct species, the gourmet, the man who gives priority in human affairs to the discriminate enjoyment of food. This can, exceptionally, be combined with other activities. The ten members of the Académie Goncourt have found that awarding an annual literary prize does not interfere with their lunch at Drouant's.

Indeed, the gourmet's tragedy is that often some other activity is necessary to allow him to fulfill his vocation. As the critic Sainte-Beuve said, "Rejoice, my little stomach, all that I earn is yours." What is more sincere than the gratification of the palate? And what is more sociable than a good meal shared? The gourmet deserves a place in the front rank of humanists. His vision of life, from the benevolent vantage point of the dining-room table, is a happy blend of the esthetic and the pragmatic.

The gourmet goes back at least as far as Rabelais, who listed sixty ways to cook an egg and created interesting dishes like pilgrim salad. Since then, there have always been dedicated men whose critical palates helped keep up the standards of the national cuisine. Sometimes they drifted into gastronomic chauvinism. The nineteenth-century gourmet, Nestor Roqueplan, affirmed that "a foreigner can never succeed in making a white sauce." But more often they were ready to appreciate good food wherever it was served. Brillat-Savarin, another codifier of the laws of gastronomy with his *Physiology of Taste,* traveled to America where he became immoderately fond of turkey. His aim was to be the La Rochefoucauld of the pantry and he hammered out hundreds of aphorisms on the order of "Tell me what you eat and I will tell you who you are," and "A dessert without cheese is a one-eyed beauty." Like Carême, he believed that everything important, from personal well-being to the destiny of nations, depended on what man was given to swallow and digest.

An even more imposing figure appeared prophetically at Paris restaurants with a white napkin knotted around his bulging neck, after World War I, when the French threw themselves into the roaring twenties and forgot austerity and suffering. Maurice Sailland was from Angers, one of the five or six gastronomic capitals of France. But in Paris he called himself Curnonsky, a name derived from the Latin *cur non* (why not). In 1927, five thousand gourmets elected him prince, and Curnonsky became a household word. He modestly said at the time that "to do justice to my duties, I would need twelve mouths and twenty-four anuses." Curnonsky looked like one of those great mounds of Charentes butter that stand in French *crèmeries,* but in fact he followed a Spartan diet of one meal a day. He was peremptory in his tastes, and when friends invited him to dinner, he ordered the menu, saying, for instance: "Make me a leg of lamb with red beans and if the skin is not crackling and if it is not the color of a baby's cheeks inside, I'm leaving." He could have made a fortune if he had been willing to compromise his standards. A margarine firm offered him an income for life if he would say that margarine replaces butter. "Nothing replaces butter," he replied. (Margarine was, in fact, invented in 1869 by the engineer Mège-Mouirès, but in 1880 the Academy of Sciences prohibited its use in government canteens on the grounds that it was indigestible.) The only favor he ever accepted was a lifetime pass on the Paris metro because he had slipped on the stairs and broken his pelvis in 1930.

To Curnonsky, art meant Watteau's "Embarquement pour Cythère," which shows some eighteenth-century courtiers picnicking, and Manet's "Déjeuner sur l'Herbe." Literature was Zola's *Le Ventre de Paris,* Anatole France's description of the restaurant in the rue Vavin whose only dish was *cassoulet,* and the wedding feast in *Madame Bovary.* His opinion of Flaubert was mixed, however. "Flaubert a gourmet," he said, "what a laugh! How could he have written in *L'Education Sentimentale,* 'the bottles of wine were heating on the stove.'" He appreciated Chateaubriand because of the incident at Dante's grave in Florence. The poet was meditating when he saw a laurel bush and picked a leaf which he put carefully into his pocket. "Your Excellency is right," said the guide. "Take a few more. There is nothing better with macaroni." As for women, the highest compliment was to name a dish after them, like Nellie Melba's peaches. Gastronomy has its political parties, Curnonsky said. The extreme right are the partisans of palazzo cooking, the elaborate, complicated *grande cuisine* which is still served in a few private French homes, with a menu of six or seven courses written in chalk on glass tablets in front of every guest; the traditional right is the "one only eats well at home" variety who grow their own vegetables, raise their own chickens, and keep a wood stove and an ancient *cordon bleu* in the kitchen; the center are the bourgeois defenders of regional specialties whose wives do the cooking; the left is the little bistro where the *patron* does the cooking, the *Entrecôte Bercy* with the *gros rouge* that makes indelible spots on the checkered tablecloth; and the extreme left is the omelet, the ham sandwich, and the snack bar.

Alas, the extreme right is vanishing. The days when Polish lords sent ten-page telegrams to the chef at the Cercle de l'Union, who was reputed the best in Paris, listing their favorite dishes, are over. Obesity was once a sign of prosperity and to be knowledgeable about food was the characteristic of a class that had arrived. After the German advance of 1914, my grandfather's contribution to the war effort was to limit the number of meat courses to three per meal. More recently, the duc de Brissac gave me an elaborate explanation of the chemical reasons why oysters should be eaten with Sauterne, which had something to do with glucose. But today the rich take sauna baths and it is the poor who are fat. Also, the connection between love and gastronomy is dying out. Both begin as forms of sublimation, the one of hunger, the other of desire, but the *cabinets particuliers* where both appetites could be satisfied exist today only in one Paris restaurant, La Pérouse. There one still hears the discreet cough of the old *sommelier* as he nears your private dining room, which is furnished with a couch. On the mirrors one can still see the entwined hearts, the dates, and the exclamation points cut with diamonds, as with a schoolboy's penknife on the trunk of a tree. But gone are the *bidets* of Larue, which were disguised as flower vases and placed in the center of the table.

The extreme left is spreading, and 18,000 Wimpy hamburgers are sold in Paris each week. Curnonsky killed himself in 1956 at the age of eighty-four, feeling perhaps that it was pointless to go on living if his palate and digestive tract no longer functioned. His parting words to a friend were: "Never eat the left leg of a partridge, for that is the leg it sits on, which makes the circulation sluggish." But his mantle has been passed to other less Gargantuan gourmets whose sacred mission it is to make a scene when *crêpes suzettes* are made with the peel of oranges instead of tangerines or when Beaujolais is used to prepare *Coq au Chambertin*.

In 1968, Robert Courtine, who writes a gastronomic column called "Pleasures of the Table" under the pseudonym La Reynière in the newspaper *Le Monde,* visited the Paris three-star restaurants, setting various traps. He ordered tomato salad and gave bad marks when the tomatoes were not peeled and seeded and when he was not asked what sort of oil he wanted in the dressing. Gastronomy is the result of a mental attitude which confers importance to the seeding of a tomato. As long as there are men like Robert Courtine who are genuinely afflicted by a bad meal, and chefs who learn Carême by heart and have nervous breakdowns over a sauce that curdles, the standards of French *cuisine* are safe.

Drink

The history of France as a nation begins not with a banquet, but with a glass of wine. The Frankish king Clovis won the support of the church when he converted to Catholicism and took communion from the bishop of Rheims with a glass of nonsparkling champagne. The grape is one of those common denominators that unites Frenchmen, like the language and an epic past. On the tympans of Romanesque churches in the wine-producing Midi, the devil is sometimes represented as a hedgehog because during the grape harvest he shook the vines and impaled the fallen grapes upon his spines. From the borders of Gobelins tapestries to the frieze of the ducal palace in Nancy, the vine is the favorite symbol of French decorative art. Kings believed it cured their indigestion and generals believed that it won wars. Marshal Joffre, a cooper's son, said one of his generals was general *Pinard* (a slang word for wine) and the ration for the troops was raised from half a liter to a liter per day after the reversals of 1915. The ability to develop a wide range of wines suited to every kind of food is often used as a metaphor for French civilization and its qualities of patience, good taste, and judgment.

The origins of wine are obscure. The genius who first realized that the fermented juice of the grape could be modified and aged and treated in a way that made it far superior to the juice of other fruit is unknown. Anthropologists are not sure whether Neolithic man drank wine. Grape seeds have been found in Dordogne caves, gathered in bunches that could indicate an early form of pressing. We know that the Egyptian pharaohs drank wine, and one patient French oenophile has traced 521 references to wine in the Bible.

Vineyards are believed to have been first planted on French soil around 600 B.C., after the Greek founders of Marseilles had started importing their own wine. By the time of the Roman occupation of Gaul the wine of the Rhone region had attained sufficient

notoriety to cause Emperor Domitian to order half the vines uprooted as a protectionist measure in favor of Roman wines. Pliny
the Elder said the Gaul wine merchants were sharp traders and
complained that a forty-liter amphora cost more than 1,000 sester-
ces, a price he could only explain by the merchants' unreasonable
pride in their own product.

But why did the matchless vintages develop in France rather
than in other wine-producing countries? Let us say that it is one
part the mystery of the soil, so that the same vine plants yield wines
as varied in their excellence as their regions of origin, one part the
early support of church and state, and one part the French pro-
pensity for training and refining the gifts of nature. In the Middle
Ages many of the best vineyards belonged to the church. The use of
wine spread as a pleasant adjunct of high observance and communion under two species. Saints drank it (Joan of Arc liked wine
in her soup) and had wines named after them (Saint-Emilion,
Saint-Estephe). Every village was girdled with vineyards tended
with monastic patience. Every French parish raised vines for its
local needs regardless of climate and soil. Two regions prospered
early: Bordeaux because it was close to a harbor, and Burgundy
because it was near Paris where the reputation of its velvety virtues
had spread. The monks kept what they needed for the sacraments
and sold the rest. "I say mass with a great Meursault," said Cardinal de Bernis, "because I want to avoid making faces when I take
communion."

French kings granted tax advantages to winegrowers (although
overproduction led to acreage control) and Philippe le Hardi and
François Premier owned vineyards themselves. The monarchy's
road construction program in the seventeenth and eighteenth centuries made it possible for regions with a vocation for wine to
export their product. Once wine became competitive outside its
home region, the vine disappeared from the northern plains and
the western hillsides, where lack of sunshine and late frosts resulted in more bad than good years. Many vineyards remained
the property of the church until the Revolution, when they were
confiscated and fell into the hands of farmers less versed in the
imperious needs of the grape. This, and the drop in European
trade that resulted from the Napoleonic wars, caused a shrinkage

of acreage and contributed to the development of specialized wine regions (as for the emperor's taste in wines, he preferred Montrachet cut with ice water).

Bordeaux had a late start on the domestic market because for centuries it was sold primarily to England. The marriage of Eleanor of Aquitaine and Henry Plantagenet led to the Hundred Years War and the overnight prosperity of the Bordeaux wine merchants, who became purveyors to the English court. Demand grew to the point that a 300-ship fleet was built to carry Bordeaux to England. Bordeaux vineyards were less fragmented than those of Burgundy and from the Middle Ages the *châteaux* belonged to the high bourgeoisie, men like Charles de Secondat, baron de la Brède et de Montesquieu, and Michel Eyquem de Montaigne, both of whom reached wider fame for their writing than for their wines. The question of which is the more lethal, writing or imbibing, was settled by Alexandre Dumas' cook, who said: "He was wrong to fiddle with books, that is what finished him." Bordeaux was always more cautious and protectionist, and kept its shipping privilege until 1776. In 1885, the Bordeaux winegrowers lobbied successfully for a classification which ranked their wines by quality, another example of the French predilection for nomenclature.

But it is the Côte d'Or, lovingly called the department of nectar because it contains the great Burgundies, that can boast the most expensive real estate in France. The saying goes that "an acre is plenty to arrange a marriage," and no girl could want a better dowry than a field or two of Pommard or Musigny. Anyone searching for changeless France should visit the vineyard of the greatest Burgundy of all, Romanée-Conti, which is grown on a surface not quite as large as the Place de la Concorde. Originally, not even millionaires could buy it because the prince de Conti and his friends consumed the entire production. Madame de Pompadour used her influence at court to get the vineyard away from the prince, but failed. The Revolution accomplished what she could not, and some Romanée-Conti can now be found on the market. The vineyards look as though they had been woven onto the landscape by the master weavers of Gobelins, and like a tapestry, they can no longer be improved, changed, or extended. That tiny strip of land produces something matchless and exquisite. A few feet away, the quality changes even though the methods of winemaking are identical. Chemical analysis of the soil cannot explain what remains one of the most satisfying and palatable of mysteries.

Perhaps the primacy of Burgundy is simply a matter of seniority. The great wines of Beaune were known from the third century. It was noted then that instead of grafting new plants onto the old, the winegrowers planted new vines every fifteen years. The soil became laden with the remains of old vines, a form of noble refuse which, after having produced fruit, contributed to the nourishment of the new plants. The prestigious past of Burgundy is not hyperbole. Charlemagne really kept a few acres of Corton for himself and his court. French army units really salute when marching past Clos Vougeot.

But wine growing did not depend only on mysterious processes that took centuries to develop. Wine, like gastronomy, has its great inventors. Dom Pérignon, who was part untutored chemist and part clairvoyant, was tending the cellars in the abbey of Hautvilliers near Epernay around 1688 when he decided to encourage rather than prevent the peculiar secondary fermentation of the local wine. Fermentation in the bottle released carbonic gas under pressure and caused the wine to sparkle. He adopted cork over oiled tow to seal the bottles and experimented with blends which were an improvement over the vintages that made them up. Champagne thereafter fought Burgundy for supremacy, and lost a battle at Versailles when Louis XIV's physician Fagon found that it damaged the nervous system and turned the blood to vinegar. But with champagne production these days running to 80 million bottles a year, not everyone seems to feel these side effects.

The bottle of wine is an emblem of French civilization. Because wine lives, ages, and changes in the bottle, it lends itself to personalization. It is attributed a soul, a temperament, qualities of wit and wisdom which are the fluid concentrate of a superior way of life. It is a way of life that can be sampled by uncorking a bottle. Something so prestigious must be beneficial, and the conviction is held that wine, like an old and loyal friend, can do no harm. It is the antidote for alcoholism, the ray of sunshine in the trenches, the glass of morning cheer, the national and patriotic beverage, nourishing, antiseptic, and tonic.

More than that, the ability to appreciate wine is seen as a sign of general perspicacity, while, as Baudelaire said, someone who drinks only water must have a secret to conceal from his fellow-man. Against the French tendency toward suspicion, wine provides a bond of fellowship, and against tightfistedness, something which it is natural to share. The measure of Voltaire's stinginess is that he gave his guests *vin ordinaire* and kept Corton for himself. On one hand the qualities of the wine—delicacy, finesse, and continuous excellence—are transferred to the people who made it. On the other, the qualities of the country are attributed to the wine, so that each bottle is said to be the expression of a thousand years of history and a fertile and harmonious landscape. Frenchmen have always found in wine qualities which defy analysis of its ingredients—Pasteur found philosophy, Montaigne wit, Baudelaire inspiration that turned a mole into an eagle, and Montesquieu a way to spur love. The role of wine has not changed since the Gothic cathedrals were built; it is still sacramental.

What has changed is its quality. Today they are making wine without grapes, thanks to a mixture of sugar, tartaric acid, water, and artificial coloring. If wine sums up a civilization, then the liquid that is sold by the giant of French wine retailers, Nicolas, with sincere-looking labels that boast of native tang, is the expression of a sour and meretricious people. In the long run, the future of all wine is not in the hands of the growers or retailers, but of the architects when they stop building cellars. But the drop in the quality of French wine goes back to the Phylloxera epidemic of 1875 and the start of government intervention in its production and sale.

The Phylloxera is a small green louse that attacks the roots of the vine. It traveled to France in 1875 with American grapes that were being used in grafting experiments, and destroyed nearly the entire French vineyard. After home remedies like urinating on the vines and burying toads near the roots proved ineffective, the cure was found in grafting French grapes onto American vines which had built up an immunity to the lice. This took time because the government's first measure was to prohibit the entry of foreign vines. Thereafter, while the French vineyard was being replanted almost from scratch, government policy oscillated between support and penalization of overproduction. Replanting was at first encouraged with tax exemptions, but led to overproduction of low-quality wines. Fear of Phylloxera generalized the use of chemical sprays and fertilizers. The use of sugar to strengthen the alcoholic content of wine was legalized.

The most serious consequences of the Phylloxera epidemic were not the destruction of the French vineyards, but the government tolerance of fraud and poor quality. Lowering the sugar tax and allowing the winegrowers to add small amounts of sugar became a mandate to produce fraudulent second pressings that were more sugar than grape. In 1906 another misguided government decision restored the traditional privilege of home distillers to produce and sell their own spirits. These three million legal moonshiners formed one of the most powerful lobbies in France. In years of overproduction, the government remedy was to buy from the wine-growers the alcohol distilled from the wine they could not sell. It was bought for industrial uses, at ten times the cost of kerosine. The government was thus directly subsidizing the overproduction of bad wine. Timid attempts to limit the planting of vineyards and to block production were defeated by the wealthy distillery industry and the wine-growing lobby. Governments nostalgic for the small farm with a few acres of vines as its principal cash crop kept up the subsidies. It was no mean achievement for the de Gaulle government in 1960 to push a law through the National Assembly which repealed the privileges of the home distillers.

There has been no serious threat of overproduction since the end of the Algerian war, when imports of cheap Algerian wines dropped by half. But the French do not need Algeria when they can produce their own bad wines, and it is hard to see how the patient and laborious traditions of the great vineyards can be reconciled with rising labor costs (the thousands of workmen who turn the upside-down champagne bottles each day by hand to assist the flow of the deposit into the neck), growing foreign demand for reasonably priced wine, and the modern businessman's insistence on a quick turnover. The production of good wine is becoming anachronistic. When the small farms are no longer subsidized, maybe they will convert their vineyards to pasture and France will become an exporter of milk. Perhaps ways will be found to mechanize the making of wine, from picking the grapes to handling the bottles. Experiments are already being made with canned wine, wine concentrates, and bottletops instead of corks.

The de Gaulle government also tried to do something about

alcoholism, which the French too often tend to regard as an inoffensive side effect of the gregarious enjoyment of life. Along with the suppression of their franchise, the home distillers are now able to obtain low-interest loans to adjust their produce to the fruit-juice market. Licenses to open new cafés have become hard to come by in a country which already has one café for 32 adults. Publicity for alcoholic beverages is banned from sports stadiums and housing projects. In the 1960 debate on home distillers, the Communists found themselves voting with the liquor lobby against the measure. The Communists argued that the suppression of the franchise for the little fellow would favor the big distillers. The liquor lobby argued that to reduce alcoholism by suppressing alcohol made as much sense as suppressing automobiles to reduce traffic accidents. In a more lyric vein, the marquis de Montesquieu, who produces a decent Armagnac, recalled that "vine leaves decorate the capitals of our cathedrals . . . wine is one of the great symbols of the Christian religion." After this first victory over the liquor lobby, the government went much further in 1966 when it built a factory in Lillebonne to make synthetic alcohol, a way of announcing that it would no longer buy the beet, grape, and apple alcohol of farmers at inflated prices.

But although the tyranny of the *bouilleurs de cru* (home distillers) seems over, France is still remarkably indulgent toward alcoholics, even though 120 Frenchmen a day die from strong drink, and alcoholism ranks as the third cause of death, after heart disease and cancer. France still leads the world in the amount of pure alcohol consumed per adult per year: 28 liters as compared with 24 liters for Italy, 9 for the United States, and 8 for Great Britain. That record is maintained largely thanks to a minority of two million persons who drink an average of half a gallon of wine per day. The working man who starts his day with a rum in his coffee and keeps a pleasant edge on, thanks to the unobtrusive but steady consumption of *petits blancs,* is still part of the French scene, as is the farmer who believes that three or four liters of wine a day cannot hurt him as long as he sweats it off in the fields, and the jolly pensioner who ruins his health because he raises his glass too often to the health of others.

Provincial newspapers still describe domestic tragedies under the rubric, "dramas of alcoholism." In January, 1968, two passengers were killed in a train accident and the inquest found that the driver had been going too fast "under the empire of alcohol" (railway workers, for some reason, enjoy one of the highest rates of alcoholism among professional groups). One out of ten Frenchmen is employed in some manner with filling the glasses of others, and signs like the following are common: "Fight alcoholism by drinking more wine." A law to punish drunken driving was not passed until 1965, after a debate in the National Assembly during which the deputies argued about the definition, not of drunkenness but of driving. At what point, they wondered, can a man be said to be driving? When he is sitting in his car, when he turns on the ignition, when he steps on the accelerator, or when he changes into first gear? The French still view the drunkometer test as an insult to their dignity and an intolerable invasion of privacy. In 1966 the municipal council of the Indre turned down a request for funds to arm the gendarmes with drunkometers. The problem is fiscal as well as social, for the taxpayer pays for the government's program of medical subsidies and is apt to grumble when he learns that in Paris 26 percent of hospital admissions are due to alcoholism and that the average cost of treatment for cirrhosis of the liver is three thousand dollars. Treatment of alcoholics accounts for one-third the total operating cost of nationalized French hospitals. Once the French taxpayer realizes he is supporting the drunkenness of others the benevolent attitude toward tippling may change.

Clothing

What is worth remembering, however, is not that the French are too fond of the bottle, for that is within the reach of any man, but that in catering to the elementary needs of the species they have specialized in the inimitable. This is as true of Schiaparelli as it is of the widow Clicquot—both ladies sell bottled joy. French leadership in food, wine, perfume, and women's custom clothing helps propagate the notion that the French inhale and exhale good taste as effortlessly as they breathe, whereas closer examination of these areas of excellence shows sustained effort and government support. In the seventeenth century, the great mercantilist minister, Colbert, realized the advantages to be derived from high fashion, which he said must be to France what gold mines are to Peru. The guild of couturiers was established in 1675. It was then that the first fortunes were made from details like the position of hems and pockets, or a clever way of folding silk. The tyranny of fashion goes back further still, for in the twelfth century women at the Capetian court wore sleeves so narrow they had to be sewn on each time and were appropriately called *manches à l'imbécile.*

High fashion was propagated by the court. Clothes were and remain the most obvious way to recognize the privileged, and a courtier boasted that there was more of a difference between his appearance and a peasant's than between that of a peasant and a naked savage. The seasonal alternation between narrow and wide sleeves, high and low necklines, draped and fitted tunics, became a feminine pastime. One generation decreed that gorgets should be worn, and the next generation discarded them as ridiculous. Under Louis XII there was a craze for Genoa velvet, and under Henri II everyone wore a ruff in imitation of the king, who was trying to conceal a scar on his neck. The aptitude of homosexuals for high fashion was already evident during the reign of Henri III. The effeminate king was said to have worn six thousand yards of lace at the 1577 Estates General at Blois. He enjoyed ironing his ruffs himself, until they were "so stiff they crackled like paper." Louis XIV set new laws for fashion. The ordinance of 1710 regulated the lengths of women's trains (eleven ells for queens). Madame de Maintenon, like Madame de Gaulle, insisted that ministers' wives keep their necklines high.

With the Revolution, the center of fashion moved from Versailles to Paris, and there was a brief period of patriotic negligence, short jackets, knickers, and Phrygian bonnets. Balzac's perfumer, César Birotteau, hated the Revolution because it had abolished powder. Fashion betrayed political opinions. Loyal monarchists wore coats with eighteen buttons (for Louis XVIII, the king-to-be) and cockades that were Tricolor on one side and white (monarchist) on the other. The austerity of the Terror was followed by the insouciance of the Directoire. Madame Hamelin walked down the Champs-Élysées naked under a muslin tunic, while the ladies known as the *merveilleuses* wore the first topless dresses.

Renewed concern with clothing led to the publication of the first fashion magazine, the *Journal des Dames et des Modes,* in 1796. Ingenious devices for advertising French fashion abroad were

Little Pandora and Big Pandora, the first fashion models. They were dolls sent to foreign capitals, with changes of costume in the latest style. Little Pandora had an informal wardrobe while Big Pandora wore only evening gowns. Even during the Napoleonic blockade, the Pandora dolls continued to reach England, Italy, and Vienna to spread the gospel of French styles to thousands of fashion-starved women.

France had a court which required sumptuous fashions for all but the last thirty years of the nineteenth century. Napoleon, like Louis XIV, realized that fashion was a way to occupy his entourage. He encouraged ostentation and scolded the wives of his generals when they wore the same dress twice. Under the Second Empire, the Empress Eugénie managed to combine fashion and patriotism by wearing materials made by the stagnating Lyons textile industry. She launched the first modern couturier, Charles Frederick Worth. Unlike the humble seamstresses who arrived through the servants' entrance, Worth was an expensive tyrant and a monster of snobbishness. To put oneself in his hands, said a fashionable lady, was to sell one's soul. It was probably Worth whom the historian Taine had in mind when he wrote this classic description of the couturier: "They say, 'I don't care if he's rude as long as he dresses me. After all, the smartest women go to him.' He says: 'I am a great artist, I compose, I have the palette of a Delacroix. A dress is the equal of a painting.' If one becomes irritated by his peremptory manner: 'Monsieur, in every artist there is a Napoleon. When Ingres painted the Duchess of A . . . he wrote her in the morning, Madam, I must see you this evening at the theater in a white dress, with a rose in your hair. The duchess cancelled her invitations, put on the dress, sent for the rose, and went to the theater. Art is God; the bourgeois are made to take our orders.' "

With the Republic, the court disappeared, but fashion remained geared to the cultivation of a caste spirit, although now it also reflected material prosperity in the growing number of women who could afford haute couture. Instead of one couturier supported by a queen or an empress, there were dozens, each of whom had an obedient following of rich clients. Fashion became an industry based on the principle that as soon as a collection is shown, it is tinged with obsolescence. The top couturiers are those with enough authority to make women obey slight and arbitrary changes from one season to the next. Only Coco Chanel remains relatively faithful to a basic line, and insists, "I am the only one who knows how to make a skirt."

Fashion was not only, as Colbert had predicted, a gold mine for France, it also served as an antidote for national misfortunes. Just as the *merveilleuses* helped Parisians forget the Terror, couturiers continued to present their collections in the gloomy years of German occupation. Balmain's fame was based on his "Occupation evening dress" and his "subway gown." When they ran out of cloth, the couturiers made hats out of newspapers, with trailing ribbons that said, "Follow me, young man." The couturiers helped French women prove that no matter how black things looked, they would never be dowdy. After the war, one of the first to show the world that France was still France was the cousin of a minister and son of a wealthy businessman, Christian Dior, who managed to convince the women of the world that lowering a hemline was a New Look. Dior's father was dismayed by his son's early penchant for women's clothes and told him: "At your age, I was more interested in undressing women." Dior showed that if it is less fun, it is more profitable to dress them.

Marketing methods are changing, but the principle of imposing a *griffe* (trademark) that is synonymous with the desires of women remains the same. It is one of the higher forms of Pavlovian reaction. French philosophers have written theories of fashion, saying for instance that "fashion is what is real in abstraction"; fashion becomes the most elegant expression of the logical French mind. Courrèges and Cardin have understood that today's couturier is no longer the creator of a perishable ball gown some duchess will wear once, but the engineer who works from blueprints for the boutiques of a thousand department stores. In gastronomy, wine, and clothing, France's vocation still lies in the production of the inimitable, but the problem in all three fields is how to adopt modern marketing techniques without a loss of quality.

9

A Woman of Iron
and Velvet

The Courtly Tradition

THE originality of woman's role in French society is that she was able for so long to exercise power while being deprived of legal rights. It is only since 1965 that a married French woman can open a bank account without the permission of her husband, and only since 1946, long after her European sisters, that she can vote. Since she could not cash a check or cast a ballot, she did the next best thing, which was to govern the hearts of the banker and the man in office.

It is to the French woman's struggle for social influence that the Western world owes romantic love. The idea of love as an art that can be learned and perfected is not, as the feudal historian Charles Seignobos maintained, an invention of the twelfth century; Ovid's *Ars Amatoria* should be sufficient proof of that. But the specific form of romantic love adopted as a value by the Christian world grew out of the French tradition of courtly love which followed the misogyny of the Middle Ages. Medieval French husbands enjoyed the legal right to beat their wives and banish them to convents for adultery. Chastisement for erring wives ranged from whipping them, to making them chase a chicken naked in the street, and to locking them in a wooden cage on a pulley system called the *accabussade* which was dunked in the river like a cray-fish trap. Men were crude and soldierly and were often away from home on campaigns. Women learned to match their ribaldry. An idea of medieval gallantry is conveyed by the following exchange between a lady and a clean-shaven knight arriving at a tourney:

"Tell us about your way with women—how many have you ferti-lized in these parts?"

"None yet, I think."

"That doesn't surprise me, for by the look of your down, your sword cannot be very keen."

"And what of your own?"

"I have none."

"That doesn't surprise me, for grass can't grow on a beaten track."

The church encouraged the lowly status of women in the writ-ings of theologians who presented her as an agent of the devil. At the apocryphal Council of Macon, the fathers nearly defeated a motion that woman possessed a soul the equal of man's. But, para-doxically, it was the church, by instituting the Truce of God, which spurred the process of refinement that led to the ideal of courtly love. Men kept from the field of battle on religious holi-days stayed home. The lords restricted to their castles began to share the peaceful pursuits of women. In the twelfth century ma-terial prosperity made castle life more hospitable to culture, which arrived in the form of the troubadours, who quite sensibly sang the praises of the ladies who protected and paid them. In further efforts to regulate warfare, the church instituted the ceremony of the dubbing of knights, which gave women an important role, for the knight swore to defend them. This oath amounted to a trans-ference of goals from God and King to fragile womanhood.

As chivalry developed its rites, the protection of women became its rationale. Chivalric society shifted the image of woman from object of scorn to subject of highest consideration. The idea arose that man should compliment, divert, and please women—in short, court them. The combined influence of the troubadours and a growing Marian cult (the feast of the Immaculate Conception was inaugurated in Lyons in 1140) contributed to the establishment of romantic love based on a devotional attitude toward women. The troubadours are the direct ancestors of the Beatles and other pop singers who embroider on the theme, "All You Need Is Love." They postulated the obligation to love and the sufficiency of love, the joys of love, the happiness in the presence of the beloved, the pain in the absence of the beloved, all the familiar permutations that still pass for lyrics in pop songs. Departing from the ribald and masculine tradition of *amour Gaulois,* were the songs and poems of the troubadours who aspired to chasteness, like the Tertiaries of Saint Francis who slept beside naked ladies to test their virtue. Physical love was mentioned only as a vague and distant promise. Original to the courtly tradition was the idea that love can lead to sentimental exaltation separate from physical satisfaction. This remains the ambiguous attitude of the Western heart, which is not content with mere bedding down.

The social importance of romantic love was that it made woman the arbiter of courtly qualities. Now it was the man who languished and was tested and had to prove himself to deserve the favors of his lady. The situation was an exact reversal of the time when Charlemagne's daughter Bertha carried her lover Angilbert on her back across the snowcovered courtyard of the Rhine castle of Lorsch so that no masculine footsteps leading to her chambers would be discovered. Women now became the dispensers as well as the patronesses of courtly love, an instrument to control masculine behavior. The troubadours spread the vocabulary and regulations of amorous service. In the feudal courts of the Midi, like Narbonne and Toulouse, women formed courts of love to legislate the relations between the sexes. Assemblies of aristocratic married women, sometimes sixty strong, gathered to study cases involving sentimental litigation and to pass judgments. It was the first instance of advice to the lovelorn. It also illustrates the invincibly juridical nature of the French mind. Finally, it was an attempt to draw up a doctrine of love. Twenty-one of these cases and judgments are contained in the fourteenth-century work of André the Chaplain, *The Art of Love.* In one unusual case, a lady married, but her former lover insisted on his rights, which the lady refused. The court of love ruled that "the marriage bond does not exclude the rights of the first love, unless the lady has decided to abstain completely from matters of love." In a period of arranged marriages, the courts of love decreed that real love cannot exist between married couples because it is not voluntary.

The gap between romantic love and marriage remains one of the conundrums of the Western tradition even in a time when most marriages are voluntary. The gracious judges of the courts of love were encouraging adultery, since love had to be found outside marriage. Courtly love was furtive and discreet, and the all-woman tribunals were as harsh with boastful lovers as with inconstant ones. Adultery as a necessary element of French married love, the *ménage à trois* and the familiar cuckold, all this was decreed by the courts of love and finds modern resonances in the words of the twentieth-century moralist who wrote that it is not when a woman spends an hour with her lover that she commits adultery, but when she returns to her marriage bed.

Courtly love veiled the lingering coarseness of an age that still smelled more of the kennel than the drawing room. While titled ladies spent their days conducting elaborate parlor games, real courts continued to sentence adulterous women to convents. In aristocratic society, lovers brought their complaints for judgment before female courts, but in civil law a woman was still regarded as her husband's property. Nonetheless, instead of perishing as a fad, courtly love endured as the condition of admission to an elect society, and its code of good manners and homage to the gentle sex endured also. The quasi-religious exaltation of woman may well have been an inversion of genuine mysticism, but at least it provided an alternative to the rigid feudal scheme which blamed her as the author of man's fall. The tradition survived, even though it had to compete in its successive forms with a rival tradition of antifeminist ribaldry.

The French woman is the product of periodic oscillations between these traditions, between the Lady with the Unicorn and Villon's *dames galantes*, Chrétien de Troyes' portrayal of woman as divine and Rabelais' estimate: "When I say woman, I mean a sex so fragile, so variable, so inconstant and imperfect that nature seems to have wandered from the good sense with which it created all other things."

The Political Mistresses

Often, *amour courtois* and *amour Gaulois* coexisted. The Hundred Years War (1337–1453) was a period of decline for the courtly tradition, since men reverted to their warrior role. But at the same time, woman's social position improved when Agnes Sorel became the first royal mistress to be recognized by a king. Charles VII made her the equal of princesses, and the lovely Agnes with the improbably high breasts (she posed for Fouquet's "La Vierge de Melun" in the Antwerp Museum) founded a female line of powerful political advisers which did not die out with the monarchy but continued to flourish under Empire and Republic and flourishes still. The name of the Roman water goddess Egeria who counseled King Numa is a common noun in French. "From time to time," Catherine de Medici remarked, "in every age, whores have directed the affairs of kings."

French governments have traditionally indulged, instead of shadow cabinets, pillow cabinets of ladies with an aptitude for mixing politics and sex. Their influence in both areas has sometimes been exaggerated; Madame de Pompadour was sexually cold and the claim that she governed France does not hold up. But certainly her weight was felt in many of Louis XV's decisions. In 1793, at the same time Madame du Barry was being guillotined as the last mistress of the *ancien régime*, Madame Roland was becoming famous as the Egeria of the Girondins, although it is unlikely that she was able to distribute her favors to all 180 members of the faction. She, too, died on the guillotine and is credited with the last words, "O Liberty, what crimes are committed in your name!" Madame Tallien was more fortunate. She was arrested and would have been guillotined if her husband, the secretary of the Commune of Paris, had not overthrown Robespierre. Credited with saving thousands of potential victims of the Terror, she was dubbed "Our Lady of Thermidor" and became the Egeria of the Directoire.

Louis XVIII had Madame du Cayla, although that was supposedly Platonic, and the fiery Republican Gambetta had Léonie Léon, who was credited with changing his mind from seeking revenge on Germany after the 1870 war to seeking a Franco-German alliance. The Third Republic became known as the Republic of Favorites. Actually, the Republic was saved by a woman when the popular general Boulanger chose to join his mistress Madame de Bonnemain in Belgium rather than make a bid for power. Her sudden departure was the result of police pressures. She died soon afterward of consumption, like Camille, and he killed himself on her Ixelles grave in 1891. "He was nothing more than a lady's man," said Clemenceau, who divorced his American wife, Mary Plummer, and never let his love life interfere with politics. But thanks to women, other politicians were helped in and out of power, and even died in office. In the days when being president of France was largely a tape-cutting, ship-launching, chrysanthemum-inaugurating office, Félix Faure confided to his adviser Louis le Gall: "How weary and bored I am with all this, always the same thing, the same faces, the same conversation. And when I think that I have three years to go . . ." The year was 1899, and the fifty-eight-year-old president had served four years of his seven-year term. To relieve the tedium of the job, Faure was a faithful devotee of the *cinq à sept* (the traditional late-afternoon romantic interlude). One of his regular visitors was the wife of his official portraitist, Adolphe Steinheil. According to Maurice Paléologue, head of the *affaires réservées* department at the Quai d'Orsay, Meg Steinheil "was expert at shaking men's loins."

On the morning of February 16, Faure told Le Gall that he felt "a little weak in the knees." He had a busy day, a cabinet meeting at ten, and afternoon appointments with Cardinal Richard, the archbishop of Paris, and the prince of Monaco. Around 5:15, the president's secretary, Blondel, saw the prince of Monaco out and ushered in Mrs. Steinheil through a side door. Half an hour later, Blondel heard strange sounds coming from the presidential office. He peeked in and saw the naked president collapsed on a couch, his hands clutching Meg Steinheil's curly head to his groin. It took some time to cut her hair away from the president's stiffening fingers. She left the Élysée Palace as his wife and daughter were summoned with a doctor and a priest. "You should not alarm us like this, my dear," said his wife, but the doctor told her Faure had suffered a cerebral hemorrhage. Meanwhile, Le Gall had got Premier Charles Dupuy out of bed to tell him the news. "God damn it," said the fat premier as he stood beside his bed in long underwear, "that's the second one who's given out on me" (Faure's predecessor, Casimir Périer, had resigned in 1895). When the circumstances of Faure's death became known, the political opposition tried to create a major scandal; but the French are pretty unflappable about the sex lives of their politicians—a lady's man has a political advantage, and Vincent Auriol's popularity in Toulouse soared after his glass eye was found in a lady's bed—and were more sensitive to the comic aspects of Faure's death. When he occupied the Élysée, General de Gaulle liked to tell the joke about Faure's doctor asking the butler: "Does he still have his *connaissance?*" (Is he still conscious?) "No, sir, she just went out through the garden door."

A far more serious scandal broke out in 1914 when the newspaper *Le Figaro* tried to smear Premier Joseph Caillaux by publishing letters he had written his mistress, signed "your Joe." Madame Caillaux, a no-nonsense French housewife with strong feelings about invasion of privacy, went to the *Figaro* offices, asked to see the editor, Gaston Calmette, took a revolver from her handbag and shot him dead. She was acquitted, but her husband was forced to resign.

The garden variety of mistress either did not last long enough to gain political influence or picked transient figures who had no influence themselves. The traditional sinecures for the mistresses of politicians were the government-subsidized theaters, the Opéra, and the Comédie Française. In 1926, the Minister of Education, Edouard Daladier, told a visitor that the Director of the Comédie Française "came to bother me about three young actresses without any talent whom he hired because they were the mistresses of ministers or former ministers. He cried on my shoulder because naturally he did not have the courage to say no when they forced those little strumpets on him . . . it is true that I have no mistress among these ladies of the Comédie . . . which for a Minister of Education is a serious breach of manners."

Daladier, however, was under the influence of the marquise de Crussol. When he was premier in 1934 and right-wing rioters tried to storm the Concorde bridge and march on the Chamber of Deputies, the press said "the red marquise" had urged him to fire on the demonstrators. In the last day of the Third Republic, when France seemed as paralyzed as a guinea pig before a python, the political mistress blossomed in the persons of the marquise and Hélène de Portes, who had what seemed like total power over Paul Reynaud. When he became premier in 1940, his dark, high-strung, always conspiratorial Egeria was in the wings, filtering appointments, eavesdropping and reading secret telegrams. When the German advance began and the government fled to Bordeaux, Madame de Portes accompanied Reynaud. Brigadier General Spears, who was then acting as Churchill's liaison officer, has left a disturbing account of the chaos over which Madame de Portes presided. Here was a near-hysterical woman with no visible talent for politics, who legally was not even allowed to vote, and she was manipulating the premier of France like a puppet. She was pressing Reynaud to conclude an armistice with the Germans. She would interrupt meetings, slam the door, stamp her foot, and make faces indicating she had important things to tell him. Spears finally complained to Reynaud's chief of cabinet, Roland de Margerie, who said: "She is ugly, messy, dirty, nasty, and half crazy, and her presence here is hard for me to bear."

Reynaud survived the war to become a deputy in the Fourth and Fifth Republics, but he no longer had Madame de Portes to rely on. On June 28, 1940, she was driving her sports car on the Saint Maxime road with Reynaud when she braked too hard and some suitcases on the back of the seat slipped and struck the nape of her neck. The car went out of control and she was killed. But her species lived on in the Fourth and Fifth Republics although General de Gaulle, like Clemenceau, was never swayed by the advice of women except perhaps in matters gastronomic. Several of his ministers carried on the tradition of female representation in the highest circles of government that began when Agnes Sorel persuaded Charles VII to oust the British from France, and the king "left his gardens and hunts and took the bit between his teeth," according to the abbot of Brantôme, sixteenth-century chronicler of the decline of the chivalric tradition.

L'amour Gaulois

As a result of the Hundred Years War, the court returned to the tradition of *paillardise* (lewdness) which preferred earthy pleasures to the romances of the troubadours. Brantôme's *Lives of Gallant*

Ladies is the antithesis of André the Chaplain's *The Art of Love.* Delicacy of feeling to deserve a woman's tenderness gave way to the basic rule: Copulate whenever you can with whomever you can. In Brantôme, who was chronicling court incidents, women were portrayed as ravenous for sex, like the virgin on her wedding night who complained that it hurt. "If you don't keep quiet I'll take out the big one," her husband said. The next day she asked for the big one. Or the still chivalric courtier who said: "I kiss your hands and feet, madame," to which the lady replied, "Sir, the best part is in the middle." Women were good at all ages: "You make a better bouillon with old hens." A man was expected to "turn his lady's windmill without spilling any water." A lady boasted she only took lovers when she was pregnant: "I never take passengers aboard my ship unless I've got plenty of ballast." When a man promised a repeat performance and did not live up to it, his lady said, "Get out, this isn't an inn." According to Brantôme, Catherine de Medici found four *godemiches* (dildos; the French is from the Latin *Gaude Mihi,* or rejoice me) in the jewel case of a lady-in-waiting. He could only conclude that "in France, the weather is set at coupling; there are whores everywhere and cuckolds everywhere."

But at the same time Brantôme was describing the easy licentiousness of the sixteenth century, the return to the courtly tradition was already under way, thanks to the growing eminence of women in literary salons. As with the troubadours, culture was the instrument of female ascendancy. The salon served the same purpose as the court of love; it made woman the arbiter and the judge of masculine behavior. Manners must be polished, feelings must be expressed in a roundabout way, all crudeness must be abolished. The rise of the *femme du monde* placed the important function of taste making in the hands of women. The salon began to function in the sixteenth century, when Ronsard and Du Bellay attended the gatherings of Antoinette de Loynes. In Italy and Spain, women were still meekly closeted with their *petit point,* but in the French seventeenth century they reigned over manners.

The Hotel de Rambouillet was a fortress of female sensibility for a quarter of a century. Men of talent obediently trooped to the lovely house in the rue St. Thomas du Louvre where Catherine de Vivonne, marquise de Rambouillet, enforced the virtues of refinement that soon lapsed into preciosity. Conversation, like her muslin bodices, was diaphanous. In the blue room, Arthénice (an anagram of her first name devised by Malherbe) received her "gallant alcovists" and her "sighers." "Do satisfy the desire that this seat has to embrace you," she said, as they arrived. Mademoiselle de Scudéry, with her Carte du Tendre (Map of Tenderness), made a parlor game of the pathetic fallacy. Each locality on the map had the name of a feeling, and each player charted his travels along the path of Love and tried to avoid the pond of Jealousy.

One of Richelieu's motives in creating the all-male Académie Française in 1635 was to counter the threatened female monopoly on culture. Although the ladies were excluded from the Académie, they soon employed their talents to groom candidates. But the *précieuses* were not merely a clique of fussy ladies who spoke in ridiculous periphrases. They were the first conscious feminists. They denounced the inferior education of women and clamored for the equality of the sexes which the foundation of the Académie at once denied.

Libertinage

Although official literary honors were denied her, the French woman had gained considerable ground from the time when it was argued that she should not be taught to read or write, so that she could neither send nor receive love letters, to the publication of the first French psychological novel by comtesse de La Fayette in 1678. Little more than a century separates Brantôme's cheerful lechery from the romantic transports of *La Princesse de Clèves*. The comtesse de La Fayette carried on the tradition of Chrétien de Troyes and Tristram and Isolde with her tale of the marriage of reason between Mademoiselle de Chartres and the prince de Clèves. When she tells her husband she has fallen in love with Monsieur de Nemours, the news kills him, and she soon follows him to the grave rather than marry her lover. The promptness with which the prince and the princess die of love was a proof of supreme abnegation, although today it might be viewed as an example of morbid psychology. *La Princesse de Clèves* is an attempt to turn a misunderstood wife into a tragic heroine. In this and in its presentation of an untarnished lady prevented by society from following the inclinations of her heart, it is a feminist novel. The comtesse de La Fayette set her novel a century back to the court of Henri II, however, for she knew that in her own time women had other means of coping with marriages of reason than doing away with themselves. The development of libertinage in the seventeenth and eighteenth centuries was a synthesis of courtly love and the cynical approach of *amour Gaulois*. Men paid elaborate court to women, but with total insincerity.

Women, on the other hand, decreed that passions should not be controlled but exploited. The French woman's contribution to morality has been to expose the insipid core of virtue. As La Rochefoucauld said: "There are few honest women who are not sick of their trade." For a seventeenth-century woman to reject a suitor because he had a mistress was considered an impropriety. The princesse de Clèves would remember the pressure of a hand all her life, whereas the duc de Richelieu at the court of Louis XV could not remember which women had been his mistresses. Love became a diversion masquerading as a passion. The eighteenth-century courtier pursued the goals of Brantôme with the language of the *précieuses*. Monsieur de Nemours could spend days analyzing one of the princesse de Clève's blushes, but that was literature, and at court what mattered was how quickly a woman could be maneuvered into bed. The libertine tradition was codified by the aphorisms of Chamfort (love is the contact between two epiderms) and the novel *Les Liaisons Dangereuses*, by the artillery officer, Choderlos de Laclos, who treated love as a strategic problem. The cool-headed technicians of love, those most gifted in deceit and pretense, are victorious over the vulnerable romantics. But their victory is meaningless, and Laclos is actually a moralist warning that technique no more replaces love than catechizing replaces faith. This, say Laclos and Chamfort, was eighteenth-century society. If it had been moral there would have been no need to write about it. The decree of the courts of love, that love could be found only outside marriage, persisted, but the chivalric behavior of a lover toward his mistress did not. When a lady told the prince de Ligne that he had made her pregnant, he replied: "Madame, when you sit on a pile of thorns, how do you know which one has pricked you?"

In the eighteenth century, the social influence of women depended less on the observance of the chivalric tradition than on

the ability to maneuver within the closed and artificial environment of the court. Although still legally inferior, women at court
were equals because they participated actively in day-to-day life
based largely on the organization of pleasure. Women formed influential friendships and lobbied effectively for special interests.
They had a hand in military and religious promotions and in the
other forms of court patronage based on influence rather than
merit. The Goncourt brothers have a tendency to interpret the
French eighteenth century as a matriarchy when they say that
"woman was the governing principle, the reason that directs, the
voice that commands; she was the universal and fatal course, the
origin and source of events. Nothing escaped her and she held
everything, even the king of France." The fact is, that as bureaucratic systems go, the court was the one in which women could
most effectively operate, since advancement depended on personal
support and intrigue. But rather than a clear-cut case of "I govern
France and my mistress governs me," it was more a matter of
women organizing influence-peddling and taste-making. The taste
makers saw the gap between social and legal status, and Madame
de Tencin, friend of Montesquieu and mother of d'Alembert, said,
"It's easy to see from the way he's treated us that God is a man."

Women at court defended the Encyclopédistes (Madame de
Pompadour was said to have written the Encyclopédie's article on
rouge), but they did not return the favor. The Encyclopédie omit-
ted any mention of the equality of the sexes. Diderot, its guiding
spirit, believed women's senses clouded their minds. Voltaire
thought women were more honest than men but weak in both
body and spirit. Even Rousseau, who appealed so directly to the
feminine sensibility that women wrote him they had read La
Nouvelle Héloise a hundred times and that the book had saved
their marriages, believed that "women are big children," whom
nature intended to be weak and deprived of man's inventive power
since their principal function is procreation. Rousseau combined
romanticism and antifeminism, which may have inspired one of
his most illustrious admirers, Napoleon, to maintain toward
women the dual attitude of contempt and passion. Rousseau's
Saint-Preux might be ready to die of love for Julie, but that did
not change the fact that she would be expected to be a docile wife.

Women and the Revolution

Not surprisingly, the Revolution, when it came, ratified the feudal concept of a proprietary relationship between man and woman. To the feudal lord she was a chattel, to the bourgeoise of 1789 she was a piece of dowried real estate. Instead of a declaration of the rights of woman, the attitude of the Convention was expressed by the Cordelier leader Pierre Chaumette: "Imprudent women who want to become men, aren't you satisfied with your lot? What more do you want? You rule over our senses, the legislators are at your feet!" The gap between social power and legal impotence grew wider with each change of regime, so that at the same time Chaumette was speaking, Gouverneur Morris, an American witness of the French Revolution, wrote in his diary, in reference to an important political figure: "His wife, I find, is acquainted with the whole affair. This is the woman's country!"

The only form of *égalité* between the sexes that the legislators of the Revolution believed in was the guillotine, which decapitated either sex with equal dispatch. The three most eminent women of the Revolution, Marie Antoinette, Madame Roland, and Charlotte Corday, were among its victims. In the case of the first two, the all-male revolutionary tribunal was punishing female interference in the affairs of men. It was taking its revenge on a chivalric tradition which, in exalting women, gave them power. Marie Antoinette had not only to be judged as a queen, but humiliated as a woman. The tribunal made her frightened and impressionable eight-year-old son testify that his mother had taught him to masturbate. Unable to extract a confession of treasonable behavior, the tribunal trumped up charges that made her seem an unfit mother, so strong was the need to demean a woman who had exercised political power thanks to her influence over her husband. Madame Roland, whose fault lay in holding a salon where the Girondin leaders met, also had to defend herself against personal attacks. She was questioned about her personal relations with the Girondins, so that it seemed as though she were being tried less for treason than for offenses against public morality. Like Marie Antoinette, she was accused of influencing her husband, who had served as Minister of the Interior. When she tried to explain herself, the public prose-

cutor Fouquier-Tinville cut her off and said: "With these garrulous women one is never done." The tribunal showed more respect
for the twenty-five-year-old Charlotte Corday, because she was
"Maratized," that is, she had slain the revolutionary leader Marat
in keeping with his own theory of the violence that cleanses. She
complied with the first rule of Jacobin logic, that to denounce is
to condemn; the proof that Marat was a traitor was that she had
found it necessary to kill him. With Charlotte Corday, the tribunal was sentencing one of its own.

The Revolution gave women the opportunity to show that they
could die as bravely as men, and Charlotte Corday spent her final
moments of freedom posing for the German portraitist Hauer. A
story gained wide credence that the executioner slapped her head
as he held it up to the populace, and it blushed.

The Great Misogynist

The Revolution adopted a patriarchal, punitive attitude toward
women, which Napoleon codified when he came to power, adding
to the bourgeois credo that woman is man's property, the soldier's
insistence on total obedience from inferiors, and the bitterness of
a betrayed husband.

The Code Civil, which legislated the inferiority of women as
no other text has done, was completed in 1804, long after Napoleon
had begun to ruminate about the infidelities of his Creole wife.
Josephine, whom he married in 1796, was six years his senior and
was almost immediately separated from her husband by the Italian
campaign. But his letters remain as evidence of his ardor. "What
are you doing at this hour?" he asked. "You must be sleeping, and
I am not there to feel your breath, to contemplate your graces, and
to smother you in caresses. Far from you the nights are long, sad,
and insipid. Close to you my only regret is that the night does not
last forever." On April 24, he sent her "a kiss for your heart, and
then lower, much lower," and in another letter he said, "You know
very well that I can't forget the little visits; you know very well;
the little black forest—I send it a thousand kisses." But when Josephine came to visit her husband on the Italian front, she was
joined by the handsome blond captain Hippolyte Charles. According to Hamelin's memoirs, she decided to spend the night in

Brescia. "I am retiring," she told Hamelin. "They will set up my table by my bed and we will sup together."

Hamelin saw three places had been set and asked who the third person was.

"It's that poor Charles," said Josephine, "he stopped in Brescia after a mission and learned I was here."

"Knowing what I knew and seeing what I saw," wrote Hamelin, "I did not find the meal very amusing. Once it was over, we retired, but as we passed through the door, a languishing voice was heard to call back Charles, and I continued on my way."

Bonaparte was so angry not to find Josephine in Milan as expected that he broke out with a skin inflammation. He did not learn until 1799 that his wife had lovers and was accepting bribes to procure contracts for army supplies. It was then that he first thought of divorce, although he did not actually go through with it until 1809. On the island of his final exile, Saint Helena, Napoleon summed up his opinion of Josephine, which might also be taken as his final attitude toward the fair sex: "She had the prettiest cunt in the world, but she lied too much."

But if the word "love" is absent from the Napoleonic Code, it is not simply because Josephine made a cuckold of the most powerful man in France. There is no reason to believe that Napoleon would have behaved any differently if his wife had been a model of virtue, for he was convinced that social order depended on the subjugation of wives to their husbands. The Napoleonic Code, where it applied to women, was a specifically antifeminist piece of legislation drafted by men for men.

Napoleon explained his point of view before the administrative tribunal he had created, the Council of State. According to the memoirs of one of its members, Tribondeau, he said: "Nature has made women our slaves! A husband has the right to tell his wife, madame, you will not go out! Madame, you will not go to the theater! Madame, you will not see such and such a person! That is to say, madame, you belong to me heart and soul!"

This patriarchal philosophy was embodied in a series of laws binding woman in a legal corset which it took her 150 years to loosen. Article 213 said: "The husband owes protection to the wife, and the wife obedience to the husband." Article 1124 said that "unfit persons according to the law are minors, exconvicts, and married women." Article 223 gave the husband the right to prohibit his wife from working, and Article 1428 made the husband the administrator of his wife's wealth. He could dispose of it without her consent. But she could not even obtain a hunting license (and later a driver's license) or attend a university without his consent. The courts upheld the husband's legal right to read his wife's mail. "The principle of the inviolability of letters must exceptionally give way," the ruling said, "before the husband's right, in view of the domestic authority conferred upon him by the law, to seek the proof of an offense against his honor or some grave lapse to the obligations of marriage of which his wife might be guilty."

Placing married women in the same category as minors led to all sorts of aberrations. A doctor could not operate on a sick child without the father's permission, which could not always be obtained in emergencies. In 1936 there were three women members of the cabinet in Léon Blum's Popular Front government (Education, Welfare, and Undersecretary for Scientific Research), none of whom were allowed to vote. As a result of the law that "the wife is obliged to live with her husband and follow him everywhere he judges it convenient to reside," there was a case in which a tubercular man divorced his wife because she refused to join him in the sanatorium. From 1804 to 1938, when half a dozen of the most glaringly unfair laws in the Napoleonic Code were abolished, French women enjoyed practically no civil rights.

The dictionary definition of woman, according to Larousse, was "the companion of man." The language itself encourages this subjugation by having only one word, *femme,* for woman and for wife. The slyest dig at the feminine sensibility, however, is the traditional beginning of the medical school anatomy lesson on the heart, describing it as "a hollow muscle."

Emancipation of Women

And yet the suffragette movement was slow to start in France because of the French woman's natural ability to work within the system rather than change it. The Napoleonic Code was one thing, and family life quite another. The husband who in principle disposed of the family wealth in fact obediently turned over his pay envelope to his wife. The wife, who legally could not open a bank account, spent 80 percent of the family budget. French women never marched through the streets breaking store windows and never crashed men's meetings wearing false beards, as the English and American suffragettes did, because French women never really felt threatened. They overcame the obstacles of the Napoleonic Code through their traditional weapons of occult influence and taste making. The French wife might be forced to live where her husband chose, but it was she who decorated the interior. Just as Marianne, the symbol of the Republic, is a woman, the French family's Chancellor of the Exchequer is a woman embodied in the opulent *caissière* who reigns serenely behind the marble counter.

In the same years that the Code became law, Madame Récamier proved that the French woman would not be legislated into submission and would maintain her areas of supremacy. From her bed, which was on a platform like an altar, she enacted laws of her own—she decreed that it should always be April.

The first French suffragette was Stendhal's heroine Lamiel (1842), whose emancipation was sexual. She was the precursor of Lady Chatterly by nearly a century. She paid the village idiot to make love to her, saying: "I must learn what it is." Lamiel was a pilot model for the modern woman, devoid of hypocrisy, matching the masculine world of money and power with charm and wit. But the French feminist movement, once it was organized, was never quite sure that it wanted to meet men on equal grounds. Premier Aristide Briand recalled that when he was a young deputy, he was invited to speak at a feminist congress. An ardent partisan of the equality of the sexes asked if she could change speaking times with him because she had a train to catch. Briand was in a hurry too and refused. "You are not very gallant," said the woman. "Thank you, madame," Briand replied, "you have just given me an opening for my speech."

In France, the progress of women depended less on feminist organizations than on the conflict between the bourgeois concept of woman as property, with its insistence on dowries and inheritances, and the humanist belief in freedom as a path to personal fulfillment. In a country which has produced ladies of letters of the caliber of Madame de Sévigné, Georges Sand, and Colette (whose spouse Willy used his husbandly prerogatives to sign stories she had written), education for women was not approved until the great educator Victor Duruy made some timid experiments in 1867. He proposed classes for young ladies in the presence of their parents. His emissaries to the provinces reported that female education was generally regarded as a social danger. The historian Ernest Lavisse, who was made Director of Women's Education, came to the conclusion that he was in charge of something that did not exist.

Another generation lapsed before the first girls' high school opened, and by 1900 there were twenty-four schools for girls in France. Ten years later, they were allowed to pass the baccalaureate examination, a visa to higher education which had been restricted to men. Men still imagined that women were lost outside a social system which dictated their conduct and relieved them from choice and cogitation. To this stereotype the French woman responded with examples like Madame Curie, who, although born in Poland, studied in France and managed to combine a scientific career with a full family life. But it was not until 1938 that special university degrees for women were done away with.

Another factor in the emancipation of women was war. With much of the active male population at the front, World War I allowed women to take on new jobs and responsibilities. In 1917 a woman named Jeanne Tardy was attached to the cabinet of the Ministry of Labor. She accurately predicted that the civil service would soon welcome thousands of her sex. While their sons and husbands were in the trenches, French women learned self-reliance. After the war, millions of widows and "white widows" (unmarried women who had lost their fathers) continued working. In 1920 a bill to give women the vote was passed in the National Assembly, but the conservative Senate pigeonholed it for several years before turning it down.

World War II remedied that injustice. Already, measure by measure, the Napoleonic strictures were being whittled away. In 1907 women were allowed to dispose of their salaries, and in 1927 they were allowed to join unions. In 1938 the principle of woman's civil incapacity ended with the suppression of the celebrated Article 213, the broadly interpreted legal obligation of wifely obedience.

With the Vichy regime, the rights of women suffered a temporary setback. Marshal Pétain believed female emancipation was partly responsible for French defeat. Instead of staying home and having children, French women had preferred to "find jobs so they could buy expensive dresses." Vichy glorified the housewife and the family of many children. A 1941 law prohibited divorce during the first three years of marriage. In 1942 a Montauban midwife was sentenced to life imprisonment in the campaign against abortion. Vichy considered the French woman a defaulting mother in need of rehabilitation. Many of these defaulters joined the Resistance movements, and others were deported. The ingenuity of the French woman in hostile environments came out in the labor camps; elderly ladies in Ravensbrück dyed their hair to escape a selection based on age. As World War I had given the French woman job opportunities, World War II gave her opportunities for heroism.

The women of Wyoming won the right to vote in the 1870's, the women of England in 1918, and the women of France in the ordinance of April 21, 1945, under the first postwar government of General de Gaulle. In the 1946 legislative elections, 39 of the 618 deputies were women. But since then, the percentage has decreased. French women are still not sure that they should become directly involved in politics, and in a recent poll only 22 percent of the sample said they would accept a woman president as easily as a man. Moreover, 80 percent said they vote the same way as their husbands, which does not necessarily mean that the husband makes the choice.

Although there is nothing in the Gaullist constitution of 1958 about the equality of the sexes, and although the general himself was known to be a man who does not consider women fit for serious conversation and who broke up after-dinner guests according to sex, *à l'Anglaise,* the Fifth Republic accomplished what the feminist organizations could not. Since 1965 the French woman has been able to open a bank account without her husband's permission, and bankers have been trying to woo the ladies into their establishments. But the French woman needs no lessons when it comes to thrift; hers is already legendary. She may look as though she spends most of her time in boutiques and beauty parlors, but she is an ant disguised as a butterfly.

Along with banking privileges, the French woman won fiscal equality in 1965. The husband can no longer make unilateral financial decisions without her consent. Two hundred articles of the Napoleonic Code had to be altered to achieve this change. But habits are harder to change than laws, and 90 percent of French couples still marry under the system of *communauté de biens,* which gives the husband considerable control over family funds. When a woman goes to a lawyer and says, "My husband wants a divorce, but he has already sold my share of the family business; what can I do?" the lawyer is apt to reply: "All you can do is cry, madame." The husband can still choose the place of residence, and if his wife refuses to follow him, he can have her salary seized if she has a job and divorce her if she doesn't. The husband still decides whether his wife can work. She can appeal, but it is hard to prove that the husband's decision is an "unfounded vexatory tactic," particularly since the French courts still invoke "the presumption of sagacity" for the husband. There is also a persisting inequality in the definition of adultery. A man can only be found guilty if it takes place in his own home, and will be sentenced to no more than a fine. A woman can be found guilty if she commits adultery anywhere, and faces a possible jail sentence.

French divorce cases seldom invoke adultery, however, because adultery is often considered the safety valve that makes marriage possible and because it is more convenient to use the catchall motive of "grave injury" to obtain a French divorce. Grave injury can be anything the imagination devises. Recent cases include a husband who wrote the name of the murderer on the title page of his wife's Whodunits, and a husband who played the bagpipes and made his wife keep time with a flyswatter.

Population Policies

A final peculiarity of the state's attitude toward the French woman is the extent to which it has tried to control the central and most intimate female function, procreation. In a first phase, which lasted roughly from the Revolution to the war of 1870, official influence restrained childbirth in accordance with deep instincts of French society. After the defeat of 1870, the French awoke to the dangers of underpopulation and the French woman, after having been told for over a century to limit the size of her family, was blamed for the country's military defeats. The government line reversed itself, from Malthusianism to biological anxiety. Today, one example of government involvement in private affairs is a vigorous family policy which pays couples to have children in order to realize the dream that haunted the general: one hundred million Frenchmen.

In the eighteenth century, France was the most heavily populated country in Europe, but that advantage was lost with the wars of Revolution and Empire. It was at precisely the same time that France was being bled by the Napoleonic campaigns that the natality rate started decreasing, not only because of the soldiers' unborn children, but also because the French became sensitive to the advantages of a small family. This was, in part, the result of the Enlightenment and its stress on man's rational control of his environment. To limit the size of one's family was a way of ordering nature that increased the chances of personal progress and prosperity. The bourgeois ideal was often expressed, "It is preferable to encourage men to have savings instead of children."

There was also a change in attitude toward the child. It was only when French parents became interested in their children that they stopped having so many. Parental indifference and brutality toward children was ingrained in *ancien régime* society. A humanist like Montaigne could not remember how many children he had. The idea that a child is an individual who deserves his parents' care and attention is the result of the Enlightenment and Rousseau's treatise on raising children, *Émile*. The declining natality rate was linked to the changing idea of the family. The greater the number of children, the less attention could be paid to each. Finally, there was concern for property. The tendency of small farmers to limit their families so their land would not be fragmented among several heirs had been noticed as early as Rabelais, who said that was one reason peasants encouraged their sons to become monks. When the Revolution redistributed the lands of the clergy, there were thousands of new landowners, traditionally thrifty, prudent men, who suddenly had a reason to limit the size of their family. The Napoleonic Code provided further encouragement by stating in Article 832 that each child had to be bequeathed a specified part of the parents' property. The Code ruled that children were equal, but in denying the father's testamentary freedom, it institutionalized the social custom of the only son. The fact that France is a 97.5 percent

Catholic country meant nothing, for social conduct has never been determined by religious factors when they are in conflict with matters of property.

The French did not wait for Margaret Sanger to find out that sexual pleasure could be distinct from procreation. Already in the seventeenth century priests complained in their sermons that the "baneful secrets" of birth control had penetrated "even into the villages." The traditional advice of a mother to her daughter is: "It is up to your husband to be careful." The French have made a science of coitus interruptus. As one French wife put it: "It's like a meal where you've had plenty to eat, and you're very pleased even though there is no dessert."

A woman who announces a new pregnancy to a relative is told: "One would think you were doing it on purpose. You really don't know how to manage." A French wife considers it her husband's duty to "inconvenience himself." A 1962 study of 1,200 Grenoble women showed that 68 percent used some form of contraception, which broke down as follows: Coitus interruptus, 71 percent; rhythm, 21 percent; condoms, 4 percent; and injections, 4 percent; while the pill and the diaphragm represented a negligible percentage. (Oddly enough, a Frenchman claims to have invented the diaphragm, and in the cemetery of La Celle, in the department of the Var, visitors can read this inscription on a tombstone: Here lies Louis Bernard Roudier—he had all the virtues of a good family man. Suffering humanity owes him the invention of rubber pessaries, for which he received the king's patent, and which his inconsolable widow continues to manufacture with the same success.) It is only since 1968 that oral contraceptives have become legal in France and can be sold in pharmacies and advertised, so it is too early to tell whether they will replace the traditional French method of birth control based on self-reliance and husbandly abnegation. My cousin René, possessor of the archetypal French family, one boy and one girl, has no faith in the pill and continues to practice what he calls "jumping off the train while it's still running," and "fireworks on the lawn."

In the nineteenth century, family planning was linked to upward mobility. The one- and two-child families of the grasping bourgeoisie became a familiar literary subject. In a novel about a family of nineteenth-century industrialists, the Goncourt brothers wrote: "Madame Mauperin was not pleased about this latest daughter . . . she had arranged matters so that she would have two children. The third was unexpected, and disrupted the fortune of the two others." There were nineteenth-century birth announcements that read: "Mr. and Mrs. X have the misfortune to announce the birth of an undesired child." France was a century ahead of the rest of the world when it came to programmed, systematic birth control. Eminent economists like Jean-Baptiste Say advised French wives to exercise "conjugal caution" in order to increase their chances of social and economic achievement. A slow population growth was hailed as the mark of a cultured and sensible nation, a stimulus to consumption, and the condition of economic security.

The French developed a Malthusian reflex. They genuinely feared that overpopulation would lead to poverty. Every child seemed to the timorous middle class a potential unemployed worker. With the Industrial Revolution and the formation of an urban proletariat, economists and political writers raised the specter of "dangerous" poor classes who would become an economic burden to the rest of society.

The Académie Française in 1851 gave a special prize to a book that extolled the wisdom of birth control. The French did not need encouragement, for this was only another aspect of foresight about money, jobs, marriage, and every other serious part of life. Valéry could not hide his admiration for the national ability to regulate birth. "The cause of depopulation is clear," he said, "it is presence of mind." Even the Third Republic feared population growth at first, because it was a weak regime whose leaders felt threatened by "the multiplication of the dangerous classes." While the rest of Europe doubled its population, France assiduously incubated only sons. In the nineteenth century its population fell below that of England, Italy, and Germany. Awareness that France was suffering from a dangerous case of anemia came with the humiliation of defeat. The Franco-Prussian war was traumatic for a country which had made a virtue of underpopulation: There were nearly half a million military casualties, the Paris Commune cost another fifty thousand lives, and worse than that, the annexation of Alsace and Lorraine by the Germans deprived France overnight of one million and a half of her citizens. For these reasons, the population dropped by two million between 1866 and 1872.

Although aware of the danger, the Third Republic was unable to change Malthusian habits. At first, a voluntary increase in the birthrate was sought. Between 1870 and 1939 hundreds of works on this newly discovered peril were written. Their authors searched every corner of French life for causes of the decline, which was attributed with utter seriousness to playing with dolls (a substitute for children), sterility induced by absinthe, the French poodle fad (another substitute), and the dangerous consequences of bicycle riding on the female reproductive organs.

Commissions were named to study the problem, and the press warned that the population of Germany would soon be double that of France. The French Academy of Medicine said it was healthier for women to have large families. The sociologist Durkheim suggested that suicides were more frequent in small families where collective bonds are weaker. But there were still years when the birthrate fell below the death rate. The First World War was partly demographic in origin. Sixty-six million Germans thought they could handle thirty-nine million Frenchmen. A German magazine said France had a feeling of "animal inferiority" toward its prolific Eastern neighbor. Von Moltke remarked that the low birthrate cost the French a battle a day in World War I. The war cost a million and a half French lives, and more millions in terms of unborn children during the war years. World War I French propaganda was particularly virulent in denouncing mothers of only sons. The classic remark was: "You smothered one son in your bed, you will lose the other on the battlefield."

As a result of the World War I slaughter, the government moved more vigorously to encourage higher natality. In 1920 a law against abortion and contraception was passed by the *Chambre Horizon Bleu* for overtly patriotic rather than moral motives. Publicity for contraceptives could be punished by a jail term for "outrage to good morals." Dr. Morucci, a respected sociologist who opposed the measures, was accused of having been bribed by the Germans and living off the proceeds of abortion. Along with these prohibitions, births were rewarded for the first time with subsidies for civil servants and "French Family" medals, bronze for five children, silver for eight, and gold for ten. Thanks to these encouragements, the population did not decline. It remained stationary at around forty million from 1920 to 1946. But France's inability to increase its population bred a mystique of powerlessness that was one of the underlying reasons for the swiftness of the 1940 debacle. The country could not physically support another bleeding. Right-wing writers, who were quick to collaborate, truly believed that France was afflicted with some biological curse, or, as Drieu de la Rochelle said: "An impotence to renew its own matter, to multiply its cells."

The next step, enacted in 1939 thanks to Paul Reynaud and Edouard Daladier's *Code de la Famille,* was to present childbearing as a profitable enterprise. Family allocations paid French mothers to produce. Today, having children means important tax deductions, outright subsidies, reductions on train fares, credit facilities, and school benefits. The nonproducing members of society—bachelors, widowers, and childless couples—help subsidize the child-bearers through higher taxes.

The allocation, which was maintained and increased by the Fourth and Fifth Republics, is no pot of gold. It is not an invitation to indolent parents to live off their reproductive capacity, but plays a modest role in maintaining the standard of living of large families. Most children's clothes are sold between the fifteenth and the twenty-fifth of each month, the period when the allocations are distributed. A nonworking mother with three children gets a basic monthly allocation of around sixty dollars (plus small prenatal and maternity payments when she is pregnant). The allocation has become part of the French mentality, and a Paris department store sells "the doll who collects allocations"—a bar of candy is sent free each of the first six months after the purchase. But thanks to housing problems and inflation, the Malthusian reflex still operates to make France the Common Market country with the lowest population density (86 per square kilometer as against 351 for the Netherlands). And this despite a remarkable population explosion between 1946 and 1966, during which the population jumped by nine million.

After a hiatus of a century and a half, the French started breeding again, thanks to the stability and relative prosperity of ten years of Gaullism, the end of colonial wars, and the repatriation of a million *colons* from Algeria who swelled the population figure for metropolitan France. But France, which had not by 1968 reached the fifty-million mark, cannot expect to double its population in an age which has both the instrument of limitation in the pill, and the necessity for limitation if material and psychological well-being is to be achieved. Like an independent Quebec, the magic one hundred million Frenchmen remained one of the general's unrealized dreams. Despite allocations and stability, the birthrate is dropping again. It was 16.6 per thousand in 1967 as against 18.1 in 1964. And in 1968 General de Gaulle said that although he would not subsidize an "amusement" like oral contraception, he would allow it, which left the French Communist Party as the only political group opposing birth control and defending an old-style nationalism that is still trying to make up for World War I losses.

While the Italian and Polish Communist Parties have encouraged birth control, the French Communists continue to call it a bourgeois perversion of the workers. In 1963 Jeannette Vermeersch, the widow of the French Communist leader Maurice Thorez, said that "birth control is a trap for the masses and a bourgeois weapon against social reform." The thought, if not the language, is that of a conservative Roman Catholic bishop.

Today's Woman

The modern French woman is the product of her gender's long struggle to affirm itself against misogynist legislation and nationalized breeding patterns. She has won acceptance in every profession and aspect of national life, despite occasional grumbling that the only place where it still says "men only" is the toilet. The writer Marcel Jouhandeau complained that women were allowed to serve on juries because they were less tolerant than men. "The gravest error of our judicial system," he said, "is women jurors, and heaven knows I am not a misogynist, but I have some precise and disconcerting memories—the sentence requested by the prosecutor is rarely sufficient for these Furies, whose punitive vengeance seems insatiable."

But this twentieth-century Portia is herself divided between romantic inclinations and practical necessities. After the battle to affirm her rights comes the internal struggle between a soft heart and a hard head. Is she to be the Lady of the Camelias or the regal *caissière*? Is she to die for love or protect her dowry? Should she seek the *grand amour* or protect her "little capital," as virginity is frequently called. The French woman is this mysterious synthesis of the calculating and the disarmed, plotting her marriage of reason while secretly yearning for elopement. She has equal opportunity but has not availed herself of it. There are no women ambassadors, prefects, or cabinet ministers. There are only 7 women in the 200-member Conseil d'État, and only 4 in the 180-member Cour des Comptes, the highest auditing body. A woman with a degree still prefers to be a housewife, and only 16 out of 1,000 French engineers are women.

The distinction between love and marriage established by the courts of love persists, and Eleanor of Aquitaine's 1163 treatise is still valid: "Love cannot impose its rights on two married persons. Lovers grant everything freely and mutually without any constraint, while married persons are held by duty to submit reciprocally to one another's will and refuse each other nothing."

When I married an American girl in the spring of 1968 in Paris, I had to spend long hours at the Préfecture de Police office which authorizes foreigners to marry French nationals. The plump, gray-haired lady who delivered the permission was sensitive to the delicate nature of her job, and when I complained about the time it took, she smiled and said: "For some, it's a blessing in disguise; it gives them time to think it over. I like to think that the marriages that come from this office are solid marriages, and when you've gone to such trouble to fill out papers you think twice before getting divorced. We used to have an office for divorces too," she added with a sigh, "but now they've taken that out of our hands." I was reflecting on the way French bureaucracy came to the rescue of unresolved hearts when she handed me the authorization and said, "Well, there you are, there is our benediction."

The ceremony in the City Hall of one of Paris' twenty *arrondissements* was conducted by a handsome lady mayor, a Resistance heroine, an ardent Gaullist, and the long-time mistress of a well-known general who had just died in an accident. When my wife went to see her to arrange a date, she was in mourning and, unburdening her own situation, said: "You can imagine the irony of my position, celebrating marriages . . ." On the designated day we arrived with two witnesses and she put on her Tricolor sash and sat at her high mahogany desk decorated with the Paris coat of arms, under a color photograph of the general and a white plaster bust of Marianne. She wore dark glasses and looked very, well, eroded. She asked us to come close to the desk and began reading the required articles from the Napoleonic Code, about the husband's obligation to give protection and assistance to his wife, and the wife's duty to live in the domicile chosen by the *chef de famille*. Her voice broke and she seemed to be weeping behind her dark glasses, but she controlled herself. Then, departing from the customary text, she told us that of course in a society there had to be regulations and administrative procedures, but that the only law that counted, finally, was the law one made for oneself. "It is easy to love," she said, "it is less easy to get along (*de s'entendre*)." Each individual finds his own way and she knew that we would find ours if we would only find the balance between emotion and reason. She was telling us the very opposite of what her mandate required. She was speaking from the standpoint of her personal tragedy, and saying that the office she represented was far less real than what a man and a woman can mean to each other outside the bonds of marriage.

As mayor, she advised couples to love, honor, and obey, and she read the list of obligations and duties required by law, but her own life contradicted every word, and with us, because of her sense of loss, she was being consistent, not with her office, but with her experience as a woman. The circumstances were special, but I like to believe that only a French woman, with her qualities and traditions, could have conducted a marriage ceremony on the theme that love and marriage are not necessarily compatible.

Still, even an unhappy marriage is preferable to spinsterhood, and the French woman marries early, after a search conducted by herself and her mother for a *bon parti*, a good match. Above all, the prospect must be *sérieux*. Seriousness is a rare blend of thrift, sobriety, pragmatism, stern father, faithful husband, and good provider. A French mother can sniff out a "serious" man the way a truffle hound can find that elusive fungus in an oak forest. It is not easy to escape. One of my cousins, a debonair fellow doing his military service in the air force, was particularly sought after by mothers in his garrison town.

"And what do you do in civilian life?" they would get around to querying.

"What I do in civilian life is not the opposite of what I am doing now," he would reply.

"You mean you are a civilian pilot?"

"No, madam, I am a flying trapezist in a circus. There is no such thing as a foolish job." (*Eh, quoi! Il n'y a pas de sot métier.*)

This irreverence was usually enough to disqualify him. Proof that "serious" men can be found and led to the altar, however, lies in the fact that six and a half of the eight and a half million French women between the ages of twenty and fifty are married, and half a million more are widowed or divorced. After ten years of marriage, according to a recent poll, 41 percent say they are satisfied, 23 percent say their life is a dull routine with a few good moments, and 36 percent say they envy single women.

The French marriage is a network of mutual obligations, a contract with each page written in increasingly fine print. The wife's role is to control her husband without making him aware of it. The typical comment of a housewife is: "I use every available weapon—clothing, the home, food . . . and the rest you can guess." Television and buying on credit are powerful new weaponry in the feminine arsenal. The working-class wife is grateful when her husband works overtime, and says "at least he won't be wasting time and money in a café." The French wife prides herself on making marvelous meals with leftovers, and also on her talent for obtaining without asking (she secretes deceit just as animals develop secondary characteristics in hostile environments).

Woman still sees herself as a negotiable commodity on the marriage market. How many girls enroll in medical school, not to become doctors but to marry one? The myth that the French girl is "easy" is contradicted by the surveys which show that 72 percent of married women under thirty said they had married as virgins. The terminology of virginity assimilates woman to a product: "A girl is like a bottle of Vichy water—it's sold sealed." The woman feels she must keep her virginity as long as it's a value for the man: "I didn't want to lose what a girl can only give once," or "I asked him to be careful because I wanted to be married intact." This is still the traditional attitude, although there are signs that French women are beginning to consider virginity less as something that should be kept to please an eventual husband than as the suppression of a burden, a rite of passage to womanhood. The new French woman is not only the one who was given the right to vote in 1946 and the right to open a bank account in 1965, but the one who intends to squander her "little capital." She is still in a minority, and the surveys show that only 12 percent of French women feel it is their right to *faire des bêtises* (enjoy premarital sex).

There is nothing puritanical about this caution toward premarital affairs. Sex is seen as another gift of nature to be enjoyed and refined. As Madame de Sévigné told her daughter: "We make love like animals, but a bit better." The French woman has demystified the functions of the body. Laurence Sterne was riding in a carriage with the marquise de Rambouillet when she told him to pull the cord. "I asked her if she wanted anything. *'Rien que pour pisser,'* she said. Grieve not gentle traveler, to let Mme. de Rambouillet piss on . . . I handed her out of the coach, and had I been a priest at the chaste Castalia [a spring near Delphi], I could not have served at her fountain with more respectful decorum."

As the heir to the libertine tradition, the Frenchman believes he has an edge on lovemaking because he takes it seriously. He is the tactician who approaches a woman like a chess player or a geometer, seeking an elegant solution to every problem—like Valmont in *Les Liaisons Dangereuses* writing a letter to one mistress on the naked back of another. As they have appropriated gastronomy, the French tend to appropriate sex, forgetting that Casanova was Italian and Don Juan a Spaniard. French sex is cerebral, and a matter of principle. Montherlant affirmed that there must be something wrong with a man who is faithful to his wife. Adultery is the norm, because marital sex is dull. Ideally, the man should be a sexual egoist at home, so that his wife does not form the dangerous habit of enjoying the marriage bed, and a sexual altruist abroad, finding his own pleasure in the satisfaction of his partner. Sexual altruism is probably the main reason for the Frenchman's reputation as a lover.

Treatises have been written to explain that the singularity of being French consists in the paradox of a totally uninhibited but totally disciplined attitude toward sex. There is no false shame or false modesty; considerable masculine pride surrounds the diligent pursuit of agreeable sensations. French lovemaking is less passionate than technically proficient, its vocabulary reminiscent of two housewives discussing a complicated recipe—do this, then do that, now here, that's right, turn a bit, not too fast, simmer but do not let come to a boil. The attitude is at once detached and overrefined. Compare the FBI agent who was dismissed because he was discovered with a girl in his hotel room, with the French police commissioner who boasted that he only made love to clothed women so that he could imagine they were more beautiful than they were.

Sexual escapades can ruin the career of an American politician, but they are viewed with amused tolerance by the French. It did no lasting damage to the president of the National Assembly, André Le Troquer, when he was named as a leader in a ring that recruited teen-age girls for *partouses* (orgies, pronounced *part-ooze*). Nor did it hurt Georges Pompidou to be publicly linked with the case of actor Alain Delon's murdered Yugoslavian body-guard, who was known to have photographed celebrities at orgies. After Pompidou returned from a visit to the pope in early 1969, de Gaulle is said to have told him: "I hope you went to confession." Don Juanism on the part of everyone from an ambassador to his chauffeur is expected, and women become practiced in handling it without offending male vanity. Gaston Palewsky, an early Gaullist who became ambassador to Rome and cabinet minister, offered a lady a ride home after a dinner in suburban Neuilly in 1945, when only government officials had cars. "No, thank you, dear Gaston," she said, "but tonight I'm too tired, I prefer walking." The French see no breach of the Hippocratic oath in a doctor's trying to seduce his lady patients. The figure of the handsome young doctor as a ladies' man who uses medical knowledge as a technique of seduction is a familiar one. There is also the figure of the older woman as the archetypal initiator; the French believe that sexual knowledge is transmitted by one generation to the next. The French woman of forty who initiates a man half her age in the essential mysteries scowls at the groping experiments of American teen-agers and college students, and asks: "How can they learn anything when they are all the same age?" Sex to the French is like any skill: It is taught; apprentices learn from masters.

Adultery is the link between the bourgeois solidity of marriage and the national reputation for naughtiness. It fits into the system as a social necessity which, in making marriage bearable, guarantees the continuity of the family. Half of the wives questioned in a poll said they would excuse their husband's infidelities in order to keep the family together, and 20 percent said they had already committed adultery as a revolt against the husband's marital authority. The misunderstood wife is, after all, a French discovery, and when Flaubert hit upon the species, his analysis was so painfully accurate that he was put on trial after *Madame Bovary* was published.

The alternative to adultery is divorce, and the French take the resigned attitude that if there are few good marriages, there are even fewer good divorces. Each year there are roughly 300,000 marriages and 3,000 divorces; thus, on the average, one marriage in a hundred ends in divorce, and two out of three divorcees remarry. But often the French wife prefers a difficult marriage to a divorce which makes the children suffer, creates material problems, and places her brutally on her own. The French woman is still like Gertrude Stein's cook, who thought the captain's cry of "women and children first" was nonsense because it broke up families. Marriage continues to be regarded as an imperfect haven from life's difficulties. Far from aspiring to endless romance and sustained intensity of feeling, the French wife expects marriage to be a routine which erodes romantic love, and resigns herself to her Saturday-night conjugal duty and the dull job of housekeeping. Or else she is not resigned and makes life difficult for her husband, like the wife of a civil servant, who went with her to see the gynecologist and said: "Madame has her period every thirty-seven and a quarter days, Madame throws the dishes on the floor on the thirty-third day of her cycle, Madame's kidneys ache when she waxes the floor, and Madame is frigid." If Madame is not frigid, she may take a lover, and anyone doubting that the mythology of the cuckold and the *ménage à trois* still flourishes should attend the Paris theater.

Every culture gets the art forms it deserves, and the French theater has boulevard comedy. Every possible variant of the husband-wife-lover triangle has been staged, but the French public still asks for more. The genre is as stylized as Japanese *noh* theater, and the audience laughs because it knows what to expect, as a kind of Pavlovian response. All these plays are based on the conventions of adultery: The buffoonery of being cuckolded, the alliance of husband and lover, the wife's ability to deceive both. When all the farcical misunderstandings have been sorted out, when no one is left in closets or under beds, and when husband and wife have made amiable amends, the play ends. No theatrical form is so artificial or remains so popular.

No other people has explored so thoroughly, in its literature and its behavior, the techniques of deceit between men and women. But thanks to the salutary tradition of love-as-a-game, when an actor declaims the key line *"mon cher,* I am dismayed to learn that my wife is deceiving me," everyone roars with laughter. Here we return to the ribald tradition of Brantôme, the round of love, her Majesty the petticoat, wicked Paris, the *Vie Parisienne* article called "How to Eat an Asparagus," which showed twelve society beauties each pulling on a large asparagus stalk in her own distinct way, the nocturnal assignations of total strangers in the lanes of the Bois de Boulogne, and the visits to discreetly elegant brothels like Madame Claude's on the rue Marignan by visiting dignitaries, listed on the official calendar of events as "visit to the president of the Senate" (there is one proverbial lady who is supposed to have two *zouaves* tatooed on her buttocks, with crossed bayonets and the words *on ne passe pas*).

The ribald tradition is still very much alive. In the spring of 1968 I was having lunch in a two-star restaurant on the Moselle river, near Nancy. An attractive young lady was eating alone and exchanging jokes with three men acquaintances at another table. As the waiter was bringing their main course, she signaled to him and deftly tucked a small object under the roasted guinea-hen wing on one of the plates. I was sitting behind her and saw that the object was a condom. It may have been a tasteless practical joke, but I felt pleased to be living in a country which has so few prigs.

The romantic tradition is less evident. Who can find time today to die of love like the princesse de Clèves? Businessmen can no longer keep the traditional five-to-seven appointments with their mistresses. Unhurried weekday adultery is vanishing from French life. It belongs to an age when women told their lovers: "But darling, I need an hour just to lace up my back." Long hours protect husbands, just as children protect wives, from the follies of the imagination, and *midinettes* (young working girls) are vaccinated against their passions by the romantic pap about Soraya and Elizabeth Taylor in the women's magazines. A cooler, more clinical and experimental attitude of the emancipated woman was caught by Françoise Sagan when she wrote at the age of seventeen in *Bonjour Tristesse:* "The words 'to make love' have a special seduction, very verbal, separated from their meaning. The word 'make,' material and positive, combined with the poetic abstraction of the word 'love,' delighted me." Sagan the teen-age novelist managed to combine the two main French currents of love, the courtly poetic abstraction with the earthy physical demand.

But the courtly tradition was an antidote to weakness which the French woman no longer needs. Why should men pretend to be at her feet when she is their equal? And yet, too often, French women behave as if they were the guardians of an archaic formalism; they still expect elaborate courtesy. They do not seem to know how to behave naturally in their new role as equals. They wonder whether they have not lost more than they have gained. Through their artifices and mannerisms they still insist on designating the weapons and the field of battle that control the processs of courtship. The French woman wants to be the queen on the chessboard, the most important piece, highly vulnerable, requiring protection, but indispensable. She is more attached to consideration than to her rights. If she is not the center of attention she behaves like a sulky child. Sex remains a reward for attentive courtiers. She feels her smile should be as highly prized as a sapphire, and that even her inanities should be listened to with silent eagerness. What happens when poets stop praising the arch of her eyebrow as the center of the world? The failure of contemporary man to meet these standards may explain the tense impatience and unpleasantness of some French women. Brigitte Bardot is predatory in her choice and rejection of men but expects to be courted like an eighteenth-century princess.

The late nineteenth-century view which came as a rejoinder to the treacle of the romantics was that the French woman is a highly specialized creature, at her best only in the three roles of shopkeeper, society woman, and whore. Today, with more than 4,000 women operating their own business, she has extended her talents to other fields and is prone to bursts of self-congratulation. Françoise Giroud, one of the best French woman journalists, writes that "our women of iron and velvet are in an enviable position today, because men go on loving them, they enjoy their company, appreciate their conversation, and respect their judgment. After traveling widely I have begun to wonder whether France is not the only country where men and women really understand each other in more ways than for perpetuating the human race—the French woman is in a sense an exclusive product, famous even when she is decried." Perhaps Madame Giroud is right and the French woman is the caviar of her sex, but I find her overextended and unsure of her real role, wanting to succeed in a man's world and at the same time to be serenaded by troubadours, and insisting on continuing to exercise the age-old tyranny of the heart which men so long pretended to accept.

She is the Amazon who refuses to cut off one breast in order to remain completely feminine, the office worker who still believes seductiveness is the way to promotion, the lady lawyer who expects her adversary to be gallant. The contrived is seen as always preferable to the natural, like cooks who put a sauce on everything. She brandishes the prerogatives of her sex in a particular form of female sententiousness. Everything is owed her, she feels, because she is a woman, and to begin with, the sacrament of love. The French woman's sensibility cannot tolerate dislike, which she claims to feel as strongly as physical pain. But because she desires to please, she expects tribute. It is all too complicated for some French friends of mine, who have purposely found wives outside their own borders and bless their decision as the condition of their peace of mind. (The number of French diplomats with foreign wives is particularly striking.) Every week in the feminine press there are articles about "What the French woman wants." Does she want marriage, does she want divorce, does she want a career, does she want six children or six lovers, or both, does she want the moon—there does not seem to be any answer, except that the French woman is always in a state of wanting, which is a special form of self-serving intensity that might become hard to bear once eternal vows are made.

So that while admiring the genius of the French woman in her various mutations—Eleanor of Aquitaine, Joan of Arc, Mademoiselle de Scudéry, Madame de Montespan, the *tricoteuses,* Madame Récamier, the Lady of the Camelias, Emma Bovary, Colette, the *grandes horizontales,* the duchesse de Guermantes, Coco Chanel, Louise de Vilmorin, Jeanne Moreau, and Yvonne de Gaulle—I find that the common denominator of all these ladies is that they ask a great deal, and that other women are more gracious and natural because they are less demanding, and I reflect on the classic and almost untranslatable remark by the poet Valéry. As a man who had been surrounded by the flower of French womanhood, he was asked his opinion by his doctor. "Well, you see, doctor," he said, "when all has been weighed and considered, and no matter how exquisite the pleasures they procure, they can finally be divided into two categories: the *emmerdeuses*—pests—and the *emmerdantes*—bores. Of course there were a few exceptional ones, you are right. They form a small and particular group. I would call them the *emmerdéesses*—peevish goddesses."

10

➤➤➤

The Sixth Element

The National Vice

"WHY are the French so thinlipped?" a Dutch visitor to Paris asked me. I said that seemed natural in a country where avarice is a virtue. Molière's Harpagon and Balzac's Père Grandet are heroes, not villains. Harpagon reached the point where he never gave his greeting, he only loaned it. Grandet, the whites of whose eyes had a yellowish tinge, devoted his life to the secret accumulation of wealth. No one knew the extent of his capital, which was tied up in gold and land, for he considered investment a prodigality. He would rather risk an accident than have a broken step on his stairs fixed. He would rather have his withered maid Nanon eat in the dining room with his guests than have her use a separate candle in the kitchen. Few men, however, can claim the sense of method and the spirit of sacrifice of a Père Grandet, who remains a heroic, ideal figure most Frenchmen can only imperfectly emulate.

I am not saying that the French tend to be misers, but that the most perfect misers tend to be French. In their first arithmetic classes they learn that adding is thrift, subtracting is spending, multiplication is hard-earned profit, and division is inheritance. According to the 1969 edition of Pick's *World Currency Report,* one quarter of all the privately owned gold in the world is in France, although that is not the only reason for lumpy mattresses. Investment is still regarded as a prodigality: 83 percent of the sample in a 1968 survey said they put their savings in low-yield savings accounts, land, or gold; 11 percent said they invested in foreign stocks, and only 6 percent showed enough faith in the productivity of the French economy to put their money in domestic stocks.

Where their savings are concerned, the French do not seem to have become aware of the Industrial Revolution. But this is less a matter of ignorance than a positive philosophy based on hoarding. Avarice remains mysterious because misers will never agree to pay what a psychiatrist charges. Is it a negation of the life instinct, a form of repressed anger, ingrown ambition, the result of a deprived childhood, or a neurotic fear of the future? Whatever it is, it takes a French writer to defend it as "a form of calculation that can be found at the origin of many virtues. One enriches one's memory with the same methods one uses to make a fortune." Accumulation is a virtue, since it is the principle of learning (*on n'en sait jamais trop*), and avarice is simply a form of accumulation. It is used as a metaphor of virtue in the language: A good general is miserly with the blood of his men, and a wise statesman is miserly with his words. It is a principle of education: Schoolchildren are taught the evils of buying on credit, as brides are given a post-office savings account as a wedding present. There are 27,000,000 of these accounts open, and they bear a 3 percent interest on a maximum of $3,000. They are a sure way to lose money, since the rise of inflation is greater than the rate of interest; the thrifty Frenchman leaves profits to the state, which reinvests his money for a return of 10 to 15 percent. Saving as an end in itself is so deeply ingrained that an internationally known writer and teacher like the late André Siegfried was shocked by conspicuous consumption in the United States and once predicted economic disaster "unless the American housewife learns to darn socks."

The French experience shows, however, that thrift is more

dangerous than spending, for hoarding is the average citizen's way of showing his lack of confidence in his government. When Premier Raymond Poincaré tried to stabilize the franc in 1928, he expressed his sense of frustration to a visitor: "Do you know what a liter jar is?" he asked. "Yes, it holds a liter, but it can also hold ten thousand francs in small bills. You fill one with your savings and you bury it, and then you fill another. That's all. In the villages now, men say of their neighbors, 'He must be at least a two- or three-jar man.' No, it's not easy to collect taxes when the money is there," and he pointed his square thumbs at the carpet. The irony was that the same persons who mistrusted the Bank of France too much to open an account were hoarding notes issued by it.

The problem of hoarding is one with the problem of flight of currency. French speculators have traditionally preferred foreign currencies to their own. When Vincent Auriol became Minister of Finance in 1936, he reported that the flight of capital amounted to 60 billion francs. He said he felt like "a receiver in bankruptcy rather than the executor of an estate." In September of that year Premier Léon Blum had to devaluate, in a tripartite agreement with the United States and England which allowed Blum to disguise the measure as a "realignment." He was widely attacked because he had promised he would not touch the franc. Confidence among the wealthy had been shaken by the Popular Front's social reforms and press campaigns against the *deux cent familles.*

In 1968 it was the government's decision to raise inheritance taxes that shook confidence and made the French revert once again to their habit of leaving the fiscal ship as soon as it springs the slightest leak. In what was called the barricades of the rich, the money fled to Germany, an ironic way to commemorate the fiftieth anniversary of the 1918 armistice. The combination of millions of Frenchmen hoarding gold or buying Deutsche marks once again threatened the franc. But unlike Blum, General de Gaulle saved the franc through sheer stubbornness. The reaction of French capital in times of financial stress is nonetheless entirely predictable. Under de Gaulle, it should also be mentioned, the gold hoarders could hardly be blamed, for they were constantly reminded in official quarters of the excellence of the yellow metal.

Avarice is also considered the highest form of self-esteem. Fiscal worth is equated with personal worth, and life is described as a machine to which money imparts movement. Conversely, charity degrades him who gives and humiliates him who receives. The Frenchman gives in church after making a mental note of what the person next to him has put in the tray, but he suspects that the beggar on the corner may be more of a miser than he is, and sleeps on a mattress stuffed with 100-franc bills. The government encourages these attitudes with its refusal to grant tax exemptions for charity, with the result that there are practically no foundations. Current law allows tax-deductible gifts to charity up to one-half of 1 percent of taxable income. How can a civil servant who knots his tie loosely to keep it from wearing understand, much less encourage, someone who wants to give away millions? The more familiar attitude is that of the millionaire on his deathbed who said: "I wish I could melt everything I own into a glass and swallow it before going."

Most puzzling is the avarice of the well-to-do, like the millionaire who invited his grandchildren for Christmas. His son brought the trees and the presents, but he grumbled that he had to pay for the electricity. Or the French aristocracy, whose forebears made a point of honor of incurring huge debts in order to keep up at court. Today their elegance and exquisite manners have become perfectly compatible with tightfistedness. The comte de Laborde took sick while visiting an Italian duke on lake Como and had to be operated on at the villa. His hosts graciously paid for the medical expenses, but as the comtesse told a friend: "Think of the expense of tipping the servants, now that we have been here two months." And when the duc de Gramont retired his loyal valet, Alfred, who had given him his cigarette ration during the war and had been entrusted with delicate telephone messages to his mistresses, he gave Alfred a miserly pension and would say with great feeling: "This inflation is a disgrace! Poor Alfred is starving to death."

Avarice is also the urge to be a sportsman without taking a risk. After thirty years of working seven days a week in order to feel financially secure, the owner of a *tabac* in Paris decided he would take Sundays off. With three friends, also the owners of *tabacs,* he rented a tiny lot, about two hundred square yards, adjacent to a large property which conducts a weekly pheasant shoot. Each Sunday he and his cronies dress up in the corduroy leggings, knee-high boots and feathered hats of the seasoned hunter, and buy forty pheasants with clipped wings from the gamekeeper of the big hunt—they can still hop, but they can not fly. They spend the day stalking the crippled pheasants on their fenced-off piece of meadow. "You understand," he said, "this way we are able to shoot all the birds we have bought. If we buy forty we are sure to return with forty." He proudly takes his brace of pheasants to a neighborhood restaurant to be prepared, and is considered quite a sport. "Good God, man," said the English hunter in a *Punch* cartoon to a French hunter aiming at a running pheasant, "you aren't going to shoot a running bird?" "*Mais non,* I wait till 'e stop."

The Sunday hunter with his private pheasant shoot is part of a certain France whose principal and mythical figure is a large red-faced man with tiny eyes carrying a huge ring of keys; he has perfected the art of locking up. He locked up his wife with restrictive legislation, and his children with moral instructions about thrift. His country is locked within its borders, as his garden is locked within high walls and his house behind steel shutters. His knowledge is locked inside his diploma, which assures him his position in life until he reaches retirement age, when his locked up pension is waiting for him. The money in his safe represents houses without bathrooms, vacations without travel, schools without playgrounds, and electric lights that are seldom turned on (per capita consumption of kilowatt-hours is three times less in France than in the United States).

With such a pronounced vocation for protectionism, the jungle begins on his doorstep. What is known in English as a welcome mat is called in French a *paillasson,* which has no connotation of welcome in it, but might be translated as: "If you must come in, at least wipe your feet." He does not tell his own family what he earns. The more money he makes, the more he withdraws from the community and becomes secretive. Wealth isolates him from his fellowman, whereas in the United States wealth means greater involvement in community affairs. The Frenchman feels he must shield himself from curious outsiders. As an American girl living in Paris said of French doctors: "They always give me the impression that they are afraid you will take over their practice if they let you in on too much." Even if he amasses a huge fortune, this type of Frenchman will keep the philosophy of *petitesse,* the virtue of smallness, and repeat to the end of his days: "My glass is small but I drink in my glass."

If the type sounds like a vanishing relic, remember that there are still more than 6,000 *notaires* in France. Whether they still write out official papers in longhand with steel nibs and blot the paper with blue sand or not, their function as wardens of the bourgeois purse remains the same (it is only since 1926 that authentic deeds can legally be typewritten). The *notaire's* life is dedicated to the dissimulation of wealth. Since one becomes a *notaire* by buying the practice of another *notaire* (it is one of the last surviving examples of the venality of offices), they start off in their profession by dissimulating the real terms of acquisition. The terms sometimes involve more than money, and one can still see, in the specialized publications *notaires* read, want ads that say *"notaire's* office for sale; matrimonial condition," which means that the *notaire's* unweddable daughter comes with the office.

From the right to draw up deeds and contracts, which was set out in detail by royal statute in the fourteenth century, the *notaire* became the confidant of property owners. It was he who arranged the best terms for a mortgage or found a safe investment that brought 12 percent interest. His professional survival depended upon his being as silent as a tomb. A social history of France could be written on the basis of notarial acts dealing with marriages, taxes, deeds, and wills. The national archives have 75,000,000 notarial acts on deposit, occupying seven miles of shelves. Today, particularly in the provinces, much of French life is still carried out *devant le notaire.* The *notaires* remain the repository of family secrets and archaic business practices. They still believe that "in this business innovations must be avoided." They still rub their hands delightedly when they learn that one of their clients has passed away and there will be an estate to divide.

Their offices still have the frayed curtains, threadbare rugs, and ink-stained desks that inspire the confidence of their thrifty clientele. They can tell you how to escape inheritance taxes on property: You arrange a fictitious sale, get it discounted, and invest the money in tax-free Pinay bonds, which were created in 1952 to lure the gold from under the mattresses. They bring a low yield but have three solid advantages: The interest rate is pegged to the price of gold, a financial amnesty was declared for buyers of Pinay bonds who were holding capital abroad illegally, and there is no inheritance tax on them. The power of attraction of the Pinay bonds can be illustrated by the fact that when Robert Meunier du Houssoy, the giant who ran the huge publishing trust Hachette, died in 1968, the price of Hachette stock dropped a bit, and the price of Pinay bonds rose a bit on the Paris stock market a few days before his death. It is estimated that one-third of French estates escape inheritance taxes, completely legally, thanks to Pinay bonds. They are France's tax-free enclave, France's Liechtenstein. Balzac saw in the *notaire* the prototype of the Philistine, unscrupulous, petty, conventional, and backward, a creature who begins life as a butterfly and ends it as a grub wrapped in a cocoon of hypocrisy, his mind dazed for the same reason that an artillery gunner is deaf, but continuing to moralize as easily as a cook makes a sauce.

The survival of the *notaire* is one of the symptoms of an attitude toward money fixed in France's past. A static conception of personal wealth, seen as something that must be hoarded and saved rather than something that should grow, is the result of centuries of fiscal and economic irresponsibility on the part of the government. Slowness to adopt new industrial and agricultural techniques comes from the belief that France can be happy without machines. There are always village sages, custodians of obstinate foolishness, who solemnly observe that the harvester will never replace the scythe. The French are still not quite sure about the telephone. If Madame de Sévigné had had one, she would not have left the prose classic of her correspondence with her daughter. Marshall Joffre refused to use it, and General de Gaulle only used it in emergencies. The Communications Minister Yves Guéna announced in the summer of 1968, the season of snarled lines, that he saw no reason to improve service on the Côte d'Azur because the extra lines would be idle nine months of the year. Sensitive to the horrors of waste, he preferred an inadequate number of lines that were always humming. France remains the only Western country where the telephone is rationed, with 400,000 requests that will take two to three years to fill.

Economic stagnation has often been rationalized as the price to pay for the preservation of the French way of life. Protectionism was a barrier against foreign values that might be attached to imported products. The anti-entrepreneurial Catholic philosophy was transmitted to the Revolution, which condemned interest-bearing loans. Profit has always been tainted in France: The noble derogated by becoming a businessman; quick fortunes were made by black marketeers, not honest men; high salaries meant that someone lower on the line would be deprived. In the 1969 presidential election, candidate Georges Pompidou had to practically apologize for his past as a bank director while in the United States success in the business community is a political asset. There is no prestige attached to commerce. The woman from a family of drapers who married a country doctor carefully explained to her son: "We were not shopkeepers. My father's window was made of frosted glass. We were wholesales [négociants], not retailers [commerçants]."

At the same time, there is a great attraction to commerce in that part of the population which sees it as the only way to rise without diplomas or the accidents of birth. Men make enormous sacrifices to buy a fond de commerce (lease on a small shop). For them it means independence, handling money, being one's own boss, and having a little fortress from which to resist change. But when Pierre Bercot, the president of the Citroën automobile works, gave a conference in 1963 before the Academy of Moral and Political Sciences, praising the idea of profit as natural to man, some of his listeners afterward chided his cynicism, while others praised his courage, as though it was exceptionally bold in a capitalist country in the sixties to praise the profit motive. Bercot thereafter became sarcastically known as "the high priest of profit." In the French mind, profit still means the same thing as profiteering.

The Franc

It takes centuries of currency manipulation to build up a lack of confidence in national finances so thorough that in the years before World War I, the French investor loaned two and a half billion dollars to moribund imperial Russia. My grandfather, with characteristic suspicion of the French economy, lost a fortune when in 1914 he invested half his capital in Russian bonds and the other half in German bonds. He had not counted on German defeat or Russian revolution, and by 1918 he was ruined. John Maynard Keynes found such flights of capital mysterious, and wondered why the French "have seldom made a foreign loan that there was any reasonable prospect of getting back again." The Frenchman dreamed of huge profits when he heard of exotic investments like the Ottoman loan, the Hellenic debt, and the Spanish railways, which swallowed up billions of francs. But where could the French investor turn? He has been periodically ruined by trusting his own governments.

From 1360, when Jean le Bon designed a coin that showed a Frankish king on horseback and called it a franc, the monarchy based its fiscal policy on arbitrary changes in the value of its currency. Every time a king could not pay his debts, the coin of the realm dropped in value. Only land and gold were not affected by these manipulations. Under Charles VII in the fifteenth century, the franc fell to one ten-thousandth its original value. Constant wars and political crises made sound fiscal measures impossible. The class of *rentiers* (possessors of a fixed income) were invariably the victims of these brutal devaluations, Kings repeatedly floated bonds they could not redeem and frightened off the nation's savings. A glass jar was safer than a king's word. The French also became suspicious of banks after the failure of John Law's Mississippi bubble in 1720. Thousands of investors who had turned their gold into shares of his colonial companies were burned. National banks existed in the seventeenth century in England, Holland, Sweden, and Hamburg, but did not conquer the French fear of "Law's infernal spiral" until two centuries later.

There are historians who believe the French Revolution had essentially fiscal causes, but after 1789 its leaders continued to float worthless bills called *assignats,* which by 1796 were worth one thousandth their nominal value. Napoleon, the great stabilizer, left as one of his principal achievements the Germinal franc, which had an astonishingly long life. A coin containing four and one-half grams of fine silver, it was minted in April, 1803 (Germinal of the year XI in the revolutionary calendar), and its value was maintained until 1927, when Poincaré put the franc on the gold standard and pegged it to the dollar at the rate of roughly five for one.

France enjoyed a stable currency for a century and a quarter, which coincided with the rise of bourgeois power. Indeed it was a condition for the survival of capitalist fortunes, based neither on land nor gold. The Germinal franc was the bourgeois franc; it allowed fortunes to come out of hiding and contribute to economic growth. The link between political power and wealth was property qualifications for voters, which were not done away with until the 1848 Revolution. France in the nineteenth century was governed by an oligarchy of bourgeois notables who held the nation's pulse because it also held its purse strings. The Germinal franc, as invariable as the platinum meter kept in the Breteuil pavilion in Sèvres, became the measure of personal worth. Victor Hugo was a great poet because he owned a town house on the Place des Vosges. A deputy receiving a delegation of workers said: "You want to have opinions on everything and you couldn't raise ten thousand francs in annual income among you."

With its distrust of the out-sized and the outsider, French industry preferred family firms, as secretive about production and cost control as the Père Grandet was about his gold louis. The bourgeois ethic of family limitation led to underpopulation. France, which could no longer count on military superiority, compensated for its manpower deficit with loans to foreign powers which diverted capital from industrial growth but helped purchase useful alliances. The Paris stock market became an instrument of foreign policy. When the government wanted to improve its relations with a foreign country, it welcomed its stock issues on the Paris exchange; in 1912, 72 percent of the stocks quoted on the Paris exchange were non-French. The Crédit Lyonnais bank, which touted Russian bonds for a quarter of a century, took pride in its refusal to invest in French industry. "Do you know how many companies this establishment has financed?" its founder Henri Germain would ask. "None, I am happy to say."

The customs tariff was an idea of Colbert's, who was Minister of Finance from 1661 to 1683, and whose tariff schedule of 1664 remained in use long after his death. Contempt for the customer begins with Colbert, who created national manufactures like Gobelins and Sèvres, and made sure there could be no competition, either foreign or domestic. Quality and costs were high, and Colbert could say what French salesmen have been telling their customers ever since: "If you don't like our product that's your hard luck." American shoppers who wonder why French salesgirls seem so determined to ignore them can tell themselves it is nothing personal. Centuries of protectionism have helped develop what, by opposition to the hard sell and the soft sell, might be called the anti-sell. The anti-sell mentality was expressed by the woman in the stationery store on the rue de Rennes, who in winter greeted customers with the words: "Shut the door quickly, you are letting the heat out." The customer is that barely tolerable nuisance who is responsible for drafts. I realized that this phobia has a summer version when on a steaming July day I lifted the cover of an ice-cream freezer in a café to pick out what the French call an Eskimo. A panic-stricken waitress ran toward me, shouting: "Close the lid, close the lid—you are letting the cold out—especially on a day like this." This restrictive mentality is the personal counterpart of economic protectionism.

Bans against foreign products were the outstanding feature of French commercial policy until Louis XVI signed a commercial treaty with England, for which he was widely criticized. But the Revolution brought back high tariffs almost at once. The Convention said it was a patriotic duty to keep foreign goods from entering France, and went further than Colbert, by abolishing the free ports he had created. Protectionism was part of Napoleonic strategy. If the French still use chicory in their coffee and spend millions to subsidize a sugar-beet industry, it is thanks to the emperor's Continental Blockade, which boomeranged when the coffee and cane-sugar colonies fell into the hands of the enemy.

Napoleon III was the first chief of state to enforce free trade with any success. It is fashionable today to write off the second French emperor, as Marx did when he said that history is repeated as farce. But however farcical the goateed, liquid-eyed emperor may have been, he was able to convince French industry that it could meet foreign competition. Thanks to him, Europe had its first free-trade period, which lasted roughly from 1860 to 1892, preceding the Common Market by a century. Protectionism returned under the Third Republic, less as an economic doctrine than a theory of the state. The goal was increase of national power through support of home industry and a favorable trade balance. New tariff laws gave the government power to raise the import duty by decree.

France in the twentieth century reverted to the comfortable mercantilism of Colbert. The belief that France is better off on its own was compatible with the huge World War I loss in men and money. Protectionism, like the Maginot Line, gave a false feeling of security. In 1938 industrial production dropped below the 1928 level. That General de Gaulle was able to reverse this trend and join the Common Market with hardly a murmur from his people is one of his major achievements. It was possible because France enjoyed a position of leadership among the Six and because the French businessman, after ten years of relative prosperity, began to understand the stimulus of competition.

France always thought economic self-sufficiency would make it immune from international financial crises. Part of protectionism is the "I've got mine" mentality, and a lack of sympathy for the financial problems of other countries. The tremor that started in New York on Black Friday, 1929, reached England first and threatened the pound. The Bank of France promptly converted its own pounds into gold. On September 21, 1931, the French government refused to close the Paris Bourse to allow England to go off the gold standard without too much leakage. The franc seemed solid, and like soldiers watching a battle from the ramparts of a fortress, France preferred to withdraw to hopefully invincible positions. But after the devaluation of the pound and the dollar, French capital began to flee because the franc was too highly valued. French goods could not be sold on world markets. There were runs on French banks, and 700 of them failed between 1929 and 1937. In 1936 the franc had to be realigned on the dollar, but that was not enough, and there were devaluations in 1937, 1938, and 1940. Reluctance to devalue had prolonged the crisis. One of the main reasons France became known as the sick man of Europe was that its currency was chronically ailing from 1936 until the general took power in 1958. Inflation became known as *le mal Français,* and its greatest victims continued to be the *rentiers.* From 5 to the dollar, the franc dropped to 500 to the dollar in the devaluation decided by de Gaulle six months after his return to power in 1958.

By changing the place of the decimal point, the Fifth Republic created the New Franc which, like the Germinal franc, was about 5 to the dollar. This psychological rehabilitation was matched by economic growth and sound fiscal policies, so that France has not had to devalue in ten years. But hoarding gold continues to divert capital from economic growth. Hoarding by private persons could be easily ended by adopting the policy of the United States and Great Britain, which makes it illegal for individuals to hold gold, although stopping this venerable privilege would meet with strong resistance. The general, of course, never claimed to be an economist, but he had the alchemist's fondness for the properties of gold: it is yellow, inalterable, has no nationality, and can be pressed into bars, ingots, or coins.

To Evade or Not to Evade

The industry which employs the greatest number of persons in France is tax evasion. Teachers do not declare private lessons, waiters and hairdressers do not declare tips, doctors and lawyers are not required by law to keep detailed accounts, and it is generally estimated that they declare about one-fourth their income. Millionaires with stables call themselves farmers, or they call their country houses cultural centers and their yachts sailing schools, which exempts them from taxes based on visible signs of wealth. According to the only serious study done on French attitudes toward taxes, those who cheat are a minority, but a large and active one.

In 1957 Jean Dubergé polled 1,049 French taxpayers, 32 percent of whom told him they thought there was nothing morally wrong about tax evasion, because "if I declared my real income I'd be ruined," or "when they set the tax rate they account for a certain percentage of fraud," or, as a medical school professor put it, "The state is an abyss which engulfs all the nation's resources, and therefore I feel it is my duty to withhold all I possibly can from the tax collector." The 42 percent of the sample who came out against tax evasion were, like old men denouncing the follies of youth, largely in fiscal categories where fraud is almost impossible. Even then, many said that while they found tax evasion wrong they understood those who indulged.

Whether they cheat on their returns or not, the French feel more strongly about taxes than most people. They are still blowing up tax collectors' offices. One exploded in Lussac, in the Bordeaux region, in 1967, and the following note was left on the scene: "Tax collector—watch out about sending the green forms too early to peasants—first and last warning." (The color of correspondence from tax offices changes from a neutral white to an ominous green to an indignant pink as one falls behind in payments.) What was Poujadisme but a political party founded on fiscal discontent? It seems incredible that a party which made tax evasion its principal *raison d'être* could have won 52 seats in the National Assembly in 1956. But when the government exempted Marshal Juin's estate from inheritance taxes as a gesture of "national recognition," it too was endorsing the notion that taxes are a punishment, since lifting them was a reward.

On one hand the French have sound reasons for mistrusting the equity of their tax systems, but on the other, they have waged successful rear-guard actions to block forms of taxation which are taken for granted in other countries. There was no personal income tax until 1917. Even then it was divided into two separate taxes, one on salaries and one on other forms of income, until 1959. There is not to this day one penny of tax on capital gains.

Income tax on a person's real wealth was a feature in Gaul when it was a colony of the Roman Empire, but when the empire dissolved in 395, the right to tax was part of its dust. Subsequently, the measure of a French king's power lay in his ability to tax. Under weak kings, wise men set forth theories that taxes could be levied only with the approval of his subjects, while a strong king like Louis XIV bolstered the countertheory that taxes are permanent and nonvoluntary, and paid Sorbonne professors to affirm that the property of his subjects belonged to the king by divine right. But the *ancien régime* was never able to enforce an equitable tax, and each new tax was notable mainly for the number of categories it exempted. The men of the Revolution were under the influence of the Physiocrats, who believed land was the only source of wealth, and they voted a property tax. Under the Directoire, this led to the system of the *quatre vieilles* (four old ones), which prevailed until World War I forced the National Assembly to vote an income tax. The Four Old Ones were taxes on land, invested income, licenses (like a hack license), and doors and windows. Only the doors and windows giving on the street were taxed so that tax collectors would not have to invade the privacy of the home. The French income tax today is still based on external signs of wealth like number of servants and kind of car, so that what is being taxed is not necessarily wealth but profligacy. The confusion of the thing itself with its external expression is a constant of French life which in the tax system gains force of law. It is like confusing a handshake with real friendship, a political speech with genuine conviction, or blushing with virtue. When proposals are made to give the income tax a more realistic basis than external signs of wealth, there are pained outcries in the French press about inquisitional methods.

Indirect taxes were abolished in the first fever of the Revolution, only to be restored by Napoleon to help finance his campaigns (he even restored the hated *gabelle,* or salt tax). They continue today to account for 75 percent of total tax revenues. Anyone protesting that indirect taxes are unfair because the poor are taxed the same as the rich on necessities of life like a pack of Gauloises or a bottle of wine should be told that the average taxpayer prefers it that way. While believing that his contribution gives him the right to complain, he is hostile to changes in the system. According to Dubergé's poll, 58 percent favor indirect taxes because they are invisible, they strike all consumers alike, and if you don't want to pay the tax you can give up the product. The French consumer likes the fact that an element of personal choice enters into indirect taxation. Perhaps some have given up smoking as a negative form of tax evasion. This does not mean that they approve of the tax structure, but that they fear any change would be for the worse. The French taxpayer is even wary of tax cuts because he fears some trick. He lives in a world where things are never what they seem, where behind the façade a group of insiders are taking some unfair advantage. School life and barracks life have taught him that as a helpless individual in conflict with an omnipotent state, all he can count on is ruse. The attitude toward taxes is part of the centuries-long deterioration in healthy relations between the citizen and the state. Indifference to tax reforms is an aspect of the *bulletin blanc* mentality. As a history professor explained: "When none of the candidates, the programs, or the parties inspire confidence, I cast a blank vote even if the election of the incumbent is the lesser evil. That way I won't have to reproach myself for having contributed to his election." Taxpayers do complain, however, about red tape. A simple request about the property tax on a piece of land can lead to an open-ended correspondence once it has been established that there are no less than eight different systems for assessing property taxes. The official booklet on French tax laws is 834 pages long and as obscure as *Finnegan's Wake*. The French tax people insist that they are constantly trying to make taxes more humane, and as an example, point to Ministerial Circular 86 of April 19, 1958, which reads: "Even when they are picked from organic matter purchased from third parties, maggots [for fishermen] must be considered products exonerated from the TVA." TVA means tax on the added value, and it is the biggest single French tax, amounting to one-third the total receipts.

It is a tribute to the ability of the French mind to discard simple solutions in favor of elegant but complicated ones. Every consumer product is subject to the TVA as many times as there are steps in its manufacture, distribution, and sale. Take a steel ingot: The iron is taxed when it is mined, taxed again when it is made into steel, taxed again when the ingot is sold to a wholesaler, again when it is used by an appliance factory to make an egg-beater, and again when the eggbeater is sold. At each step, only the increase in the cost of the product is taxed, which favors low-profit, high-volume production. The rate varies from 6 percent for staples like sugar to 20 percent for luxury products like records and furs. The time lost in paper work and accounting at every step is staggering, and the effect on the economy is the reverse of that intended. Instead of encouraging price stability, retailers automatically increase their prices on everything from bread to television sets, explaining that "it's because of the TVA." The consumer accepts what he does not understand.

Even a simple measure like withholding income tax from salaries is impossible in France because of the opposition of employers, 80 percent of whom refuse to cooperate because "it's not our job to be tax collectors." The French tax structure remains one of the most complicated and least democratic of any Western nation. Indirect taxes lighten the tax load of the rich, and personal income tax is still in its infancy, even though the number of families paying it has quadrupled from 3,000,000 in 1954 to 12,000,000 in 1968. The system is, however, relatively lenient. Payment is usually open to arrangement following protracted negotiations. The state cannot jail a citizen for a tax offense; it can only seize his property, except for his bed, anything sealed into the wall, a month's supply of food, professional tools, military equipment, and the fur coat that he or she may be wearing.

The reforms of the Fifth Republic have tended to lighten the tax load of corporations and nonsalaried income. The minority of Frenchmen who own stocks are tremendously advantaged since they pay no capital gains tax and enjoy a 50 percent exemption on dividends, intended to encourage stock investment. In addition, there are several perfectly legal ways for wealthy men to evade inheritance taxes, like buying Pinay bonds or tax-free forested land. The days when the clergy and the nobility were exempted from the *taille* (*ancien régime* income tax) are not over; the privileged groups have simply changed. Today they are the owners of capital and the farmers, whose income represents 12 percent of the national product, but whose taxes are only 1½ percent of the total. Government tends to regard the farmers as the sacred cows of the French economy. They not only have their own tax system, but their own social security and their own bureaucracy. All the Ministry of Agriculture lacks to become an independent government is its own army and its own courts.

Despite tax advantages, the Frenchman remains suspicious of the stock market and of big business as a whole. Is it because industry is the denial of a rural civilization and a lost *douceur de vivre?* Is it the memory of the brutal changes that accompanied the Industrial Revolution, child labor and the exploitation of the proletariat? Is it the esthetic awareness that whatever industry touches it sullies, or the moral attitude born of financial scandals which involved people in high places? Or is it the collaborationist stigma of big business during World War II? In any case, the French behave as though the four statues on the corners of the Paris Bourse were antithetical—Justice contradicting Fortune and Abundance contradicting Caution. Only 3 percent of the population owns stocks, as compared with 10 percent in the United States. In 1958 the total value of stocks was less than 1 billion dollars, while private ownership of gold totaled four times that amount.

The belief prevails that the market is for insiders eager to fleece the retired civil servants barely subsisting on small pensions and the pale spinsters who live with their cats. Investment is considered a form of gambling rather than an expression of confidence in the country's economic growth. There is some basis for this belief, since the French market is so lacking in regulation that it invites wild speculation. There is no French equivalent of the Securities Exchange Commission. There are no margin requirements, which makes the Paris Bourse the temple of inside tips, paper profits, and fortunes made and lost on margin. French companies, far from making their balance sheets attractive to investors, downgrade their profits for tax purposes. Finally, the stockbrokers are a tiny clique (83 in Paris), appointed by the government from father to son. They are, curiously, prohibited by law from giving market advice to their customers. They are considered neutral agents of the sale and purchase of stocks.

A Little Help from the State

French capitalism has been shaped by protectionism, mistrust of industry, periods of unsuccessful flirtation with foreign bonds, an attachment to gold resulting from inflation and currency manipulations and, more important than the rest, an ever-spreading practice of government planning. The French economy has been described as bisexual, part free enterprise and part state-controlled. The national preference for trained rather than natural growth finds an ideal target in the economy. Every French regime has manipulated economic levers to attain its goals. The Fifth Republic encourages the decentralization of industry with rebates on electricity and railway transportation costs that come out of the taxpayer's pocket. Government is also the nation's biggest employer: 400 companies, including most of the energy and transportation companies, are nationalized or mixed.

Vigorous state intervention was also a feature of the *ancien régime;* the state had a monopoly on gunpowder, weapons, and dockyards. Louis XIV made the sale of Nicot's weed (named for Jean Nicot, a sixteenth-century diplomat who imported tobacco into France) a royal monopoly, and in 1810 Napoleon made tobacco a government-operated industry, which today contributes roughly 5 percent to the budget. Distribution is handled by 50,000 concessionaires (*tabacs*), who sell postage stamps as part of their duties, generally with bad grace. The purpose of the government-run firm (Régie des Tabacs) which controls the manufacture and sale of cigarettes is to spur the consumer to smoke more. In 1959 its director, Grimanelli, deplored that France was only sixth in tobacco consumption, behind the United States, Belgium, Holland, Great Britain, and Switzerland. The French government finds itself in the peculiar position of stimulating lung cancer, while other countries are trying to devise legislation to curtail smoking.

Nationalization of the instruments of production, Marx's principal demand in the *Communist Manifesto,* came about as a result of war, not revolution. France recovered Alsace-Lorraine after World War I and placed the potash mines and the railroads under government care. Using its right to exploit German patents, the government built and operated an ammonia plant in Toulouse. Shares in Turkish oil companies were another item in the World War I bounty which led the government to become the principal shareholder in the Compagnie Française des Petroles. Between the wars the government diversified. It bought an interest in shipping lines in 1920, held 25 percent of the stock when Air France was formed in 1927, set up a government-run broadcasting system in 1928, took over the ailing Transatlantique steamship line in 1933, and nationalized the railroads and the armaments industry in 1936.

The last and biggest nationalization wave came in 1946, during General de Gaulle's first brief period of power. The image of big business had been tarnished by widespread collaboration with the Germans, and the business community was too guilt-ridden and afraid of purges to resist the measures. Gas and electricity were nationalized, as were the 4 largest banks, which totaled among them half the deposits in France, and the 34 biggest insurance companies. The coal mines were nationalized, and today are part of a huge industrial complex called the Charbonnages de France, which also manufactures rubber, fertilizers, chemicals, and synthetic fibers.

The government took over the country's biggest car works from the collaborator Louis Renault. Since so many public industries have ancillary activities, one can never be sure today whether a given product is made by the state or by private firms. State-run Sud Aviation makes washing machines, and the state-run Havas agency makes the distressing advertising shorts that are shown to a captive audience during intermission in French movie houses.

The government believes that because it is disinterested it is in a better position to run businesses. The experience of private enterprise, on the contrary, is that it is successful insofar as it is interested in profits. Some state-run businesses survive only because they are subsidized, just as in the nineteenth century the state kept sailing clippers afloat after the steamship had made them obsolete, and encouraged the use of canals after railways had provided cheaper and quicker transportation. Government-run businesses are not managed primarily to make money, but are part of an overall program of political and social goals. The railroad runs a huge deficit because hardly anyone pays the full fare and because seldom-used lines are kept up to save declining regions. It encourages featherbedding to keep down the unemployment rate, and railway express rates are set ridiculously low. It has been seriously suggested that the railroad would cost the taxpayer less if it were free. The government spends three times more on making up the 25 percent deficit in the railroad budget than it spends on highway construction. The size of the deficit doubled between 1961 and 1965.

Another danger is political appointments. Just as men with no diplomatic experience are named ambassadors in the American foreign service, Frenchmen with no business experience are named to high posts in nationalized industries. Yvon Morandat became head of the Charbonnages de France on the basis of his record as a Resistance hero, and Paris police prefect Maurice Papon was named head of Sud Aviation, even though it was rumored that he once asked where the propeller on a jet plane was. With political appointments, the government acknowledges that top executive talent is not needed to run these firms, and would in fact balk at policies like mining coal that can not be marketed or making Caravelle airplanes that are sold at a loss to enhance French prestige. Private businessmen, like contractors who have to work in close cooperation with the nationalized sector, complain that as soon as the state is involved, costs double. A contractor who has built 25 apartment buildings on the Côte d'Azur said that he has never been able to get the people from the gas, electricity, and water departments to agree to install their services together in the same utilities ditch. "Government departments are only interested in raising costs to make their balance sheets look good," he said, "and the civil servant is jealous of the entrepreneur. 'What are you complaining about?' he says. 'You are feathering your nest.' They push the poor but honest attitude to the point where it paralyzes business."

Nationalized industry is a part of the overall government system of economic planning. The government decides it should help an underprivileged region like Brittany. It builds a plant in a region with idle manpower, even though it is uneconomical. A site will be picked in the Vendée countryside to make automobile gear shifts, with the assurance that deficits will be met at the end of the fiscal year by the government. Planning is a euphemism for self-fulfilling prophecy. It is like predicting that an individual will eat more if he gets fat. The government sets economic goals and then implements them with its many levers. The planners hope for a steady rate of growth, venture without risk, a form of capitalism sheltered from uncontrollable booms and busts. Economic growth is provoked, just as oysters are provoked into secreting cultured pearls. The Commissariat du Plan, with its 4,500 consultant-experts, sets long-term objectives. It builds up a library of industrial data, makes market studies, predicts business trends, coordinates the expansion of competing firms in the same fields, and helps firms obtain government financing for projects it approves.

Planning becomes a vast cartel of private and government-run businesses, controlled by public administration and financed by government-run banks. The First Plan (1947–53) put France back on its feet after the war. It channeled Marshall Plan aid, rebuilt heavy industry, and was credited with soaring production and a 30 percent rise in the standard of living. The Second Plan

(1954–57) was aimed at curbing inflation despite the cost of the Algerian war and the 1956 Suez expedition. The Third Plan (1958–61) was intended to adapt France to the competition of the Common Market, but its goals were not attained, while the Fourth and Fifth Plans (1962–70), were generally aimed at social and economic development. The Fifth Plan had some notable successes. It helped the port of Le Havre handle a greater amount of tonnage than Antwerp in 1967, for the first time in its history. In doing so it awakened the sluggish Le Havre notables to the advantages of expansion and competition.

But it was shaken in its objectives by the economic repercussions of the May-June disorders in 1968. The nature of the Plan, however, is to incorporate events into its previsions, and an interim report was published in November, 1968, to explain that May-June was a warning tremor rather than a real quake. Thus the omniscient Plan absorbed the student-worker revolt. The revolt, said the report, was caused by youths' refusal of a future that seemed plotted for them, coupled with fears of an uncertain future. This is like saying that a man has killed himself because he hated life and loved it too much. It is less an attempt to explain than a method for encompassing all possible explanations. Anyone accustomed to a free-enterprise economy will find the Plan a highly technical example of wishful thinking. But General de Gaulle called it "an ardent obligation," and experts are already working on the Sixth Plan (1971–75). But in a Common Market framework the definition of national economic goals will become less meaningful. Holland has given up its Plan, and concentrates on good management rather than a planned economy.

The French Brahmins

The key figure of the French economy is not, however, the Planner, but the Controller. Millions in public funds are spent to subsidize archaic farms and firms, but each cent is repeatedly controlled by the Ministry of Finance. Once payment is authorized it is controlled again by a civil servant called an *ordonnateur* who issues a payment warrant, and once the money is spent an Inspector of Finance makes sure it has been well spent. The French system is a unique combination of economic waste and financial overscrupulousness. It helps explain why in France there is plenty of pork-barreling but almost no graft. The Inspector of Finance, a post created by Napoleon to audit the expenditure of public funds, has grown in stature to become something very different from a mere auditor. The disparity between the ostensible task and the real power of the inspectors is enormous. They are young men who do well in their exams at the school which recruits high civil servants, the École Nationale d'Administration. They graduate at the head of their class, called the "boot," which gives them the pick of civil service careers, including the foreign service. The fact that the boot almost always picks the Inspection of Finances is an initial proof of its prestige.

The young inspector takes on the tedious job of traveling through France auditing the accounts of tax offices, prefectures, and nationalized industries. He counts the wagons in railroad yards, and the pastepots on secretarial desks. He is met by unsmiling old-timers who resent his poking into the details of their work. He is the itinerant conscience of the public administration, checking on the honesty and efficiency of his fellow civil servants. But the inspectors form a tiny elite who soon gravitate from what they themselves call Purgatory to the command posts of the nation's economy. Only six examples of this rare species are produced each year. In 1968 there was a total of 237 active and 121 retired inspectors. The list is a guide to the French corridors of power and includes former Premier Maurice Couve de Murville, cabinet ministers, the president of the National Assembly Jacques Chaban-Delmas, and the directors of half a dozen of the principal banks.

Inspectors of Finance are traveling accountants in their twenties, on an $8-per-diem and a $300-per-month salary, *chefs de cabinet* in their thirties, cabinet ministers in their forties, and chairmen of the board in private industry in their fifties. They run the economy by virtue of having nosed ahead by a few percentile points in a final examination. Seldom has such a minute initial advantage, comparable to the tenths of seconds that divide Olympic runners, made such a difference in men's lives. Once the pale and overworked student in his early twenties has passed this essential hurdle, the rest of his life will seem like an anticlimax as he finds the doors of leadership opening automatically before him. This closed caste continues to be recruited among the middle and high bourgeoisie. A 1952 study on their social origins showed not a single one from a working-class or farmer background, while 80 percent came from bourgeois families, and 48 were the sons of high civil servants.

The days when the students had to appear for final examinations in tails ended in 1914, but formalism and icy articulateness are still highly prized, as is the image of the well-rounded individual who can discuss the quarrel over Manet's "Olympia" as fluently as the means of stimulating investment in an underdeveloped economy. Chaban-Delmas is still remembered for his brilliant ten-minute dissertation on the pediment of the Paris church of the Madeleine. Graduates like to pattern themselves on the eighteenth-century *honnête homme,* and are expected to maintain the delicate balance of cordiality and distance which marks the civil service elite. The director of the ENA, in a little speech to graduating students, makes a passing reference to correct behavior with the opposite sex. "Be good," he says in English, "and if you can't be good, be careful."

No other country has such a narrow and irreversible system of selection for the nation's levers of command. The English Old Boys' establishment and the American Ivy League mafia seem broadly based and democratic when compared with the method of tapping six young men each year to be ordained as high priests of the national economy. The dogma transmitted by each generation to the next is an intellectual method that is juridical, Cartesian, and conservative. At the outset, the inspectors are given full responsibility on their rounds of verification. They arrive unannounced in a provincial prefecture, like judges before whom the accused must prove his innocence. Their careers depend on accomplishing this meticulous control without error, no matter how varied the problem. One week the inspector will be controlling the books of a nationalized bank and the following week those of a hospital or a cigarette factory. They must be able to assimilate new situations and not be intimidated by specialists.

Early in their careers they become dry technocrats concerned with bookkeeping, remote from human problems. Under the system of mutual control, the inspector writes his findings in one column of a report and the agency under inspection can reply in a parallel column and show him up. This encourages circumspection and an obsession with always being right, qualities not necessarily at a premium in private business. The inspectors are soon detached from the job for which they were trained, to direct some of the public services which they had previously inspected. Their technical competence is also much in demand in ministerial cabinets, although the Fifth Republic has set a style for "technical ministers." The belief arises that cabinet ministers are manipulated by technocrats, that "it is the Inspectors of Finance who run France."

After fifteen years of public service, the inspector can resign and take a job in private business where his knowledge of the administration will be as much in demand as is a retired American general's familiarity with the Pentagon by a firm with defense contracts. The inspector who becomes chairman of a private bank is on close personal terms with the people he has to deal with at the Ministry of Finance. Perhaps he says *tu* to the minister's *chef de cabinet*. He knows the vocabulary and the short cuts through a maze of regulations. A company that has frequent dealings with the state needs its Inspector of Finance as badly as an explorer in the Amazonian jungle needs a guide. Since at the peak of his government career his salary will not exceed $15,000 per year, the only motivations to remain in public service are the chance for one of the plums, like Governor of the Bank of France, an idiosyncratic preference for low-paid, uninspiring work, or the notion that private industry is somehow sullied compared with the selfless integrity of high government service. These reasons still keep many inspectors from making the leap to affluence. Roughly one-third take private jobs when they reach the age of forty, a practice known as *pantouflage* (putting on a pair of comfortable slippers). More and more, the ruthless selection and the long years of badly paid government service are being considered an apprenticeship for worldly rewards: a listing in the *Bottin Mondain* (the Paris Social Register), which enumerates in conventional symbols the decorations, membership in one or two good clubs like the Interallié, and a castle in the country. The idea is that if you cannot have one of the handful of government jobs in which you can dictate to the wealthy, the next best thing is to join them. Whatever side of the teller's cage the inspector is on, his economic philosophy is based on strong state intervention.

Passage from the public to the private sector is exactly the reverse of what takes place in the United States, where the top talent from the business and legal communities is recruited for public service at considerable personal sacrifice. Having proved his value in private enterprise, the American executive is in demand for top government jobs. The French high civil servant, having proved himself at the service of the state, is in demand by the business community. The Inspector of Finance becomes a Président-Directeur-Général, an executive title created by Vichy law in 1940 and borrowed from the German *führer-prinzip*. The inspector joins a group where he can feel at home, for 50 percent of his fellow executives are, like him, graduates of a *grande école* like the ENA or the military engineering school, Polytechnique. As an official in the Ministry of Finance said: "When I want to call someone at IBM Paris, I look down the executive list and I see twenty persons who were in my class at X [Polytechnique]." It is all very cozy.

Since the French executive is formed most often as an engineer or a public servant, he tends to be more concerned with the technical and administrative side of business. There is a growing reaction to the limitations of this training, and some firms, like Schlumberger Limited, refuse to hire graduates of the ENA.

An example of the maddening attitude of the ENA graduate was given me by an American banker who went to see Jean Dromer, an ambitious and capable Inspector of Finance and close collaborator of then Minister of Finance Michel Debré, about opening a Paris branch. The American, in fluent French, said he was going to develop three main points, and he went on to discuss related matters. About five minutes later he was interrupted by Dromer, who said dryly: "But monsieur, you have not mentioned your third point," like a teacher correcting a wayward student. This is the slide-rule mentality which continues to consider every problem in terms of the parallel columns of an accountant's report, where the inspected official has a right of reply. The men in power coopt in the succeeding generation those most capable of adhering to the same mentality that made them successful. Mental habits become starched like their collars. The fetish for an elegant, irreproachable presentation is such that a

French executive admits: "In France, when a problem is well presented the solution is adopted even if the solution is not as good as the presentation."

The Divine Right Patron

Business, like every other area of French life, is burdened with archaic attitudes and traditions which have outlived the era for which they were suited. The feudal period of French business, in which the *patron* or boss patterned his relations with employees and executives on those between a lord and his vassals, is only now changing under the pressure of international mergers, competition, and foreign investment in French firms. In the nineteenth century business dynasties were formed like fiefs; the Schneiders in the Creusot, Michelin in Clermont-Ferrand. Their owners felt vested with a mission of total authority over the public and private lives of their employees.

The Schneider brothers, who built a huge foundry at the time of the first railroads in the 1830's, turned the pastoral township of Le Creusot into an austere industrial colony. They built low-rent housing, hospitals, schools, and churches which the workers and their families were ordered to attend. Two and one-half percent of the workers' salaries was withheld for the upkeep of these facilities. The Schneiders strengthened their control, thanks to alliances with church and state. They were mayors of Le Creusot from father to son and some became deputies. Eugene Schneider, the best-known and most flamboyant lord of Le Creusot, was president of the National Assembly. The expression "divine-right *patron*" was coined for him. He had a private theater built in the turreted castle that overlooked Le Creusot from a hilltop, and he acted in plays, like a Roman emperor, before an audience of his family and a few discreet friends. After his fatal heart attack in 1942, which followed by a month the English bombardment of his factory, the bishop of Autun came to sprinkle holy water on the statue erected in his honor in the center of town. Several generations earlier, in 1888, the Vicar-General of France had come to Le Creusot to deliver a sermon to the workers on the theme that intellectual work is more demanding than manual labor. Strikes, as the state attorney under the Second Empire said, were the blackest ingratitude against a management devoted to spreading well-being. Regiments of soldiers were sent to Le Creusot to break a strike in 1870 and were personally handed two cigars apiece by one of the Schneiders. The Autun courts gave Jean Valjean-type sentences to arrested strikers and petty thieves (three months in prison for stealing two kilos of coal).

In some of its social programs Le Creusot was far ahead of its time. The infant mortality rate was 30 percent lower than the national average. The health and pension plans were models adopted later by other industries. But was this form of paternalism different from the feudal lord's awareness that a serf cannot work the land on an empty stomach? Le Creusot grew, reaching a population of 38,000 in 1914, but it was no less ugly and sooty. There was no public transportation because the Schneiders believed in the virtues of walking. Even the fair grounds and the public gardens and walks belonged to the company and could be closed if the workers grew restive. The education was clerical, and children were herded weekly to the confessional from the age of seven. Workers removed their caps in the presence of Schneiders. The personality cult was encouraged. When Adolphe Schneider fell from a horse in 1845 and his head splattered like a watermelon on a sharp rock, the blood-stained rock was kept like a holy relic.

When Eugene Schneider succeeded his father in 1898, he raised the minimum pension from 360 to 365 francs, like a king making the traditional gift to the nation upon succeeding to the throne. Like kings, the Schneiders reached their majority at the age of six, and their coronation consisted in lighting a blast furnace. In 1874 six-year-old Charles-Prosper was badly burned during the ceremony. The workers had free coal in the winter, free coffee in the summer, and a company orchestra whose members were paid regular wages during rehearsals. The Schneiders also had a royal passion for building—a home for orphans, a maternity clinic, a sports stadium, and workshops for apprentices went up over the years. It was incomprehensible to the Schneiders that with all these advantages the workers should strike. Finally, Eugène Schneider formed a company union, which expressed in its statute the wish "to establish and maintain with the company directors relations based on dignity, discipline, and respect."

The French word for scab (*jaune*) was coined because the head of the union lived in a yellow house. The Schneiders ruled Le Creusot until World War II, firing workers suspected of Socialism and controlling everything from employees' funerals to the cost of gas and electricity. Le Creusot declined along with the iron age, but although the fiefs no longer exist, the ideology lingers. Shy, jug-eared François Michelin inherited a rubber products empire from his dying grandfather when he was twelve years old. The fact that he was unable to qualify for a *grande école* did not matter, for he surrounded himself with graduates of Polytechnique imbued with respect for the dynastic character of the firm. Michelin won control of another dynasty, Citroën, after its founder André Citroën gambled himself into debt at the Deauville casino.

The pecking order in such firms is established according to family connection or rank in competitive examinations rather than performance in the job. Nepotism also exists in the nationalized industries, and Pierre le Faucheux, the capable former director of Renault, sent his nephew to direct the stagnant United States operation in the early 1950's. The nephew got things done because he had a direct line to the home office. There are French families that breed executives the way Irish families breed priests. Once ordained, the struggle in this life is over. Raoul de Vitry, president of France's biggest aluminum producer, Pechiney, has six sons, four of whom are like himself Polytechniciens. There are also firms like the French Sears Roebuck, La Redoute, in which the Président-Directeur-Général, who happens to be the son of the founder, visits the plant each day like a laird making the rounds of his manor, in the belief that his employees will be stimulated to higher productivity by the sight. This does not prevent mail-order sales in France from being only 1 percent of the total retail trade, as against 8 percent in the United States.

The French *patron's* attitude toward his workers is that they are paid to do a job, not to have a voice in the operation of the firm. They are expected, like good children, to be seen on time and not heard. After World War II, General de Gaulle passed a law which made workers' committees (*comités d'entreprise*) mandatory for firms with more than 50 employees. Fear of these committees has led *patrons* to perform acrobatics with their books and their personnel to keep the legal number of full-time employees from reaching the fateful 50. Some themes of divine-right *patronat* are still articles of faith: that some degree of unemployment is a useful means of pressure against the workers; that the *patron* is master of his own house, so that union activities must be barred from the plant—overzealous union delegates are transferred to plants far from their homes or fired on trumped-up cases of professional negligence; that the government should allow cheap foreign labor into the country—Citroën has a high percentage of Spanish and Portuguese workers with no job security, and maintains gray-uniformed private policemen officially called interpreters to intimidate unruly migrant workers; that French products should concentrate on the domestic market and neglect the export market; that investments should be made with extreme caution; and that secrecy about technical developments and balance sheets is the cardinal virtue. When General de Gaulle visited the purposely drab, unobtrusive Michelin headquarters in Clermont-Ferrand in 1959, the members of his entourage were kept outside. I once listened in astonishment as the commercial director of one of the leading manufacturers of scales in France repeated the nineteenth-century argument that increasing the workers' wages would only lead them to squander more money in cafés.

It is only since 1968 that unions have won the right to recruit, hold meetings, and collect dues on company time. "It is a revolution," said the business monthly *Entreprise*. "Your father taught you never to forget a wedding or a birth, to buy a drink from time to time for the workers that complain the most, and if necessary, to slip a man a bill now and again. . . . But above all no unions. They are professional agitators . . . but now a modern executive must admit the existence of the unions."

The habit of authoritarianism makes the French executive reluctant to delegate responsibilities; he spends an inordinate amount of time on policelike surveillance of his staff. The French director of an American-controlled firm in Paris insisted on personally examining the huge pile of daily incoming mail. His American chairman gently mentioned the amount of time it took. "A secretary can do it," he said.

"No, I'd rather do it myself," said the director. "That way I can ferret out mistakes."

"If this was the States," confided the American, "I could tell him 'look, this is a goddam waste of time,' but here I've got to find some Machiavellian subterfuge to get him out of the habit without his realizing it, so that his feelings won't be hurt."

In another Paris company, the director is famous for listening in on his staff's telephone conversations on a special hookup. A French firm is reluctant to fire an executive who doesn't measure up, not only because of the severance pay involved, but because it is afraid he knows too much and will peddle it to the competition. I asked a French PDG what he thought about Carlsen, the head of General Motors, going to work for Ford. "That would be impossible in France," he said. "If the head of Citroën wanted to go over to Peugeot, Peugeot would never hire him, they would be afraid he would do the same thing to them." Suspicion extends to technical innovations. When Sven Nielsen, the Danish-born magnate of French publishing, decided to sell books with the pages already cut, his competitors predicted his demise, saying "the French reader wants to cut the pages himself." Nielsen today controls a highly successful federation of more than a dozen publishers.

Close cooperation between private industry and government can also lead to counterproductive practices. When Chrysler took control of the Simca automobile firm in the 1950's, Chrysler executives were sent to work alongside their Simca colleagues. One Chrysler director watched his Simca *vis-à-vis* spend half an hour on the telephone with the *chef de cabinet* of the Minister of Posts and Communications pleading for an extra telephone line. At the end he looked up triumphantly and said: "I've got it."

"If you were the head of an American company and spent that much time on that kind of trivia, you wouldn't last long," the Chrysler man said.

The French executive, his American counterpart found, takes longer to do almost everything. Hiring a secretary is like casting a difficult part in a play. The French PDG is overfond of the prestige attached to his job and tends to neglect its commercial aspects. The commercial director of an English firm who was spending one day in Paris tried to see the PDG of a French firm, but he had not arrived on the day the PDG "receives" and no exception could be made. An American executive grows impatient because his French counterpart does not stick to business, because his interests are not rigidly compartmentalized. The Frenchman refuses to be regimented and is proud of his broad cultural interests. The French executive tends to be aloof with his employees. It does no good, as the U.S.-trained director of a Paris private bank found out, to say "My door is always open—if something is wrong come in and see me." No one ever does. The employee too has become affected by the long tenure of the divine-right *patron*. He still receives his thirteenth month, a custom that perpetuates paternalism, since it is a gratuity rather than an earned pay raise, and makes accounting a nightmare.

Lack of mobility is common to both employees and executives. In some regions of France there is unemployment while in others good jobs go begging. The French workingman will not migrate where the jobs are. He is in a cocoon made up of family, cronies, and habits, and the prospect of a better salary will not induce him to leave it. The rent freezes that prevailed until 1964 were a major factor in the sedentary nature of French labor, for once a family found a long lease at a low rent, they refused to move. Mobility was tied to the housing shortage. The same is true of executives; those in Paris consider a transfer to the provinces a personal humiliation, while those recruited in the provinces tend to view a promotion to the Paris headquarters as an unacceptable hardship.

Americans working with French businessmen also tax them with being overly sarcastic and negative in their thinking. They have a compulsion for finding reasons why things cannot or should not be done. One American who is on a board of directors with about a dozen French executives reports it is like a miniature National Assembly. Parties are formed, speeches are delivered, and political rhetoric is adapted to business decisions. Petty jealousies, intrigues, and affectations of mystery interfere with business policy.

The human element was one reason why Renault had such problems in the United States. Renault attacked the American car market after World War II like a French foot soldier attacking a German Panzer division. There was no market research or study of legal requirements for imported cars. A young man working in the New York office was sent urgently to Los Angeles where 300 Renaults were stranded at dockside; U.S. customs would not let them enter the country because their headlights and taillights did not comply with the state of California's motor vehicle laws. Because of competing clans in the home office, it took years to get decisions to move from a hangarlike Broadway showroom to one more consistent with French elegance, on Park Avenue, and to get better finish and paint jobs on export models, doors that didn't fall off when you yanked them, and to develop a new sales concept to sell the Renault as a second car. These are problems non-French firms seldom have. It is the kind of thinking that led the Marseilles olive oil industry to sneer when a Dunkirk firm began to market its oil in plastic bottles thereby winning the lion's share of the market, and led it to neglect the by-product of detergents, a gap that was filled by Procter & Gamble. The French PDG drowns in detail, he feels he must do both his job and his subordinates', whom he underpays since he is unwilling to give them any responsibilities.

The *patronat* does little to change its image. Since 1854 there has been an equivalent of the National Association of Manufacturers, first called the Committee of Ironworks (Comité des Forges), and renamed the National Council of French Patrons in 1945. It maintains traditions of secrecy and political influence. When Roger Priouret, one of the most reliable writers on economics, asked to see the Comité des Forges archives to prepare a book on the French *patron*, he was turned down. The council, however, was unable to keep the secret of its pay-offs to deputies at election time.

Price-fixing is another nebulous notion. Fixing the price of drugs is perfectly legal. Pharmacies have a monopoly on the sale of drugs, and nationwide prices are fixed at a profit margin of 32 percent. The French attitude is to avoid competition and to regulate prices whenever feasible. Nor have there ever been any French antitrust suits. Many large firms were absorbed by the state. A private firm like Hachette, which prints, publishes, and distributes a high percentage of France's written matter, would in the United States have long since been dismantled as a trust illegally controlling the market. But in France, Hachette is useful to the government; one of its publishing houses, Gallimard, was known as Gaullimard.

The *patronat*, however, did not have the ear of de Gaulle, but the days when a government could be toppled as was René

Pleven's because he was about to make the social security system more costly for employers seem to be over. Today the *patrons* have, rather than a consistent political doctrine, a sum of complaints about the cost of the *force de frappe,* the subsidies to peasants, the counterproductive anti-Americanism, and the threat of participation, in which the workers would have a voice in the operation of the plant. Many *patrons* feel that this "third way between capitalism and Communism" is quite simply the way of chaos.

The Breeze of Change

Still the French attitudes toward money are slowly changing, both on the individual and corporate level. In the present phase, old and new patterns coexist. There is a mixture of suspiciousness and daring. A banker trying to persuade investors in Lyons with portfolios of $50,000 and $100,000 to buy into the American market met with polite refusals. "The U.S. economy can't hold up with all these racial problems," he was told. Bankers complain that long-term capital is chronically rare because the government savings accounts drain off a high percentage of potential investors' money.

But at the same time, the basic option to compete on the international market has been taken by French business, and habits of centuries are in the process of changing. The Oréal company, which makes toilet articles, is largely responsible for persuading the French to wash their hair. They still use five times less soap per capita than Americans. As one of my aunts once said: "I take a bath once a year whether I'm dirty or not." Oréal marketed Dop shampoo in inexpensive little plastic cubes which became a fad and created a habit. There are still musty general stores called *au petit profit,* where withered and bent old ladies sell a few buttons and a spool of thread (400,000 stores have an annual volume of business of less than $4,000), but there are also more than 1,000 supermarkets. The lady who asked her husband "Why are American housewives always forgetting their shopping bags?" after attending American movies in which she saw them carrying the groceries in paper bags, is becoming an exception. The French are still not entirely reconciled to advertising and tend to agree with the philosopher Alain, who said: "Imagine a pretty girl who would hire a lawyer to argue the case of her looks." But advertising budgets are growing and advertising has made the big breakthrough now that French television has agreed to accept commercials and the Commissariat for Tourism is using private ad agencies to attract foreign visitors.

The threat of American companies is another incentive to the French businessman. American businesses with French branches are not concerned with national economic policies. If a factory is not making money, it is closed down, regardless of the employment picture. Conversely, conflicts arise between French branches and home-office policy. The French branch of the Freuhauf trailer company obtained a contract to supply trailers to Red China, but it was vetoed by the home office. American branches in France tend to become sales counters, with research facilities remaining in the home country. Large firms specialize: IBM makes electric typewriters in Holland and 360 computers in Montpellier. Other companies have European branches simply to assemble parts made in the U.S. As Servan-Schreiber pointed out in *The American Challenge*, the logic of business forces the United States to practice a sophisticated form of economic colonialism, a challenge which may spur the French to renovate their own business practices.

In 1969 the French business world was shaken by the first takeover bid in its history, a sign that the period of stagnant management and contempt for the stockholder is coming to an end. BSN (Boussois-Souchon-Neuvesel), a small, dynamic, market-oriented glass firm with young executives, made a vigorous although unsuccessful bid to take control of the largest French glass manufacturer, Saint-Gobain, a tradition-bound, incentive-stifling firm. A move which in the United States would have seemed commonplace, seemed revolutionary in France.

The monopoly of *fils à papa* and graduates of *grandes écoles* in top jobs shows signs of ending too, as does the secret shame of profit. A firm like Télémécanique, the third biggest manufacturer of electromagnetic contactors in the world, promoted a skilled workman with a sixth-grade education to the executive level. The salaries of its executives are made public. Employee salaries have increased, thanks to a profit-sharing program, and employees own

15 percent of the company's stock. To accept the profit motive, to change jobs in response to new opportunities, are concepts which French management is in the process of digesting. Raoul de Vitry, head of Pechiney, recalls that when he was hired as a young government mining engineer, he had the following conversation with the director:

"What is your present salary?"

"One hundred thousand francs."

"I can give you eighty thousand."

"With what title?"

"I would prefer that you did not ask me for a title."

"What about a contract?"

"I would prefer that you did not ask me for a contract."

The promising young executive was expected to make a financial sacrifice and forgo job security as proof of his zeal to join the firm.

The economic habits of the French have changed more in the last twenty years than in the previous century, despite the persistence of old ways. It used to be said that the Frenchman wins his bread (*gagner son pain*), but today he defends his beefsteak (*defendre son biftek*). Bread consumption has gone down from 185 kilos per person in 1914 to 110 in 1962. Only Americans and Canadians eat more meat than the French. The ideal French beef would have two rear ends and be all steak, but until such an animal is bred, the French will continue to export the front end of the beef and keep the rear end. The standard of living has doubled since the war. The number of private cars went from 2,000,000 to 5,000,000 between 1953 and 1963. Families who scorned bathtubs are now buying dishwashers and installing swimming pools. Most incredibly, the French are beginning to pay rent. The principal reason there was practically no new housing built between the two World Wars was that deputies were elected in 1921 on the promise of freezing rents for World War I veterans. The law was passed and extended year by year because no government was strong enough to rescind it. Seldom has an electoral promise been so catastrophic for a national economy. Poor housing too is a French constant, and in the complaints the three estates were asked to draw up in 1789, the Paris Third Estate said that workers were spending 50 percent of their income on rent. A major effort in housing has been made since 1964, however: 400,000 units have been built. Taxes on the sale of property have been reduced from 22 to 11 percent.

But most important, frozen rents have thawed. They rose 64 percent between 1963 and 1967. A cousin of mine almost had apoplexy when he was told the rent on his three-bedroom apartment overlooking the elegant Parc Monceau was going to be raised to $100 a month. It is the kind of apartment with two living rooms, a dowdy one that is lived in and another one splendidly furnished in Louis XVI, with an eighteenth-century bronze clock, portraits of ancestors by Nattier, a Savonnerie carpet, and a *bonheur-du-jour* signed "Riesener." It is only disturbed for eminent guests. Then, and only then, are the baccarat brandy decanters, the marquise de Sévigné after-dinner mints, and the box of stale Cuban cigars brought forth, as though from a safe-deposit box. The showpiece salon, like Gabriel's designs for the Place de la Concorde, is merely another example of the French love of façade. News of the rent increase induced my cousin, who had just inherited a fortune from his parents, to take in paying guests. He used to boast that he spent less on rent than on cigarettes.

Many Frenchmen can, however, escape high rents by becoming homeowners with the help of government financing. Credit for buying a house or an apartment is easier to obtain than for a pack of Gauloises from the corner *tabac*. The main problem in the building trades is not credit but controls, such as those regulating the size of the halls, the design of ironwork balconies, and the required number of doors between bedroom and toilet. Shopkeepers are beginning to sense the advantages of buy-now-pay-later, which not so long ago was called "the open sore of commerce." The French still cherish the notion of the tiny profit (Paris waiters will dissert on the nuance between the service charge and the tip which is considered a voluntary supplement to the often compulsory service charge), they still consider the income tax a violation of the Rights of Man, and they still enjoy petty fraud, like traveling first class on the metro with a second-class ticket, or spending hours on the telephone to get a $2 parking ticket fixed.

But Gaullist stability spurred consumer spending. The general

ended inflationary colonial wars and devalued the franc in 1958
to give French exports a strong position. He concentrated on public investments to develop industry, although 80 percent of industry is still located above a line running from Marseilles to Le
Havre, and what is under that line constitutes a French Mezzo-
giorno. He joined the Common Market and accepted its free-trade
rules, which forced French business to become more competitive.
This in itself seems almost miraculous when one looks back on the
centuries of protectionism exemplified by the Code Méline of the
late nineteenth century that was so detailed some of its articles
were drafted for the protection of specific factories.

The French have always been poor salesmen, but now at least
they admit it. Businessmen are saying "We have to be like the
Japanese. Sell a product first, and manufacture it afterward." The
victims of the era of *petitesse* will be the thousands of anachronistic small businesses and farms that the government helps shore
up as a nostalgic reminder of a France that was. One sign of its
end is that for the first time in its existence, the National Assembly approved legislation for a rise in the inheritance tax in
October, 1968, thereby violating the sacred precept: No one has
the right to prevent a thrifty man from leaving his fortune intact
to his heirs. A lawyer friend reports that disputes over wills continue to make up the bulk of his practice. In the summer of 1968
I was watching television in the café of an Auvergne village. The
drama turned on the will left by a rich recluse, and the attempts of
his greedy relatives to cheat his loyal servant out of her share.
The spectators sat transfixed, and there was an audible gasp of
amazement when the *dénouement* came and the servant revealed
she was the dead man's widow. The bad younger brother went to
a sideboard to mix himself a stiff drink, and someone in the café
said: "He needs it." There is nothing dated about the Balzacian
themes of avarice, family hatreds, and contested wills.

What cannot be litigated is fought over. Much violence in
France is concerned with property rights. It was predictable that
the home and the office of the leading executive in a bid to take
over the Saint-Gobain glass works in 1969 would be bombed.
There is not much difference between a farmer firing his shotgun
at poachers, and a motorist yelling the traditional battlecry "prevent me or I make a misfortune" over his favorite parking space.

Particular to the 1968 French student-worker revolt, however, was the respect for property. Looting was insignificant.

The sixties has been a boom period for the European economy, and France has moved with the tide, despite depressed areas and an underpaid, under-organized labor force. One could reverse what André Siegfreid said about America: The French will have understood money when they stop darning socks. There are still men like Père Grandet, like the wealthy Normandy farmer who built a wooden case for his transistor radio so that he could lock it to keep his wife and children from wasting the battery. But whatever these nineteenth-century survivors do with their gold napoleons, France seems condemned to economic expansion and conspicuous consumption.

I I

>>>->>>->>>->>>->>>->>>->>>->>>->>>->>>->>>->>>((<-((<-((<-((<-((<-((<-((<-((<-((<-((<-((<-((<-((<

A Catalog of Oversights

F RANCE is not a synchronized country. It is like an ungaited
horse, each of whose legs is proceeding at a different cadence.
That is why statements about the French tend to cancel each other
out: volatility and tradition; planning the future and predicting
the past; the periods of one-man rule that impose political authority by stifling political life, and the periods of party rule in
which authority is absent but political life abounds; the handshake and the slap; euphemism and bombast; the incurable pettiness of the middle classes and the equally incurable addiction to
grandeur. The French credit themselves with wisdom for establishing social patterns that do not require change, but this
stabilized civilization makes change difficult in the areas where it
is needed. Is the harvester really better than the scythe? Do we
not risk revealing too much by advertising our product? Should
the Ministry of Communications improve telephone service in
holiday areas that have only seasonal affluence? Is it really useful
to have a teacher-student ratio in the university? Questions such
as these are still being asked, with implied self-satisfaction about
the way things have always been done. It is the same kind of self-

satisfaction that makes the French often say that Americans are children. The opinion that there is something fundamentally naïve and innocent about America's vision of the world is one that reflects not only a glib and uninformed judgment, but a lack of understanding about themselves. For to assert that others are children is to imply that one is oneself mature, whereas politically, the French are chronically immature, going through regimes the way a central heating system burns fuel.

The opposite of looking for anomalies in a country is to generalize about it, and although at the outset of this book I pledged to avoid generalizations as I would certain smug and boisterous acquaintances, I found myself running into them. It is inconvenient never to generalize about minor practical matters, like Dickens complaining that "there is not a door or a window in all of Paris that closes," or even about larger matters, like Sir Philip Thicknesse's unflattering capsule definition: "The French are generally speaking very curious, confident, inquisitive, credulous, facetious, rather witty than wise, eternal babblers; in a word they are at all times what an Englishman is when he is half drunk." Generalizations are unavoidable, but, like a politician elected by a narrow margin, they should be taken as valid for only part of what they are supposed to represent.

One fairly safe area of generalization concerns the pleasures a country provides. Only an incurable dyspeptic would dispute a generalization like "French food is often very good." I may not have done justice to the delights of living in France. One of the basic tests for a nation is, after all, that its inhabitants like it enough to live there, so that there is no serious population drain due to migrants, expatriates, or defectors. The most immediate delight is the absence of heaviness. Go to Germany or Belgium and return to France, and you will see what I mean. It is like passing through a decompression chamber and entering a lighter atmosphere. Lightness means tipped foils instead of sabers, a sauce without flour, a dress that is elegant because it is without superfluities, the ability of an employer to rebuke a subordinate without offending him, politeness without obsequiousness, irony disguised as flattery, indifference disguised as attentiveness, gestures that are understood before they are completed, the importance of nuance, like the difference between sports and athletics or between strength and power, and knowing the right tone to adopt, the precise gradation between familiarity and deference when bantering with a lady. Lightness is present in a hundred details of daily life, from the conversations in which topics are skimmed rather than exhausted, to the landscapes themselves, which never seem lush or barren, and seldom brood. The French conduct their human affairs with an absence of ponderousness, a happy lack of repetition and insistence. One of the most wounding remarks one Frenchman can make to another is: "It is useless to insist."

Another delight is the specifically French subculture of restaurants and cafés. I go to certain restaurants less for the food than to observe the families of serious eaters, four generations all looking alike at different ages, their napkins tied to their necks like flags around a pole, staring at their plates in silent concentration, their lips moving only to allow the passage of food, the youngest raising their wine glasses with the same aplomb as the oldest. Among the highest examples of a civilization, I would find it hard to choose between the cathedral builders and the café haunters. The natural habitat of some fairly common French types is the kind of café you can spend your day in because it combines the right degrees of familiarity and impersonality. No one can make demands on you as in home or office, and the surroundings are inviting, counterconversations start up easily and are just as easily broken off, deals are made, bets are placed, girls are picked up, someone is always waiting to use the telephone, and couples neck soundlessly for hours in corners. I have always admired those who wrote in the noisy privacy of cafés, settling down in the morning with a café crème, a croissant, and a blank sheet of paper, and filling it as the café filled, the ring of the cash register like the ring at the end of the typewriter carriage, the shouted orders and the hum of voices background music for the arrangement of words on a page, the cardboard saucers piling up as the measure of a day's work.

To explain France, I had to mention the café subculture, just as I should have mentioned certain categories of employment whose contribution to the advancement of the species is doubtful, like the concierge. The function of the concierges as guardians of property gives them an invincible armor of respectability. They are official voyeurs and snobs, and it is not often one can get the best of their righteousness. The sculptor César, when he arrived unshaven and corduroy-clad at a dinner given by one of the Rothschilds, was intercepted by the concierge, who led him to the servants' entrance. In his lilting southern accented French he told her: "I am the great sculptor César, and I make more millions in a week than you will ever see in a lifetime. For I am an artist, me, but you are a tramp, a tramp you have been, and a tramp you always will be."

The concierge identifies with the occupants of the building she watches over; she is by virtue of her job an ad hoc member of the bourgeoisie or aristocracy. It is rare to hear class differences sincerely condemned in France, even by Communists, the general assumption being that they are necessary and practical. Men are defined more by the order to which they belong than by their beliefs. What Jouvenel said in *La République des Camarades* is still true: "There is less difference between two deputies, one of whom is a revolutionary while the other is not, than between two revolutionaries, one of whom is a deputy while the other is not."

Because each in its way represents the qualities of its order, I have always preferred the mansion of the fourteenth-century merchant Jacques Coeur in Bourges to Versailles. It was built on hard work, thrift, and foresight; it was both castle and storehouse, and the sculptures on its chimneys and walls express a consistent antipatrician iconography. Instead of acanthus leaves and salamanders, fleur-de-lys and unicorns, there are only edible plants and animals, a sheep munching on cabbage, a hare nibbling lettuce; instead of courtiers in attendance, there are burghers eating a stew, choosing fruit from a basket, and playing chess. The mantelpieces are sculpted like the crenels of a fortress from behind which prosperously dressed burghers smile and wave. Jacques Coeur's motto was "flies can't enter a closed mouth," and one chimney shows a court jester with his lips sealed by a padlock, an ironic comment on the idle babbling of courtiers, while on another he has had carved a parody of a joust: laughing burghers watch peasants charge each other on donkeys, with wicker shields, blunt-pointed lances, and scarves over their faces. Jacques Coeur not only mocked the nobles, he was cleaner than they were. Although built two centuries earlier, his house has better plumbing than Versailles, with sit-down toilets and a steambath that used steam from the kitchens.

I should have included a profile of the durable fellow, not Jacques Coeur, but the bourgeois, from the time the word "burgensis" first appeared, in a 1007 charter establishing the free city of Loches. The bourgeois, hard bent on profit when everyone else was concerned with either survival or profligacy, defined themselves as those who had something stored away. Kings hired alchemists to make gold, but then invariably borrowed it from bourgeois merchants like Jacques Coeur. Once they had built up an inventory, fathers and sons became dedicated to upward mobility and a life without risk, while politically they subscribed to the doctrine of Syracuse: Long life to the tyrant, for if he dies a worse one will come. Their function was to profit from revolutions, not to make them. As they profited from the Reformation even though it did not take in France. Calvin did for the bourgeois what Marx did for the worker. He rid him of his guilty conscience. After Calvin, there were no more wills from last-minute penitents returning to the church the profits acquired by usury. And as they profited from the king's minister Colbert, who made nepotism respectable, finding sinecures for his six sons, dukes for his three daughters, and making his three brothers respectively a minister, a general, and an archbishop. What is more natural for a man than to take care of his family?

The bourgeois is the indoor man, his landscapes are paintings and art objects and every other form of accumulation. A lexicon of bourgeois phrases could also be accumulated: good accounts make good friends; drowning the fish; I could not do otherwise; there is no such thing as a small profit; happiness is the misfortunes one has avoided. It would include a chapter on misalliances: if his daughter wants to marry the chauffeur, I doubt that this is love; it is more likely an aberration of the senses; of all the ways a young girl has of finding happiness the foresight of her father is the surest; you will often find that the same key opens the strongbox and the heart. The bourgeois sensibility saturates French life. When they say the bourgeoisie is dead, they might as well say the Code Civil is dead or the instinct for thrift is dead. A sign I saw recently outside Lyons said: *Restaurant ouvrier, cuisine bourgeoise* (working-class restaurant with bourgeois cuisine).

The vocabulary of profit and loss gives the bourgeois away. Language, as much as one's face, is a badge of identification. But the attempt to explain the thought processes of the French through the structural principles of their language remains to be made. The French persist in grading languages like milk, theirs being grade A. In the writer Paul Morand's reception speech at the Académie Française, in March, 1969, I came across the assertion: "To write in French is to see flowing the waters of a mountain stream, next to which all languages are muddy rivers; it is to live in a crystal palace." A crystal palace is not everyone's idea of a model home. No one will deny that French, along with Greek and Latin, is one of the three languages that has had a major role in the Western world, spreading as a literary and a colonial tongue, and pidginized by the natives. The term "lingua franca" originated because the Crusaders, wherever they came from, adopted Provençal French as a matter of convenience. But after Greek, Latin, and French, it is the turn of English, which has supplanted French to become the lingua franca of business, science, and outer space, and the essential second language for Europeans. How much of French resistance to English membership in the Common Market is due to fear of England as a linguistic Trojan horse?

Perhaps every nation has, because of language, thought patterns which are fixed like radio frequencies; straying from them means overlapping with other frequencies, with resulting static. Efforts to adjust to a new frequency are as unsettling as arriving by car in London and having to drive on the left side of the road. Take the case of the French specialist in American civilization who, visiting the United States for the first time in ten years, went to Harlem and saw written in large letters on a storefront, the word "soul." He pondered the significance of his discovery. Soul, he thought; *l'âme*, the sum of moral and intellectual faculties. What can it mean in this connection? For a Frenchman, logical and Cartesian, it is puzzling. He hailed a passerby who told him "soul means black; it means soul brother and soul sister."

Ah, he thought, soul designates a race. But pursuing his inquiry, he was told by a Negro college professor that soul referred only to black music. Then it is a musical term, he thought, this becomes increasingly complicated. He asked two musicians, one Negro and one white; the white musician confirmed that soul was a quality of black music, but the Negro said "Man, when Van Cliburn plays Tchaikovsky, he's got soul." Well, thought the specialist, each is arguing that soul extends to the race of the other, how paradoxical.

In a magazine he came across the argument that soul was a cultural style developed by the urban ghetto population, while in another magazine he learned that there was not only soul music, but soul food, soul hairstyles, and soul clothing, and that certain persons were blessed with soul while others were not. Marlon Brando was not because he was too rational (ah, then, soul was a form of the irrational), but he was startled to read that George Wallace, whom he had considered the arch foe of the Negro, was credited with having soul. A Negro pastor in Atlanta, however, insisted that only Negroes had soul, and he wondered that a man whose vocation it was to shepherd the souls of all the faithful should be so restrictive about that commodity. The more he tried to define soul the more it eluded him. A recording star told him soul was the erotic quality of Negro singing, and he wondered how there could be such a confusion of the spiritual and the physical. Several times he was told: "If you were American, asking that question would be proof that you haven't got soul." Ah, he thought, then soul can be defined by what it is not. Finally, he put the question to a Memphis country-music disk jockey, who in the midst of connecting with "all you out there" and slapping the records on the turntable, turned to him and said "Why, man, soul is the intangible." The professor's urge to define was satisfied. Here was a definition broad enough to accommodate everything he had been told. "And you know," he said, "that young fellow gave me the best reply even though of all those I talked to he had one of the lowest levels of instruction." Basically, soul is a concept totally foreign to French experience.

A trip to Paris by someone not attuned to French thought patterns could be equally perplexing. What to make of the case of the divorced father who locked himself in his country house with his two children and threatened to shoot them and himself if the police attacked? It all seemed like make-believe, with the father and his children cheerfully posing for photographers from the mass-circulation magazine *Paris-Match,* and the young son allowed to fetch milk and return to the house without police interference. On those occasions he could have fled to safety, but he went back to his father voluntarily. When the siege had lasted a week, the police were ordered to attack. The father, keeping his promise, killed his children and himself. It was never learned who had given the order or why. If there was tragedy in the incident, it was in the way human problems are dealt with in abstract terms by remote, anonymous bureaucrats.

The state does not make mistakes because no one can be found to whom a mistake can be attributed. Callousness is natural to *étatisme.* Blunders are settled by administrative reprimands within the department. Rare are the blunders of such magnitude that they shake up the bureaucracy, the way the false arrest of Captain Dreyfus shook up the army. What France needs, since it has no system of checks and balances, no Congressional investigative committees, Supreme Court, or crusading newspapers, is more Dreyfus cases.

So often in France things are the opposite of what they seem. There is still a Paris newspaper with the word "Intransigent" in its title, in a country where survival is founded on transigence. It is at the moment when someone tempts fate by writing that France is bored that France erupts, and when every one predicts disorder that the French are orderly. But their unpredictability operates within the unchanging charter of Big Brotherism. There is no more illuminating reading about France than the decisions of the Conseil d'État, which reveal the unexpected areas of life where the responsibility of the state is invoked. When the state is everywhere, it is everywhere held responsible. It is held responsible because a young lady suffering from otitis had a facial nerve severed during treatment in the state hospital of Montpellier. It is held responsible because it delivered a firearms permit to a young man in Tregastel who subsequently shot and killed someone he mistook for a thief. Such farfetched appeals to the state, upon which the Conseil d'État must rule, are a measure of the extent of state control. What does democracy mean in such a context? Basic democratic concepts, like the people's right to know, are nonexistent in France, where the right to know is a commodity the government rations according to its policy goals.

Even independent newspapers like *Le Monde* sometimes knowingly play up government leaks, and become the instruments of national policies because fundamentally they see their role as one of leadership rather than information. I wonder whether the respected editor of *Le Monde,* Hubert Beuve-Méry himself, would approve without qualification the people's right to know.

As for democracy at work in the political system, it is striking to see in a French political campaign that the election posters are pasted on at night. According to an antiquated ruling, they are officially illegal, but they are tolerated if they are put up while the police isn't looking. This practice sums up the nature of the electoral process in France; it is tolerated and tinged with clandestinity, there is something shameful about it. It is as though the French had not yet really felt the distinction that exists between a change in regime through the electoral process and a change through revolution and *coup d'état.* The electoral process remains suspect inasmuch as it cannot be completely controlled and permits the overthrow of the custodians of regulations. Regulations are sacrosanct, even though those in power are only able to function by breaking them. A prefect is a man who is able to violate the regulations, like a bartender sneaking drinks, and is thus able to do favors for people and obtain results. Conversely, the real anarchist is the one who insists on minute enforcement of the regulations, like the man who always traveled free on the railroad because he knew the regulations by heart. When the conductor asked for his ticket, he would say "but you are not wearing white gloves as you should be."

Using the weapons of the state against the state is a form of anarchy the French system makes necessary. It also encourages a mental climate in which everyone has strong convictions and is thus unwilling to change his mind. Intellectual resourcefulness takes precedence over intellectual honesty. There are excellent reasons why France should not have entered World War II (the Germans would have finished off Poland and left France alone to attack Russia), or why Algeria should have stayed French (the *colons* would be massacred and Algeria would go Communist otherwise).

The French are not open to conversion, political, social, or otherwise. The mental attitudes are frozen, the arguments are tested and often inherited, and cancel each other out.

Every ideology knows the troops it can count on. Only the party in power grows, not because its reasons are better but because it has the power to obtain results. Often, when I have heard intelligent Frenchmen argue, I have felt that each one was trying not so much to convince the other as to explain and clarify his own position to himself. The preference persists for creating intellectual systems that do not have to be translated into practical programs. The mind is seen in the Cartesian sense of a private domain where one has total authority over one's ideas. And then events occur that do not fit any intellectual system, like the 1968 May-June riots, which were described as unpredictable because no one had predicted them. The historians set to work to turn such events into a coherent drama. No wonder that France has never had a Shakespeare or a Schiller or any great playwrights who have used national history as their subject. French history is already so theatrical there is little that playwrights can add after the soliloquies have been delivered and the last words been said. The only major play inspired by the French Revolution is Buchner's *La Mort de Danton,* and it took Shaw to write about Joan and Arthur Miller to write about Vichy France.

There are a number of other things I should have mentioned in this book: the importance of being "correct" (proper) and the love of carbon-monoxide-saturated Sunday outings by the side of the road. The way language smooths over the little difficulties of life: A friend of mine in Paris had an irritation which his wife thought was gonorrhea; he agreed to see the family doctor but was embarrassed because the doctor was a woman. He went to be examined, not knowing exactly what he should do, when she said: "And now, would you please show me the litigious object?" The futile search for a laundry that doesn't starch shirts, and the starchiness of social life. But the antidote to starch is the old anarchist reflex. You will always find a Paris taxi driver to tell you that "everything is rotten, it can't last, if things don't start moving we're going to blow up the boiler." But it does last, thanks to the fine balance between tradition and changeability. The French are creators of styles not because they are particularly inventive but because they require change. At the same time there is nothing they admire so much as longevity, the power to go on, which made de Gaulle the natural successor of Pétain.

I think it was Virgil Thompson who pointed out that when the French admire a writer or a painter, they tell him to "continue." In schools, teachers tell their best students to "continue." An inspector arrived at a military academy one day and was startled to see that one of the cadets was a Senegalese. "Why, you are a Negro," he said.

"Yes, sir."

"Eh bien, continuez, mon ami, continuez."

Predictions about this changeable people are hazardous, but I think it is safe to say that France and the French will continue.

Index

58933

GRAMONT, SANCHE DE
    THE FRENCH.

DATE DUE

DEC 20 1996			